# TOWPATHS

"Rivers are ungovernable things, especially in Hilly Countries. Canals are quiet and very manageable."

—Benjamin Franklin, 1773

# Towpaths

## A Collection of Articles from the
## Quarterly Publication of the
## CANAL SOCIETY OF OHIO

*Celebrating 50 Years, 1961-2011*

Edited by Boone Triplett and Bill Oeters

Canal Society of Ohio, Inc.
550 Copley Road
Akron, OH 44320
www.canalsocietyohio.org

ISBN-10: 1453789588
ISBN-13: 978-1453789582

The Canal Society of Ohio, Inc. is a 501(c)(3) non-profit organization. Any proceeds from the sale of this publication are to fulfill the obligations of its charter.

Printed in the United States of America

# TOWPATHS

No. 1      Canal Society of Ohio, Inc.      1963

## Canawlers!

With this issue we graduate from mimeographed bulletins to a regular, quarterly journal. Stories of canal days, complete with pictures, will be regular features. Should you have canal material that would be of interest to our members, we suggest you send it in. Pictures must be sharp and clear and glossy prints. Stories should be short and factual. Your material will be returned and due credit given.

* * *

'Photo by Dr. W. V. Gollar, Defiance. The Miami and Erie Canal crossing of Little Flat Rock Creek. Just south of the village of Junction, Paulding County. The Miami and Erie met the Wabash and Erie at Junction - hence the name. Still in place in 1962.

113 Commercial Ave., S. E., New Philadelphia, Ohio

**Volume I (1963), No. 1, p. 1**. First Cover of *Towpaths*. The familiar "rope" logo made its debut in the very next issue and has been a staple ever since.

# TABLE OF CONTENTS

# OHIO'S CANAL SYSTEM

Sesquicentennial Issue, 150 Years of Ohio's Canals

## OHIO & ERIE CANAL

## MIAMI & ERIE CANAL

## BRANCH CANALS

## EPILOGUE

## INDEX

# PREFACE

Flashback to the early 1960s. Outside of an 8th grade Ohio history class, few people had ever heard of the canals. What remained of Ohio's 1,000 mile inland navigation system was being eradicated. Canal beds make for ideal highway right-of-ways after all. Locks and other historic structures were being wiped out and nobody really seemed to care. Except for a small group of individuals, primarily from Northeast Ohio, who decided to form a society dedicated to the preservation and promotion of Ohio's once-great canal system. These folks formed the Canal Society of Ohio.

When the CSO was founded, there were no operating canal boats in the state. No towpath hiking trails were being developed. There were no historic villages, museums, or visitor centers in Ohio related to the canal system. Canal-themed "parks" were strictly of the roadside variety. National heritage corridors? Hardly. Ditto for restoration projects. Canals were something to avoid. Fast forward to the present, say, a sunny June weekend in Cuyahoga Valley National Park. My, how times have changed! We in the CSO would like to think we had something to do with all of that.

There seems to be a misconception about the CSO. Outsiders commonly mistake us for a "big money" organization but the CSO is strictly a non-profit group. While members do pay modest dues ($20 a year for a family is quite a bargain), that money is given out in the form of grants as stated in the articles of incorporation. Same goes for any royalties from this book. "Canawlers"* within our organization, even the officers, are all volunteers who share a passion for canals. The fact that we are all afflicted with "canal fever" is evident at our two annual tours, something that seems to have remained constant throughout the years.

Besides the tour invites, another CSO membership perk is a subscription to *Towpaths*. Back in 1963, the founders decided to publish something more than just a mimeographed quarterly newsletter. *Towpaths* is a scholarly research journal devoted exclusively to the study of canals, and this book is a compilation of those collective efforts over the past half century.

Selecting articles for inclusion in this book was a difficult task. The journal has evolved since the early 1960s, growing from basic broad-themed subjects in the beginning to more detailed topics in recent years. So there was a concern that the material would not "mesh." Plus, the membership felt that the articles should be arranged geographically. We eventually decided to include as broad a spectrum of authors as possible across the entire 50 years, drawing occasionally on newspaper or first person accounts to fill in the gaps. Geography seemed to take care of itself. By not relying too heavily on a handful of strong contributors, the finished product is more representative of the whole CSO membership.

The book starts with an introduction providing some background on the CSO followed by a "Construction and Operations" chapter that covers the canal era from 1825-1913. (We stretch it from 1783-1929.) Next is a condensed version of the 1975 Sesquicentennial issue that outlines each of Ohio's

---

* "Canawler" or "Canaller" is an authentic term referring to a person who lived or worked on a canal boat and can be applied today to anyone with an interest in the topic. This was verified in an article titled "Canawler?" by T.K. Woods in *Towpaths*, Volume XII (1974), No. 2, pp. 18-19.

27 navigable canals. More research has grown that number to 40. Then we focus attention on the two major canal systems in Ohio: the Ohio & Erie and the Miami & Erie. For the Ohio & Erie, we begin in Cleveland and end up at the southern terminus in Portsmouth. Going the other way along the Miami & Erie, the journey starts in Cincinnati and finishes in Toledo. Both main line canals connected Lake Erie with the Ohio River.

Those two were the major ones but significant branch canals such as the Pennsylvania & Ohio, Sandy & Beaver, Walhonding, Muskingum River Improvement, Hocking, Cincinnati & Whitewater and Milan are grouped into a chapter all their own. Finally, we wrap things up with a brief epilogue—a recruiting pitch for our humble little organization. Chapters such as "Stories" and "Since 1961" were considered but the narrative seems to flow better if these are placed in proper geographical sequence.

Nearly 3,000 pages of *Towpaths* material have been published in the past 50 years but only a small percentage of it could be represented in the book. An anthology of articles is hardly the format for putting together a comprehensive history of the Ohio canal system anyway. That's not the goal here. Even for selected articles, some editing was necessary. These portions are indicated by a "[…]" symbol. Space concerns also led to the omission of bibliographies and footnotes. (See the original articles for references.) And in lieu of using [*sic*] notation, spelling and other minor errors were corrected by the editors. Otherwise, the material appears as originally written. Despite these limitations, the CSO is proud of *Towpaths* and is happy to celebrate its 50th anniversary by presenting this collection.

Acknowledgements should be given to Terry Woods and Larry Turner for their assistance in picking articles and to Dave Badger for proofreading the text.

**Anybody remember "Cal Naller"?** He made a brief appearance as CSO mascot in 1972 then disappeared.

# INTRODUCTION

*An appropriate place to start would be the Canal Society of Ohio's articles of incorporation. These define who we are and what we do.*

Volume XIX (1981), No. 1, p.1

## CANAL SOCIETY OF OHIO, 1961-1981

To commemorate the 20th anniversary of the incorporation of the Canal Society of Ohio, this issue of *Towpaths* reviews the purposes of the Society as stated in its Articles of Incorporation:

"The Canal Society of Ohio, hereby called the Society is formed for the purpose of collecting and preserving information relating to the history of the Ohio Canals; of accumulating and cataloging such books, papers. documents, relics and articles of interest as will tend to illustrate the history of the Ohio Canals; to receive by deed, devise, bequest or other means, property having historical significance in Ohio Canals; of devoting all of such property and other historical material in the education of school children and in awakening the interest of the adults in the history of the Ohio Canals; of the collection and distribution of Ohio Canal historical information among the people of Ohio, by means of lectures, public meetings, exhibits and in the designation of historical canal sites so that a better understanding may be had in relation to the Ohio Canals.

It is a further purpose of this organization to conduct the affairs of the Canal Society of Ohio wholly without profit and to use all money and property received by the Society for the benefit of the people in Ohio."

§§§§§§§§§§§§§§§§§§§§§§§§§§§

*L.W. "Lew" Richardson was the first editor of* Towpaths *and one of the organization's founding fathers. His 1974 article describes the early history of the Canal Society of Ohio.*

Volume XII (1974), No. 2, pp. 23-24

## AS WE WERE by L.W. Richardson

A Canal Society of Ohio officer has suggested that an account of the formation of the Society and the early years should be written and has asked this "old timer" to contribute to that end. The task was accepted only when it was realized that the "baby" is now a "teen-ager" and should be aware of its heritage, however humble. What follows is a combination of not-too-reliable memories and some scanty notes. Hopefully, others will come forward to fill the inevitable gaps in the story.

It really began about 1958 when the late Ted Findley and the writer met and discussed a mutual interest, the canal system of the State of Ohio. Ted was an expert on the history of the Ohio & Erie Canal. Most of our limited knowledge concerned the Miami & Erie Canal and the western region. An exchange of information and much canal talk was the natural result. Through Mr. Findley we met Ted Dettling, an authority on the canals of the Akron area. We three were quite concerned with the rapid disappearance of the remaining canal structures and with the seeming lack of awareness by the general public of this important phase of Ohio's history. The possibility of organizing a group that could influence a change in this situation was discussed, but with no conclusion.

However, in the late summer of 1960, Ted Findley called to say that he and Ted Dettling had decided to call a meeting in Akron, in October, to explore the idea and see if such a group could expect public support. The response was far greater than anyone had anticipated. Over 40 people sat down to dinner at the Portage Hotel. Ted Findley chaired the round-table discussion that followed. The interest was evident and committees were appointed to draft a Constitution, apply for a Charter and make other necessary plans.

The first regular meeting of the Canal Society of Ohio was held in March, 1961, in the Valley View Town Hall. This is the first slate of officers elected: President, T.H. Findley, New Philadelphia; 1st V-P, James G. Cowles, Cleveland; 2nd V-P, L.W. Richardson, Lakewood; Secretary-Treasurer, Dr. L.P. Carabelli, Akron; Corresponding Secretary, H.W. Dosey, Cleveland Heights; Historian, Miss Harriet Leaf, Akron; Directors, Miss Terry Green, Valley View; J.D. Robinson, Parma; Carl Pockrandt, Akron. Unfortunately, Dr. Carabelli, because of ill health, was unable to complete his term of office. Harry R. Valley, Lakewood, was elected in his stead.

The Society sponsored its first field trip, July 15-16, 1961. A small group met at the "crossing of the Tuscarawas" on Saturday, the 15th, then followed the line of the canal to New Philadelphia, the overnight stop. On Sunday morning the tour continued south to the triple lock on the Walhonding Canal at Coshocton. President Findley prepared for the tour our first "guide", listing all canal structures and points of interest along the way.

The first annual meeting was held in Columbus, June 15-16, 1962. About twenty-five attended a get-together at the Hotel Deshler on Saturday. Sunday morning, the group met at the terminus of the Columbus Feeder, followed it to Lockbourne, then went up the Ohio & Erie through Groveport and Canal Winchester to Lockville.

Through these first few years, the Society grew slowly but steadily. When the first roster was printed in 1963, it listed 133 members.

Soon after the Valley View meeting, President Findley began mailing to members at regular intervals, a mimeographed news-letter that he titled, TOWPATHS. In 1963, the first regular, quarterly, TOWPATHS, began publication. This writer was the editor and the booklet was printed in New Philadelphia. The first number, because of a breakdown of communications, was a typographical disaster, but that problem, at least, improved with practice. At first the contents were, in large part, copies of laws and reports as contributors were slow in responding. The President and editor filled in the gaps.

There were many who contributed to the success of the Society, too many to name individually. One man, however, must be recognized. This was Ted Findley. His knowledge, dedication, and boundless enthusiasm kept the organization alive and healthy in those first difficult years. They must also be grateful to the officers and members of the Summit County Historical Society. They provided meeting places, in the old Perkins house, and moral support and their help was invaluable.

It is true that I am biased, but on the whole I think that we founding fathers can be proud. There is no question that the Canal Society of Ohio has been responsible for the increased interest, throughout the state, in the old canals. Additionally, the files of TOWPATHS, in the capable hands of Frank Trevorrow and Terry Woods, now offer the researcher a rich store of canal history.

§§§§§§§§§§§§§§§§§§§§§§§§§§§

*Generally acknowledged as the "George Washington of the CSO," Ted Findley's vision was instrumental in the establishment of the organization. Published posthumously, his enthusiasm for the topic shines through in this aptly titled article.*

Vol. XI (1973), No. 1, pp. 8-11

### ONE CANALLER'S ENTHUSIASM, PART I by T.H. Findley

In these historical studies which I have made, if I have learned anything from them at all, it is this…Whether you know it or not; whether you believe it or not; whether you like it or not; you and I are descendents of the groups of people who took part in the great westward trek of the white races during the late 17th and (early) 18th centuries in which the cowards never started and the weaklings died on the way.

I'm not a native of Ohio. When I first came over into your state 30, 35 years ago (this was written in the early 1960's) and first started to travel its highways, I noticed along those highways a weed-grown ditch—far too straight of line to be natural, far too large to be a drainage ditch for the highway. It excited my curiosity and I made inquiry.

I found that the weed-grown ditch was all that remained of a once great transportation system that had been the pride and joy of several generations of Ohioans. Here and there an old timer could remember having swum in it in the summer, having skated on it in the winter, and occasionally one could even remember a boat drawn by horses or mules…but few, if any, could tell me when it was started, how long it took to build, how much it cost, what its purpose was, or how long it was in use.

So, I went to the State Capitol at Columbus. I gained access to and poured over old maps and records. I joined the Ohio State Historical Society to gain the benefits of their records.

I learned that the ditch was interesting from a great number of angles...political, economical, financial, romantic and engineering.

POLITICAL, because what is today a weed-grown ditch made the State of Ohio...there isn't any question about that. Between 1820 and 1840 the population in Ohio tripled. The population of Indiana quadrupled, and Illinois increased its population five times. In the late 1830s, the little village of Toledo, on Lake Erie, reported that every 24 hours 3,000 immigrants were passing through on their way to settle the lands of the west, by way of the canal systems.

Thirty-seven counties of the State of Ohio today contain 65 percent of its population and, without exception, those 37 were the canal counties. All of the great cities of the state were canal ports. Cleveland grew from a little village of 500 people in 1825 to one of the great cities in the world because it was the terminal port of the Ohio and Erie Canal.

Akron did not exist previous to the digging of the canal system, but was founded as a direct result of the Irish laborers housed in contractor's shacks while they were constructing the system of 21 lift locks within the present city limits of Akron.

Canton, Youngstown, Columbus, Cincinnati, Dayton, Toledo all were canal ports and received such impetus during those early days that their neighboring cities have never been able to catch up to them.

Without what is today a weed-grown ditch, there is a strong possibility that the people of Ohio might have been French or Spanish speaking.

For previous to the digging of the canal systems in the state, the cheapest means the farmers had of disposing of their products was to build a raft, load that produce on the raft; wait for the spring floods, float the raft down the Ohio River, to the Mississippi, trading with the French and Spanish at St. Louis and New Orleans...and where people's trade is, that's where their heart is more than likely to be.

Aaron Burr, with his Blennerhassett Island scheme, was a traitor to his country, but he was indeed an astute politician, and he knew an empire could be carved out of these western colonies because of their almost complete isolation from the seaboard by reason of the tremendous mountain chain running through the states of New York, Pennsylvania, Maryland and Virginia.

ECONOMICAL, because during the War of 1812 the Government could buy a cannon in the city of Philadelphia, Pennsylvania, for $400; but to transport that cannon over the mountains to Perry who was building his fleet on Lake Erie, would cost them $1,800 in freight charges. To put a barrel of flour in Fort Meigs up near to what is now Toledo would cost $100, although that barrel could be bought in New York or Philadelphia for $3.00. It has been estimated that the freight charges alone that the Government paid during the War of 1812 would have constructed every road and canal in the states of New York, Pennsylvania and Ohio.

ECONOMICAL, too, because previous to the digging of the canal systems, wheat in Ohio...when it could be sold...brought 25 cents a bushel. When the canals were finished, it jumped immediately to 90 cents and a dollar.

In the year 1825, before the canals were started, they could produce a barrel of the finest flour in Cincinnati for $3, when it was selling in New York or Philadelphia for $8 a barrel. But to transport that flour to New York or Philadelphia would cost them $25. When the canals were finished, they could ship it for $2.50!

FINANCIAL, because of the interesting and courageous way in which they financed the internal improvements. When the Canal Commission reported to the State Legislature in 1825, the estimated cost of the canal system was to be $5 million. And in that year the entire tax duplicate of the State of Ohio was only $56 million.

They had the courage and the foresight to place themselves into debt for nearly 10 percent of the entire valuation of the state at the time to build the great internal improvement. That last canal bond was retired in 1903. Before they were through they dug 1,000 miles of canals in the state and had spent $16 million.

ROMANTIC, because a race of people grew up and died with the old canal system. They were Americans in the full sense of the word, but the manner of life that they led, and the language that they used to explain the tools of their craft have completely died out from our way of life, with no further need for them. Men and women were born and raised on canal boats, received their education…religious and otherwise, on the boats; grew to manhood and womanhood, married, acquired boats of their own; raised their children, died and were buried…all without having strayed far from the canal.

In 1857, on the Ohio & Erie Canal alone, there were 25,000 people directly employed on a total of 2,000 boats on the 309 miles of its length.

Volume XI (1973), No. 2, pp. 13-16

**ONE CANALLER'S ENTHUSIASM, PART II by T.H. Findley**

ENGINEERING was perhaps the most amazing feature of Ohio's Canal system. To dig an artificial ditch never less than 26 feet wide at the bottom; never less than 40 feet wide at the top; containing never less than four feet of water, 309 miles across a wilderness of what was then the state of Ohio, bridging rivers, tunneling through hills, filling in valleys with crude instruments of that day, is an engineering marvel.

Previous to the year of 1816, there had been several attempts to improve the internal river systems of the state, that being their main means of transportation between the Lake and the Rivers. But, notably, in that year a group of Cleveland men secured permission from the State Legislature to institute a lottery. This lottery was to raise the sum of $64,000. That amount of money was to be used to improve the channel of the Cuyahoga River, from the tiny village of Cleveland at its mouth on Lake Erie, to the point where it began veering to the east…by hand digging the shallow water to remove snags and sawyers, then constructing a 7-mile turnpike road over the old Indian Portage to the headwaters of the Upper Muskingum (Tuscarawas) River. The modern Portage Path Street in present Akron, Ohio traces much of the route of this proposed road. The channel of the Tuscarawas would also be improved, again by hand digging the shallows and removing the snags to the forks of the Muskingum (present day Coshocton, Ohio).

This would open a trade route between Lake Erie and the Ohio River. Produce could be loaded on a flat boat at Cleveland, laboriously poled up the Cuyahoga to the Portage Road, transshipped onto wagons; wagonned across the seven mile turnpike road, reloaded onto flat boats, and floated down the Tuscarawas and Muskingum Rivers to Marietta on the Ohio.

But the plan fell through because of the sparsely settled condition of the state and the general lack of money. After several years, those who had purchased tickets had their money returned and that particular scheme forgotten.

The first specific progress toward an Ohio Canal System came in December, 1818. Governor Brown, in his inaugural address, strongly urged the State Legislature to appropriate funds for the surveying of canal routes within the state. That suggestion didn't get much response, but he kept plugging away.

Finally, in January of 1822, the Legislature appropriated funds for surveying the canal routes, and in the very early spring of that year a party of men started out. It's hard for us to visualize the condition of the state 150 or so years ago, because we have absolutely nothing in the state at the present time with which to make comparison—almost completely covered with immense hardwood forests, the creeks and river bottoms almost completely choked by the debris of centuries of spring and summer floods. What roads there were consisted mainly of pitiful little trails that followed the original Indian and game trails, for the most part, over the ridges and hilltops. Settlements consisted of lonely little cabins perched high on a hillside, or clusters of cabins at the principal fording places of the rivers, since Ohio's streams were her main avenues of transportation. It was through this wilderness that the party of canal surveyors started out.

There wasn't a graduate engineer within the confines of the State of Ohio at that time…they had to borrow one from the State of New York. There weren't adequate surveying instruments to be had and many miles of the canal levels were laid out with a carpenter's level, a rifle barrel, a compass, and a home-made "T".

This party of men surveyed 900 miles of line (five principal routes) and reported to the Legislature that any one of them was feasible, with a plentiful water supply.

The FIRST ROUTE was from Youngstown in the valley of the Mahoning River, through the valleys of the Conneaut and Ashtabula rivers, to Ashtabula.

The SECOND was from Cleveland up the valley to Akron, down the valley to the Tuscarawas to the Muskingum and down the Muskingum Valley to Marietta on the Ohio.

The THIRD was from Marietta to the Killbuck branch of the Muskingum, through Wooster and Millersburg, to Lake Erie.

The FOURTH…the shortest of all…from Portsmouth at the mouth of the Scioto, up that river valley through Columbus, then along the valleys of the Black and Huron rivers to Lake Erie.

The FIFTH route was from Cincinnati, then the largest city west of Pittsburgh with a population of 25,000, up Mill Creek into the valley of the Miami River, to the valley of the Auglaize, then down the Maumee valley into Lake Erie.

Then the arguments started. Even in those days, representatives in the Legislature were after the most for their particular sections of the state and they realized they couldn't build a canal along each of the routes. A debate about which route to use went on for two or three years until February of 1825 when the Legislature passed the Canal Enabling Act which provided for the building of two canals. The first one…a portion of the far western route was to be built from Cincinnati to Dayton, the completion of the rest northward dependent entirely on the granting of lands by the U.S. Government through the Indian Territory north of Dayton.

Mainly due to political reasons, the other route was a compromise of three of the original survey routes. It started at the present site of Cleveland; went south to Akron; crossed the divide to the Tuscarawas valley and followed it south through Fulton and Dover; down the Muskingum valley to a spot just above Dresden. The route then turned west through Newark to the little village of Lockbourne on one of the tributaries of the Scioto; then down the main Scioto River through Circleville to Portsmouth on the Ohio River.

On the 4th of July, 1825, a vast crowd estimated at 6,000—and that would be a tremendous crowd for those days—together with the State Militia, principal state officers, and invited guests, plus Governor DeWitt Clinton, the great canal governor of New York State, met at a point three miles south of the village of Newark to break ground for the Ohio & Erie Canal.

The same party moved westward to Middletown, so-called because of its location mid-way between Cincinnati and Dayton, to break ground for the western canal on the 21st of July.

By the fall of that year, there were 3,000 men and 2,000 animals at work on the northern section of the Ohio & Erie alone. A workman's wages in the early days of canal construction amounted to about $6.00 a month. The workday then was from sunup to sundown and there were 26 working days a month! Nearly every farmer along the route wanted to be a canal contractor; in October 1826, bids were opened in the New Philadelphia courthouse for 110 sections of the canal. There were better than 6,000 bids on those 110 sections!

In the beginning, many farmers and their sons took on a section (half mile) or two of canal. They were glad to get work, glad to get the money. But many of them soon came down with "Canal Fever". Many modern doctors have diagnosed the symptoms—breakbone fever, ague, shakes—as Malaria, but they didn't recognize it as such in those days. Ministers preaching from the pulpit said it was a visitation from the Almighty for man daring to tear up his handiwork in the beautiful state river valleys. There are records of a young doctor in New York State who lost his license because he dared suggest that this Canal Fever might be due to the bite of a fly or mosquito. The medical profession believed the "Fever" was due to the miasmic air (fog) along the river bottoms early in the morning. Cabins were built high on the hillsides so the people could get as far from those morning mists as possible.

The "Fever" drove most of the farmer-contractors away from their jobs. And the Irish took over. They called him a Wild Irish Bog Trotter. He was tough, he could take it. But in spite of the fact that he was tough, there is a dead Irishman buried for every yard of canal constructed in the northwest corner of Ohio.

The first section of the Ohio & Erie was completed on July 4th, 1827 and the first canal boat traveled from Akron to Cleveland. Canal water reached Dover in 1829, in 1830 it reached Roscoe, and in January, 1832, seven years after work was begun, the Canal Commissioners reported that the entire system was completed as provided for in the original Canal Enabling Act, with the exception of the lift locks into the Ohio River at Portsmouth and Cincinnati.

This was just the beginning; before they were through they dug 1,000.75 miles of canal. This job is even more awe-inspiring when one remembers that it was all done with pick and shovel, and wheelbarrow. The horse scraper wasn't invented until the railroads came in. Those thousand miles of canals in Ohio joined the canals of neighboring states, so that, in the 1840's, it was possible to board a boat in New York and go to Cincinnati, Chicago or St. Louis!

**Ted Findley, Co-founder and Early President of the C.S.O.** Checking a map of the Ohio & Erie Canal against the wall of Lock No. 14 in Tuscarawas County.

# CONSTRUCTION AND OPERATIONS

*Probably the canal society's most prolific and well-known contributor, Frank Trevorrow provided material for* Towpaths *over a period of four decades. He died at the age of 107. His articles alone were published as a book in 1973.*

Volume III (1965), No. 3, pp. 5-6

### WASHINGTON'S FORESIGHT by F.W. Trevorrow

The proposed and very controversial Ohio-Erie Canal is again prominent in the news. In news articles, various claims are made as to who first proposed joining Lake Erie with the Ohio River by canal. George Washington's, if not the first, were among the earliest.

As the War for Independence neared its end, Washington became deeply concerned with the problem of settling and holding the regions west of the Alleghenies. He was convinced that an inland water transportation system was essential to this end. He explored the rivers of New York in 1783, particularly the connections with Lake Erie and the northern reaches of the Susquehanna. His views were stated in his letter to Chevalier de Chastellux, a Major-General in Rochambeau's army, on October 12, 1783. Washington said, in part, "I could not help taking a more contemplative and extensive view of the vast inland navigation of these United States…would to God we may have the wisdom to improve them."

Settling and securing the western lands with a system of inland water transportation continued to be uppermost in Washington's mind at the close of the war. Thomas Jefferson was also thinking along the same lines. On March 29, 1784, Washington, in a letter to Jefferson, said, "My opinion coincides perfectly with yours respecting the practicability of an easy and short communication between the waters of the Ohio and Potomac." Then he questions Jefferson, "Query, have you not made the distance from the Cuyahoga to New York too great?"

Washington owned extensive property in Western Pennsylvania and Virginia which would increase in value with settlement. He was frank to admit a personal interest in western expansion. In September, 1784, he visited his properties and explored the southern tributaries of the Ohio for the nearest connections between them and the James River and the North Branch of the Potomac. Returning to Mount Vernon, Washington wrote to Gov. Harrison of Virginia on October 10, 1784, at great length on the subject of Internal Navigation. From his own explorations and Lewis Evans' map of 1775, he made his recommendation for a system of internal communication reaching from the Virginia seaboard to Lake Erie.

Washington recommended that Commissioners be named to survey the possible routes to the Ohio River. Upon the survey reaching the Ohio, he said, "The navigation of this river being well known, they will have less to do in the examination of it, but nevertheless, let the courses and distances of it be taken to the mouth of the Muskingum, and up that river to the carrying place with Cuyahoga, down the Cuyahoga to Lake Erie…Let them do the same with Big Beaver Creek…and also with the Scioto."

The river courses Washington named in his letter were paralleled by the original Ohio-Erie Canal within about forty years. Big Beaver Creek, or Beaver River, as it is now called, would form the southern reach of the proposed new canal. Most interesting of all, however, is perhaps the fact that what Washington called "the carrying place with the Cuyahoga" is now the city of Akron.

§§§§§§§§§§§§§§§§§§§§§§§§§§§§

*To recognize the 150th anniversary of the groundbreaking on the Ohio canal system, the* Towpaths *editorial staff published a special commemorative issue in 1975. This introduction covers the period from 1803-25.*

Volume XIII (1975), No. 1, pp. 1-4

## 150 YEARS OF OHIO'S CANALS:
## OHIO'S CANAL SYSTEM, AN INTRODUCTION by TOWPATHS' Editorial Staff

On July 4th 1975 the citizens of Newark, Licking County and Ohio will celebrate the 150th anniversary of the launching of work on this state's canal system. Independence Day one hundred and fifty years ago celebrated two events which had far-reaching effects upon the growth and prosperity of an infant state which, at that time was home for less than a million people.

One was the formal opening of the National Road, while the other was perhaps of even greater importance—the construction of an immense system of artificial waterways. This latter event was of such importance that the Governor of New York, DeWitt Clinton—the foremost proponent of canal construction in the country—and his staff made what at the time was considered to be a long and hazardous journey from Albany, New York, to a wilderness clearing south of Newark, Ohio, just to attend the festivities. At Newark the New York delegation was met by local Militia which acted as an escort throughout the celebration.

On the big day itself, an enormous crowd gathered at a point later known as "Four Mile Lock" for the official "ground breaking" on the Ohio & Erie Canal. Governor Clinton delivered the principal address, eloquently depicting the great benefits that must follow the building of the great system of canals that had been authorized by the State Legislature. Governor Morrow of Ohio followed that with an equally impressive message.

Then followed the "earth breaking". Governor Clinton placed the first shovelful of dirt into the barrow, Governor Morrow the second, followed by Judge Wilson of Licking County, and he in turn by Judge Schofield of Fairfield County and then by a "host" of anxious volunteers until the barrow was more than filled.

Many of the dignitaries from New York and Ohio next travelled on to Columbus, where the group dined and the two Governors again engaged in oratory. They finally arrived at Middletown, Ohio, where on July 21st, 1825, a similar "earth turning" ceremony was held, this time inaugurating work on a western Ohio waterway—the Miami Canal.

Agitation for improved transportation in Ohio began almost as soon as there was an official State of Ohio—in 1803. The first scheme was to improve the channels of the Cuyahoga and Upper Muskingum (Tuscarawas) Rivers and connect the two at their closest points with a 7 mile wagon road. The first State Legislature authorized a private company to hold a lottery to raise sufficient funds ($64,000 was the goal) to complete the project. There just weren't enough people in the state at that time with cash money to raise such a stupendous sum, however, and the whole idea fell through.

In 1807, Thomas Worthington, U.S. Senator from Ohio, introduced a bill into the upper house of Congress directing the Secretary of the Treasury to investigate and report back to Congress on a plan for developing a system of government sponsored canals and highways to link the "new" west with the "old" east. On April 4, 1808 Albert Gallatin presented his now famous "Report on Roads, Canals, Harbors, and Rivers". In it he approved all the popular projects then under consideration and suggested others that would have benefited nearly every state in the union. Gallatin also suggested that the whole vast scheme could be paid for in ten years out of normal government revenue.

Conditions were changing, however, even while the various states lined up to get "their" share of the money. The U.S. Embargo Act, closing its ports for foreign shipping, was beginning to injure United States commerce. Congress didn't think it would be a good idea to make large expenditures at such a time and Gallatin's recommendations were not acted upon. The War of 1812 came along next and all grandiose plans for internal improvements were dropped "for the duration". By the time the country and economy returned once more to some degree of normalcy, administrations (and attitudes) had changed in Washington. The Federal Government was no longer willing to sponsor internal improvements and individual states were encouraged to "do it on their own".

New York was one state determined to improve its transportation system even if its residents had to finance a canal entirely by themselves. New Yorkers were certainly not against receiving outside help if it could be obtained, however, so in 1816 Thomas Worthington, who was now Governor of Ohio, received a request from the New York Canal Commission for aid in financing construction of their Erie Canal. A committee appointed by the Ohio Legislature to study the request returned a favorable report. Four days later, however, the Ohio Senate struck out that portion of a resolution offering financial aid, but a close relationship developed between New York Canal Commissioner DeWitt Clinton and Ohio's Governors Thomas Worthington (1814-1818) and Ethan Allan Brown (1818-1822).

Worthington and Brown marshaled their forces and agitated for a Lake Erie to Ohio River canal at every opportunity. Various committees were formed to study the question and several resolutions proposed, but it wasn't until January 31, 1822 that an Act was passed by the Ohio State Legislature that authorized surveys to be run over five specified possible routes.

That Act also caused an Ohio Canal Commission to be formed and authorized it to hire an "expert engineer" to oversee these surveys. But Ohio in 1822 could not boast of a single school of engineering within the state's borders. In fact, there was probably no one even living in the state of Ohio who could lay claim to the title of engineer. Fortunately, and due to the good offices of DeWitt Clinton, one of New York state's top engineers, James Geddes, was employed to run the Ohio surveys.

In 8 months Geddes and one or more of Ohio's canal commissioners ran 900 miles of surveys. All the routes specified in the Act hadn't been examined by the end of 1822, however, when Geddes was called back to New York. A supplementary Act was passed to provide $4,000 of additional funds to complete the surveys in 1823. However, Ohio was unable to obtain a senior engineer from New York. Each of Ohio's acting canal commissioners, Micajah T. Williams and Alfred E. Kelley, made trips to the Erie during 1823 to gain some first hand knowledge in canal building.

A young New York engineer by the name of Seymour Skiff was hired in the spring. It was hoped he would be the nucleus of an Ohio engineer corps. Unfortunately for all concerned, Young Mr. Skiff was in the field only 14 days when he contracted a disease (probably Malaria) that hit nearly every member of the surveying teams that year. He was taken to Worthington to receive medical attention, but died shortly afterward. As the result of the death of one of their chief engineers, plus the delays due to sickness, little progress was made during the remainder of 1823. Therefore, it took another surveying season before a final report could be made—a season in which the nucleus of an Ohio engineer corps was formed around another young engineer from New York (Mr. W. Price) and an Ohioan (Samuel Forrer).

At their first meeting in 1822 the seven man Board of Canal Commissioners decided that the ideal route for a Lake Erie to Ohio River canal would be one that benefited as many of Ohio's citizens as possible. With this idea in mind, they proposed a route that would come up from the Lake through the valley of the Cuyahoga River, then run to the Ohio River by two different routes. One leg would go east from the Cuyahoga summit, through the established communities in Columbiana County, to the Ohio River. The other leg was to run in a south-westerly direction crossing the Scioto valley as far above Columbus as possible, then across the divide and down the valley of the Miami River to the Ohio near Cincinnati.

The survey teams were able to locate a route from the Cuyahoga summit to the Scioto valley, but at a point some eleven miles *below* Columbus. And from there, though they tried many routes, they were unable to supply a canal with sufficient water to get it into the Miami valley. They were also unable to bring a canal from the Cuyahoga summit through Columbiana County. Therefore, the third Canal Commissioner's Report proposed what was considered to be a politically acceptable Lake to River canal route and in February, 1825, the State Legislature passed an Act authorizing, in effect, two canals.

One, what remained of the Commissioner's "diagonal route", was to leave the Lake by way of the Black or Cuyahoga valleys, south by way of the Killbuck or Tuscarawas valleys to the Muskingum, then over to the valley of the Scioto by a number of smaller streams and perhaps a tunnel through the dividing ridge, then down to the Ohio near Portsmouth. And to satisfy the relatively populous and politically powerful southwestern corner of the state, a short canal was authorized to be built from Cincinnati (the western terminus of the "diagonal route") up the Miami valley to or near Dayton. This Miami Canal was to be completed through to the Lake "at an early date". So less than five months later, just north of the Licking summit, the State of Ohio embarked on an ambitious program of artificial waterways that, together with the private endeavors, would total nearly 1,000 miles and would, as one prominent historian puts it, "bring the World to the Wilderness".

§§§§§§§§§§§§§§§§§§§§§§§§§§§

*Once Ohio's massive internal improvement project was undertaken, the job fell to the Irish to do the actual digging. The following article by William D. Ellis tells their story.*

Volume III (1965), No. 3, pp. 1-4

## HOW CAME THE IRISH TO DIG THE CANALS? by William D. Ellis

Our great gift from the Irish was that they dug the Ohio Canals. By the time they had reached Ohio, they were expert. They had dug the Enfield Canal and the Farmington in Connecticut, then the Champlain and the great Erie across New York.

Then they came to the biggest of them all, the Ohio Canal System.

These were rugged, melancholy men, great red-haired Gaels and small, wirey, flat muscled, enduring men from Castle Shannon, Glengariffe, Coolnalaema, Londonderry, Belfast, Dublin and Counties Cork and Galway…any part of Eire where the economic misery was deeper than in eighteen inches of cold Ohio muckland.

These were the men who took over construction after the first blazing summer and the first freezing winter thinned out the ranks of our Ohio farmer-contractor types.

The sullen, lead-eyed Irish pushed the scoops and shovels and oxen through 900 miles of Ohio rain and ague for $10.00 to $12.00 a month, giving up only one Irish for every three miles of canal bed. They cut the canal straight and steadily through roots and rock, leaving a track of slack water behind them that would float a billion dollar commerce and lift the west out of the stagnating depression that froze us in 1818.

But it took a special kind of foreman and a special kind of contractor to handle them. As G.K. Chesterton put it,

> "The great Gaels of Ireland
> Are the men that God made mad.
> For all their wars are merry,
> And all their songs are sad."

They worked with a tight lipped anger. And why not? Contractors in America advertised for men to work the canals in newspapers in Belfast. But if they needed 500 men, they advertised for 1,000. It kept the price down.

From Belfast, the fare was cheaper to Canada, so some Irishmen landed at Nova Scotia and walked south. But most shipped to Baltimore or Boston for seven pounds sterling.

Now when they hit port, a passenger broker greeted them at the dock. A passenger broker was a parasitic form of life who worked on a commission for a boarding house. He led off as many Irish immigrants as he could to his employer's boarding house. To the boarding house, the Irishman found himself in debt. Contractors or other brokers bought up the debts from the boarding house proprietors and vessel captains, and Mr. Carnahan, Monahan, Cochran or Hogan often found himself bound to a work contract to pay off his debt.

Now very often by the time he had dug his way across New York State, he was free and clear, but he was only trained in digging, blasting, ditching, clearing and pipe laying. So he stayed on the canal.

In addition to the track of slack navigation the Irishman left behind him, he also left a trail of settlements named "Little Dublin," "Irish Grove," "Irish Hill," "Paddy's Land" and "Irish Town". And he left a trail of little shrines. A few Irish priests worked the canals on a circuit basis. Before the priest's arrival, the canal men would throw up a scalan, a little sanctuary of latticed branches where the priest heard confession, gave communion and said mass.

As the canal men pushed the canal forward, these were not torn down behind them. On the contrary, some grew, like St. Mary's-of-the-Flats in Cleveland, manned by Pastor John Dillon from County Limerick, Ireland.

I'll not go into the horrendous fights between Corkonians and Far-Downers, with which you are already familiar, in which one kind of Irishman tried to preserve the canal jobs for his own kind. You'd expect a constant battling among the men from the nation which once had 600 kings or ruling Tuaths.

But they could cooperate, too, in a quiet and highly effective way…to register their grievances with contractors who were too rough.

Although Alfred Kelley largely protected the men from contractor abuses on the Ohio Canal system, there were still some contractors who, being paid in good currency, paid their men in wildcat currency; ran company stores with exorbitant prices for pants, boots, cloth, bed ticks and rations; and absconded without meeting the payroll.

So the Irish canal diggers used what they called the Whiteboy system. "Midnight legislators" met after dark to hear an Irish canal man who had a grievance. If they agreed the contractor was unfair, "enforcers" were elected to pay a visit.

The first step was usually a reasonable Whiteboy letter. "Dear Sir: This will give ye civil notice that you will discharge from your pay your manager, Mr. J.S. Thompson, who is unfair as foreman. If Thompson leaves the canal in six days, there will be no trouble."

Experience taught the contractors not to ignore such a note. The enforcers were always selected from men from another canal system.

If the message was not heeded in six days, there would be a contractor cemented into the berm of the canal, head down, feet up.

Some say that the Hibernian movement in America began with the canals. Irishmen are not easily organized, except over serious troubles; and the canals were trouble enough to command a large space in *The Boston Pilot.*

*The Boston Pilot* was an Irish-American newspaper cherished on the canal. A single copy of it would work its way from hand to hand, from Cleveland to Akron, to New Philadelphia, Coshocton, Newark. But it could never quite make it to Canal Winchester. By the time the paper reached Newark, it had been torn to a hundred fragments, which were lovingly rolled in an oiled deerskin.

*The Pilot* kept Irishmen informed about where the best paying canal jobs were, but it urged them to get off the canals as soon as possible.

Yet, later generations of thoughtful Irish politicians and philosophers have said, that hard as the canal work was, it was a great thing for the Irishmen. They reason this way. As Irishmen moving west across the nation on the canals bought their way clear of debt, many dropped off along the route to establish farms and businesses.

Had it not been for the canals, they might have remained in a concentration on the east coast, becoming an unhappy minority group.

But via the canals, the Irish people spread themselves across the land, salting and peppering the whole nation with their wonderful Irishness…rising in a very few generations to positions of affluence and leadership.

§§§§§§§§§§§§§§§§§§§§§§§§§§§§§§§§

*While much of the credit for building the canals goes to the Irish, German immigrants played a key role as well. Brad Bond, long-time* Towpaths *editor and an outstanding writer/researcher to boot, contributed this article on the topic of stone masons.*

Volume XLIII (2005), No. 3, pp. 58-61

### MASON'S MARKS by Brad Bond

In 1999 Ron Petrie published in the Newsletter my request for help in preparing an article on the marks masons inscribed on stones cut for lock walls. The only answer to the request was from Bill Trout III in Virginia. He had published a description of mason's marks on the Old Belt Line Bridge built in 1891 over the James River. He counted marks on 313 of the 2727 visible pier stones and found 53 different marks suggesting at least 53 different masons supplying the stones for the 10 piers.

Bill Trout also sent Mike Starkey's report on mason's marks on the locks and culverts of the Kanawha Canal through the James River Gorge. These are reproduced below. The construction date is variously in the 1820s to 1840s.

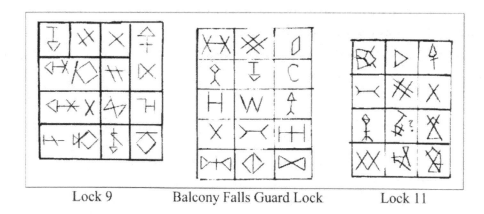

| Lock 9 | Balcony Falls Guard Lock | Lock 11 |

It is surprising how infrequently and erratically these marks are found. Apparently it was a choice by the contractor whether to pay by the piece or the hour. If by the piece, the stonemason had a stake in labeling his work so as to get credit for it. If the mason who cut the stone was not involved in installing the stone in a lock wall, it became a matter of chance as to whether the mason's mark faced out or not. If the stone was square in the long cross-section, there was only a 25% probability of the mark showing in the finished wall; 50% if the cross-section was rectangular, and the mason knew to put his mark on the narrower side.

Testimony concerning Lock 1 on the Muskingum Navigation shows a stonemason charged with installing the lock stones, which were boated to the site already cut to size. I've found no mason marks on any of the Muskingum stones.

The mason's mark was a unique signature for a particular construction project, but probably not for a career. The symbols used were much simpler than those used in earlier centuries in Europe where a stonemason enjoyed higher prestige.

A visit to the Internet provided examples of mason's marks found on stones from the cathedral in Cologne, Germany, the probable country of origin for Zoar's stonemasons.

At the guard lock on the Zoar side of the Tuscarawas River, dated 1830, the following symbols appear: XI, XIII, XIIII, II, LII, and two, more complex marks:

These marks do not show up on the opposite side of the river where an undated guard lock permitted access to the slackwater above a dam from the Ohio & Erie Canal. It looks as though a different set of masons provided these stones. That would make eleven Zoar residents acting as stonemasons, if both guard locks were built in 1830. (The purpose was to provide navigable access for canal boats to the four mills – saw, flour, planning and woolen – along the mill race on the Zoar side.) If they were done at the same time, it's significant that none of the mason marks are duplicated on the two locks.

Stones for each of the six walls of the guard lock were cut by a different mason as shown in the figure below, and all the marks are facing out. Stones that make the bend in the wall are cut in the shape of a pentagon with two right angles where the stone meets the adjoining wall. Since the sum of angles in a pentagon is 540 degrees, this leaves 360 for the remaining three angles or 120 degrees apiece which would be the face angle. It looks as though the masons may have cut the stones on the site, installed them themselves and cooperated on who cut the pentagons. The famous Zoar flour mill that straddled the Canal was built seven years later. Lock 10 was also constructed by Zoarites but it was refurbished in a 1900s repair by the Daley Brothers, and the original stones are not exposed.

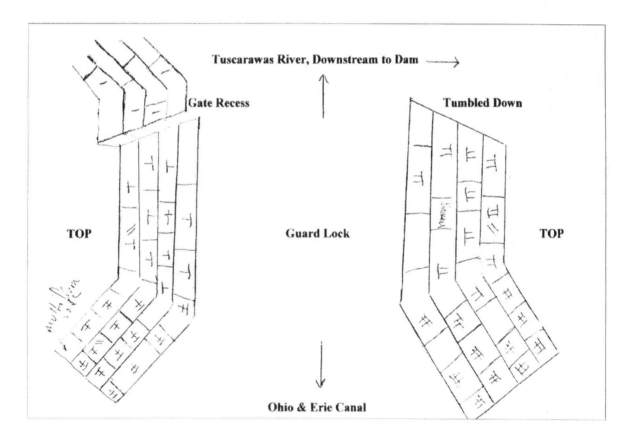

Marks on the walls of Lock 29 at Peninsula on the Ohio & Erie Canal are Roman numerals; III, IV, V and VI. These stones were probably cut at the nearby Deep Lock quarry. Were there six stonemasons? If so, what happened to the stones cut by I and II?

At Lock 21 west of Newcomerstown ten of the 25 coping stones are marked with an abutting **XX**, with right angles instead of the 45 degree angles shown here and a square instead of a diamond in the middle. It's possible that the same stonemason cut them all, and the unmarked stones are reversed so that their marks are hidden. Only eight of the other hundred or so stones show marks. Some sixteen at the upstream end are rough-cut and appeared to have been installed under different management.

Neil Sowards sent a mark from the lock that allows boats from the St. Marys feeder into the Grand Reservoir. It's an **X** with a third line through the middle. During the restoration of Lock 38 in the CVNRA a mason mark was recorded in the shape of a triangle with a handle. Finally, there's the mark found at Waverly, which looks like one of those found at Balcony Falls by Mike Starkey.

§§§§§§§§§§§§§§§§§§§§§§§§§§§§

*So when all the digging was done, how many miles of canals had been dug in Ohio? There are some discrepancies in the following table, which appeared in the very first issue of* Towpaths, *but 1,000 miles is the generally accepted figure. (Ohio & Erie and Miami & Erie totals include branch canals.)*

Volume I (1963), No. 1, p. 2

### CANAL MILEAGE IN OHIO by Chief of Engineers, U.S.A. 1896

| | |
|---|---|
| Miami and Erie Canal | 301.49 |
| Ohio and Erie Canal | 512.26 |
| Pennsylvania and Ohio Canal | 76. |
| Sandy and Beaver Canal (Less 6 miles included in the Ohio Canal) | 79. |
| Whitewater Canal | 32. |
| | 1000.75 |

*After the Irish and Germans completed their work in the Cuyahoga Valley, the first boats were ready to navigate the Ohio & Erie Canal between Akron and Cleveland. The following article was submitted by noteworthy canal author Terry K. Woods, a former CSO president and* Towpaths *editor. Also a member of the "Canal Buffs Hall of Fame," he ranks with Trevorrow and Bond as one of our exceptional contributors.*

Volume X (1972), No. 1, pp. 6-8

### OHIO'S FIRST CANAL BOATS by T. K. Woods

The first canal boat in Ohio was built in Akron sometime prior to July 1827 and was named, appropriately enough, the STATE OF OHIO.

That section of the Ohio & Erie between Akron and Cleveland was officially opened July 4th, 1827, but the STATE OF OHIO, carrying the Governor and other dignitaries, left for Cleveland the day before. It was soon met by an Erie Canal boat that had been purchased in Buffalo, brought across the lake, towed up the Cuyahoga, dragged into the canal at Akron, and re-christened the ALLEN TRIMBLE.

The two boats stopped for the night in Boston, then continued on the next day. The PIONEER, constructed earlier that year in Peninsula, and itself loaded with passengers and a band, came up the canal from Cleveland and met the other two boats some six miles above the village. A salute was exchanged and the three journeyed on together.

The Governor said in his speech later in the day that, "The boats were cheered by thousands assembled from the adjacent country side, at different points, to witness the novel and interesting sight", of Ohio's new transportation system in operation for the first time.

Local histories fail to mention that the three boats were forced to stop some distance outside the village. Records show that water wasn't let into the "Cleveland Bends" till April 1828 when Lock #44 was completed. Lock #43, at the foot of South Water Street hill, wasn't completed until July 29, 1827. Then boats entered Merwin's Basin for the first time, reached the river through a temporary cut, and unloaded.

Though Lock #42, 1,000 feet south of Broadway and 500 feet south of the old Grasselli Chemical Plant on Independence Road was operational, research indicates that the initial flotilla on the Ohio & Erie stopped at Lock #41, at the foot of Harvard Avenue. This lock is better known to canal buffs as "Five Mile Lock".

The ceremony and speeches were scarcely over when Captain Guy unloaded the ALLEN TRIMBLE which had arrived with a cargo of flour consigned to Merwin, Giddings & Co. This firm also sent the first boat from Cleveland to Akron. John Blair bought an Erie boat, the HENRY CLAY, and started a freight and passenger line in Cleveland. He painted a sign on the boat's side, "The Farmer's Line – Night and Day". He also acquired the STATE OF OHIO under Captain Wheeler, the CANTON under Captain Bremigan, and the SUN under Captain Munson.

The SUN, a passenger packet, started running day and night between Cleveland and Akron on July 25, 1827. It left Cleveland at 8:00 P.M. on Monday and Friday evenings and departed Akron for the return trip on Tuesday and Saturday afternoons at 5:00 P.M. With 42 locks and three aqueducts to negotiate, that 37 mile trip took over 20 hours.

The canal was closed for the winter at Christmas time, but that first season saw 1,811 tons of freight and 6,020 passenger miles originate or terminate in Cleveland. It was the beginning of a prosperity that transformed Cleveland from a tiny village to the largest city in the state.

An interesting footnote to this story is the fact that when the Ohio & Erie Canal was begun in 1825, the exact location of its northern Terminus was left undecided. An estimate made in 1825 indicated it would cost $6,000 less to terminate the canal on the west side of the Cuyahoga. The village of Cleveland donated $5,000 to the Canal Fund and Chief Engineer Bates located the route on the east side of the river. This made Cleveland the northern Terminal. It's doubtful if $5,000 was ever more wisely invested.

Much of the information contained in the above article was gathered from a series of articles by W. S. Kelly in the 1945 *Plain Dealer*.

**State of Ohio canal boat**. A 1959 photograph of the remains. *From* Towpaths, *Vol. II (1964), No. 2, p. 1.*

§§§§§§§§§§§§§§§§§§§§§§§§§§§

*Countless articles have been written about canal boats. Few have been presented as concisely and as colorfully as this piece by John C. Vanderlip.*

Volume II (1964), No. 3, pp. 1-3

## CANAL BOATS by John C. Vanderlip

Born simultaneously with the opening of the canals was a new type of boat, a far cry from the clumsy, old river scow that could navigate only with the current. This new breed of boat adopted the best features of the old Durhams, incorporated the better points of cabin design from the Arks, and came up with the last word in overland travel. No more dusty, bumpy trips on the stage! Freight rates would be halved and then halved again, towns and cities that were weeks apart were now only days between by this modern conveyance which seemed to glide effortlessly at the end of a long tow rope extending from the towpath where the horses or mules were employed to pull the boat.

Highest on the canal's social ladder was the packet, and a haughty queen she was! She held precedent over all other boats as points of contest, such as entering locks or passing midstream, and never missed an opportunity to remind her subjects of her royal birthright. Considered strictly a passenger boat, she was the best equipped and the most elaborate. She was named after the fast sail boats that plied the Atlantic coastal waters and allowed only hand luggage aboard.

A step lower than the packet was the line boat, and a versatile craft was she. One could move his whole family, including the kitchen stove, below her decks even to the point of doing a little housekeeping en route. Although she was designed primarily as a utility boat, in later years she was used almost exclusively to forward freight, especially the type that could be stowed below decks.

Next, below the line boat, came the freight boat which usually was built either for bulk cargo, such as coal or gravel, or was constructed similarly to the line boat with space under her deck to carry her load. The bulk carrier was sometimes referred to as the three cabin boat, with a cabin in the bow for the crew, one in the stern for the Captain and his family and a small stable sandwiched between the cargo bins midship for the mules.

Besides these three basic type boats, there was the shanty boat, where sometimes a second and third generation was reared that never lived on solid ground, plus a variety of makeshift craft built either for limited service or constructed by rank amateurs.

Although there seems to be different opinions as to whether or not a timber raft would be considered in the boat category, we do know that it was despised by every one on the canal. It consisted of from five to ten parts, called cribs, which were locked through separately and then lashed together to form a slow moving, clumsy contraption that delayed every boat in the vicinity.

A few boats were steam driven but it seems that they were unable to compete with horse and mule power. First, construction and operating costs were much greater and, second strong objections were raised in their use on account of the commotion of the water to the detriment of the canal banks and to other boats.

Last, but not least, we had the State Boats—the guardians of the right of way. To these floating black smith and carpenter shops was entrusted the job of maintaining the canals, even to the extent of working right through the winter if their services were needed. Each boat had a certain portion of the canal to maintain and did yeoman service when washouts and breaks occurred.

§§§§§§§§§§§§§§§§§§§§§§§§§§§§

*Animals provided the motive power for canal boats. Lew Richardson's "Power on the Towpath" was the first true* Towpaths *article.*

Volume II (1964), No. 1, pp. 1-6

### POWER ON THE TOWPATH by L.W. Richardson

CANAWLERS—This issue is devoted to motive power on the canals. Because of space limitations, the application of mechanical power to canal propulsion has been ignored. A future number will be concerned with the numerous attempts, in Ohio and elsewhere, to utilize the power of steam and electricity to move canal boats.

\* \* \*

Building America's canals, with little experience, limited in talent, and the primitive equipment then available was a monumental task, but one that was accomplished with an astounding degree of success. Routes and grades were surveyed, hydraulic problems solved water supplies established and locks and other structures so well built that, when undisturbed, many are in good condition after a hundred years or more.

Cheap and efficient operation of the canals was, on the other hand, a goal never quite achieved. The long history of canals is also the story of man's endless experimentation with every known source of power, in an effort to find the best way to move a heavy boat through a narrow waterway.

The first canals in recorded history depended on the energy of men for tractive force, augmented when possible by primitive sails. We accept the fact that the Chinese, with a seemingly endless supply of cheap manpower, still depend largely on these two methods. We know, too, that sails are used in modern times in the Low Countries of Europe. It is more difficult to accept the fact that, as recently as the turn of the century, teams of men were pulling canal boats in Germany, Holland, Belgium and England. A German authority, Dr. Mitzen, in 1890 calculated that men could tow boats up to 26 tons at 1½ miles per hour, 11 miles per day. He neglected to tell us how many men! An interesting footnote to this use of men as draft animals was the development, in England in the 1800's, of a new trade, the "leggers". On the Birmingham Canal there were two tunnels, each about two miles long and built with low roofs and no towpaths. At the portals men awaited traffic and for a fee propelled the boats through by laying on their backs and pushing with their feet on the roof and walls of the bore.

When the first canals were built in America, the use of men on the towpath was, in most instances, expressly forbidden, although it was considered proper to labor with pikes and sculling oars in canalized rivers and streams. There were exceptions to the general rule, In 1856 "Porte Crayon" described in Harpers a trip on the Jericho Canal in Virginia "…the barge was propelled by two slave boatmen, who each took hold of a long pole, and by the help of a peg and withes, rigged it horizontally, one at the bow and the other to the stern…so that the ends projected over the towpath."

On the eastern canals, oxen were the principal means of power, at first horses were reserved for fast packet service. Oxen were powerful; Harlow in *Old Towpaths*, states that, "One yoke of oxen drew, on the Middlesex, a raft of timber calculated to weigh 800 tons," but they were very slow, even with a light tow they did little better than a mile an hour. Sails were used extensively but were not dependable and at times were even slower. Thoreau, in his A Week on the Concord, comments, "With their broad sails set, (the canal boats) moved slowly up the stream in the sluggish and fitful breeze."

By the time the canal fever had reached Ohio it was generally conceded that horses could supply, if not the cheapest, at least the most dependable power. Before the end of the period the mule had replaced the horse to a great extent. But there were still problems. An account of the troubles one Ohio "canawler" experienced in the early days is found in *The Life and Reminiscences of the Hon. James Emmitt*, published in Chillicothe in 1888.

"In 1836, Mr. Emmitt organized the Eagle Line of passenger and freight packets, to ply the canal between Portsmouth and Cleveland. He owned one half the stock in this company, and Ransome and McNair of Cleveland, the other half. The company owned one hundred and thirty horses and twelve boats.

"The horses were stationed at what was then regarded as proper intervals, between Portsmouth and Cleveland. In their endeavor to do a great deal of business, the proprietors of the Eagle Line often worked many of their horses forty-eight hours at a stretch. The result was, that they killed a great many of them from overwork, and reduced the others to an almost worthless condition. They operated this line for about two years, and during this time, their gross receipts from passenger traffic amounted to fourteen thousand dollars, and from freight twelve thousand dollars. When they balanced up their affairs, at the end of the first year, the three partners had to pay in six hundred dollars each to make good their losses.

"The other boat lines, competitors of the Eagle Line, were the Troy Ohio Line, owned by Pease & Allen, which had equipment about equal to that of the Eagle; the Troy and Erie, owned by Standard, Griffith & Co., and the Farmers' Line, operated by Chamberlain & Co.

"They all lost money, owing to the same causes that operated against the Eagle Line—trying to do a heavy business with a light equipment of horses. They all worked their horses to death, and their profits disappeared in replacing the animals whose endurance had been overtaxed. After running along in this way about a year, the competitive lines concluded to consolidate their teams, and to accomplish this they organized the Towing Path Company, and by throwing their live stock together they had control of about six hundred horses. The arrangement did not affect the ownership of the boats—or floating stock—

at all. It was designed merely as an economical arrangement for moving the boats over the line. But it didn't produce satisfactory results, either, as the actual cost of towing a boat was twenty-six cents a mile. No money could be made, in the face of such an expense account, and in the fall, after the formation of the company, a dissolution of partnership was agreed upon. All of the animals belonging to the company were assembled in Cleveland, preparatory to a redistribution, and it can be honestly said that it was the most wonderful collection of old, broken-down, sore-headed horses ever gotten together in Ohio. There were probably five hundred animals in this grand round up of worn out nags, and they presented every form of disease, deformity and dilapidation the horse is subject to. It was a wonderful collection of equine freaks. Some members of the company added their canal boats to the general heap and terms of redistribution were agreed upon. The horses and boats were all numbered and valued, and every man drew by lot to the value of his stock in the company.

"Mr. Emmitt secured, as his share of the wreckage, three horses of questionable usefulness, and a canal boat. With his share of the spoils, Mr. Emmitt started for Waverly. The harness was lost off one of the horses, and a few days after leaving Cleveland the boat was locked in the ice, where it was held for several days. Two of the horses died on the way home.

"It was plain to all interested, after the nonsuccess of this experiment, that some better method of caring for the towing stock had to be devised. The horses had to be worked fewer hours and given more rest between tricks. It at first seemed impossible to do this without increasing the number of horses and placing the stations closer together, which would entail a very heavy expense. But finally someone conceived the idea of erecting a stall on the boat, amidships, capable of accommodating three or four horses, and of carrying the horses 'off trick' right on the boat, where they could be fed and rested with the greatest possible convenience and economy. It was a happy scheme for the boatmen, and its great utility was promptly recognized. The expenses of boating were reduced fully two thirds, and money making was made possible on the canal. After the system of carrying the horses on board the boat was inaugurated, the cost of towing canal craft was reduced to seven cents a mile. Had is system been adopted from the start, the proprietors of the early canal lines would have made fortunes, instead of losing considerable money, as they did."

While the adoption of the on-board stable reduced expenses, it must be noted that it did not always improve the lot of the animals. In the last years of the canal era, it was reported that the four mule teams on the Susquehanna double boats were often worked a thirty six hour trick without rest.

The search for answers was not always one of trial and error, as the one just quoted. Before many years the engineers were applying professional knowledge to the problem. This is illustrated in The Report of the State Engineer on the Canals of New York, 1863.

"Expense of Towing...Boats. Speed At Two Miles per Hour."

"'When a boat is moved in a canal whose cross section does not exceed 6.46 times the cross section of the boat, it has a peculiar obstacle to surmount. The water in front will be elevated, and falling from this height it tends to escape along the sides, but cannot accomplish this as in an indefinite fluid, and carries forward with it a portion, the more considerable, as the interval between the sides of the boat and the canal is reduced."

There follows a half page of algebraic calculations based on French experiments and concludes that the resistance of a boat of 76 tons capacity, 78½ ft. long and 14½ ft. wide is 245 lbs. and that the cost of towing would be 14.31 cents a mile. It continues:

"From numerous experiments in France, ordinary horses exerted an effort of 143½ lbs. for six consecutive days, at a speed of two miles an hour; then the number required to tow (the boat described) would be 245/143 or 1.71 horses."

It may be that Ohio horses were not "ordinary," in any case, experienced and knowledgeable canal operators had long known that unless the canals were enlarged to accommodate larger boats, that could be moved more efficiently, the system was doomed. At the time of the New York report just quoted, the Erie had been improved once and was then, according to the Engineer, in need of another enlargement.

§§§§§§§§§§§§§§§§§§§§§§§§§§

*Tow animals were the unsung heroes of the canals. Imagine hauling a 200,000 pound load over this distance up this elevation.*

Volume II (1964), No. 1, p. 7

**HORSEPOWER**

A large Ohio canal boat would weigh 20 tons and was capable of hauling 80 tons – a gross load of 100 tons. On a haul from Cleveland to Akron this 100 ton load would be lifted 395 feet and pulled 37 miles. All with only three or four horsepower.

§§§§§§§§§§§§§§§§§§§§§§§§§§

*Here's a little snippet from the November 7, 1849, edition of the* Onondaga Standard *contributed by Richard N. Wright. There is no evidence that rats were actually used as tow animals.* ;-)

Volume VII (1969), No. 4, p. 51

**TALL TALES OF THE CANALS – "A Whopper"**

"They tell us of big rats on the line of the Ohio Canal, & one of them is said to have towed a boat, using his tail as a towline. That's a whopper – of a rat, we mean. If we should attempt to beat this rat story, we would tell of a mosquito in the Montezuma swamp on the Erie Canal, who stole a boat pole for a tooth pick".

*Dozens of articles have appeared in* Towpaths *on the topic of canal commerce. Cargoes included wheat, timber, coal and other bulk goods such as ice in the days before refrigeration. Here we turn to another "all star" contributor, the late George Crout, former curator of the Middletown Canal Museum.*

Volume XVI (1978), No. 1, pp. 1-4

## ICE BUSINESS ON THE MIAMI AND ERIE CANAL by George C. Crout

On January 13, 1870 the **Middletown Journal** reported: "Heavy work forces are at work at the Ice Houses along the canal, packing away the crystal. Ice dealers and ice packers have been harvesting all week. The late cold weather made splendid ice on the ponds around town. It will range in thickness from 5 to 8 inches – clear and solid. The business of ice packing in this vicinity, this season, will be no mean item in the aggregate, as many hundred tons will be cut, and considerable capital will find its way into the hands of laborers, and thence into the pockets of our merchants. The crystal ought to be cheap next summer, and our citizens can calculate upon keeping cool."

While most people think of the canal as a mode of transportation, the harvesting of ice was once one of the most important industries along the canal, with surplus water from the canal being used to fill the ice ponds which paralleled its banks.

Middletown and Hamilton were well located for the ice business, for they were within easy shipping distance from Cincinnati, the Queen City of the West, and a major city. With a large German population beer was a favorite drink and ice-cold beer was preferred. In the summertime the ice was shipped to Cincinnati on canal boats.

One firm, the Knoor Ice Company had ten storage houses at LeSourdsville, now a popular lake resort, and cut from a forty acre area. A load was shipped south each summer day and when it became very hot, two shipments were made.

Middletown had its own large brewery, the Sebald Brewery, which operated its own ice pond. It was a six-acre lake.

Ice houses in the immediate vicinity of Middletown in the last quarter of the 19th century included besides those mentioned, several others. The Collins Company harvested from a pond of six to seven acres. The Doty Pond just north of the old Doty Lock covered about three acres. Adley's had two ponds, one on each side of the canal, covering perhaps seven acres. Cunningham's, near Dick's Creek, covered four acres. The largest was at LeSourdsville as noted, but south of it was one at Rockdale of about six acres.

Each pond had one or more ice storage houses. Sawdust was used for packing and insulation, and was brought down by canal boat from northern Ohio where forestry was still a major occupation, and piled up for the ice season.

The writer had the opportunity to interview one of the ice cutters, Julian Rice, some twenty-five years ago. He recalled his work on the ponds as a boy, and said that the ice cutters used tongs, hooks and ropes with pulleys to hoist the ice into the store houses, and then later a continuous chain conveyor with hooks to lift the ice and store it more rapidly was invented.

The **Middletown Journal** reporter stated as early as 1870 that "an elevator was used for carrying the ice from the pond to the house, and the process of filling was very rapid. The machinery was operated by an engine. A great number of hands were employed, which made the sight rather interesting to look at."

In 1884 the same newspaper reported that the ice merchants "have been reaping their harvest during the past week on their large ponds near this place. Several hundred men are engaged in the business. The ice-chewers will have a good harvest this season."

The thickness of the ice varied from winter to winter, but in an interview Rudolph Schiebert, another Ohioan who remembered ice-cutting days, said he remembered "one winter they cut fourteen-inch ice off the old canal." This seems to indicate that after the ponds were harvested and if it were cold enough, ice could be cut from the canal itself.

In the winter, ice cutting or ice harvesting was a cold way to make a dollar a day, but with construction work down, several hundred laborers were available. When it was felt that the ice had reached its maximum thickness, large, flat-bottomed sleds loaded with special equipment pulled out for the frozen ponds. They carried such tools as spud bars, pike poles, tongs, augers, ice-saws, ropes and pulleys, snow scrapers and ice markers. Two draft horses pulled the sleds.

When a good spot was found, the horses were hitched to a five-pronged ice marker which made indentations in the ice about thirty inches apart. They marked in one direction and then in the opposite to produce cross-hatched lines making the surface look like a giant checkerboard.

Men dressed like lumberjacks drilled holes in the ice with ice augers, then the ice saw with its large teeth, powered by men's muscles, began cutting the blocks of ice which were freed by the spud-bar men. To pick up the free-floating ice, a chute was lowered into the water, and the pike polers guided the crystal cakes to the chute.

At first a cowsucker, an iron frame, was dropped over the end cake. Attached to it was a long rope which ran through a pulley, hooking to a single tree, pulled by a horse ridden by a slender young boy. This pulled the ice up into the house. This method was replaced by a conveyor line powered by a steam engine. The ice saw also became motorized, and mounted on a sled.

But this was not the end of mechanization. Eventually the ice-making machine itself was invented, and manufactured pure, clear ice at any time of the year. The Sebald Brewery brought the first such machine to Middletown, and before long the icehouses were deserted and another industry was gone. The era of delivered, man-made ice also ended when the modern refrigerator put an ice-making machine in every home.

§§§§§§§§§§§§§§§§§§§§§§§§§

*Another bulk commodity shipped along Ohio's canal system was iron. This article from Lloyd Manley provides a nice mix of technical detail and eye-catching artwork.*

Volume XXXVII (1999), No. 4, pp. 79-80

## STEEL MANUFACTURE AND THE P. & O. CANAL by Lloyd Manley

In the highly competitive blast furnace industry, transportation costs were critical and often made the difference between profit and loss, especially when many miles separated the furnace from its raw materials and markets. This is because the ore, limestone and fuel are heavy and bulky while the finished products can weigh huge amounts. Boats and ships were and are to this day the most economical means of moving this freight. The P. & O. Canal was vital to the early success of the iron industry in the Youngstown area. The first blast furnace in Ohio was a small charcoal-fired smelter in Mahoning County built in 1804. It used the abundant kidney ore. By the time the canal came into use others were operating and the industry boomed. Pig iron and finished products could easily travel by boat to the iron fabricators in Pittsburgh, Cleveland and Akron. Several blast furnaces were built on the bank of the canal to utilize its low-cost freighting. Raw materials were available close to the waterway and not too distant from the furnaces.

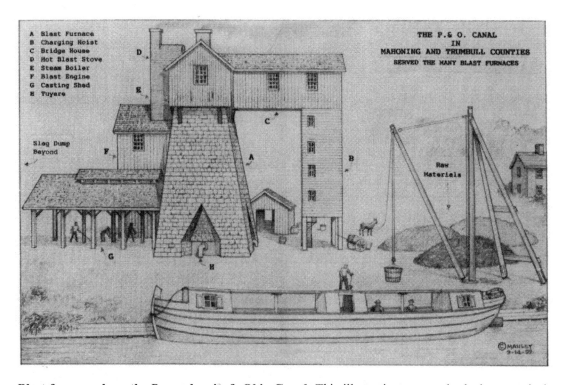

**Blast furnace along the Pennsylvania & Ohio Canal**. This illustration accurately depicts a typical three-cabin freight boat and iron foundry. *Drawing by Lloyd Manley.*

Until 1846 charcoal was the principal fuel, but in that year experiments using the local hard coal without conversion to coke were successful. Expensive charcoal and coke were not required, a significant saving. Many larger and more efficient furnaces were built because, unlike fragile charcoal, the coal could support a much heavier burden of ore and limestone without being crushed (which would retard the air blast). About this time coal began moving on the canal to Cleveland to fuel a rapidly expanding fleet of steamships on Lake Erie. Not until 1856 when the Cleveland & Mahoning Railroad reached Youngstown was this business threatened.

In 1846 a large vein of high quality iron ore was discovered near Niles, close to the canal. It could fill the needs of the numerous large furnaces built after 1850 and some of its ore would be shipped to Cleveland and other cities. In 1846 the first rolling mill began operation near Youngstown. It could convert cast pigs to malleable wrought iron much faster than the old forge hammers, and long bar stock and rails could be produced at low cost. The industry would continue to expand for 100 years or more becoming a major steel mill complex. However by 1860 the canal had lost most of its business to railroads which were faster.

§§§§§§§§§§§§§§§§§§§§§§§§§§§

*In addition to ice and iron, canals also moved people. Short excerpts from this famous journal entry by ex-president John Quincy Adams are common but it rarely appears in its near entirety. Too bad, since it is one of the best passenger accounts of travel in an Ohio canal boat ever written.*

Volume IV (1966), No. 2, pp. 17-19

## TRAVEL ON THE CANAL by John Quincy Adams

In 1843, The Astronomical Society of Cincinnati invited the President of the United States, John Quincy Adams, to lay the cornerstone of a new observatory to be built in that city. The President accepted with reluctance, his interest in science overcoming his distaste for travel. The journey involved going from Boston to Buffalo by train, to Cleveland by lake steamer and then to Cincinnati by canal boat and stage coach.

His account of the trip through Ohio is of interest not only for the vignette of canal travel but is also a rather startling reminder of a far less complicated age. The small Presidential party shared a packet boat with numerous other passengers and the Chief Executive enjoyed no more privacy or comfort than the others.

After the ceremony, the hill on which the observatory was to stand was renamed Mount Adams by the grateful Cincinnatians.

The following excerpts are from Vol. XI, The Memoirs of John Quincy Adams, 1876.

- - -

"Nov. 1. - - - From this place (Cleveland) there are two modes of proceeding to Columbus, distant two hundred and thirty-two miles - - - one by land stages traveling night and day, with excessively bad and very dangerous roads; the other by canal boat on the Ohio Canal, which will take us four days to reach Columbus. We were advised by all means to take the latter mode, which we concluded to do, and took passage in the canal boat ROB ROY, Captain Phillips. She was to depart at two o'clock P. M., and in the mean time I was to undergo a reception - - - Mr. Andrew made the address to me, which I answered as usual, and shook hands with the men, women, and children; after which we dined at the American Hotel, and embarked in the canal boat ROB ROY.

"Akron, 2nd. - - I came on board the canal packet boat ROB ROY yesterday very unwell with my catarrh, hoarseness and sore throat, and some fever. This boat is eighty-three feet long, fifteen wide, and had, beside the persons I have named, about twenty other passengers. It is divided into six compartments, the first in the bow, with two settee beds, for the ladies, separated by a curtain from a parlor bed-chamber, with an iron stove in the center, and side settees, on which four of us slept, feet to feet; then a bulging stable for four horses, two and two by turns, and a narrow passage, with a side settee for one passenger to sleep on, leading to the third compartment, a dining hall and dormitory for thirty persons; and, lastly, a kitchen and cooking apparatus, with sleeping room for cook, steward and crew, and necessary conveniences. So much humanity crowded into such a compass was a trial such as I had never before experienced, and my heart sank within me, squeezing into this pillory, I reflected that I am to pass three nights and four days in it. We came on board the boat at two o'clock, the time when she was to depart, but it was four before she left the wharf. We were obliged to keep the windows of the cabins closed against the driving snow, and the stoves, heated with billets of wood, made the rooms uncomfortably warm. - - -

"3rd. - - In the course of yesterday and this day we passed through the places named in the margins of Wednesday's page (the names of 45 towns between Cleveland and Columbus.) We reached Massilon last evening after dark, and, it being a considerable place, there were symptoms of a desire on the part of its inhabitants to give me a reception. - - - We finally persuaded them to let us pass on quietly. As acquaintance became familiar with my fellow passengers, time slipped away more cheerily. They are all kind and obliging, the young ladies very lively and good-humored. The weather has been so harsh and churlish that we have not been tempted to open our windows, or to stand on the deck of the boat to see the country around us. The banks of the canal are so muddy that there is no comfort in walking. We see that we are in a beautiful country, with a deep rich soil, but much of it along the borders of the canal is woodland, and with the wood cut down, and the stumps standing, like the pins of a bowling green, and presenting an aspect rather of desolation than plenty.

"In the common dining room and dormitory I made out with no small trouble and inconvenience to write for about two hours in the forenoon of yesterday and this day, and one hour of each afternoon, in this diary, - -. I write amidst perpetual interruptions, in the presence of half a dozen strangers, who seem to think me a strange, sulky person, to spend so much time in writing. The most uncomfortable part of our navigation is caused by the careless and unskillful steering of the boat into and through the locks, which seem to be numberless, upwards of two hundred of them on the canal. The boat scarcely escapes a heavy thump on entering every one of them. She strikes and grazes against their sides, and staggers along like a stumbling nag.

"We passed, in the course of last night, through a settlement of Germans, called Zoar, a community under an absolute ruler, and this day through Gnadenhutten, originally a Moravian settlement, but now fallen into the ordinary track of breeding towns. This afternoon the sky cleared off, and on approaching a place called Roscoe, several of us landed, and walked about a mile, when we were obliged to return to the boat.

"4th. - - About one o'clock this morning Mr. Grinnell came to my settee and awoke me, to communicate to me a letter just received - - - inviting me to visit - - that place (Newark) - where we were to arrive about sunrise. On reaching Newark we landed - - - -. After breakfast we went to the Town Hall, I believe, crowded with goodlooking persons of both sexes, and there a gentleman welcomed me with a complimentary address - - -.

"We returned to the boat, and proceeded, to terminate our navigation at Hebron. Here we took leave of the Macy family, Mr. Russell, and Miss Langdon, whom we had found charming traveling companions. They proceed in the boat to Portmouth, where the canal reaches the Ohio River. We are henceforth to go by land stages to Cincinnati."

§§§§§§§§§§§§§§§§§§§§§§§§§§§§

*Understandably, canawlers harbor a certain amount of resentment towards railroads. Our attitudes are reflected here by another former President of the United States, Martin Van Buren.*

Volume XLIII (2005), No. 3, p. 62

## CANAL VS. RAILROAD, II

Martin Van Buren, Vice President (1833-1837), and former governor of New York State wrote the following, contributed by Larry Turner.

"Dear President Jackson:

"The canal system of this country is being threatened by the spread of a new form of transportation known as railroads. The federal government must preserve the canals for the following reasons:

1. If canal boats are supplanted by railroads, serious unemployment will result. Captains, cooks, drivers, repairmen and lock tenders will be left without a means of livelihood, not to mention the numerous farmers now employed and growing hay for horses.
2. Boat builders would suffer, and tow line, whip and harness makers would be left destitute.
3. Canal boats are absolutely essential to the defense of the United States.

"In the event of the expected trouble with England, the Erie Canal would be the only means by which we could move supplies so vital to waging modern war.

"As you may well know, Mr. President, railroad carriages are pulled at the enormous speed of 15 miles per hour by engines which, in addition to endangering life and limb, roar and snort their way through the countryside setting fire to crops, scaring livestock and frightening women and children. The Almighty certainly never intended that people should move at such breakneck speed."

§§§§§§§§§§§§§§§§§§§§§§§§§§§

*Railroads so severely damaged the canal business that the state leased out the waterways to private interests. The lessee period from 1861-78 is a constant source of controversy among historians of the Ohio canal system, as tackled by Terry Woods in 1971.*

Volume IX (1971), Vol. 4, pp. 55-56

### MAINTENANCE OF OHIO CANALS DURING THE LEASE by T.K. Woods

The state-owned canal system was leased in 1861 by a company consisting of William J. Jackson of Piqua, Joseph Cooper of Cincinnati, Colonel. A. Medberry of Roscoe, Thomas Brown of Dayton, Thomas Moore of New Philadelphia, and Kent Jarvis of Massillon. The lease was to run for ten years at a cost to the company of $20,075 per year, payable semi-annually in advance.

Apparently, this arrangement was agreeable to both parties as the lease was renewed in 1871 to the same company at the same terms. Then, in 1878, the company abandoned the lease and the canal system came under state control again in 1879.

Some historians charge that the canals were not properly maintained while leased and were practically useless when returned to the state. Other authorities claim that canal maintenance during the period of leasing was no worse than that conducted by the state and that this was just an excuse the state used for its subsequent abandonment of the system.

Turning to the contemporary newspapers, the *Akron Beacon Journal* for 1881, we find that the northern division of the Ohio & Erie was closed for one week on June 10, 1881 for water to be drawn off and repairs made.

During this one week period, "the lower west wing wall of Lock #5 and both wing walls of Lock #6 are to be repaired. One pair of gates will be put in at Lock #16 and a set of gates at Lock #19, two pairs at Clinton, one pair at Fulton and two pairs at Navarre. Peninsula Lock will be repaired; the heavy traffic and short time allowed for repairs prevent its replacement.

"Three new towpath bridges are to be built. One bridge 80 feet long will be constructed at Goose Pond waste weir, another 45 feet in length at Lock #36 (17 Mile Lock) and still another at Lock #39 (11 Mile Lock).

"Some 'grouting' will be done to a number of locks to prevent them from leaking. Several sand bars will be removed and other repairing done." The *Beacon* reporter then adds a significant paragraph, "The work done heretofore has not been of a permanent character and for this reason, more work needs to be done this year. If two wing walls were built every year, the locks would be in excellent shape, but now several years will be required to accomplish this."

That the canal had to be drained for repairs during a time of heavy traffic indicates that there was a dire need for repairs. It also appears that the wooden gates and towpath bridges had not received proper periodical maintenance. Otherwise, there would have been no need to replace so many complete wooden structures in 1881.

This leads to the conclusion that the canals were not properly maintained by the Lessees, at least not in the final few years prior to 1878. Since the state renewed the lease in 1871, the maintenance during the first ten year lease can be assumed to have been satisfactory.

§§§§§§§§§§§§§§§§§§§§§§§§§§

*Canal water has never really had all that great of a reputation, as evidenced from this passage in the Report of the Chief Engineer of the Board of Public Works.*

Volume V (1967), No. 4, p. 48

## WATER POLLUTION IN 1879

"In the manufacture of paper and starch, and in other manufactures along the line of canals, a large amount of chemicals are used; after use these chemicals become very offensive, and the residuum is allowed to flow into the tail races, and from thence in to the canals, to the great detriment of their navigation.

"These chemicals poison the waters so as to kill fish in the canals, and make the water so very offensive that the stock cannot drink it. They also produce a stench that is very disagreeable and unhealthy to persons living along the lines. It is also a serious damage to the boatmen, as, from its alkaline property, it produces a foam or suds, at or in the locks, during the commotion of the water produced by filling and emptying the same, which often rises so high as to run into the windows and doors of the boats."

§§§§§§§§§§§§§§§§§§§§§§§§§§

*During the early 20th century, the state spent considerable time and expense in improving the canal system. For a discussion of this period, we return to the writings of Frank Trevorrow. It is the third installment of the articles referred to in the editor's note.*

Volume XXVIII (1990), No. 1, p. 1 & pp. 5-9

## OHIO'S CANALS—THE FINAL YEARS, PART I: The 20th Century Improvement Program by Frank W. Trevorrow

EDITOR'S NOTE: The three articles in this issue of <u>Towpaths</u> were contributed by Frank W. Trevorrow, charter member of the Canal Society of Ohio, honorary trustee, past president, author of significant historic research and publications on Ohio's Canals, marine architect, and advisor on canal lore to all of us in the canal following. Not to be outdone by Frank's many contributions is his devoted wife Marjorie, who has hiked uncounted miles on the towpaths these many, many years as Frank's faithful assistant.

### CANAL IMPROVEMENTS

Canal supporters gained a measure of success with the passage of the Act of April 6, 1902 by the General Assembly "to provide for the retention, maintenance and supervision of the canals of Ohio, their water supplies, reservoirs, dams, feeders, and adjacent lands, to encourage the building of canal boats and the extension of cheap transportation." The Board of Public Works recommended to the Legislature the enlargement of the canals to a minimum depth of five feet to accommodate 100 ton boats. It was argued such an improvement would not necessitate enlargement of existing structures. A Joint Board in Control and Management of Lakes, Reservoirs and State Lands dedicated for public use, consisting of the Board of Public Works, the Chief Engineer and the Ohio Canal Commission was created in pursuance of the Act. Land leases, water rents, oil leases and land sales were reviewed. Two unrelated events occurring in 1902 were the purchase and conversion of the well-known boat *River Mills* to a State boat and the construction of a new lock to connect Long Lake at Akron with the Ohio & Erie Canal at the Summit Level.

Chief Engineer Chas. F. Perkins continued his advocacy of improvement in his 1903 Report, recommending the inauguration of plans for the systematic improvement of the Northern Division of the Ohio & Erie Canal and all of the Miami & Erie. The Southern Division of the Ohio & Erie from Dresden Junction was to be maintained in its then present condition His estimate for improvement to five foot depth was:

| | |
|---|---|
| Dresden to Cleveland | $573,186.33 |
| Cincinnati to Toledo | 964,602.41 |
| Total | 1,537,788.74 |

These amounts were submitted to the Legislature in January 1904 and formed the basis for subsequent Legislative action.

The condition of the canals made improvement imperative if they were to continue to operate. The Ohio & Erie was reported to be navigable by 80 ton boats from Cleveland to Trenton, by 60 ton boats to Newcomerstown and with ordinary repairs, it could have been navigable to Dresden. From Columbus to Waverly, it was navigable by 50 ton boats. Below that place, it had been closed for many years. The collapse of the Great Miami and Mad River aqueducts in July 1903 closed the Miami & Erie at Dayton, but it was navigable above Dayton to Toledo.

The supporters of the canal system achieved their greatest success with the passage of Senate Bill 258 which Governor Myron T. Herrick approved May 6, 1904. The Act provided for an appropriation of $75,000 for 1904 and $125,000 for 1905 for the reconstruction of the Northern Division of the Ohio & Erie Canal. The appropriation was not to be available until new water leases aggregating $30,000 per year for terms of not more than five years were negotiated by the Board. The Board had no difficulty in achieving that goal by the end of 1904. Perkins termed the Act: "Decidedly the most important and meritorious step for the retention and improvement of the canals." The Act was signed by Warren G. Harding, President of the Senate. The Act provided that the appropriations were to be expanded for the reconstruction in accordance with plans and specifications prepared by Chief Engineer Perkins. The Improvement was expected to involve a total expenditure of $573,064.33, substantially the estimate Perkins submitted in his 1903 report.

Two considerations may have favorably influenced the decision to rehabilitate the Ohio canals. New York had undertaken the construction of the Barge Canal replacing the Erie Canal with greatly increased capacity. The Federal Government was about to undertake the canalization of the Ohio River. It was thought Ohio's canals would then be in the strategic position of forming the natural link in the waterway system joining the Eastern Seaboard with the Ohio and Mississippi rivers, a concept prevailing since the beginning of the Ohio canal system.

Actual construction began in June 1905 after four month's delay caused by an injunction brought by one of the bidders. After dismissal of the injunction, contracts were awarded for rebuilding the whole line of the Ohio & Erie Canal from Cleveland to Akron in three work sections. Section 1 comprising locks 22 to 27 inclusive, sluices between locks and Sand Run aqueduct was awarded to McGarry & McGowan. Section 2 comprising locks 28 to 35 inclusive, Peninsula aqueduct abutments and removal of the center pier went to P. T. McCourt. Geo. W. Carmichael & Co. was awarded Section 3, locks 36 to 41 inclusive, culverts, sluices and wasteways between locks, Mill Creek and Tinkers's Creek aqueduct abutments. The contract for the steel superstructures for the three aqueducts was awarded to the King Bridge Company. D. E. Sullivan & Co. was awarded the contract for dredging the canal, Cleveland to Akron. At the southern end of the Improvement Clifton Bros. of Zanesville was awarded the contract to build a new outlet lock to the Muskingum River and repair the other two locks on the Dresden Side-Cut. This work was important because the Federal Government had appropriated $110,000 for a dam and lock on the river between Zanesville and Dresden, contingent on Ohio improving the connection of the Side-

Cut with the river.

Although no appropriation for work on the Miami and Erie was made for 1905, Perkins found it necessary to increase the estimate for that canal to $1,214,798.41 for additional dredging in Cincinnati and the replacing of all wooden locks between Loramie Summit and Defiance with concrete structures. The Legislature acted favorably again in 1906, providing $100,000 for the Ohio & Erie and $150,000 for the Miami & Erie in 1906 and $150,000 for the Ohio & Erie and $206,000 for the Miami & Erie in 1907.

On the Miami & Erie, contracts were made in 1906 for steel truss aqueduct superstructures at LeSourdsville and Sunfish Creek with Capital Construction Company. Frank Davis received the contract for reconstruction of locks 32 to 43 inclusive, comprising all the locks between Middletown and Lockland, excepting lock 36 at Hamilton, awarded later. Schneider Bros. held the contract for locks north of the Summit, No. 14, "Saw Mill", north of St. Marys and No. 36 and No. 37 at Defiance. Six Mile Creek aqueduct was awarded to David Beard.

The contracts made in 1906 for the Ohio & Erie included all the locks within the city of Akron. No. 1, to No. 7 inclusive to P. T. McCourt, No. 8, to No. 14 inclusive to S. W. Parshall and locks No. 15 to No. 21 inclusive to McGarry & McGowan. Lock No. 16 at Trenton was contracted to J. W Kisner. Other work contracted included sluices, Mud Run culvert and dredging. The specifications for lock reconstruction called for the use of old lock stone to the extent of about one-third of the mass, to be imbedded in the concrete in layers, each separated from another by not less than eight inches and no stone to be laid nearer than twelve inches of the top, face or end of wall. At lock No. 16, Trenton, it was decided to use the stone from the old lock to protect the canal bank between lock No. 16 and No. 17 where the river had encroached. The new lock was hence all concrete. Much original stone was thus hidden from future canal researchers.

T. D Paul, engineer-in-charge of the northern section of Ohio & Erie, noted in his report: "Ever since the removal of Three Mile Lock, No. 42, the five mile lock has been too shallow for even a four foot canal, and to get a five foot depth, the only feasible plan was to lower and rebuild the entire lock." This is a rare mention of "Three Mile" lock, which must have been located just north of Clark-Pershing bridge, and was removed when the new outlet to the Cuyahoga at South Dille street was made in 1872.

Work on the Miami & Erie proceeded at a faster pace in 1907 with the larger appropriation. Contracts for locks 30, "Lower Greenland" and 31, "Dines" were placed with Frank Davis, and locks 24, "Upper Carrollton" and 27, "Sunfish" with Fauver & Renich. A. Koenig received the contract for locks 28, "Franklin", and 29, "Upper Greenland". Other important contracts placed were for dredging, Miamisburg-Middletown with Thos. Strack, and Amanda Aqueduct with T. N. Harrison. North of the Summit, lock 34, "Paper Mill" was contracted to Schneider Bros., lock 43, "Bucklin's" to Oberle & Sawyer and Providence Dam to John Weckerly. Lock 44, Providence Guard & Lift lock was repaired by State forces.

On the Ohio & Erie contracts were placed for work south of Akron with Jas. Wildes for Clinton Guard lock and locks No. 1 and No. 3, with S. W. Parshall for locks No. 2 and No. 13 and with Fauver & Renich for locks No. 4, No. 11 and No. 12. Contracts for lock No. 6 to No. 10 inclusive was awarded to

Daley Bros. of Bolivar, lock No. 14 to H. Minnich and lock No. 15 to J. N. Kisner. Other important 1907 contracts were: to Burns & Engle for Wolf Creek Aqueduct with the superstructure contract to Capital Cons. Co. J. S. Kisner received the contract for rebuilding Walhonding Dam and dredging the canal, which would serve as an important feeder to the canal at Roscoe. Franklin Bros. received a large contract for a new Reservoir in Summit County. Rebuilding sluices, wasteways and culverts between locks was included in the lock contract or was performed by State forces.

Generous appropriations were made in 1908, $245,000 for the Ohio & Erie and $281,000 for the Miami & Erie. The resignation of J. C. Wonders, engineer-in-charge of the Miami & Erie Improvement, to become the first State Highway Commissioner was a sign of the times. On the Miami & Erie, contracts were let for locks 12 and 13 at St. Marys, 35 and 38 at Defiance, 41, "Texas" and 42, "Rice's" and locks 45 to 52 inclusive, Maumee to Toledo. Kinnear Bros. held the contract for locks 45 to 52, S. W. Parshall for locks 12 and 13 and Schneider Bros. for locks 35, 38, 41 and 42. Important contracts were also let for Middletown Dam to Carver Contr. & Transp. Co., Crescentville Aqueduct to D. F. & C. R. Snider and the Miami river Aqueduct of two eighty foot spans to Capital Const. Co. Kinnear Bros. received the contract for the Loramie Waste Weir, T. H. Watson for the Lewistown Weir and Bulkhead and H. F. Romaine for the revetment wall of the West Bank of St. Marys Reservoir. On the Ohio & Erie 1908 contracts covered mainly river work. The contract for Cuyahoga River bulkheading was placed with Standard Cons. Co., Zoar Dam and Regulator and Hilton Dam at Trenton to Daley Bros., and Sugar Creek Dam to Clark & Medley.

Appropriations were greatly reduced in 1909, providing $140,000 each for the Ohio & Erie and the Miami & Erie. On the Miami & Erie, B. Neihaus contracted for locks 22, "Snider's", 23, "Dryden's" and 25, "Lower Carrollton". Williams & Morse contracted for lock 26, "Miamisburg" and 36, "Upper Hamilton". All locks south of Dayton were thus under contract for rebuilding. North of lock 21 at Dayton to Lockington Summit, no rebuilding was undertaken. North of the Summit three stone masonry locks, 8, 24 and 30 did not require rebuilding. Except for locks 12 and 13 at St. Marys and 14, "Sawmill", none of the wooden locks between New Bremen and lock 32, "Vial's" were rebuilt. Lock 1 at New Bremen was rebuilt in 1910 under a separate appropriation. Locks 32, "Vial's" and 33, "Schooley's" were contracted to T. H. Watson & Son.

Most major contracts for the Ohio & Erie had been placed before 1909. The few contracts placed in 1909 were for lock 5-A, a culvert and towing path embankment with W. M. Brode & Co., and for a retaining wall between locks 5 and 5-A with I. H. Watson & Son, all at Massillon. Perkins noted in his 1909 report the failure to include rebuilding the five-span Walhonding Aqueduct on the mistaken assumption that only nominal repairs were required, thus omitting a vital structure necessary to complete the line to Dresden.

Contract prices for work on the Improvement Program ranged from five to eleven thousand for lock rebuilding to vastly larger amounts for river work, of which the following are examples:

| Dredging: | Cleveland to Akron | $79,741.64 |
| | Walhonding Canal | 22,843.70 |
| | Zoar Canal to Dover | 11,212.21 |
| | Miamisburg to Middletown | 46,278.47 |
| Miami River Aqueduct | | 22,456.19 |
| Middletown Dam | | 26,844.98 |
| Cuyahoga River Bulkhead | | 35,148.66 |
| New Reservoir, Summit County | | 29,772.64 |

Troubles to the Improvement program began to appear in 1908 with the abandonment of contracts by McGarry & McGowan, Fauver & Renich and P. T. McCourt. Serious trouble was reported on the condition of lock 28 "Deep Lock" on the Ohio & Erie at Peninsula. P. T. McCourt held the 1905 contract and completed it the same year. On trying to pass a dredge through the lock in 1909, it was found that the wall slanted inward due to sagging of the concrete forms and also that the concrete was of poor quality. The poor quality of the concrete was attributed to certain ingredients of Cuyahoga River gravel. The walls were refaced, wing walls and wasteways extended and gates reset at the State's expense. Poor quality concrete was also evident at lock 34, "Red" or "Jaite" Lock. The faulty work of McCourt led to charges later of fraud and mismanagement of the whole Improvement Program.

By 1910 all major work on both canals was under contract or completed. Only $60,000 was appropriated for the Miami & Erie and nothing for the Ohio & Erie. No appropriations were made thereafter. Perkins was replaced as chief engineer in May 1910 by Jas. R. Marker, appointed by Governor Harmon. Marker submitted a report to the Governor in September highly critical of the Improvement Program and charging gross mismanagement and fraud. As a result, the Improvement Program came to a virtual halt. After the expenditure of over one and one-half million dollars, with most of the important structures rebuilt, the canals were not navigable and would remain that way until the devastating floods of March 1913 ended the possibility of resumed operation to all intents and purposes.

§§§§§§§§§§§§§§§§§§§§§§§§§§

*All that work was undone by the 1913 flood. A canawler who lived through it, "Dillow" Robinson of Independence Township, provides this harrowing account.*

Volume XI (1973), No. 1, pp. 5-8

### THE 1913 FLOOD by "Dillow" Robinson

That was the first year I worked as a member of the State Boat crew. A State Boat always kept one man through the winter to help with chores and one thing and another. Since it was my first year, I was the one picked to work with the Captain throughout the winter of 1912-1913.

Well, it was in late March, and it had been raining for two or three days; the Captain and I walked up to the feeder gate and looked at the water. It was coming up so fast that he said, "Well, let's go back and get the boat out of the lock chamber". We usually wintered our boat in Fourteen Mile Lock. Then the Captain said, "I'll harness the team, you get the towline out, and we'll bring the boat up here to the bridge; it'll be safer than down in the lock".

Well, before he got the team harnessed, a man that lived over at the Brecksville Station came down the path and he said, "Do you boys want any help?" And we assured him that we did so he harnessed the other horse. Then the Captain came up to me and said, "Huey Burns is goin' to drive the team; I'll steer and you take care of the bow. When we get to the bridge you take the bowline and tie it to the bridge's framework".

So we towed the State Boat up to the bridge and when we arrived. I put the bowline around the framework. Huey Burns and the Captain unhitched the team and tied the towline to a tree on the towpath side of the canal and secured another line to a tree on the heelpath side. Then they ran still another line from the stern to a tree farther down the towpath.

We next tried to push the boat down into the canal so we could get the bowstem under the iron framework, but the water was too high by then and no matter how hard we tried, we couldn't accomplish it.

The water was coming up awfully fast by then so we all moved off the boat to the near-by Brady Napp house. A little while later, a retired Policeman or Fireman from Cleveland came into the house. He lived in a boat that was beached down the canal a piece. He was called Long Jack Geiger.

Then there was another man, lived in a boat, went by the name of Peg-Leg John. He mended umbrellas and kitchen utensils and used an old canal boat as his home and place of business. Two of our party waded out to his boat, got him on the back of one of them, and carried him up to the Brady Napp house.

We were all in that house for about two days and two nights. Nobody slept much. What sleep we did get was in a chair. Everybody was jumping up from time to time, running outside, and trying to see just how high the water was.

Irv Murphy, the Feeder Tender, went out once and, while he stood at the approach to the bridge, it suddenly lifted under the pressure of the swirling water, took a quarter turn, and sank into the canal. When we heard of this, the Captain and I hurried out to see what had happened to the State Boat.

Somebody must have been looking out for us; as the bridge made that quarter turn, it sheared the bowline and left the boat riding safe in the choppy water, still secured to the trees. Our big worry then was, where was the bridge? If it was underneath the boat, we would have the devil's own time getting it off when the waters receded.

After two days and nights at the Brady Napp house, the rising waters forced us to higher ground and we all moved up to the home of a farmer named Carter. We stayed there for four or five more days.

After a time the water began to recede and we went out to look at things. Our fears that our boat would come to rest on top of the sunken bridge when the water went down were unfounded. The flood water rushing over the bridge floor had gouged a deep hole into the canal bed below. Then, when the bridge was torn off its abutments, it dropped into this hole and left the boat floating free above it.

So we got back on board, loosened the other lines, and float down stream toward Fourteen Mile Lock. And that's where we ended up after the flood—just about where we started from.

There were a couple of big breaks in the towpath of that section, but no harm had come to the Pinery Feeder Dam. So when the flood pretty well dried up, we brought the team from the Carter Farm back to the winter barn in Brecksville and we set about fixing up the damage that the flood had done to our section of the canal.

There was nothing wrong with the feeder dam so once we completed our repairs to the banks, that section had a good head of water. But the stretch south from the Pinery Narrows to Akron was almost completely destroyed. Our State Boat continued working our section, maintaining it only for hydraulic purposes, till about 1920—seven years after the flood, but there was no commercial traffic after 1913.

Actually, there had been very little traffic after about 1906 or 1907 when they rebuilt the locks out of concrete and dredged the channel. Our State Boat made what I think was the last trip down the canal through Canal Fulton. The reason for that was, we were in Akron; we built a long retaining wall to be done down in Fulton. On the way, we planked the aqueduct at Wolf Creek (Barberton).

They had a State Boat at Fulton, run by Johnny Moore, but he had only one man to help and he didn't have any tools or implements or anything. So we went down there and we leveled some of the towpath that had become piled up from the dredging. We weren't down there too long and then we went back to Cleveland.

We had plenty to do around Cleveland even though there wasn't any traffic. We always had four or five men working for us, though generally only four. I left the canal when I was about 23 and I've done a lot of things since, but I've never forgotten my life on the canal.

§§§§§§§§§§§§§§§§§§§§§§§§§§§

*While 1913 is generally accepted as the end of the canal era in Ohio, the book was not officially closed until 1929 with formal ceremonies at Middletown.*

Volume XXXIV (1996), No. 3, pp. 38-39

### CLOSING THE MIAMI & ERIE CANAL by George Crout

It was at Middletown that the Miami & Erie Canal had officially begun on July 21, 1825, and it was here that in November, 1929, it was officially closed. According to contemporary accounts both events were appropriately celebrated. While the story of the groundbreaking has been widely recounted, the closing seldom has been noted, yet, it too was a major event. Local and state authorities decided on the date, Saturday, November 2. At midnight officials went to the State Dam and turned the water off; foot by foot it receded, and, within 12 hours, the first section dug from the dam to St. Bernard was almost dry.

The commemorative program began at 12 noon with a Jubilee Luncheon at Hotel Manchester, presided over by George M. Verity, President of the Armco Steel Corporation. Many dignitaries were introduced and made brief remarks. Representing the State of Ohio was Attorney General Gilbert Bettman, who had assisted the movement to abandon the canal, and State Senator, David H. De Armond, author of the bill to close it. Frank Raschig represented the State Highway Department. Congressman Roy G. Fitzgerald of the Third Congressional District was principal speaker. Representatives of all major railroads of the area were present, as well as city and county officials of various governmental units of the Miami Valley, along with Chamber of Commerce officials. Celebrity Jeff Davis, King of the Hoboes, an invited guest, was popular with the crowd.

Local civic leader, George H. Sebald, Chairman of the Middletown Committee of the Miami Valley Superhighway Association, presided over ceremonies following the luncheon. Sebald was credited with originating the plan to fill in the canal and convert the right-of-way to a state highway from Cincinnati to Toledo. Later I-75 would be built following a more direct route, but many sections would be converted to parkways.

Thousands turned out that Saturday afternoon to witness a Towpath Jubilee Parade, depicting the evolution of transportation from the Indian travois to the airplane. Fortunately, film was taken of the event and has been transferred to videotape. The parade ended at a reviewing stand erected on the east side of Yankee Road at the canal bridge.

In the 1825 ceremony two governors, DeWitt Clinton of New York and Jeremiah Morrow of Ohio, had each lifted a spadeful of earth, officially beginning construction of the Miami Canal. As part of the closing ceremonies, this symbolic gesture was recreated, the reporter noting: "The pages of history were turned back. The two spadefuls of dirt which the Governors had borrowed at the beginning of construction were returned."

As a permanent remembrance of the event a boulder monument was unveiled, reading in part that "this Ohio property was rededicated Nov. 2, 1929 to its original purpose—Transportation". In Middletown the old canal route became Verity Parkway, in Hamilton, Erie Boulevard, and in Cincinnati, Central Parkway.

Over 104 years separated the official opening and closing of the canal. The Ohio canal system represented the biggest public works effort of the early 19th Century, and led to rapid economic development in the state.

However, as George Knepper in his history of Ohio noted, "even under the best conditions, the canal's lifespan was limited, because...the railroad was on the rise". Dr. William E. Smith wrote that the canal could have been made into a barge canal, deepened and widened, but that "the public was in no mood to save it." However, its closing led to new uses of the land, parts of which were developed into recreational and historical areas.

# OHIO'S CANAL SYSTEM

## MAP OF OHIO CANAL SYSTEM
## 1825-1913

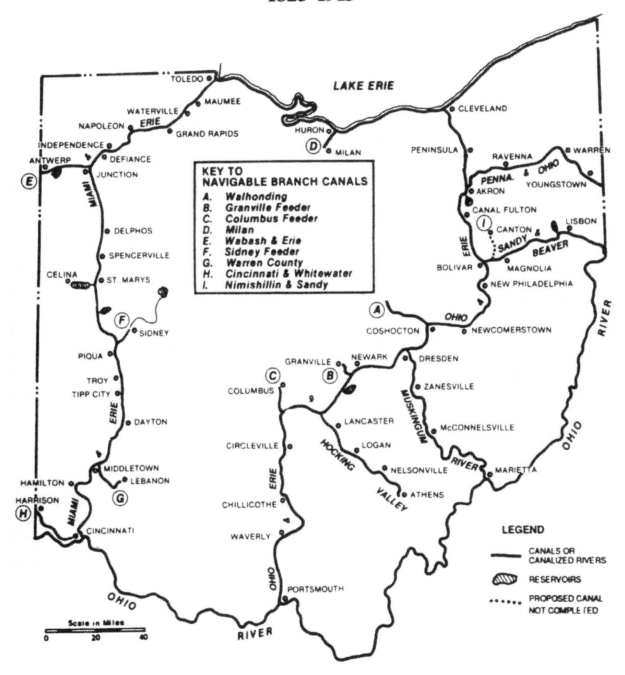

**KEY TO NAVIGABLE BRANCH CANALS**

A. Walhonding
B. Granville Feeder
C. Columbus Feeder
D. Milan
E. Wabash & Erie
F. Sidney Feeder
G. Warren County
H. Cincinnati & Whitewater
I. Nimishillin & Sandy

**LEGEND**

— CANALS OR CANALIZED RIVERS

▨ RESERVOIRS

••••• PROPOSED CANAL NOT COMPLETED

Scale in Miles
0   20   40

**"Official" CSO map of the Ohio Canal System.** *From* Towpaths *Vol. XXVIII (1990), No. 1, p. 4.*

*The 1975 sesquicentennial issue provided a capsule summary of each of Ohio's 27 navigable canals. Much of the material was assembled by the* Towpaths *editorial staff and compiled from earlier issues. Here, history repeats itself as this commemorative 4-part 150th anniversary edition (the only issues of* Towpaths *to ever feature a color cover) has been modified and updated. "New" canals have been added, bringing the total number to 40, and the order of presentation has been rearranged to be consistent with the format of the book. Summaries were written by the* Towpaths *editorial staff except where noted.*

*First up is "Ohio's Grand Canal," followed by no less than 15 separate and individual canals associated with the Ohio & Erie.*

Volume XIII (1975), Nos. 1-4, pp. 5-68

## SESQUICENTENNIAL ISSUE, 150 YEARS OF OHIO'S CANALS

### 1. THE OHIO & ERIE CANAL

The Act of 1825 that authorized building the Ohio & Erie Canal specified that construction should begin near the Licking summit, and it did, but the Canal Commissioners had decided to construct and open the canal in sections from north to south so communications with eastern markets via the Lake and New York's Erie Canal could begin immediately upon the opening of the first section. […]

Completion of the first 38 miles of canal between the new village of Akron and Cleveland was scheduled for the fall of 1826, but a number of things conspired, the delays mounted, the spring of 1827 came and went, and still a great deal of work remained on that northern section. […]

So a big push was put on in 1827 to open the canal by July. All the workmen in that northern section were taken off nonessential jobs and put to readying the canal bed, towpath and structures for navigation. The official opening was July 4th that year, but none of the feeder dams were yet finished nor were many of the lock bypasses and tumbles that insured an even head of water between levels. As a result, the water supply for the rest of 1827 and well into 1828 was intermittent and navigation was difficult at best. Still, when the canal was closed from cold weather in December of 1827, over 1800 tons of freight had been moved between Akron and Cleveland.

Sickness, competition for workers from other canal projects and an occasional inept or unscrupulous contractor continued to plague construction of the canal, which delayed the scheduled openings of several canal sections. But the 28 mile section from Lock #1 in Akron south to the lock just below the newly formed town of Massillon (Lock #5) opened in August, 1828; the section to Dover in 1829; to Newark in 1830 and to Chillicothe in 1831. Then, with the exception of the lower lock into the Ohio River near Portsmouth, the Ohio & Erie Canal was completed and its entire length open for navigation on October 15, 1832.

Two sloop locks, each of six feet lift and with chambers of 25 feet by 100 feet joined the Ohio & Erie Canal to the Cuyahoga River about ½ mile above the river's mouth. These locks, Nos. 44 & 43, allowed the largest class of sloops and schooners then navigating the lake to enter Merwins Basin and pick up or off-load cargo at the many warehouses lining its shore.

From here, the Ohio & Erie Canal used 42 locks to overcome the remaining 389½ feet of the Cuyahoga slope to the Portage summit at Akron. There were also three aqueducts in this section: one across Mill Creek, nine miles from Cleveland and one across Tinker's Creek, thirteen miles from Cleveland. The other, at Peninsula, carried the canal from the eastern to the western side of the Cuyahoga River. About ten miles from this point the canal abandoned the valley of the main Cuyahoga for that of the Little Cuyahoga to the vicinity of Lock #16, then the old outlet of the Summit Lake to the northern edge of the Portage summit—some 38 miles from Cleveland. [...]

The Portage summit was nine miles long and passed through a natural body of water—Summit Lake. The level of this lake was dropped approximately five feet to drop the level of the summit so it could easily receive water from the upper Tuscarawas. Attempts to build a towing path along the eastern shore of Summit Lake or support one from the bottom all failed due to the extremely mushy conditions of the area. It was necessary to build a floating towpath, from light timber dowled together, across a portion of the lake.

The first lock on the Tuscarawas slope was located on the west side of the river in the present city of Barberton. A few rods south of Lock #1 the canal crossed Wolf Creek above a dam, then remained on the west bank to Clinton, where it crossed to the east bank of the Tuscarawas on slackwater above a dam and stayed on that side of the river for the next 28 miles through the towns of Fulton, Massillon and Bethlehem (Navarre) before again crossing to the west bank, this time on the "Tuscarawas Aqueduct", a short distance above Bolivar.

The canal remained on the east bank now for 57 miles to Roscoe, where the Walhonding River joins the Tuscarawas to form the Muskingum. On the way it passed through the towns of Dover, Lockport, New Castle, Trenton, Gnadenhutten, Seventeen, Port Washington, Newcomerstown, Evansburg and Lewisville. Sugar Creek in Dover was crossed upon a slackwater above a dam. The Walhonding River was crossed upon a long three-span aqueduct. This aqueduct was unique on the Ohio & Erie in that its southern abutment was an integral part of a double lock (Locks #26 & 27) that lowered the canal into Roscoe Basin.

For the next 14 miles the east bank of the Muskingum River was followed through Adams' Mills to Webbsport. This is the lowest level between the Portage and Licking summits. There were originally 29 locks between this point and the Portage summit to handle the 238 foot change in elevation. [...]

After Webbsport, the Ohio & Erie Canal left the Muskingum valley and ascended the valley of the Wakatomaka for about nine miles. Then, passing through a gap in the divide, it ascended the valley of the Licking River to the summit level in Licking County, touching as it did the towns of Hartford's, Frazeysburg, Nashport, Lickingtown, and Newark. This was a distance of 32 miles with a total ascent of 160 feet that was overcome with 19 locks. There were three aqueducts on this relatively short stretch. One was across the main branch of the Wakatomaka one mile above Frazeysburg. Another was across the North Fork of the Licking River at Newark and the third was across the middle or Raccoon Fork of the Licking River and this one was also located in Newark, about one mile from the second.

One of the more unusual features on the Ohio & Erie Canal was in this section at the "Narrows of the Licking". Here, the Licking River flowed through a narrow, rocky defile leaving little room along its banks to dig a canal. The engineers solved the problem by damming the Licking at the narrow end of the gorge and leading the canal through the valley along the resulting slackwater pool. At one point it was necessary to blast a towpath along the face of a sheer rock wall. […]

The Licking summit, itself, was 14 miles long and touched the towns of Hebron and Millersport. Three aqueducts were located along the summit level. One was located at Hebron; another, two miles south of Hebron and the third across the South Fork of the Licking some three miles from Hebron. […]

Water was supplied to the summit level by the "Granville Feeder" at the northern end of the level and by the Licking Reservoir, now known as Buckeye Lake. […]

In order to have the summit level low enough to get the maximum benefit from the reservoir, it was necessary to dig a three-mile long "Deep Cut" through the dividing ridge. The cut began near the feeder aqueduct, extended to the south and was 34 feet deep near its center.

From the summit the canal descended southwardly along the valley of Walnut Creek for some 18 miles passing through the towns of Baltimore, Havensport, Carroll, Lockville, Waterloo, Winchester, Raneysport and Sharps' Landing. The canal crossed, then recrossed Walnut Creek to take advantage of the terrain before crossing a level plain between the valleys of the Walnut and Big Belly and followed the latter to Lockbourne just above the Big Belly's junction with the Scioto. Lockbourne lay just some 30 miles from the Licking summit by canal. The 202 feet difference in elevation was overcome by 30 locks. […]

From Lockbourne to the Ohio River near Portsmouth the canal generally followed a course south through the Scioto valley touching the towns of Holmes' Landing, Millport & Bloomfield, Circleville, Westfall, Yellowbud, Deer Creek, Andersonville, Clinton Mills, Chillicothe, Sharonville, Waverly, Jasper, Cutler's Station and, by crossing the river after leaving the canal, Portsmouth. The first 15 miles of this section ran along the east side of the Scioto, crossing Walnut Creek near Bloomfield, about 7 miles below Lockbourne, upon a slackwater above a dam. At Circleville the river was crossed on an aqueduct; a lock with a 9½ foot drop was built into the stonework of the western abutment.

Eleven miles below Circleville the canal crossed Yellow Bud Creek by an aqueduct and, 14 miles below Circleville, it crossed Deer Creek on another aqueduct. Yet another aqueduct was used to cross Paint Creek, some two miles below Chillicothe, and Sun Fish Creek, 21 miles north of the Ohio River, was crossed on a twin arch culvert. Two more stone culverts were required in this last stretch of canal: a one arch affair across Camp Creek, 17 miles above the Ohio River, and a three arch job across Scioto Brush Creek 8 miles north of the junction. The total length of this section was 87 miles and 24 locks were required to lower the canal 211 feet. An outlet lock allowed canal boats to venture out into the Ohio River. […]

As originally constructed, the Ohio & Erie Canal was 308.14 miles long (exclusive of feeders) and used 146 locks to overcome a difference in elevation of 1,207.35 feet. It also used 5 guard locks and 203 culverts. In order to cross streams or rivers, aqueducts were used 14 times and slackwater pools & dams 8 times. In addition, there were 6 dams used exclusively to provide slackwater pools for water supply.

The Ohio & Erie Canal was noted (as indeed were all of Ohio's canals) for its competent, but unspectacular engineering. The dimensions of the canal's prism and locks were carbon copies of those used on the Erie. The minimum widths were 40 feet at the waterline and 26 feet wide at the bottom with a minimum depth of 4 feet. The Commissioners, however, wisely dictated that these dimensions were to be exceeded whenever the resulting cost would not be significant. It wasn't unusual, therefore, at least during the early days of the Ohio & Erie Canal, to come upon sections that were 100 feet wide and 12 feet deep. Aqueducts were designed with wooden flumes resting upon stone piers and abutments and, at least one of these aqueducts (the one at Circleville), was covered. Locks were the standard mitered gate type made of stone, with a closed chamber measuring 90 feet long by 15 feet wide.

The size of the lock chambers determined the maximum dimensions of the boats that could be used on the canal. Boats 80 feet long by 14 feet wide and 4 to 4½ feet deep, drawing up to 3 feet of water, loaded, soon became standard on the Ohio & Erie and other state canals. The earliest boats were sharp prowed, built for speed and able to carry only about 45 tons of cargo each. Slow evolution in their design made later boats fuller of line and more blunt in the bow and stern. These changes allowed Ohio boats to carry between 80 and 85 tons of cargo each run. [...]

The Ohio & Erie Canal experienced relatively little modernization during the years, but some changes were made in the interest of efficiency and better navigation. Some aqueducts were replaced by culverts. Some slackwater stream crossings, such as those at Wolf Creek and Sand Run, in what is now Summit County, were replaced with short aqueducts. [...]

Early in the history of the canal a 2½ mile branch was constructed from the main canal near Webbsport through Dresden to the Muskingum River which had been "improved" and made navigable to the Ohio River at Marietta. Advocates of retaining Ohio's canal system suggested that the northern portion of the Ohio & Erie, from Cleveland to the Dresden Side Cut, should be improved by deepening the channel to a minimum depth of five feet and rebuilding or repairing the structures as needed; then the Side Cut and the Muskingum Improvement could be used to complete a direct route to the Ohio River.

In 1904, the State Legislature appropriated $200,000 to begin the rebuilding. $75,000 was to be used during 1904 with the remaining $125,000 to be used in 1905. Additional funds were authorized through 1909 for a total appropriation of $790,000. All of the locks from the northern terminus to Lock #16 in Trenton (Tuscarawas) plus the three locks that lowered canal boats into the Muskingum River had been rebuilt or repaired with concrete. Also, much of the channel within that stretch had been deepened with steam dredges. The Board of Public Works estimated that another $590,000 would be required to finish the project. The public and the Legislature had grown disenchanted with canals by 1910, however, and no more appropriations were forthcoming. Most of the southern portion of the Ohio & Erie Canal was officially abandoned by the State Legislature in 1911.

While the dredging and repair work were being conducted along the northern portion of the canal, most "Canallers" put up their boats "temporarily" until navigation could once more be resumed. For many, the temporary hiatus became permanent. Some portions of the canal, like that section around Navarre, never held water after 1907 when it was drained for repairs. The final blow came in March, 1913 when devastating floods destroyed much of what remained of the canal. Many of the lock gates in Akron were dynamited by nervous citizens in an attempt to allow water to drain from their town. From Lock #12 in Akron to Brecksville, the canal was virtually destroyed by the flood.

After the flood some local traffic was conducted in the section above Massillon and a State Boat patrolled that section north of the "Pinery Narrows" until the late 1920's, but the canal was useless as a means of long-distance transportation. Any tombstone erected to the Ohio & Erie Canal would have to bear the inscription—"Born—1825; Died—1913".

*In addition to the main line of the Ohio & Erie Canal, the state also constructed a sidecut at Dresden to provide access to the Muskingum River and a number of short feeder canals to augment the water supply. Many of these were navigable. A summary of these is given below, arranged from north to south.*

## 2. THE LONG LAKE FEEDER

Only a few hundred feet long, the Long Lake Feeder provided water to the Ohio & Erie Canal from the Portage Lakes at the "true" summit just south of Akron. The Portage Lakes Reservoirs were created by state engineers from a series of shallow natural lakes and low-lying swampy areas to supplement the summit level water supply. Long Lake remains the outlet.

When the canal was in operation, the Long Lake Feeder provided a connector between the Ohio & Erie Canal and the Portage Lakes. It was navigable for excursion boats into the 1920s. The guard lock which once existed on the feeder was removed in 1955 when Manchester Road was widened.

## 3. THE ZOAR FEEDER

When the main canal was constructed, a feeder of a few rods was built to supply it with water from a point just below Lock #10 in Tuscarawas County to the Sugar Creek crossing. This feeder was navigable and, jointly funded by the State and the community of Zoar, a guard lock was constructed at its head. A dam across the Tuscarawas shunted water into the feeder. […]

In 1908 the original feeder dam was replaced by a concrete one. Sometime prior to this the guard lock on the west bank was removed and water entered the canal through a simple gate. […]

## 4. THE TUSCARAWAS (TRENTON) FEEDER

This navigable feeder was built at the same time as the Ohio & Erie Canal. It was slightly over three miles long and had minimum prism dimensions of 18 feet wide at the bottom, 32 feet wide at the water line and 4 feet deep. It joined the main canal just below Lock #16 near the village of Trenton (now Tuscarawas) and supplied the canal with water for 30 miles to the Walhonding Feeder at Roscoe.

Canal boats were able to enter the feeder through a guard gate at the main canal. A guard lock at the Tuscarawas River allowed boats to leave the feeder, cross the river and go up Stillwater Creek to Uhrich's Mill some seven miles from the Ohio & Erie Canal. A low, cheap dam of brush and stone across the river answered the double purpose of providing slackwater to the mill and diverting water into the feeder.

Boat traffic virtually ceased long before the mill was abandoned in 1891, but the feeder was used as a water source for the Ohio & Erie until the 1913 floods. […]

## 5. THE WALHONDING FEEDER

Not to be confused with the later 25-mile long Walhonding Canal, the original 1830 Walhonding Feeder was about a mile long and provided water to the Ohio & Erie Canal at Roscoe Basin. Supplanted when the Walhonding Canal was completed in 1841, the dam at the head of this navigable feeder was torn out by an ice jam in 1875.

## 6. THE DRESDEN SIDECUT
### from information provided by F.W. Trevorrow and C.K. Swift

Residents of the Muskingum River valley were undoubtedly disappointed when the decision was made to direct the route of the Ohio & Erie Canal away from their valley at a point somewhat below Adams' Mill. The State did want products from the Muskingum valley brought to market through the Ohio & Erie Canal, however, so in 1830 work was begun on the Dresden or Muskingum Sidecut which would allow canal boats to leave the main canal at Webbsport and enter the Muskingum River.

The sidecut was built under the direction of Benjamin Tuttle and was 2 miles long. It crossed Wakatomika Creek on an aqueduct and used three locks to descend to the level of the river at Dresden. The sidecut was opened in 1832 and canal boats and small steamboats began operating on the Muskingum near Dresden during periods of high water.

During the early 1900's an attempt was made to renovate the northern portion of the Ohio & Erie Canal. The three locks at Dresden were rebuilt of concrete in 1905. The Dresden Sidecut was finally abandoned along with the rest of the Ohio & Erie Canal after the 1913 flood.

## 7. THE GRANVILLE FEEDER

When the Ohio & Erie Canal was being constructed through Licking County it was decided to augment the water supply to that section immediately north of the Licking Summit by running a feeder from Raccoon Creek. A contract for the feeder was let in 1831.

The village of Granville lay approximately 1½ miles above the proposed head of the feeder. At the request of the City Fathers, the feeder was made navigable by the State and Granville financed and constructed an extension into the village. The feeder was in operation by 1832 and the extension into Granville was being used by 1833. [...]

The entire feeder plus extension was a little over 6 miles long, contained two locks, the one aqueduct and its minimum dimensions were 18 feet wide at the bottom, 32 feet wide at the waterline and 4 feet deep. Severe floods on the Licking in July of 1834 caused extensive damage to the Granville Feeder and the Raccoon Creek Aqueduct was destroyed. The canal was out of service for the rest of 1834 and a new three-arch stone aqueduct was completed in 1835.

[...] When the Licking Reservoir was expanded in 1836, the Granville Feeder was no longer needed as a water supply.

The Granville Furnace ceased operations in 1838 and the feeder lost its primary source of traffic. After this date the Granville Feeder was virtually abandoned though some water remained to power mills in the 1870's.

## 8. THE COLUMBUS FEEDER
### from an article by L.W. Richardson, originally published in TOWPATHS No. 1, 1966 with additional information supplied by John Droege, Barnett Golding and Gilbert Dodds

The line of the Ohio & Erie Canal, as finally determined, was an excellent compromise between the various proposed routes. [...] There was one flaw in this plan, however. The resulting canal route did not pass through Columbus which was not only the capital of the State, but a lusty, growing community with considerable influence.

It was to be expected that immediate steps would be taken to correct this situation. Canal engineers reported that the supply of water from the Buffalo Swamp area to be impounded into the proposed Licking Reservoir had to be augmented by a feeder from the Scioto River. It naturally followed that the feeder would be navigable and that its terminus would be at Columbus.

Surveys for the feeder were begun in 1824, even before construction was started on the main canal. [...]

As originally constructed the Columbus Feeder was 11¾ miles long. The lower half of the feeder was built to the same prism dimensions as the main canal and the upper portion had minimum widths of 32 feet at the water line and 18 feet at the bottom with a minimum depth of 4 feet. It left the Scioto River between present Mound and State Streets in Columbus from a slackwater pool formed behind a dam across the river. The feeder then remained on the east bank of the Scioto through the communities of Four Mile Lock and Shadesville; and there moved away from the river to the east, crossed Big Walnut (Big Belly) Creek in slackwater above a dam and joined the main canal at Lockbourne a short distance below. The towpath was carried across the slackwater pool formed in the Big Walnut by a floating bridge which was designed to open in the center allowing for ice and driftwood to pass.

A 14 foot difference in elevation between Columbus and Lockbourne was overcome by two locks; one four miles below Columbus and the other on the north bank of Big Walnut Creek. Water obtained from the Scioto at Columbus and the slackwater crossing of the Big Walnut supplied the Ohio & Erie from Lockbourne to the slackwater crossing of Walnut Creek. Stone guard locks protected the Columbus Feeder from high water at both locations.

Construction on the feeder began with the usual ceremonies at the Columbus terminus on April 27, 1827. [...] One interesting sidelight on construction of the Columbus Feeder was that 45 convicts from the nearby penitentiary had there sentences commuted from confinement to "hard labor on the Columbus Lateral Canal" and dug the first mile south from Columbus.

Completion of the feeder was promised by June 1st of 1831 but there were the inevitable delays and water wasn't let into the channel until September 13, 1831. At 8:00 P.M. on Sept. 23rd the firing of cannon announced the arrival of the canal boat GOVERNOR BROWN from Circleville. The standard welcoming ceremonies were held before the BROWN headed back to Circleville, accompanied for a short distance by the Columbus Band and a large group of citizens. Two freight boats, the CINCINNATI and RED ROVER, arrived in the afternoon of Sept. 26th and the LADY JANE arrived soon afterward. The "Port" of Columbus was a reality! [...]

A 7 acre "widewater" in the feeder some three miles south of Columbus was a popular amusement center known as Lake Park. During the 1870's, 80's and 90's, Lake Park featured a dance hall and "safe swimming" (the "widewater" was only 2 to 4½ feet deep). Other attractions at the Park included a picnic grove, refreshment stand, fishing, sailboats and rowboats. Canal boats left the state dock in Columbus at the foot of Main Street every 2 hours for the Park. A round trip ticket plus admission to the Park cost one dime!

The last boat went down the Columbus Feeder to the main canal in 1904 and seventy-three years of canal service to the Capital city came to an end.

*Several minor privately financed waterways also connected to the Ohio & Erie Canal. Boats were known to have navigated these canals; hence they meet the criteria for inclusion. Arrangement is again from north to south.*

## 9. OHIO CITY'S CANAL
### from OHIO'S CANALS by F.W. Trevorrow

Prior to the opening of the Ohio & Erie Canal the land on the west side of the Cuyahoga River at its mouth was mostly occupied by a farm owned by the Carter family. Once the canal was completed, however, there was a great increase in the amount of shipping and commerce at the mouth of the river. […]

A village on the west side of the river was incorporated as Ohio City in 1836. Soon after incorporation, Ohio City authorized the digging of a branch canal to run north from opposite the outlet of the Ohio & Erie Canal. […] This canal was to draw traffic to the docks and warehouses on the west bank.

The Ohio City Canal eventually disappeared, possibly when the Detroit-Superior Viaduct was built. The site of the canal is now Sycamore Street. A vestige of the canal still remains—the slip alongside the Huron Cement Dock. From the new River Road bridge, the line of the canal can be clearly seen south from the cement slip to the railroad bascule bridge.

## 10. MESSENGER'S COAL CANAL
### from an article by Larry Turner and Brad Bond,
### originally published in TOWPATHS No. 3, 2003

The Messenger coal canal was dug in 1847 to connect a tramway from the coal mines and coke ovens of Rogues' Hollow with the Ohio & Erie Canal below Lock #2 near Clinton. Five years later the C. C. & C. Railroad won the right to build along the west side of the Canal and added a drawbridge to cross the coal canal. Shortly after a railroad accident involving the bridge in 1854, the coal canal was abandoned as spurs were built into Rogues' Hollow.

## 11. THE ZOAR IRON FURNACE SIDECUT
### from an article by Terry K. Woods, originally published in TOWPATHS No. 2, 1996

The Zoar Society purchased an iron mine and foundry about ¾ of a mile west of the Ohio & Erie Canal in 1831. A short canal connected the foundry with the Ohio & Erie Canal at a widewater about midway between locks No. 8 & 9. Canal boats were then able to carry pig iron north to Cleveland and the Lake. The Society at one time owned four canal boats.

Including the Zoar Furnace Sidecut, eight distinct and separately named canals existed and operated at one time or another within the borders of Tuscarawas County.

## 12. THE ZOAR SIDECUT

In 1830 the Zoarites built a guard lock and sidecut on the opposite (east) bank of the river into the village. Boats could thus leave the main canal, cross the river above the dam and enter Zoar through the sidecut to service its planing, flour and woolen mills.

About 1833 the Zoarites built a flour mill over the main canal a short distance below the feeder. Water from the feeder was diverted to power the mill. Though boats undoubtedly used the feeder and sidecut for the first few years after the canal was opened, there are no records of such journeys. It is probable then that boat traffic ceased on the new sidecut, and it was used almost exclusively as a hydraulic race, shortly after the "new" mill was constructed.

Over the years the "new" mill fell into disrepair and it was shut down prior to the turn of the century. [...] The guard lock on the Sidecut remained and is still (1975) in an excellent state of preservation.

## 13. THE DOVER HYDRAULIC
### from the 1996 CSO Tour Guide by Earl J. Olmstead of the Tuscarawas Historical Society

In 1806 Christian Deardoff, the founder of Dover in 1807, built the first mill in Tuscarawas County. It was located on Sugar Creek about three quarters of a mile above the Tuscarawas River. He operated this mill quite profitably for a number of years. However, when the state constructed the dam across the Sugar Creek for the canal crossing, Deardoff's mill site was ruined. In compensation, the State granted Deardoff perpetual water rights on the canal. A dam higher up on the creek was constructed to feed a hydraulic race. (This was later known as "The Calico Ditch".)

This hydraulic ran through much of the present site of Dover and entered the canal about 1,000 feet above the Sugar Creek crossing. Deardoff opened the Dover Mills on the hydraulic in 1848. It soon became known as the Cascade Mill and another Dover mill was constructed at the junction of the hydraulic and the canal in 1843, numerous other industries sprung up along the Hydraulic. Canal boats could enter that waterway from the main canal to load and unload cargo. [...]

The Hydraulic continued to operate until long after the First World War. The last vestiges of the ditch and the remains of the second Dover mill were razed in the late 1960's.

## 14. NEW PHILADELPHIA LATERAL CANAL
### from the 1996 CSO Tour Guide by Earl J. Olmstead of the Tuscarawas Historical Society

When the citizens of New Philadelphia found out that the main channel of the canal was not going to run through their city, they protested most vigorously that the canal commissioners agreed to a plan for a by-pass that allowed boats to cross over the river on the slackwater, behind the newly constructed Baker Dam, to the east side of the river. (This dam was located just north of the West High

Avenue bridge.) While the stock books were opened as early as January 26, 1828 and a charter was granted to build the NEW PHILADELPHIA LATERAL CANAL, little progress was made. During the Andrew Jackson administration, the federal government solved the perplexing problem of a budget surplus by returning this money to the various States. After filtering down through the various state organizations, a local partnership, Seaton & Leonard obtained a loan of $20,000 to build a saw and grist mill on the new Lateral Canal. By sometime around 1836 or 1837, the Lateral was operational. The State, for their part, constructed a short Sidecut and one lift lock that allowed boats to exit the canal and enter the slackwater pool, be poled across the river behind the Baker Dam, where they could enter the Lateral. A guard lock on the east side of the river, at the head of the Lateral, provided access to the Lateral Canal. The lateral skirted around the south side of the city, finally emptying into the river three miles downstream. Almost immediately, the location became a beehive of activity. Saw, flour and woolen mills were constructed on the Lateral, and later the New Philadelphia Electric Plant was added to the ever-growing business activity. But, with the coming of the railroads in the 1850's, the canal traffic rapidly diminished. By 1864 the lock on the right bank of the river lay in ruins from the lack of use and repair and the Lateral became only a hydraulic race, but as such, lived on for many years.

## 15. THE LANCASTER LATERAL CANAL
### from information supplied by F.W. Trevorrow, C.R. Goslin,
### Robert McDonnell of Ohio University and Blanche M. Cook

The first attempt to canalize the Hocking valley was initiated by a group of Lancaster businessmen shortly after the route of the Ohio & Erie Canal was fixed through Fairfield County. This group, which included Ohio's U.S. Senator Thomas Ewing, received a Charter from the State in 1826 to build a 9 mile lateral canal connecting Lancaster to Carroll on the Ohio Canal. The Lancaster Lateral was carrying traffic by 1832, used two locks of 2 feet lift each and was built to somewhat smaller prism dimensions than those used on the Ohio & Erie.

The State acquired the Lancaster Lateral in 1836 as part of its mammoth Internal Improvement expansion. It was to be incorporated into the proposed Hocking Canal which was to run from Carroll to Athens while passing through Lancaster, Sugar Grove, Logan, Nelsonville and Chauncey. [...]

After the State took over the Lancaster Lateral, it was widened, the two locks removed and its summit cut down so there was one continuous long level from Carroll to Lancaster. The shallow Lateral Canal remained a problem area, however, particularly during dry seasons when fully loaded boats had to be lightened across this stretch at State expense. Finally, in 1856, the Lateral Canal was widened and deepened to the full dimensions of the rest of the Hocking Canal which were the same as those on the Ohio & Erie.

## 16. THE CHILLICOTHE HYDRAULIC
### from an article by Brad Bond, originally published in TOWPATHS No. 4, 2001

The Ohio & Erie Canal had been open four years when the Chillicothe Hydraulic Association was formed to plan, finance and construct a canal to supply water from Paint Creek. A bill to introduce the Paint Creek Lateral Canal Company had been introduced in the Ohio Senate on December 12, 1834. The route crossed over Paint Creek on an aqueduct before connecting with the Ohio & Erie Canal at the 5th Street Basin in today's Poland Park.

The Paint Creek connection to the basin is shown on an 1843 map but is missing on an 1857 map and again in the 1875 atlas. The hydraulic aqueduct and dam were wiped out in a flood several years after being built and from then on the hydraulic was apparently supplied with water from the O&E Canal.

Several industries sprung up along the Hydraulic including grist mills, an ashery (for extracting potash used to make soap), a brickyard, candleworks and a woolen mill. An 1847 paper mill evolved into the Mead Paper Co., today Chillicothe's major employer.

Was the Hydraulic Canal used by boats? John Grabb answers this question as follows: "George Watson, a veteran canal boatman, was 89 years old in 1931 when he remembered distinctly transporting materials to and from various industries along the hydraulic canal with his boat *Nellie Kiel*. He said boats could pass anywhere."

By 1871 the Hydraulic was no longer in use and the city council contracted to have it filled in. Then the 5th Street basin became a dumping ground and malaria-breeding swamp. It was drained and filled in the late summer of 1884.

*The Miami & Erie Canal was not known by that name until 1849 and was actually comprised of all or parts of three separate canals. These were, 1) The Miami Canal; 2) The Miami Extension Canal; and 3) The Wabash & Erie Canal.*

## 17. THE MIAMI & ERIE CANAL

The Board of Public Works first suggested in 1845 that "for the sake of convenience" the entire canal route from Cincinnati to the Lake be designated by the name of the Miami & Erie Canal. Then, by an Act of the Legislature on March 14, 1849, that designation became official. This canal then was 249 miles long and, as originally constructed, had 15 aqueducts, 3 guard locks and 103 lift locks.

All the locks on the Miami & Erie Canal from Cincinnati north to the Loramie Summit and south from the Lake to the guard lock below Independence were of stone masonry and of the standard mitered gate type with closed chambers measuring 90 x 15 feet. Between those two points, however, the canal route had run through sparsely populated country where there was very little good building stone. [...] From Defiance to the Indiana line and from Junction to the Loramie Summit, all locks were constructed of wood. [...] Locks #8, #24, and #30 were rebuilt of stone in the 1850's.

[…] When the Extension was built, the Board did specify that the minimum depth be 5 feet, but also opted to increase the minimum widths to 50 feet at the waterline and 36 feet at the bottom. These specifications were also used on the canal from Junction to the State line, but the minimum dimensions from Junction to the Lake were increased to 60 feet at the waterline, 46 feet at the bottom and 6 feet deep. […]

The City of Cincinnati grew tired of its little used junction with the Ohio River and, in 1863, all of the canal from Broadway to the river, including the ten locks into the river, was abandoned. Experience had also proven that the Maumee River connection at Toledo was the most practical northern terminus. Therefore, in 1864, both the Maumee Side Cut and the two locks at Manhattan were abandoned by the State. The remainder of the canal north of the Swan Creek Aqueduct was officially abandoned in 1871.

After this, the Miami & Erie Canal existed for nearly four more decades and, in fact, was slightly busier than the Ohio & Erie. The larger dimensions of much of the canal made it possible for steam propelled canal boats to be *somewhat* practical. It was on the narrower and more shallow southern portion that the Electric Mule experiments were conducted in 1903. […]

The Miami & Erie Canal received some attention from the State during the attempted rebuild of the canals of 1904-1909. The channel was to be dredged to a minimum depth of 5 feet and a number of locks, including the remaining wooden ones, were rebuilt with concrete. When the Legislature lost interest in 1910, the canal was finished. The 1913 flood merely put a period to that finish.

## 18. THE MIAMI CANAL

The Miami Canal was part of the "package" authorized by the State Legislature in 1825 and ran from Cincinnati on the Ohio River to Dayton. Nearly everything that can be said about the Ohio & Erie Canal concerning its dimensions, lock sizes, boats, construction, engineering, etc. can also be said about the Miami Canal.

The eyes of the nation were focused upon the through Lake to River route, the Ohio Canal, so much of the work force was placed on the northern portion of that canal to ready it for navigation by 1827, but sufficient forces remained on the western canal so that water could be let into that section between Middletown and Howell's Basin at Lockland some 12 miles above the Ohio River, in October 1827. Two boats, the WASHINGTON and the CLINTON, had been built and an inaugural trip planned for the 4th of November. A break in the embankment near Mill Creek Aqueduct delayed those festivities until November 28 when the two boats, loaded with dignitaries, left for Hamilton and Middletown. Somewhere along the line, the procession was joined by the SAMUEL FORRER. The entire party returned to Cincinnati by canal two days later.

The remainder of the route north to Dayton was ready for a formal opening and dedication by July, 1828. […] On July 3rd, 1828, after suitable ceremonies at Cincinnati […] a canal boat […] amid the booming of cannon, the music of bands and the waving of flags and decorations of all kinds, proceeded northward. [...] The next day, July 4th, 1828, the formal opening of the Miami Canal was held in Dayton on the banks of "The Basin" at the canal's northern terminus.

For some reason work on the canal south of Howell's Basin went slowly, even though it was along a twelve mile long "level". It was 1829 before that waterway wound its way around the western slopes of Cincinnati's hills and on across Main Street. It wasn't until 1828 that the contract was even let for the extension into the Ohio River. That extension continued from "12 mile level", east of Broadway, and, using ten locks, descended to the river down present Eggleston Ave. Each of the locks had an eleven foot "drop". This river connection was completed in 1833, but appears not to have been used much. High water, "silting up" of the lower locks, and the need to trans-ship cargo anyway, caused the "working" southern terminus of this canal to become the end of the "12 mile level" along 11th, or Canal, Streets. The last two miles of that level were literally lined with boat line offices, warehouses, forewarders, merchants, and a variety of shops and factories.

Lockport Basin was located at the end of the level. It provided additional docking space and a place to turn and maneuver boats. It soon proved to be inadequate, however, and a larger basin was built just to the south. It was called "Cheapside Basin" and lay below Court Street and extended almost to 8th Street.

After leaving the city limits of Cincinnati, the canal entered the valley created by Mill Creek and followed it for some 20 miles while passing through the communities of Cumminsville, Carthage, Lockland, Crescentville and Rialto. Then the canal entered a series of natural ponds that were the source of Mill Creek and connected that valley with the valley of the Great Miami River. Two aqueducts were used in this section. One carried the canal from the east to the west bank of Mill Creek about one mile north of Carthage. Another aqueduct took the canal across Beaver Run near Crescentville.

The Miami Canal next entered the Great Miami Valley and followed the east bank of that river through the towns of Port Union, Lesourdesville, Excello, Amanda and Middletown. Gregory's Creek at Lesourdesville and Dick's Creek at Amanda were crossed upon wooden troughed aqueducts. About two miles north of Middletown, the canal received a feeder from the Great Miami River. [...]

This lower division was 44 miles long and contained 32 locks to overcome a difference in elevation of 212 feet. [...]

The upper division on the Miami Canal began at its junction with the river feeder. From there it followed the left, or east, bank of the river for 22 miles to Dayton and touched the towns of Franklin, Miamisburg, West Carrollton and Alexandersville. It then terminated in a basin at Dayton. There were 22 locks in this section which were needed to overcome an 85 foot difference in elevation.

Clear Creek, a short distance below Franklin, was crossed upon three stone arches—each arch having a chord length of 40 feet. Crane's Run, just above Alexandersville, was crossed upon a wooden trunked aqueduct and Holds Creek, a bit below Dayton, upon a twin arch stone culvert with arches of 22 feet chord each. This division of the canal was supplied with water by a one and a half mile long feeder from the Mad River. [...]

Upon completion, the Miami Canal immediately began fulfilling its goal, that of providing a convenient, dependable transportation between Dayton and Cincinnati. [...] In 1829, a Dayton merchant summed up the area's initial reaction toward the Miami Canal by saying, "The country, particularly the farmers, already feel the advantages in an increased price for their articles and a regular market, as what is not consumed around here is now boated to Cincinnati."

## 19. THE MIAMI EXTENSION CANAL

The Canal Act of 1825 included a promise that the Miami Canal would be completed through to the Lake "at an early date". Residents and Politicians from the communities along the proposed route continued agitating to make that date as early as possible. [...]

To aid in construction of this extension, the U.S. Congress had granted sections of public lands along the proposed route to Ohio on May 24, 1828. Ohio was also granted 500,000 acres of government land, within the State's borders, to aid in the payment of the canal debt or interest already incurred. A stipulation to this grant was that the lands could not be used for any other purpose. This same act also provided that the canals already under construction in Ohio should be completed within 7 years and that the Miami Extension should be begun within 5 years (1833) and completed within 20 years (1848). Otherwise, all proceeds from the sale of these lands would belong to the U.S. Government and not to the State of Ohio.

[...] The land sale fund reached the desired goal in 1833 and, in April of that year, a 17 mile section of canal from Dayton to three miles south of Troy was authorized by the Legislature. The first 17 sections (8½ miles) were put under contract in June of 1833.

An outbreak of cholera in Dayton and Troy made it understandably difficult to obtain canal workers and construction went very slowly. The additional 16 sections of that division were not let until late in 1833 and the second division of 15 miles (to just north of the mouth of Loramie Creek) was placed under contract near the end of 1834. It was originally estimated that at least a portion of this extension would be navigable by October, 1834; but continuing outbreaks of cholera, a very wet spring, rising construction costs, etc. combined to delay the opening until very late in the season of 1836 and then, only to a point 3 miles below Troy. The entire extension from Dayton to the mouth of Loramie Creek (two miles north of Piqua at the State Dam across the Great Miami) was opened to navigation in July of 1837.

The Ohio Legislature, in 1836, authorized a vast program of canals, railroads and turnpikes. Included in this package was the further extension of the Miami Canal from Loramie's Creek to a point on the proposed Wabash & Erie Canal. This portion of the Extension was to be funded from borrowed monies as well as those obtained from continued sale of the government lands. This newly authorized portion of the Extension was built in three divisions. The first, a 32 mile segment to St. Marys, was let to contractors in 1837. The second, a 12 mile stretch containing the "Deep Cut" in 1839. Severe economic problems caused by the "Panic of 1837" resulted in irregular payments to contractors. Work on the canals slowed, some contractors were forced to abandon their jobs and the need to rebid them caused further delays. Therefore, it wasn't until November 1843 that these two divisions were opened to traffic.

Because the expenditures along the line were much higher than the original estimates, and because the economic chaos left in the wake of the "Panic" made it extremely difficult for the State to meet the interest due on its existing canal debt, the legislature hesitated to authorize construction of the final section. Since all monies raised from the sale of the government land grants would revert to the federal treasury if the canal were not completed, however, the cost of abandoning the project appeared to be even higher than continuing. So, on February 29, 1843, the last 33 mile segment was authorized. Bids were received at St. Marys on June 15, 1843. Contrary to previous practice, and in an apparent attempt to minimize the expensive process of releting abandoned contracts, the State awarded the entire 33 miles to a "prime" contractor. […]

The contract called for work to be completed by November 1, 1844, but, as with nearly every other portion of Ohio's Canals, completion was delayed and it was 1845 before boats were running along the entire 115 mile "Extension". […]

As actually constructed, the Miami Extension proceeded north from Dayton for nine miles on the east bank of the Great Miami River after first crossing Mad River on a wooden troughed aqueduct. Here, the canal crossed to the west bank of the Great Miami on another aqueduct. The Great Miami Aqueduct, as the latter was called, and the Mad River Aqueduct were sources of frequent interruptions of traffic on the canal in later years due to breaking down or being washed away by floods. Lock #20 was located at the southern end of the Mad River Aqueduct and three more (Nos. 19, 18 & 17) between the two aqueducts.

Including Lock #12 at Troy, there were five locks (Nos. 16 to 12) in the 12 canal miles north of the Miami Aqueduct. […] Twelve miles above Troy, the canal crossed Loramie Creek on an aqueduct and immediately ascended the "staircase of locks" at Lockington—Nos. 5, 4, 3, 2 & 1. In addition to these five locks, there were six more located between Troy and the Loramie Aqueduct. A dam at Piqua supplied water to the canal between Locks #9 & #8. The canal was 34 miles long from Dayton to the Loramie Summit, used 20 locks to overcome a 113 foot difference in elevation and passed through the towns of Lockville, Marysville, Tipp City, Cowlesville, Troy, Piqua and Lockington.

The Loramie Summit, itself, was 23 miles long and passed through the towns of Woodbourne, Newport, Berlin, Minster, and New Bremen. Water was fed into its southern portion by the Sidney Feeder and at its northern end by Loramie Reservoir which impounded 1,828 acres of water from Loramie Creek. Just above Lockington, Turtle Creek was crossed on a mile long embankment through which the creek flowed in a twin arch masonry culvert, each arch having a 16½ foot radius.

The descent to Junction, a distance of 57 miles, began at Lock #1 at New Bremen and passed through the towns of St. Marys, Kossuth, Spencerville, Acadia, Delphos, Ottoville, Hamer, Mandale, St. Andrews and Charloe. There were 32 locks in this segment to drop the canal a total of 217 feet.

Eleven locks brought the canal to the level of St. Marys, 8 miles from the northern end of the summit. The largest artificial body of water in the country at that time, Lake St. Marys, or Grand Lake

Reservoir of 15,748 acres, was created just west of St. Marys and supplied the canal with water the rest of the way to Junction. […]

There were six aqueducts in this segment. One, the St. Marys Aqueduct was located between Locks #11 & #12; the "Six Mile Aqueduct" was just above Kossuth; the Jennings Creek Aqueduct was at Delphos; the Little Auglaize Aqueduct was just south of Melrose and the Blue Creek Aqueduct was just north of Melrose. A sixth aqueduct carried the canal across Flat Rock Creek just above (south) of Junction. The "Deep Cut" was one mile north of Kossuth. It was nearly 6,600 feet long, ranged from 50 to 52 feet deep and took 400 to 500 men nearly four years to complete. This cut allowed the canal to cross the St. Marys Moraine, a formidable east-west ridge of hard blue clay that separated the St. Marys watershed from that of the Auglaize. The Miami Extension from Dayton to Junction was 115 miles long, followed by the valley of the Great Miami north to the summit and the valley of the Auglaize north to Junction. A total of 52 locks were used to overcome a total rise and fall of 330 feet.

## 20. THE WABASH & ERIE CANAL

[…] The "Ground Breaking" on the Wabash & Erie Canal had taken place at Ft. Wayne, Indiana on February 22, 1832 […] with construction continuing on southward until the canal reached its southern terminus at Evansville in 1853. With the 18½ mile section completed eastward from Ft. Wayne to the Ohio line in 1843 the Wabash & Erie Canal in Indiana totaled 375 miles. With the 87½ miles in Ohio added on, this canal was 462½ miles long—the longest canal in the country.

Meanwhile, the Ohio portion of the canal was inching its way south and west along the Maumee. The entire canal was under contract by Oct. 1837 and the Board of Public Works expected it to be navigable by the 1st of October, 1839. By the next year, however the "Panic of 1837" had slowed the economy to such an extent that the general lack of funds from sales of the government lands plus a great deal of sickness along the route, virtually stopped construction. […]

Depressed economic conditions persisted during 1840 and grew considerably worse. […] It wasn't until 1842 that more of the canal was opened, and then only in piece-meal fashion. […]

On a Monday early in July, 1842, the JESSE L. WILLIAMS arrived in Defiance from Ft. Wayne. […] On July 4th, 1843 a celebration of the opening the entire line was held in Ft. Wayne, Indiana. The festivities included cannon salutes, free meals, free drink, and much oratory.

The route of the Wabash & Erie Canal began near the mouth of the Maumee River at the town of Manhattan. An outlet lock in the river gave boats access to the canal which followed the west, or left bank some 34 miles to the head of the Maumee Rapids as it passed through the towns of Toledo, Port Miami, Maumee City, Waterville and Otsego. Rivalry for the northern connection with Lake traffic was so great that the commissioners met at Perrysburg in 1836 to resolve the issue. The decision, a compromise, was to extend the canal to Manhattan and also to provide side-cuts at Toledo and Maumee. Nine locks were used to overcome a 63½ foot difference in elevation. Swan Creek, just below the Toledo Sidecut, was crossed upon a wooden troughed aqueduct.

At Providence, a dam across the Maumee formed a slackwater pool that the canal entered and followed for approximately 1¼ miles. A short side-cut from the pool, on the east bank of the river, led to Grand Rapids then back to the river. After leaving the slackwater, again on the left bank, the canal used an independent channel once more for 3½ miles to Texas. Three locks were required to ascend 25 feet. From Texas to Independence, the canal traversed a 22 mile "level" while passing through the communities of Damascus, Napoleon and Florida. The Independence Dam formed another slackwater pool that the canal followed for 4½ miles before crossing to the right bank at Defiance. The canal left slackwater here and rapidly climbed 35 feet using four locks. From Defiance to the Junction with the Miami Extension, the Wabash & Erie traveled 8½ miles and used three locks to rise 23 feet. Then, the canal ran 18½ miles to the Indiana Line and used six locks to ascend 28½ feet. Water was supplied from the two slackwater dams and from a 2,500 acre reservoir located six miles east of the State Line. Indiana abandoned their portion of the W. & E. in 1877. Disgruntled Ohioans then dynamited the Reservoir in 1887 and that part of the canal from the State Line to Junction was abandoned in 1888.

*There were a number of side cuts or short branch canals constructed for the Miami & Erie Canal to reach near-by communities or areas, and several of the canal's feeders were navigable. The navigable branches and feeders of the Miami & Erie Canal were…*

## 21. THE HAMILTON SIDE CUT

This side cut ran approximately two thirds of a mile to the village of Hamilton from a point on the main canal some 28 miles north of the Ohio River. The side cut was 80 feet wide.

## 22. THE BASIN EXTENSION CANAL OR COOPER'S NEW LINE

Extending from the basin at the northern terminus of the original Miami Canal in Dayton, this private canal was eventually taken over by the state and became the main line of the Miami & Erie Canal through Dayton. The Miami Extension Canal from the terminal basin to the Mad River Aqueduct was abandoned and filled in the 1870s in favor of the Basin Extension route.

## 23. THE SIDNEY FEEDER

This was a navigable feeder that followed the Great Miami River from its confluence with Loramie Creek, northeasterly and passed through the town of Sidney, some 14 miles to Port Jefferson. Here, a dam across the river, fed water into the feeder. Lewistown Reservoir, of 6,332 acres and now Indian Lake, was created at the head of the Great Miami as the principal water source for that portion of the summit. Water flowed down the river for 18 miles to Port Jefferson where it entered the feeder. It is related that one man at least, felt the Sidney Feeder would bring such a degree of prosperity into the area that he sold his business in a place called Chicago, Ill. to relocate to Port Jefferson!

## 24. THE GRAND RESERVOIR OR LAKE ST. MARYS FEEDER

The Grand Reservoir, or Lake St. Marys, was built to impound the water of several natural springs and Beaver Creek, a tributary of the Wabash, during the wet season to supply nearly 50 miles of Miami Extension during dry seasons. First contracted in 1837, the construction of the reservoir was long, difficult and caused a great deal of controversy and ill-feeling among the local residents. A basin some nine miles long and from two to five miles wide containing 15,748 acres, was formed by building a two mile long embankment across the eastern end of a natural valley and a four mile long embankment across the western end. These embankments were from 10 to 20 feet high and were finally both completed and the valley "closed up" in the fall of 1842. […]

A three mile long feeder allowed water to flow into the canal between Locks #11 and #12 at St. Marys. The feeder was navigable and a wooden lock in the east embankment allowed canal boats to be lifted to Lake level and extended the navigation to Celina and Montezuma. There was no towing path along the Lake and boat crews were required to take on their animals after going through the lock and laboriously pole their craft across the Lake. Several steamers navigated the Lake in the last few decades of the 19th Century.

The wooden access lock to the Lake became so deteriorated by 1852 that a new one of Dayton stone was built that year as well as a new iron bulkhead. A return feeder from between Locks #6 and #7 was also constructed in 1852 to direct surplus water from the canal into the reservoir.

As with many of Ohio's canal reservoirs, Lake St. Marys still exists as a recreational area. […]

## 25. THE GILEAD OR GRAND RAPIDS SIDE CUT

After the Providence Dam was constructed to supply the Wabash & Erie Canal across the Maumee River, the state constructed a short side cut canal to appease milling interests on the Gilead (now Grand Rapids) side of the river.

This short ½ mile long canal and its bulkhead lock survive into the present day.

## 26. THE MAUMEE SIDE CUT

This side cut was one and a half miles long and needed six locks to overcome a fall of 65 feet. It left the main channel 8½ miles south of the head of the Toledo Side Cut and locked into the Maumee River at the "Point", in lowlands directly across the river from Perrysburg. A rock bar, allowing only Lake Craft of shallow draft to navigate up-river to Maumee and Perrysburg hastened the early decision (1864) to abandon the connection with the river.

## 27. THE TOLEDO SIDE CUT

Toledo was one of the three communities selected to be a northern terminus of the Wabash & Erie Canal by the Board of Public Works at their August, 1836 meeting at Perrysburg. The side cut left the main channel just above (south) of the Swan Creek Aqueduct. It was approximately one mile long, followed Swan Creek and used two locks to descend 15 feet where it entered the creek just above its junction with the Maumee River. After the main canal north of the Swan Creek Aqueduct was abandoned by the Acts of 1864 and 1871 and the Maumee Side Cut abandoned in 1864, the Toledo Side Cut became *the* northern terminus of the Miami & Erie Canal.

*Several other canals may be classified as branches although all of these, except for the Milan Canal, intersected with one of the two main systems. (One, the Muskingum, is a river improvement although some sections are canalized.) Some of these are "branches of branches" such as the Middlebury Branch or Lateral Canal, Cuyahoga Feeder and South Feeder which were all part of the Pennsylvania & Ohio Canal system. Another, the never-completed Nimishillen & Sandy Canal, was to link up with the Sandy & Beaver Canal.*

## 28. THE PENNSYLVANIA & OHIO CANAL
### with specific information supplied by D.S. Weaver
### Historian of the Portage County Historical Society

Alfred Kelley, one of the Ohio State Canal Commissioners, ran a survey along the Cuyahoga and Mahoning valleys in 1823 as a possible route for the planned Lake Erie to Ohio River canal. His findings were that it would be feasible to lead a canal through those two valleys, but since the route would run through portions of both Ohio and Pennsylvania, he recommended that a private company be authorized to build the canal rather than the State of Ohio.

Early in September of 1825, a public meeting of the citizens of Portage and Trumbull counties was held in Ravenna to consider the possibility of building a canal from the Portage summit on the Ohio & Erie Canal, through their counties, to the Ohio River. […]

A bill to incorporate a company to build a canal "between some suitable point on the Ohio river, through the valley of the Mahoning, to some suitable point on Lake Erie, or to some point on the Ohio & Erie Canal", was introduced into the State Legislature. […] Finally, on January 10, 1827, the Pennsylvania & Ohio Canal Company was chartered by the State of Ohio. The state of Pennsylvania followed suit on April 14th. […]

Citizens along the proposed route no doubt expected construction to begin almost immediately, but they were disappointed. The P. & O. Canal was to connect the Ohio canal system and the Pennsylvania canal system. And while the Ohio Canal from Akron north to the Lake was completed in

1827, the Pennsylvania "Main Line" didn't reach Pittsburgh until 1831. Therefore, in 1828, the P. & O.'s Board of Directors voted to postpone the opening of stock subscription books.

[...] 1833 saw a revival of meetings along the proposed P. & O. route. By this time, however, two rival projects were being promoted to connect the two State's canal systems. One of these was the Sandy & Beaver Canal [...] the other project (was) the Pennsylvania & Ohio Railroad. [...]

A meeting of all interested parties was held in Warren, Ohio on Nov. 13, 1833. Over 100 duly elected delegates were in attendance. [...] Promoters for the three projects presented their cases, described the proposed routes of their lines and detailed the advantages they offered over the others.

After the convention was adjourned, the committee representing the Philadelphia Board of Trade made a trip by carriage along the streams and across the summits of the two proposed canal routes. The railroad route was not studied as it was supposed that financial support for a railroad would be impossible to obtain. Their report showed a preference for the Pennsylvania & Ohio route because of the great supply of water that could be brought to the summit. [...]

This report gave a big "push" to the fortunes of the Pennsylvania & Ohio Canal Company. Their charter was renewed by both the Ohio and Pennsylvania State Legislatures in 1835. A new Board of Directors was elected at the next stockholders meeting held in New Castle, Pa. on May 21, 1835. The Board promptly selected James Dunlop Harris and Colonel Sebried Dodge as Principal Engineers on the project.

Another survey of the line had been made during the Company's hiatus and a few changes made in the route. As per the survey of 1828, the canal was to have left the Ohio & Erie Canal on the Portage Summit, south of Lock #1. It was then to have passed through Wolf Ledges, over Wolf Run, through the community of Middlebury, then north to the Big Cuyahoga River near Franklin Mills. In 1831, however, several influential men from Middlebury tapped the Little Cuyahoga just below that community and built a mill race that flowed into the Ohio Canal between Locks #5 and #6 north of Akron. A new town named Cascade (later known as North Akron) was formed from that point. North Akron soon began stealing much of the "thunder" from South Akron and Middlebury: so much so, that when the P. & O. was resurveyed in 1835, Middlebury had lost much of its political "clout". The town of Cuyahoga Falls also had considerable voice in the new route. That 1835 survey routed the canal through North Akron and Cuyahoga Falls, by-passing Middlebury. Middlebury was given a short branch canal to keep its residents happy.

After the changes of 1835, the western terminus of the P. & O. was at the Ohio Canal's "Lower Basin" in South Akron, immediately below Lock #1. The canal then stepped down one lock to the level of the Cascade Mill Race which it entered and followed to a point near present Arlington Street. There it crossed the Little Cuyahoga upon slackwater created by the Mill Race dam and ascended a "staircase" of nine locks to Cuyahoga Falls where it ran along the left or south bank of the Big Cuyahoga River through Monroe Falls to Franklin Mills. At this point a rocky gorge forced the canal to enter the river through "Lower Lock" and navigate a slackwater pool for approximately one mile. Then, the "Upper Lock" with a 19 foot lift allowed the canal to leave slackwater and follow the valley of Breakneck Creek for a short distance before crossing to the north bank upon slackwater then running to the beginning of the Portage Summit some 2½ miles west of Ravenna. There were 16 locks on this 14 mile long western division to overcome a 112 foot rise.

The summit level itself was 2½ miles long and contained a Deep Cut that was nearly 5,000 feet long and over 40 feet deep in places.

The eastern division began at Ravenna and, entering the valley created by the West Branch of the Mahoning River, ran north along the left bank through Campbellsport and Newport before crossing to the south bank just below McClintocksburg. At Newton Falls, the canal crossed the East Branch upon a stone masonry aqueduct of three 50 foot spans. The valley of the Mahoning River was reached just below Newton Falls and the canal followed the river's south bank to Warren where it crossed upon slackwater. The canal then followed the north bank of the river through Niles, Girard, Youngstown, Campbell and Lowellville before entering the State of Pennsylvania. Still running along the north bank of the Mahoning River, the canal crossed the Shenango River upon an aqueduct and joined the Beaver Division of the Beaver & Erie Canal at "Western Reserve Basin", approximately seven miles south of New Castle, Pennsylvania.

The entire canal was 82 miles long (67 miles in Ohio)[*] and used 54 locks to overcome 424 feet of rise and fall. In addition, the canal contained two aqueducts, nine dams and 57 road bridges. The locks were the standard mitered gate type with a closed chamber measuring 15 by 90 feet. Most of the locks were constructed of finished and dressed stone. A few were "Composite" Locks (rough stone construction with plank lined chambers) and at least one lock, near Girard where little good building stone was available, was of wooden construction. Minimum prism dimensions were the same as on the Ohio & Erie – 40 feet wide at the waterline, 26 feet wide at the bottom and 4 feet deep. The eastern and western divisions obtained water from the many slackwater crossings and the summit level (as originally built) received water from the seven mile long Big Cuyahoga Feeder.

Contracts were let for the entire canal in half mile sections on Aug. 20, 1835. Construction officially began on September 17, 1835 when the two engineers, Dodge and Harris, drove iron stakes into the exact center of the Portage Summit – a mile and a quarter west of Ravenna. A little work was accomplished yet in 1835 on the eastern portion of the summit, but it wasn't until the next year that work was begun in earnest all along the line. [...]

At first, the stock sold well and work progressed steadily. Then, in 1837 a cholera epidemic struck – 29 canal workers died of the disease in Franklin, Ravenna and Shalersville Townships, alone, between April 30 and September 15, 1837. Little progress was made during these months and immediately following the sickness came the severe economic problems brought on by the "Panic of 1837". All work on the canal was suspended for the remainder of that year.

A $420,000 "Plunder Law" stock subscription by the State of Ohio enabled the Company to resume construction in 1838. The main canal from its western terminus to the Little Cuyahoga crossing,

---

[*] The main line of the Pennsylvania & Ohio Canal was actually 83.45 miles long, all but 9.89 miles in Ohio, according the reports of Engineer Dodge.

and the branch into Middlebury, was completed in May, 1839. That same month, the ONTARIO began regular runs from Warren, Ohio to Beaver, Pennsylvania. The summit level was completed by August 15, 1839, but wasn't able to carry traffic as its water supply wasn't finished yet. By the end of 1839 the canal was nearly done, but the Company's treasury was once again empty. A $50,000 donation from the State of Pennsylvania "did the trick" and the entire line was completed early in 1840. On April 3, 1840 the MOHAWK of Beaver and the TIPPECANOE of Warren ran the entire length of the P. & O. Canal.

The official opening celebration of the Pennsylvania & Ohio Canal began on August 4, 1840 when four gaily decorated Packet Boats left New Castle with a party of Pennsylvania dignitaries. At the State Line they were met by delegations from Warren and Youngstown. [...] On the 6th [...] two boats carrying the Akron delegation joined the flotilla and the entire fleet of six new and freshly painted craft, with pennants and flags flying, glided past the cheering throngs lining both banks of the canal between Tallmadge and Mill Streets in Akron. As soon as all six boats had locked up into the Lower Basin, they were welcomed with booming cannon and prolonged and enthusiastic cheers from another huge crowd.

At the conclusion of the ceremonies at the Basin [...] another sumptuous feast was held with much oratory and drinking of toasts. With so much "high living" crowded into only three days, it's somewhat surprising that just one of the participants, Major General Seeley of Warren, succumbed to an "Attack of Apoplexy".

Starting in 1840, the Pennsylvania & Ohio Canal enjoyed a decade of freedom from serious competition and was relatively prosperous. [...]

At first nearly all P. & O. traffic was carried in either Ohio & Erie or Beaver Division boats. By 1843, however, local boat builders had plied their trade so well that 149 boats were listed on the P. & O. "register" and that number was rapidly increasing. More boats required more water on the summit. So, early in 1844, the firm of Prentess and Whittlesey received a contract to construct two reservoirs (Muddy and Sandy Lakes) and the South Feeder. This project was completed late that year and gave the summit level and an additional 12,000,000 gallons of water every 24 hours!

The Cleveland & Pittsburgh Railroad was completed to Ravenna in 1851 and to the Ohio River at Wellsville in 1852. Passenger traffic, which had totaled nearly 9,000 persons per year in 1847 and 1848 and nearly 5,500 in 1852, practically disappeared in 1853. Through freight and items that required rapid transit also went to the railroad. However, local traffic of coal, lumber and other heavy cargo doubled between 1850 and 1854.

The Cleveland & Mahoning Railroad began construction in 1853. In 1854 its directors gained control of the P. & O. Canal Company. When the railroad was opened to traffic in 1856, canal toll rates on coal and iron were raised 50%. This made it cheaper (by 27¢ per ton) to ship by rail. The State was petitioned in 1861 for permission to abandon the canal, but no action was taken. In 1863 the C. & M. Railroad was leased to the Atlantic & Great Western Railroad. Then, in 1862 or 1863, all the P. & O. stock owned by the State of Ohio was sold to the railroad for $35,000! The canal carried limited traffic after this date though some revenue was generated by leasing water rights.

The canal was abandoned in 1868. [...]

During the spring of 1874 "night raiders" filled in the canal junction at Exchange Street and cut the banks at one or two places along Main Street. The offenders were never caught and the canal within Akron was filled in […] the Pennsylvania & Ohio Canal was gone!

## 29. THE MIDDLEBURY BRANCH OR LATERAL CANAL

This side cut was constructed along the Cascade Mill Race from the Little Cuyahoga River crossing south to the warehouses and mills of Middlebury. The Middlebury Branch was the first portion of the P. & O. Canal to carry traffic when the JOSEPH VANCE left Akron and arrived at the "port" of Middlebury on May 9, 1839. The branch was built to the same dimensions as the main canal, needed no locks and was 1¼ miles long.

Boat traffic was soon discontinued on the Branch, but, as part of the hydraulic race, was carrying water long after the rest of the P. & O. was gone.

## 30. THE CUYAHOGA FEEDER
### by Dudley Weaver, Historian – Portage County Historical Society

The feeder was 7 miles long, used three locks, one aqueduct and joined the main canal 1¼ miles west of Ravenna.

Boats could lock into the feeder from the P. & O. summit and go to one of the three basins. One basin was located at 3 miles, another basin at 4½ miles and the third at either 6 or 6½ miles from the main canal. There were loading platforms at each basin. […]

A dam across the Big Cuyahoga River near the long gone community of Feeder Dam shunted water into the feeder. Boats could not enter the river, itself, as it would have required a 22 foot lift lock and the probable use of such a lock did not justify its expense.

[…] The Canal Company decided to abandon the summit and eastern division in 1868. The next spring (1869) farmers along the upper Cuyahoga River, upon learning that Brady Lake and Pippen Lake Reservoirs were not being filled, destroyed the feeder dam and reclaimed hundreds of acres of land that had been underwater.

## 31. THE SOUTH FEEDER
### by Dudley Weaver, Historian – Portage County Historical Society

The South Feeder and the Muddy Lake and Sandy Lake reservoirs were built in 1844 to provide additional water to the summit level of the P. & O. Canal. The feeder was 9 miles long, but only that portion from the main canal to the outlet of Muddy Lake was navigable. This section was about one mile long, was built to the same dimensions as the main canal and contained one lock. The South Feeder went out of service in 1868 or 69 when the Muddy Lake outlet was dammed up.

## 32. THE SANDY & BEAVER CANAL

Residents along the eventual route of the P. & O. Canal undoubtedly thought of that canal only as a means of transportation for themselves. It was touted by its promoters, however, as an east-west link between the Ohio and Pennsylvania Canal Systems. The Legislatures of the two states felt that way and responded with support, both moral and financial. The Sandy & Beaver Canal was also, ostensibly at least, to be an east-west interstate link. In actual fact, the S. & B. Canal was initiated, promoted and financed by the citizens of New Lisbon, Ohio and surrounding area. Quite a bit of funding did come from one or two Philadelphia merchants, but local people supported the canal far beyond their normal means.

New Lisbon was the seat of Columbiana County and both had been founded in 1803 as Ohio came into the Union. New Lisbon soon became one of the more prosperous and influential towns in pioneer Ohio. In 1822-23 the State Canal Commissioners attempted to run one end of the Ohio Canal down the Little Beaver River. When this proved to be impossible, New Lisbon found itself some 45 miles east of the new transportation system, 25 miles west of the Ohio River and, literally, "high and dry". The city fathers, therefore, began investigating means and methods to connect their community with the Ohio Canal, the Ohio River, or both. […]

The Big Sandy Creek entered the Tuscarawas River at Bolivar, across the river from the Ohio Canal. The Little Beaver River entered the Ohio River at Glasgow, Pa. Branches of both these streams originate just a short distance apart and not too far from New Lisbon. It was obvious to the consultants that any canal from the Ohio Canal to the Ohio River would have to follow the valleys of the Little Beaver and Big Sandy. On July 16, 1827 a meeting was held in the Columbiana County Court House to discuss the "Canal Question". That meeting resulted in a petition to the State requesting a charter to be granted authorizing a private stock company to construct a canal from the Ohio River to the Ohio Canal. The Sandy & Beaver Canal Company was granted a charter on January 11, 1828. […]

The next step toward making the branch canal a reality was to have a detailed survey of the route made by a recognized engineer. An application was made to the U.S. War Department for such a man and, in 1828, Major D.B. Douglas, a professional engineer from the U.S. Military Academy, came to New Lisbon to survey the proposed route of the Sandy & Beaver Canal. […]

A report on the completed survey was handed to the S. & B. Canal Company President on Feb. 1, 1830. It called for a canal 90½ miles long with 100 locks, seven aqueducts and three feet extra depth on the summit to act as a reservoir. The most unusual thing about this route was the recommendation of a 2,700 foot long tunnel to take the canal through the ridge dividing the valleys of the Big Sandy and Little Beaver. […]

Promoters of the P. & O. Canal scheduled a meeting in Warren, Ohio in the fall of 1833 to convince the money men that their project was the first one to back. The Sandy & Beaver Canal Company sent a delegation firmly convinced that their project would win out. The Sandy & Beaver's high hopes were dashed when the Philadelphia Board of trade concluded (after examining both routes) that there wouldn't be sufficient water on the summit of the S. & B. to support heavy traffic during dry seasons and threw their support to the Pennsylvania & Ohio Canal.

A meeting of the Sandy & Beaver stockholders was held in Waynesburg on January 17, 1834. There it was decided to continue the project in spite of the setback at Warren. […]

Two experienced engineers, Edward H. Gill from the Schuylkill Navigation Company and Hother Hage from the Susquehanna Division of the Pennsylvania System, were hired by the Sandy & Beaver Canal Company. On September 10, 1834 they were directed to a re-examine the route with particular attention to improving the water supply on the summit. Their report was issued on October 13, 1834 and recommended that two large reservoirs, and several smaller ones, be built to supply the summit and beginning of the western division.

With the water supply question apparently answered, little time was lost in getting the canal started. A ground-breaking ceremony was held at Dam #1 on the eastern division, just a mile or so above New Lisbon at the present site of the McKinley Boy Scout Camp. Five sections (2½ miles) of the summit level were let that same year, but most of the remainder of 1834 was spent by the engineers going over the route and attempting to shorten and improve the line here and there.

By the time good weather arrived in the spring of 1835, Gill had reduced Douglas' 1828 line from 90½ miles to 73½ miles. The summit level gained the two big reservoirs and an additional tunnel. […]

By the spring of 1837, over $900,000 had been spent on construction and acquiring real estate. Thirty one miles of canal were finished, but could not be used as an attempt had been made to construct the entire line as a whole rather than in stages as on the Ohio & Erie. The effects of the "Panic of 1837" hit the Sandy & Beaver earlier than it did some other projects as the Company's treasury was empty to begin with. Therefore, in April of 1837 the work forces, which had once numbered more than 2,000, were reduced to less than 200. […] With the exception of a small maintenance crew, the canal was shut down in the fall of 1837.

The Sandy & Beaver project lay dormant for nearly seven years. Then, in 1844, with the country's economy once more fairly stable, talk of reviving the project began. Meetings were held all along the route. Early in 1845, Philadelphia subscribed $350,000 and Ohio $100,000. Stock sales had added $30,000 to the "kitty". An additional $20,000 was required to get construction started again and it was obtained during a special sales "promotion" on June 6, 1845. The Sandy & Beaver Canal Company was ready to try again.

E.H. Gill had stayed around the area for about a year after the shutdown then left for greener pastures. When the project was revived, W. Milnor Roberts was hired as Chief Engineer. The departure of the perfectionist Gill and the need for economy meant that adequate, but "cheap" engineering was the guideline for canal construction in the "40's". Locks of rough stone lined with plank replaced the magnificent stone structures, such as Lusk's Lock, which were characteristic of Gill. […]

As completed, the Sandy & Beaver Canal left the Ohio River through a stone gate near Glasgow, Pa. (a proposed extension up the west bank of the Ohio River to Beaver Falls was surveyed, but never constructed) and followed the Little Beaver, east, for 8 miles to a point just opposite Fredericktown. It then followed the Middle Fork for approximately 19 miles to the beginning of the summit level, some 2 miles above New Lisbon. The eastern division was 27 miles long (17 miles of it in slackwater). 57 locks overcame 465 feet: the last 120 feet required 15 locks in a little over a mile at Furnace Hollow. This division touched the towns of Jamestown, Martinsburgh, Sprucevale, Williamsport, Middle Beaver, Elkton, New Lisbon and Lockbridge.

The summit level began at the "paper village" of Lockbridge and wound its way for 14 miles along the valleys of Cold Run, West Fork, Willards Run and Sandy Creek. A reservoir on Cold Run and one on the West Fork of the Little Beaver (now Guilford Lake) supplied the summit level with water. The communities of Guilford, Dungannon and Hanover lay along this stretch. Two tunnels, the 300 yard Little Tunnel and the 1,060 yard Big Tunnel, carried the canal through the ridges separating West Fork & Willards Run and Willards Run & Sandy Creek, respectively.

The western division began at Kensington and ran 32 miles to Bolivar, 5 miles in slackwater, while passing through the towns of Kensington, Lynchburg, East Rochester, Minerva, Pekin, Oneida, Malvern, Waynesburg, Magnolia, Sandyville and East Bolivar. This division contained one aqueduct (across the Tuscarawas at Bolivar), 2 small reservoirs near Kensington, 10 dams and it required 33 locks to descend 220 feet.

The eastern and western divisions were completed and opened to traffic in 1846. Little Tunnel was also completed in 1846, but the Big Tunnel wasn't ready to pass traffic until 1848. On January 7, 1848, the THOMAS FLEMING left New Lisbon and headed toward the summit. Its story has been told many times; of how the craft became grounded at Frost's Mill in the Pine Hill region and had to spend the night there; of how the construction crew and a team of oxen arrived the next morning to pull them out; of how the boat was again delayed when a rock fell from the roof of Big Tunnel; and of how, finally, the THOMAS FLEMING reached Hanover late on the 8th. The THOMAS FLEMING went on to Bolivar on the 9th and became the first craft to navigate the entire length of the Sandy & Beaver Canal and satisfied the letter of its charter which required the canal to be navigable within 20 years. The story of the THOMAS FLEMING was told and retold until it was common to hear a version in which the boat was the only one to navigate the canal and it was "drug along the dry canal bed in places by teams of oxen just so the contractors could be paid".

That trip did prove one thing, though; that the summit (the Big Tunnel in particular) wasn't yet ready to carry regular traffic and it took two more years of hard work before it was. Lists of boat arrivals and departures at New Lisbon appeared in the local paper for several years. We are able to tell from their ports of origination and their destinations that the summit level and the entire canal carried a limited amount of traffic during 1850 and 1851.

Then, on April 12th, 1852 the Cold Run Reservoir Dam gave way causing a great deal of destruction. Miraculously, no one was killed. This was a serious blow to the canal. Though the larger Guilford Reservoir was still intact, it couldn't begin to supply all the water required on the summit during an exceptionally dry season. To make matters worse, the flood caused by the breaking of the Cold Run Dam lost the canal whatever good will it had enjoyed from the local population. Nervous citizens living below the breast of the Guilford Reservoir organized. Anti-Canal meetings were held and petitions circulated naming the Sandy & Beaver Canal a public nuisance and demanding that the Cold Run Reservoir not be rebuilt and that the level of the Guilford Reservoir be kept four feet below the spillway!

The summit level was practically dry and virtually abandoned. Canal boatmen had never cared much for the tunnels, anyway. The last boat to pass through the Big Tunnel was the HIBERNIAN in the late spring of 1852. The Company failed in 1853 as great chunks of canal land were sold to satisfy long overdue judgments. Both the eastern and western divisions were used for a year or two more, but the very dry summer of 1854 stranded a number of boats near the summit and they never moved again. Floods in the early 1860's destroyed the few remaining portions of the eastern division. Somehow, a group from Sandyville obtained the six miles of canal from that village to the Ohio Canal at Bolivar. This section was offered to the State and became a feeder to the Ohio Canal on April 9, 1856. The feeder was still carrying traffic as late as 1860. A flood in 1884 washed out the Tuscarawas Aqueduct. It was never rebuilt and the last bit of the Sandy & Beaver Canal was finished.

## 33. THE NIMISHILLEN & SANDY CANAL

The Ohio & Erie Canal was routed down the Tuscarawas River through Stark County, some 8 miles west of Canton – the County seat. A new town called Massillon was founded on the banks of the canal and, for a time, threatened to replace Canton as the county's most prosperous community.

Canton's merchants wanted to get in on some of that canal trade; so in the early 1830's, the Nimishillen & Sandy Navigation Company was formed and received a Charter authorizing it to build a branch canal from Canton to some point on the Ohio & Erie Canal at or near Bolivar. A Mr. Fields made the original survey and it was intended to run the canal south from the village for a mile to the "Forks of the Nimishillen", down the valley of that creek for 12 miles to the Big Sandy then down its valley for 7 miles to Bolivar and the Ohio Canal. When the route of the Sandy & Beaver Canal was finalized, the Canton Group altered their plans and decided to tap into the S. & B. just below the junction of the Nimishillen and Big Sandy Creeks.

[…] The first meeting of the infant Nimishillen & Sandy Navigation Company was held on December 25, 1834 and […] Joshua Malin was hired as engineer. He had the first division of 4½ miles located by January 30, 1835. Two reservoir sites were located just north of Canton. Malin was confident that either of these reservoirs would be sufficient to supply the canal with water until it reached the "Forks". Contracts for the first ten sections were let by May 15th, 1835 and the southernmost 5 sections by June 20, 1836. […]

When the canal company was organized in 1834, its directors fully expected the canal to be finished and operating within two years. By the fall of 1836, however, the outlook was not nearly so bright. […]

The "Panic of 1837" undoubtedly put a stop to the Nimishillen & Sandy Navigation Company, but just how much was accomplished before the shutdown isn't presently known. It is known that the canal was finished from its northern terminus to the "Forks". Neither of the reservoirs appear to have been built as that section was never even filled with water. If an early canal existed between the North Industry works and the Sparta Forge, it would have been abandoned about 1840 when both the iron works were. Sections 8, 9 & 10 were used as the race to the Browning or Goodwill Mill in North Industry for some 25 years. Some historians believe that the Star Mill south of Canton and the mill in East Sparta may have also used the bed of the old canal as a mill race, but that hasn't been confirmed. In Canton, the ditch down Walnut Street remained open for years and east Tuscarawas St. was still crossing it on a "temporary" type bridge as late as 1884 or 85. Finally the "ditch" in Canton was filled in, the mills in North Industry and East Sparta burned down or were torn down and the Nimishillen & Sandy Canal was forgotten.

## 34. THE WALHONDING CANAL
### condensed from OHIO'S CANALS by F.W. Trevorrow

"Twenty five miles to nowhere". So in a few disparaging words did one writer describe the Walhonding Canal. The characterization was accurate, but only because plans for extensions of this branch of the Ohio & Erie did not materialize.

The survey of the canal was completed and prepared for contract by William H. Price Resident Engineer in 1836. The cost of the entire branch was estimated at $387,467. Construction began in 1837 when 18 miles were put under contract. The remaining eleven sections were let in the spring of 1838. The Board of Public Works optimistically reported that the canal would be completed by October 1839, but construction was delayed and it did not open until 1841. In each year of construction the cost kept increasing. The estimate was raised to $450,000 in 1838. By the end of 1840 $491,365 had been spent. The whole cost reported after completion was $607,269.

Throughout the construction period, the Board of Public Works urged the legislature to authorize funds to proceed with the extensions. Surveys, plans and estimates of the cost of the Vernon and Mohican extensions were submitted in 1838, The Vernon Canal, from the junction of the Vernon and Mohican Rivers to Mount Vernon, would have been 21 miles and 64 chains long, had 17 locks with 141 feet of lift and cost an estimated $360,509. The Mohican Canal, from the termination of the Walhonding Canal to Loudonville, would have been 23 miles and 68 chains long, had 11 locks with 94 feet of lift and cost an estimated $416,736.

The extensions were resurveyed in 1839 by Nathaniel Medberry and an application for money to begin construction was made to the Commissioners of the Canal Fund. Bids for contracts were advertised in 1843, but when the Commissioners advised "no funds" no bids were accepted. A final try was made in 1844 with the same results and all thought of extending the Walhonding Canal was forgotten.

The Walhonding Canal, itself, began at the junction with the Ohio & Erie Canal in Roscoe Basin. It then followed the right, or south, bank of the Walhonding River for six miles to where it crossed the river upon slackwater above a dam. The canal next followed the left bank for 12½ miles through the towns of Warsaw and Walhonding to the junction of the Vernon and Mohican Rivers. The left bank of the

Mohican River was followed for approximately 5 miles to where it entered the river about ¼ mile within Knox County a short distance below the point where Flat Run emptied into the river. As originally built the Walhonding Canal was 23½ miles long and used 11 locks to overcome an 85 foot rise. A triple lock (three separate lifts built into one stone structure) was located where the canal left Roscoe Basin. There were also two guard locks along the route of the canal.

All the construction experience obtained from building the Ohio & Erie was applied to the Walhonding. Minimum prism dimensions as well as lock type and sizes were the same on both canals. Locks on the Walhonding were often referred to by name rather than by number (a practice generally followed all along the Ohio Canal System). Resident engineers tried to discourage the practice by affixing metal number plates to all the locks, but the custom of using names continued. As near as can be determined by location the Walhonding locks referred to by name are #13 – Mohican Guard; #10 – Fry's; #9 – Gamble's; #7 – Warsaw; #6 – Crawford's; #5 – Walhonding River Crossing and #4 – Feeder Lock.

The dam on the Mohican supplied the canal with water as far as Six Mile Dam. It also provided slackwater for 1½ miles up the Mohican to the long gone community of Rochester. Six Mile Dam, then, supplied the canal with water to its junction with the Ohio & Erie. […]

Lack of traffic and failure to extend the canal led to its neglect. […]

All of the Walhonding Canal above the Six Mile Dam was officially abandoned in 1896. The remainder was used as a feeder to the Ohio & Erie until the latter was abandoned after the 1913 floods. Those six miles of the Walhonding continued supplying water to a hydro-electric plant near the Triple Lock for many years. According to local tradition, Capt. Billy Sweet brought the last boat through the Walhonding in 1900 and, assuming that no more boats would follow, he is said to have sunk his craft in the lower chamber of the Triple Lock. The legend is a good one and there was, indeed, a sunken boat in the Triple Lock for many years. However photos indicate that the boat was the State or Maintenance boat for that section of the Ohio & Erie that was probably stored in the lock chamber for the "duration".

## 35. THE MUSKINGUM IMPROVEMENT
### from information provided by C.K. Swift, F.W. Trevorrow, Norris Schneider, and the Washington County Hist. Soc.

The Dresden Sidecut allowed residents of the Muskingum Valley to ship and receive goods via the Ohio Canal, but steamboats could only navigate that far up the river during periods of high water. A privately financed dam and short stretch of canal around the falls at Zanesville was constructed by the Zanesville Canal and Manufacturing Company which got a charter from the State in 1814.

The State of Ohio authorized an "improvement" of the Muskingum River from Marietta to Dresden and appropriated $400,000 on March 4, 1836. At this time the facilities at Zanesville and Symmes Creek were taken over by the Canal Commissioners.

Actual construction of the Improvement began in the spring of 1837. For nearly six years traffic on the river was hindered by this construction and it was necessary to offload and transfer cargo around each dam site until it and the adjacent lock were finished. By 1838 the small lock at Symmes Creek was in operation allowing steamboats to trade between Zanesville and Dresden. After an additional delay to repair undermined dams at Marietta and Beverly, the Muskingum Improvement was opened to traffic on September 17, 1841 when the first toll was collected at Zanesville from the steamboat TUSCARAWAS.

As originally built, the Improvement was 91 miles long, contained 11 dams and used 12 locks to overcome 125½ feet of rise. Most of this route was in slackwater, though five short stretches of canal were located at Zanesville, Taylorsville (Philo), McConnelsville, Beverly and Lowell. [...]

Locks built during the State's improvement of the river originally were to have closed chambers measuring 120 feet long by 22 feet wide. In 1838 these dimensions were changed to a standard of 175 feet by 36. The actual lock chambers were all somewhat less than standard, however, with lengths of from 157.4 to 160 feet and one chamber had a clear width of but 33.3 feet. The Symmes Creek Lock, originally built by a private company, remained 120 feet long in the chamber by 22 feet wide. [...]

By 1856 the cost of keeping the Muskingum Improvement in repair was more than its income. [...] In 1886 the U.S. Government agreed to take over the Muskingum Improvement after the State had paid over $12,000 in collected tolls. The Government took over on April 10, 1887 and the steamboat GENERAL H.F. DEVOL was the first boat to go down the river free of tolls.

On October 16, 1958 the U.S. Government transferred the Muskingum locks and dams to the State of Ohio. Also included was a bonus of $235,000 in lieu of demolishing the structures. The Ohio Department of Public Resources then began a ten year program of restoration on the Muskingum Improvement.

Today, the original locks on the Improvement are all in operation except that the Ellis dam & lock replaced the Symmes Creek dam and lock in 1910 and the Marietta lock was moved from the Harmar to the Marietta side in 1891 and removed entirely in 1969. Locktenders now lock pleasure craft through from daylight to dark. The State provides a house for the locktenders at Devola, Beverly, Rokeby Lock and Philo. The locktender's house at Zanesville is used as an office. Parking areas, restrooms and boat landings have been provided at each lock.

## 36. THE HOCKING CANAL
### from information supplied by F.W. Trevorrow, C.R. Goslin,
### Robert McDonnell of Ohio University and Blanche M. Cook

Construction of the Hocking Canal began at the southern terminus of the Lancaster Lateral in 1836 and proceeded south. It had originally been planned to run much of the canal in slackwater by damming the river at various points and allowing the canal to use the resulting pools for navigation. State engineers were forced to change these plans shortly after construction began due to the frequent shifting of the river bed.

This change of plans and the economic chaos caused by the "Panic of 1837" caused work to go very slowly. It was 1840 before the 32 miles of canal from Lancaster to Nelsonville was completed and only four more miles were completed by 1841.

When first completed, the Hocking Canal was 56 miles long and contained 26 lift locks (to overcome a rise of 203 feet) plus 5 guard locks, 34 culverts, 8 feeder and slackwater dams and an aqueduct with an 80 foot span over Monday Creek. Included in its 56 mile length were 7 miles of slackwater. The first such pool began at Rush Creek, 16 miles below Carroll and ran for 1¼ miles. The second began near Green's Mills, 22 miles from Carroll, and ran for 5 miles to Hocking Falls. The third pool, 2¼ miles above Athens, was ¾ of a mile long. […]

Extensive coal mines and salt deposits in the Hocking Valley plus a smattering of early industries provided a fairly steady volume of traffic to the canal for nearly 30 years. Receipts on the Hocking remained relatively high for fully 10 years after the peak had been reached on other Ohio canals. The fact remains, though, that receipts for the entire life of the Hocking Canal amounted to only $288,469 while the cost of the repairs, superintendents and collection for the same period was reported as $407,256! […]

Devastating floods during the summer of 1873 virtually destroyed the southern portion of the Hocking Canal. By this time receipts had fallen to the point where it was no longer economically feasible to repair that section so, in 1873, all of the canal from Nelsonville to Athens was abandoned. The 7 miles below Chauncey, including the Athens terminal, was given to the city of Athens by the State Legislature in 1874. The northern portion of the Hocking Canal carried some small amount of traffic for nearly 20 years more; but finally, in 1891 it too was abandoned and all operations ceased. Those portions of the canal lands necessary for trackage were then leased to the Columbus, Hocking Valley & Athens Railroad.

## 37. THE CINCINNATI & WHITEWATER CANAL
### from information supplied by F.W. Trevorrow

The State of Indiana authorized a canal down the valley of the Whitewater River to a point on the Ohio River some 30 miles below Cincinnati at Lawrenceburgh in January, 1836. Some Cincinnati merchants felt that a branch canal constructed from a point on the projected Whitewater Canal to Cincinnati would retain much of the trade that might otherwise be drawn off to Lawrenceburgh. Later that same year, 1836, the Cincinnati group "borrowed" Darius Lapham from the State's Engineers and had the route of the proposed canal surveyed.

The Cincinnati & Whitewater Canal Company was formed in 1837 and stock books immediately opened. A little over $90,000 was raised by stock subscriptions and the State of Ohio, as required by the "Plunder Law" of 1836, pledged $45,000. In addition, the City of Cincinnati pledged $40,000. The actual cost of the canal amounted to $542,928. The money required for construction above that amount obtained from stock sales and pledges was raised upon bonds and certificates.

The Cincinnati & Whitewater Canal tapped the Indiana canal about a mile below Harrison in a slackwater pool formed by a dam across the Whitewater River. Water for the entire 25 miles of the C. &

W. was provided by this pool. Upon leaving this slackwater, the canal maintained that level for two miles until, entering the State of Ohio, a 4 foot lift lock was located. Dry Fork was crossed on a four-span wooden aqueduct. A lock with an 8 foot drop was located just below the aqueduct. The canal then crossed the Great Miami River on an eight-span wooden aqueduct, negotiated a lock with a 5 foot drop and passed through the community of Cleves. From here the canal used a 990 foot long tunnel to pierce the ridge that separated the Great Miami and Ohio River valleys. The masonry arch of the tunnel extended an additional 800 feet into the open cuts to keep them from filling with wash and debris.

After emerging from the tunnel the canal followed the north or right bank of the Ohio River through the towns of Northbend, Addyston, Delhi and Anderson's Ferry to Cincinnati. Locks for this canal were built of common limestone lined with timber and plank – a composite lock. The two aqueducts were constructed of wooden trusses supported by wooden arches resting on stone abutments and piers. Four stone culverts were used to cross minor water courses.

Construction on the canal was begun in 1839 or 1840 and the first boat through the C. & W. reached Cincinnati in November 1843. The canal was used for a few years, but the main Whitewater Canal suffered four severely destructive floods in six years. The Whitewater Canal Company went into receivership in 1855 and after that, this canal was practically useless. Deprived of its principle source of traffic, the Cincinnati & Whitewater Canal withered and died.

In 1862 the canal was sold to the Indianapolis & Cincinnati R.R. which constructed its Plum Street Depot on or near the canal's Cincinnati terminus. Most of the towpath to Harrison was soon covered with iron rails and wooden ties – so ended the Cincinnati & Whitewater Canal.

## 38. THE WHITEWATER CANAL

Technically an Indiana canal, 8 miles of the Whitewater Canal were within the boundaries of Ohio from Harrison to Elizabethtown along the right (west) bank of the Great Miami River.

## 39. THE WARREN COUNTY CANAL
### Condensed from an article by L.W. Richardson – TOWPATHS No. 3, 1968

After "turning the earth" on July 21st, 1825 to begin construction on the Miami Canal, Governors Clinton and Morrow and their aides traveled to Lebanon for a dinner at the Indian Chief Tavern. There they dined with a number of the most influential men in the State as well as the most ardent canal supporters. Among these men were ex-Governor Ethan Allen Brown, ex-Senator and future President William Henry Harrison and the Kentucky statesman Henry Clay. Also present were financiers Rathbone and Lord who were engaged in selling Ohio Canal Bonds in the eastern money markets. Though it is not recorded as fact, it is highly probable that the idea for a branch canal from Lebanon to the main line, if not actually first suggested here, was at least seriously discussed among people who could help make it go and the project given a great impetus.

Since only the community of Lebanon could expect to derive many benefits from such a branch canal, the major burden of financial support fell upon the people within the town and the more solvent folks in the county's eastern half. A local man, Judge George Kesling, financed and arranged for a survey and worked unceasingly to get the project under way. Such a project was a formidable one for so small a community to undertake, however, and it wasn't until February, 1830 that an Act was passed incorporating the Warren County Canal Company and authorizing it to construct a canal from Lebanon to Middletown.

Stock was sold on a subscription basis, but sales were slow and hard cash came in even slower. It was nearly three years more before the requests for bids appeared in Lebanon's paper. [...]

By the fall of 1835, money from the stock subscriptions was just about gone and, with the canal less than 30% finished, it became evident that outside help was needed. Therefore, in January, 1836, a resolution was presented to the State Legislature asking that the State complete the work which was estimated would cost $128,000. The State responded favorably and completion of the Warren County Canal was included in the vast Public Works "package" that the Legislature authorized in 1836. [...]

The canal was to be completed within two years, but rising costs, abandoned contracts and the necessity to relet them at higher bids all contributed to delay the actual opening of the canal until 1840. The first boat to navigate the Warren County Canal was the COMMERCE which arrived at the Lebanon basin from Hamilton on June 9, 1840. A gala dinner was prepared at the Golden Lamb to celebrate the event. The next day several hundred citizens were treated to rides down the canal, through the locks and back to town. Two days later the COMMERCE left for Cincinnati with 200 barrels of flour and whisky and several lady passengers.

The Warren County Canal joined the Miami Canal just above Lock #12 (Lock #32 by the later numbering system) near the point where ground was first broken on the main canal. It terminated at Lebanon at the basin north of Turtle Creek, between Broadway and Mulberry Streets.

The channel crossed the broad valley between the Great Miami and Little Miami Rivers in a long curve from Middletown southeast, down Muddy Creek to the Turtle Creek valley, then northeast up that stream to Lebanon. There were no extensive excavations or fills, the terrain being generally favorable for canal building except that the gravelly soil along the terminal moraines made it difficult to hold water in the channel. Structures consisted of the usual scattering of culverts and three aqueducts: one over a branch of Turtle Creek, the others crossing branches of Dick's Creek.

Because of the nearly fifty feet difference in elevation between the two terminals, six locks were required. Lock #1 was at the foot of Clay St. in Lebanon. Locks #2, #3 and #4 were within the next two miles down the valley. The combined "lift" of the four was 28 feet. Within a short distance of the western terminus, the canal descended another 16 feet through Locks #5 and #6. All the locks were built with Dayton stone.

At the western end of the canal, water [...] was brought by a feeder about three miles long from the Miami Canal above Middletown and entered the channel just above Lock #5. At the eastern end, water was obtained from both branches of Turtle Creek. A dam was built across the East Fork above the basin and a reservoir covering about 40 acres was constructed on the North Fork. [...] Although water was fed to the long level between locks #4 and #5 from both ends, the engineers decided to introduce water from Shaker Run directly into the canal. This was disastrous; every storm washed mud and gravel into the canal filling the channel for hundreds of yards in both directions. [...]

Traffic was not heavy on the canal. Unfortunately, Lebanon could not generate paying loads in either direction. Frequent breaks halted passage for long periods. Faults in the original design added to the problems. A major break at Shaker Run in 1848 was not repaired and all through traffic ceased. In 1852, the State was petitioned to repair the canal and the resident engineer of the Miami Canal reported favorably, but the report was not acted upon and the Board's 1856 report stated that the canal, all water rights and other property had been sold to J.W. Corwin and R.H. Hendrickson for $40,000. The State and the canal company had spent $228,600 on its construction!

After the sale, the tangible evidence of the canal's existence began to disappear. The right-of-way reverted to farm land, roads and railroads obscured the channel and lock stones were used for barn foundations. Only one structure remained, the North Fork Reservoir. Left intact it remained in place for local residents to swim and fish until 1882. July of that year was one of unusually heavy rains. The reservoir filled and even began to spill over in spots. This had often happened in the past and no alarm was felt. This time, however, the embankment had been weakened and, about four o'clock one afternoon, it collapsed sending a tremendous volume of water roaring across the Dayton Pike and down the course of North Fork. [...] Damage amounted to thousands of dollars, but fortunately no lives were lost. And so ended the last tangible remains of the Warren County Canal.

## 40. THE MILAN CANAL
### by Claude Latham of the Milan Museum

Milan, Ohio, located some eight miles south of Lake Erie on the Huron River, was an early gathering place (1817) for pioneers from all over the Firelands. Merry's Mill, here, was one of the few places in the area where grist could be ground and basic goods bought and sold.

Until the 1820's, the people near Milan were, by necessity, self sufficient. By the early twenties, however, the amount of produce coming from the land was far greater than the local need. There was a ready market in the east, but the roads of the day made it nearly impossible to get there with heavy loads. When the Erie Canal opened in 1825, all this changed and the residents of northern Ohio saw an easy way to get the products of their labor to New York markets.

David Abbot, a resident farmer at Fries' Landing, built a schooner named MARY ABBOT in 1827, loaded it with produce and sailed to New York City. [...] The feasibility of shipping by water to New York was thus established. That same year, the residents of the area became aware of the business possibilities in shipping grain. A group of local businessmen applied to the State for, and were granted, a charter to build a canal from Fries' Landing to Merry's Mill Pond in the village of Milan, a distance of 3 miles. A canal was necessary to reach roads that could be used during most of the year. The area around Fries' Landing was low lying and wet.

Construction was started in 1831 and completed (with the State's help) in 1834. The Milan Canal towpath was continued past Fries' Landing as far as Abbottsford and was utilized in towing ships to Lake Erie. Ralph and George Lockwood and Hamilton Coulton built warehouses at Abbottsford and Fries' Landing and went into the business of storing grain and shipping it to Buffalo by Lake Schooner.

Construction of the canal was well under way when the Company's directors decided to deepen the channel to 13 feet, thus allowing Lake Schooners to go all the way to Milan. This eliminated the need to trans-ship grain at Huron. On July 4, 1839 the first schooner, the KEWANNEA, arrived at the Milan basin. The Milan Canal was 40 feet wide at the water line, 13 feet deep, 3 miles long and used two locks to overcome a difference in elevation of 7 feet. The stone locks were of the standard mitered gate type with closed chambers measuring 110 feet long by 40 feet wide.

A business boom in Milan was immediate. Fourteen warehouses soon lined the basin at the foot of the hill. Grain was hauled by wagon from as far away as Columbus. Very little money was used in the business transactions. Instead, farmers were given bills of credit on a mercantile store and he usually left Milan with purchases of salt, leather, cloth, shingles, plows, etc.

Soon after the grain business was established, the shipbuilding trade developed on the north side of the basin utilizing the white oak timber of the area. More than 75 Lake Schooners were built between 1841 and 1867. The last schooner built here was the EXILE in 1867. The flood of 1868 destroyed the feeder dam at Milan and, as business didn't warrant reconstruction (no freight was carried on the canal after 1865), the canal was abandoned.

The IDAHO, a schooner built in Milan in 1863, returned to the canal for repairs in 1873. It entered the lower lock at Fries' Landing and was allowed to deteriorate. Part of the hull remains today. A portion of the Milan Canal is still in use. The Norfolk & Western R.R. runs their tracks along the towpath for which they hold a 99 year lease.

§§§§§§§§§§§§§§§§§§§§§§§§§§

*So many locks and numbers! Just remember that in Ohio, Lock #1 was always found at the highest elevation or summit level and that numbers counted up from there. (Exceptions to this rule were the original Wabash & Erie lock numbers and the easternmost section of the Pennsylvania & Ohio Canal.)*

Volume XXXIII (1995), No. 4, p. 52

## LOCK NUMBERING by F.W. Trevorrow

The system of numbering locks for identification was universal on canal systems in both Britain and the United States. Ohio adopted the plan of numbering locks on its system by designating the top lock at the summit as "Lock 1." In spite of the insistence by canal authorities that locks be referred to by number in reports, locks were often referred to by colloquial names. Colloquial names were taken from those of adjacent land owners, such as "Kettlewell", or legends, "Johnny Cake," or places.

On the Ohio & Erie Canal, the lock numbers began with number one at each of the two summits, Portage at Akron and Licking. From Akron, the locks were numbered north to Cleveland, one to 44, and south to Adam's Mills, one to 30. There the numbering was continued on the Dresden Side-Cut to include numbers 31, 32 and 33.

From the Licking Summit, south to Newark, the locks were numbered north, one to 19 at Webbsport and south, one to 55 at Portsmouth.

The locks on the Miami & Erie Canal were numbered from the Loramie Summit south, one at Lockington to 53 at the Ohio River in Cincinnati, and north at New Bremen to 50 at Toledo. Similarly, on branch canals, locks were numbered from the junction with the main canal to the terminus.

At Toledo, after the canal was abandoned through the city and the Side-Cut built, two locks on the Swan Creek Side-Cut were designated 51 and 52 and the original locks, abandoned at Manhattan, retained their original numbers, one and two.

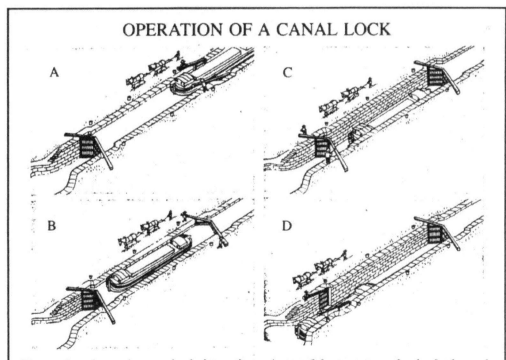

## OPERATION OF A CANAL LOCK

These drawings show a lock in action. A canal boat enters the lock through the upper gates which are then closed. As water flows from the lock the boat is lowered to the lower gate level of the canal. The lower gates are opened and the boat proceeds into the lower canal level and continues its journey. (R. K. Andrist, *The Erie Canal*, Troll Associates, Mahwah, N.J., 1964, p. 63)

*So where did these canals get all that water? What follows is a "classic"* Towpaths *article which explains it all, written originally by Frank Trevorrow and edited 34 years later by Brad Bond.*

Volume XLII (2004), No. 1, pp. 7-20

## WATER SUPPLY OF OHIO'S CANALS by Frank Trevorrow

This article first appeared in **Towpaths**, Vol. VIII, Nos. 2 and 3, 1970. It did such a fine job of describing one of the most crucial issues of planning a canal that no one has addressed the topic broadly for Ohio's canals since. Details have been reported, temporary feeders not covered in 1970 have been discovered, but the essential outline remains as he described it. And it appears worthwhile to reprint it here with a few additions and a few deletions. The editor hopes he will be excused the alterations.

Location of adequate water supplies guided the explorations of the Ohio Canal Commissioners and engineers when the initial surveys of possible routes for the canals to connect Lake Erie with the Ohio River were made. The Geddes survey of 1822 was charged by law to examine five possible routes, each commencing on the dividing ridge at the sources of the northward and southward flowing streams. The five routes were: the Grand and Mahoning, the Cuyahoga and Tuscarawas, Black River and Killbuck Creek; the Maumee and Great Miami; and the Scioto and Sandusky. The Cuyahoga and Tuscarawas route was viewed with the most favor due to the presence of the Portage Lakes, making it the easiest to supply with water at the summit.

The state was committed to the Maumee and Great Miami route for the canal through the western part of the state. Explorations of that route established those rivers as adequate sources of supply for the canal below the Loramie summit. The early reports were vague as to the supply north as far as the Maumee. Since construction of the canal north of Dayton had not been authorized, the problem of the supply of water to the northern section of the Miami & Erie Canal was left to a later date.

### Ohio & Erie Canal

The selection of the Cuyahoga and Tuscarawas route for the Ohio & Erie Canal in preference to either the Black River-Killbuck Creek or the Sandusky-Scioto River routes touched off an acrimonious debate. The Black River-Killbuck Creek route had few partisans, but Sandusky used all possible influence in trying to secure the canal by way of the Sandusky-Scioto route and deprive its rival, Cleveland, of the northern terminus.

Vitriolic editorials and letters appeared in the Sandusky newspapers, accusing the Commissioners and engineers of yielding to political pressure from Cleveland, and even impugning Alfred Kelley's integrity. Equally harsh editorials appeared in Cleveland papers in retaliation. Nevertheless, Geddes' opinion of the Sandusky-Scioto route prevailed. He said in his report: "These streams [Sandusky - Scioto] have their sources almost wholly in the country of prairies, than which, a more unfavorable tract for the production of durable water does not exist in the state."

Once the decision was made in favor of the Cuyahoga-Tuscarawas river route, the Portage Lakes were made into a system of reservoirs on the Akron or Portage Summit, as it was called, by lowering the level of the lakes about five feet to obtain the full volume of the Tuscarawas. A dam across the headwater of the Tuscarawas, south of Akron, diverted the river into the lakes.

North of Portage Summit, a series of dams in the Cuyahoga and Little Cuyahoga rivers with connecting feeders supplied the canal below the locks in Akron. Two feeders were taken out of the Little Cuyahoga, one between Locks 15 and 16, and the second between Locks 21 and 22. A dam at Peninsula, where the canal crossed from the west to the east bank of the Cuyahoga on an aqueduct, provided an important water supply between Locks 30 and 31. Nearer Cleveland, at a point known as the Pinery, another dam served to supply the canal between Locks 36 and 37 with water for the remainder of its length. This dam is still supplying water to the canal for conveyance to a steel mill in Cleveland.

South of Portage Summit, the first supplement to the Portage Lakes water supply was taken into the canal at Wolf Creek where Lock 1 South terminated the summit level. The creek was dammed and turned into the canal below the lock. Six miles further south the canal crossed to the east side of the Tuscarawas at Clinton in the pool of a dam which added to the water supply. Nimisilla Creek and Mud Creek also fed the canal between Clinton and Massillon.

At Massillon, it was originally intended to build a dam in the Tuscarawas to provide a feeder if a deficiency in the water supply was found to exist. In 1841, James Duncan, a prominent Massillon industrialist persuaded the Board of Public Works, to adopt a plan for a feeder from Sippo Creek instead of the River dam. This source of supply ended abruptly in 1848 when the reservoir dam on Sippo Creek was breached and the feeder washed out.

The abandonment of the Sandy & Beaver Canal enabled the State in 1857 to obtain the western portion from Sandyville to Bolivar to serve as a feeder. This entailed possession of the aqueduct across the Tuscarawas, which joined the Sandy & Beaver with the Ohio & Erie. The aqueduct proved to be a heavy liability. Maintenance of the structure was very expensive.

The next feeder was taken into the canal at a dam in the Tuscarawas at the industrious community of Zoar. The feeder included a lock and a short branch canal to Zoar, to enable the community to load its produce from its warehouse directly into canal boats. At Dover, 18 miles below Zoar, Sugar Creek was crossed on a dam, forming another important water supply point.

The feeder at Trenton, or Tuscarawas, as it is now called, 10 miles south of Dover, served a dual purpose. Canal boats could move 3 miles up the feeder from Trenton to the Guard Lock at the river and then up Stillwater Creek to Uhrichsville. The Trenton feeder supplied over 30 miles of the canal to Roscoe where water from the Walhonding Canal and river was introduced. The Walhonding was the final feeder on the descent south from Portage Summit into the valley of the Muskingum River at the Webbsport-Dresden level.

Ascending from Dresden, the canal followed Wakatomika Creek for about a mile, then, taking a southerly direction through a gap in the hills at Nashport, it entered the Licking River valley just east of the Narrows. A dam at this point served not only to furnish water to the canal, but also solved the problem of the passage of the Narrows. By creating a slack-water pool in the Narrows and building a stone-walled embankment along the north bank, canal boats were able to navigate the Narrows after entering through a Guard Lock. Unfortunately, it was necessary to blast away an Indian hieroglyph in the shape of a hand on the north cliff face of the Narrows to construct the embankment. The hieroglyph was known as the Black Hand and gave its name to the Narrows.

Continuing its ascent, the North Fork of the Licking River was introduced as a feeder to the canal at Newark and another from Raccoon Fork came in a mile southwest of Newark. Five miles south of Newark, at the north end of the Licking Summit level, the canal received the Granville Feeder. This was a navigable branch slightly more than six miles long extending canal navigation to the town of Granville. The feeder also took water from Raccoon Fork near the town.

The supply of water to the Licking Summit, on the dividing ridge of the watershed between the Muskingum and Scioto Rivers was decided upon in 1825. The 3rd Annual Report of the Board of Canal Commissioners said:

"The question of supplying the Licking Summit and the lower levels dependent upon it for water, is one of the most interesting and important which present itself for consideration in relation to this route. To accomplish this object, or at least aid in its accomplishment, it is proposed to construct a large reservoir contiguous to the summit."

The Licking Reservoir occupied a natural basin nearly eight miles long by about one-half mile wide and originally covered about 2500 acres. An artificial bank of about four miles in length, two miles of which formed the towing path, was raised across low ground to form the western side of the reservoir. A feeder from the South Fork of the Licking at Kirkersville entered the reservoir at the southwestern end to augment the natural drainage into the basin. The reservoir was enlarged by about 500 acres in 1836. The addition was called the "New Reservoir" and was situated west of the original towing path embankment. Gates between the two reservoirs were constructed at opposite ends of the towpath.

The Licking Reservoir was intended to supply the canal south from the summit to Lockbourne, 30 miles, except for small feeders from Walnut and Blacklick Creeks. At Lockbourne, the canal received the Columbus Feeder. Dams in the Scioto at Columbus and at the point where the Feeder crossed Big Black Walnut Creek diverted water into the feeder to supply the canal south of Lockbourne to Circleville. Two dams in the Scioto, the first two miles south of Circleville, the second, known as Tomlinson's Dam, six miles below Chillicothe, furnished the water supply as far as the southern terminus of the canal at Portsmouth.

## Miami & Erie Canal

The water supply system of the Miami & Erie Canal was relatively simple, with only one summit, the Loramie Summit, extending 23 miles from Lockington to New Bremen, to be supplied. The lower reaches of the canal were supplied by the waters of the Mad and Great Miami rivers to the south and by the Maumee to the north.

A controversy over the method to be employed in supplying the Loramie Summit lasted for four years after the extension of the Miami Canal was authorized in 1836. The matter at issue was the advisability of the employment of reservoirs as against flowing streams for the summit supply.

The route proposed in 1825 for the Miami Extension followed the valley of Mad River for eighteen miles north of Dayton. Then, following the valley of Jackson's Creek, it crossed over to the valley of the Great Miami and ascended to the summit. The supply to the summit was to be provided by a feeder from the Great Miami. Below the summit, and where the line lay in the Mad River valley, the canal was to be supplied by a feeder from the headwaters of Mad River.

The reason for proposing this line was explained in an 1841 Board of Public Works report: "At the time [1825] the practicability of supplying canals with water by means of reservoirs, upon an extended scale, was doubted by many, as no existing example could be referred to. The attention of the Engineers was, therefore, directed to the adaptation of the canal to the permanent streams of the country, in order to feed from them. Upon this system, Mad River could not but be an important feature in this plan."

In 1830, a board of engineers was appointed by the Canal Commissioners to reexamine the route of the Miami Extension. The board consisted of Samuel Forrer, Wm. H. Price and Jesse L. Williams, three of the ablest engineers in the State's employ. They rejected the 1825 line because of the inadequacy of Mad River. Instead, they recommended the canal follow the Great Miami River valley from Dayton to the mouth of Loramie Creek, thence along that stream for one and one-half miles and ascend by means of a flight of locks to the south end of the summit level.

The report of Forrer's group stated: "As part of the general outline of the plan of this contemplated canal, it is necessary to construct a number of reservoirs." It was proposed to construct one in the main valley of Loramie Creek, on the line of the canal, extending from Cynthiana (Newport) to Lockington, with two additional reservoirs in branches of that creek, another near Lewistown in the head branches of the Great Miami, and a fifth, the great reservoir near St. Marys. To add to the resources of the Great Miami, it was also proposed to construct a feeder from Mad River, which would be introduced into the Great Miami above Port Jefferson.

Notwithstanding the creation of reservoirs to supply the Ohio & Erie Canal, which were then in use, the Act of 1836, authorizing the Extension of the Miami Canal instructed the Board of Public Works to substitute feeders from living streams wherever it could be done without detriment to the interest of the State. Under the impression that it was then indispensable, the Board authorized a survey and estimate of the Mad River Feeder preparatory to placing it under contract. The line of the feeder went from De Graff on the Great Miami to a point on the Mad River 3 1/2 miles below West Liberty in Logan County. At some point in the consideration, it became a navigable feeder, extending navigation of the Sidney Feeder by 21 miles. If extended to West Liberty, as suggested, another 3 1/2 miles would have been added. Extension to Urbana for an additional 8 miles was also considered.

The question of the need or desirability of the Mad River Feeder was raised repeatedly from 1838 until 1841. Surveys in 1839 disclosed that the Lewistown Reservoir could be made much larger than originally contemplated, and that the quantity of water from Mad River was much less than anticipated, so that the Mad River Feeder could be dispensed with. After 1841, no more mention of it appears in the reports.

It seems that the Legislature did not have a clear understanding of the plan of the Lewistown Reservoir system. The waters of the reservoir were to be brought to Port Jefferson in the bed of the Great Miami where a dam diverted them into the Sidney Feeder, which was navigable to Lockington.

From queries put to the Board, it seems that some members of the Legislature thought the navigable feeder extended all the way to the reservoir. The hopes for these navigable feeders were so great in some quarters that it is related one man sold his business in Chicago to relocate at Port Jefferson, which, in his opinion was to become the greatest wheat shipping port in the world.

The final plan of reservoirs on the Miami & Erie consisted of the Lewistown, Loramie Creek and Mercer County reservoirs. The Lewistown Reservoir, originally of about 1,000 acres, was enlarged to 7,200 acres in later years. Instead of a reservoir in the line of the canal, one of 1,850 acres was built on a branch of Loramie Creek in 1843-4 under contract with P. W. Taylor & Co., at a cost of $22,000. The Mercer County Reservoir, supplying the canal from St. Marys to Junction, was commenced in 1837. Originally planned to cover 12,000 acres, it was enlarged to 17,000.

The Mercer County Reservoir, or Grand Lake St. Marys, as generally called, always held an importance commensurate with its size. Large enough to accommodate small steamers, it became the main artery of travel between Celina and St. Marys. The discovery of oil and gas in the bed of the lake in the 1890s resulted in a forest of oil derricks sprouting all over its surface. This forest took the place of the natural forest of trees, which were drowned when the lake was formed.

Water from Mercer County Reservoir was fed through a 3 mile long feeder to the canal between Locks 11 and 12 at St. Marys. An odd feature of this reservoir was the provision of the Dry Feeder in 1852. It was taken out of the canal between Locks 6 and 7 and ran west along the Montezuma road (OH 219) for about 4 miles where it turned north to enter the reservoir. The purpose of the Dry Feeder was to supply the reservoir when there was a surplus of water at the summit.

A lease of water power to mills at Celina in 1853 by the then Acting Commissioner was a source of annoyance to his successors, as it was contrary to the purpose of the reservoir. Water was supposed to go only to supply the canal, but that leased at Celina was discharged into Big Beaver Creek, a branch of the Wabash, and lost to the canal. Succeeding Commissioners pointed out that the same amount of water flowing into the canal could have been used several times over at mills along the line, returning to the canal after use at each mill, and thus would have returned many times the revenue paid at Celina.

The supply of the line of the Wabash & Erie Canal from the Indiana line to Junction was provided by the Six Mile Creek Reservoir. Located seven miles east of the state line, it covered 2,500 acres, with an embankment 10 1/2 miles long around it. The reservoir was filled by the waters of Six Mile Creek, on which it was built, and from Little St. Joseph River via the Indiana Canal. The effectiveness of the reservoir was materially reduced in 1858 when the Wabash Valley Railroad was built. The ditches of the railroad cut off half of the natural drainage to the reservoir. By 1874, the Wabash & Erie Canal in Indiana had become unfit for navigation and the Ohio section fell into disuse. The reservoir was still used to supply water to the Miami & Erie at Junction until finally destroyed in 1886 when dissidents dynamited the banks.

The waters of the Maumee River supplied the northern portion of the Miami & Erie. The dam at Independence, terminating the slackwater begun at Defiance, diverted river water into the canal at Lock 40 for the line to Bucklin's, Lock 43. There, a short slackwater section extended to Providence Dam, the last point of supply of the northern line. Located at Grand Rapids, the Providence Dam was a constant source of trouble. The riverbed was solid rock, and failure to blast out a deep enough channel resulted in stranding of boats in times of drought. The height of the dam could not be raised without flooding adjacent property.

South of the Loramie Summit, the story of water supply to the Miami & Erie Canal was associated with that of intense industrial development. At each of the dams in the Great Miami River, which diverted water into the canal, rights were secured by manufacturing establishments. Thus, the great industrial concentration of the Great Miami River valley began a few years after the canal came into operation.

The first dam south of Loramie Summit, Piqua dam, fed the canal through a guard lock just south of Lock 8. An arrangement with the Piqua Hydraulic Company, organized in 1866, permitted the withdrawal of water between Locks 3 and 4 at Lockington, returning it between Locks 10 and 11, the fall being 60.2 feet. It was conducted to Piqua through a wooden aqueduct across Loramie Creek. The wooden aqueduct was later replaced by a cast iron siphon.

Next below Piqua was the Troy dam. A feeder from this dam, known as Dyke's Race, followed the canal for some distance before the water was introduced into the canal below Lock 14. The Troy Hydraulic Company leased the water at this point, taken from the head of Lock 10 and returned to the canal above Lock 12. The Troy dam supplied the canal all the way to Dayton.

At Dayton, a dual system of feeders existed. One feeder was taken from Mad River some distance above the city through the hydraulic canal. A second was taken from the river a short distance above a dam located near the point where the canal crossed Mad River on an aqueduct. This feeder entered the canal below Lock 20, the aqueduct lock on the south bank of Mad River.

The next dam was at Miamisburg. This work was associated with the Carrollton and Miamisburg Hydraulic Company. The last dam, located at Middletown, was of great importance, as it supplied the line for the remainder of the distance to the Ohio River, and until 1855, part of the Warren County Canal. The hydraulic works associated with the Middletown dam and feeder was influential in the establishment of numerous paper mills at the locks south of Lock 28.

**The Reservoirs Today**

Many of the dams are still serving a useful purpose in furnishing water to industry. The greatest value of the canal water supply system was realized, however, when, in 1898, the reservoirs were dedicated forever as public parks. From its long abandoned canal system, Ohioans have the Portage Lakes, Buckeye Lake, Lake Loramie, Indian Lake and Grand Lake St. Marys. These reservoirs now constitute the great recreational areas of the State of Ohio.

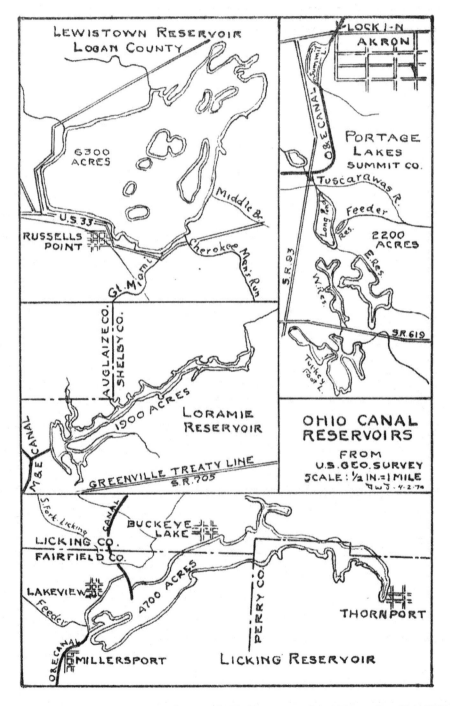

**Ohio Canal Reservoirs**. *Map by Frank W. Trevorrow from* Towpaths, *Vol. VIII (1970), No. 3, p. 37.*

# OHIO & ERIE CANAL

*This recent collaboration between Larry Turner, perhaps the CSO's most dedicated canaller, and Boone Triplett, the current editor of* Towpaths, *is a Canal 101 history of Cleveland. Residents of Wayne and Medina Counties respectively, both claim the legendary Chippewa Canal as their own.*

Volume XLVI (2008), No. 2, pp. 21-50

### CLEVELAND: HISTORY OF A CANAL CITY by Larry Turner and Boone Triplett

Mistake by the Lake? Hardly. Anyone with knowledge of canal history knows that Cleveland was carefully selected as the northern terminus of the Ohio Canal. By the end of the Nineteenth Century, the small wilderness village at the mouth of the Cuyahoga River had expanded into the nation's seventh largest city, an international commercial center with a population of nearly a half million. This is the story of how Cleveland came into being, beginning as an isolated pioneer outpost on the edge of the American frontier and evolving into a mighty transportation crossroads thanks in large part to the Ohio Canal. [...]

None other than Benjamin Franklin first brought to the attention of George Washington the importance of the real estate at the mouth of the Cuyahoga River in 1765. Recognizing this as the midway point between forts at Presque Isle (Erie, PA) and Detroit, Franklin believed that the site was of military importance. Washington's interests in the Ohio Country were more motivated by land speculation. As a reward for his service to the crown in the late French conflict, Washington was allowed in 1770 to claim thousands of acres of prime river bottomland along the Ohio, Great Kanawha, and Little Kanawha Rivers in what is today West Virginia. [...]

Before Washington could develop his vast holdings west of the Appalachian Mountains, a series of disagreements with the mother country led to a conflict known the world over as the American Revolution. Despite his somewhat lackluster list of martial achievements and primarily because he was a Virginian in what was being viewed by some as a New England conflict, Washington was placed in command of the Continental Army in 1775. More military setbacks would follow for George Washington, such as those at Long Island and Brandywine, but independence was finally won after nearly eight years of war. By 1783, the Ohio Country belonged to the United States of America. [...]

George Washington delivered a farewell address to his soldiers in 1783 and immediately turned his attention to the trans-Appalachian region. It was his greatest fear that the Ohio Country

**George Washington, 1772.** *Painting by Chas. W. Peale.*

would be "tipped" towards British Canada or Spanish Louisiana as all transportation avenues then led directly towards foreign interests. Convinced that a waterway must be opened from the Atlantic Ocean to both the Ohio River and Great Lakes, Washington spent more than a month in the saddle in 1784 personally scouting potential water routes up the Potomac Valley to tributaries of the Ohio. [...]

So what does all of this about George Washington have to do with Cleveland? In a famous letter to Virginia Governor Benjamin Harrison, Washington would write:

"Mount Vernon, October 10, 1784.

Dear Sir:

Upon my return from the western Country a few days ago...I shall take the liberty now, my dear sir, to suggest a matter, which would (if I am not too shortsighted a politician) mark your administration as an important era in the Annals of this Country, if it should be recommended by you, and adopted by the Assembly. It has been long my decided opinion that the shortest, easiest, and least expensive communication with the invaluable and extensive Country back of us, would be by one, or both of the rivers of this State which have their sources in the Apalachian mountains. [...] I need not remark to you Sir, that the flanks and rear of the United States are possessed by other powers, and formidable ones too; nor how necessary it is to apply the cement of interest, to bind all parts of the Union together by indissoluble bonds, especially that part of it, which lies immediately west of us, with the middle States...The preliminary steps to the attainment of this great object, would be [...] to appoint Commissioners...Let these Commissioners make an actual survey of James river and Potomack from tide-water to their respective sources...and the nearest and best Portages between these waters and the Streams capable of improvement which run into the Ohio...The navigation of this river (*i.e.*, the Ohio) being well known, they will have less to do in the examination of it; but nevertheless, let the courses and distances of it be taken to the mouth of the Muskingum, and up that river (notwithstanding it is in the ceded lands) to the carrying place with Cayahoga; down the Cayahoga to Lake Erie, and thence to Detroit. Let them do the same with big Bever creek, although part of it is in the State of Pennsylvania; and with the Scioto also. In a word, let the Waters East and West of the Ohio, which invite our notice by their proximity, and the ease with which Land transportation may be had between them and the Lakes on one side, and the rivers Potomac and James on the other, be explored, accurately delineated, and a correct and connected Map of the whole be presented to the public..."

Thus with this specific mention of "Cayahoga", Washington should receive a great deal of credit for envisioning the city of Cleveland and for recognizing the importance of transportation infrastructure in the development of the new nation. [...] His thoughts on the topic were shared with Thomas Jefferson who enthusiastically agreed. The correspondence between these two founding fathers on the topic is extensive. Washington was overjoyed when old war buddy Rufus Putnam established the first permanent settlement in the Northwest Territories at Marietta, stating in 1788 that "No colony in America was ever settled under such favorable auspices as that which has just commenced at the Muskingum. If I was a young man, just preparing to begin the world, or if advanced in life and had a family to make provision for, I know of no country where I should rather fix my habitation." [...]

Connecticut held to the legality of the Royal Charter of 1662 which stated that its claims extended all the way to the "great western sea". Resolution finally came on September 14, 1786, when Connecticut was allowed to reserve a 120-mile strip of land west of Pennsylvania and south of Lake Erie. This piece of land north of the 41st Parallel became known as the Connecticut Western Reserve and comprised of some 3,500,000 acres, with the westernmost 500,000 acres or Firelands set aside as compensation for Connecticut residents who had homes burned down by British soldiers during the Revolution. Sold to a group of 49 shareholders representing the Connecticut Land Company for $1,200,000 or 40 cents an acre (the money was used to fund a public school system), the company appointed General Moses Cleaveland as chief surveyor. One wonders if President George Washington, who made his first surveying venture into the western wilderness as a boy of 16, wished he could have joined Cleaveland's 44 man expedition in 1796. […]

**General Moses Cleaveland**.
*Ohio History Central.*

Moses Cleaveland departed New York for the Western Reserve in June 1796. A prominent citizen of Connecticut, lawyer, legislator, and general of Connecticut militia, Cleaveland was described as wearing such a serious look that "strangers often took him for a clergyman". He was a gifted administrator whose skills were as an organizer. Traveling along the lakeshore by bateau, Cleaveland arrived at the "capital" of New Connecticut on July 22, 1796. […] Cleaveland planned to call the town "Cuyahoga" but was convinced by his fellow surveyors to name it after himself.

On October 18, 1796, Moses Cleaveland and his surveying party left Cleaveland. […] His report to the Connecticut Land Company would state, "While I was in New Connecticut I laid out a town on the bank of Lake Erie, which was called by my name, and I believe the child is now born that may live to see that place as large as Old Windham." The population of Windham, Connecticut, in 1790 was 2,700. Found among Cleaveland's possessions after his death in 1806 was a copy of John Heckewelder's map on which the missionary himself had scribbled a prophecy: "Cujahaga will hereafter be a place of great importance." […]

Cuyahoga County was Ohio's smallest in 1810, numbering 1,457 persons. Cleveland counted only 57 residents by the same census but in that year of 1810 may have added its most influential citizen ever. The nephew of General Cleaveland's commissary, Joshua Stow, the newcomer boarded in John Walworth's office and passed the bar on his 21st birthday to become the first lawyer in Cuyahoga County. Alfred Kelley had arrived. […]

George Washington's vision became DeWitt Clinton's reality. Washington's Patowmack Company would only manage to circumnavigate the Great Falls of the Potomac three years after the general's death in 1799. Even by the early 1850s, both of Washington's canals (the Chesapeake & Ohio along the Maryland bank of the Potomac and the James River & Kanawha) stretched westward nearly 200 miles, each in a desperate grope to reach the Ohio River. Both were hundreds of miles short of their goal as the geography of the southern Appalachians was just too formidable. The situation in Pennsylvania was nearly as challenging. That state would have to resort to portage railroads to get over the mountains and by the time the Pennsylvania Mainline Navigation System was completed from Philadelphia to Pittsburgh in 1834, the Erie Canal had enjoyed a nearly decade long monopoly on all the Western trade. DeWitt Clinton and New York were able to take advantage of an east-west gap in the mountains through the Mohawk valley to complete a vital all-water link between the Atlantic Ocean and the Great Lakes.

**New York Gov. DeWitt Clinton**.

DeWitt Clinton was a lifelong politician, state legislator, United States Senator, lieutenant governor, and multiple-term mayor of New York. In 1812, Clinton ran for President of the United States on an anti-war platform against James Madison. Clinton was supported by the dying Federalist Party, who stood for a strong and centralized national government and Federal money for internal improvements. The electoral tally was close, 128-89, but Clinton lost the election to Madison. Three years of war put all discussions about internal improvements on hold but after "Mr. Madison's War" was over, the attention of the United States Congress returned to the internal improvements question. The Bonus Bill of 1817 was drafted by John C. Calhoun who stated: "Let us then…bind the Republic together with a perfect system of roads and canals. Let us conquer space." Madison shocked the legislative branch by vetoing the bill. The President cited Constitutional reasons but many believed that as a Virginian, Madison harbored resentment towards those rival "Yorkers". Calhoun was stunned by the veto. DeWitt Clinton was outraged.

Clinton resolved to do this thing himself. He was elected governor of New York in 1817 and immediately appropriated money from the Legislature for canal construction. Like George Washington, Clinton was a visionary. Clinton's "Great Western Canal" was to run 363 miles from Albany on the Hudson River to a small village at the mouth of Buffalo Creek on Lake Erie. This would later become the city of Buffalo, which like Cleveland was made great by the canal. Many thought Clinton to be mad and political opponents derided the Erie Canal project as "Clinton's Folly". No canal in America up to that time, or any engineering project for that matter, had been so large in scope or magnitude. But Clinton persevered. He was even voted out of the governorship during construction, only to be re-elected just in time to see the project through to completion. At the conclusion of the maiden voyage aboard the *Seneca Chief*, Governor Clinton emptied a cask of Lake Erie water into New York harbor and from that moment New York City has been America's leading commercial center. This "Wedding of the Waters" on November 4, 1825, was no less of a transportation accomplishment to its era than the driving of the

Golden Spike to complete the Transcontinental Railroad in 1869, the first motorized flight by the Wright Brothers at Kitty Hawk in 1903, or even Neil Armstrong's first step on the moon in 1969.

Through all of this, Cleveland remained rather primitive. General Cleaveland had been dead for more than a decade but with a population of 606 by 1820, his namesake city had not yet reached a quarter of the size of Old Windham. Ashtabula (929), Euclid (809), Newburgh (756), Painesville (1,257), Tallmadge (742), Chagrin Falls (733), and Huron (651) were all larger. [...]

Alfred Kelley had been Cleveland's first lawyer, state legislator, community leader, and bank president but by 1822 was ready to assume his most important role of all. Agitation for canals had begun in Ohio. When "Clinton's Folly" was completed in New York, there would be an almost unlimited market

**Alfred Kelley**.

back East for exporting Ohio products but Ohio had almost no transportation infrastructure of its own to transport these materials to the lake. Water was, and still is, the cheapest means for moving goods so the logic behind constructing a canal from the Ohio River to Lake Erie was almost self-evident. Alfred Kelley certainly knew this. So when Ohio created a Board of Canal Commissioners in 1822, Kelly was appointed. Shortly thereafter, he and Micajah Williams were named Acting Commissioners who would assume responsibility for overseeing work in the field.

One of the first acts of the Ohio Board of Canal Commissioners was to employ a surveyor to run prospective lines across the state. James Geddes of New York was hired for the job. Prospective routes were: 1) Grand and Mahoning Rivers (probably dismissed early on as the southern terminus would have been in Pennsylvania), 2) Cuyahoga-Tuscarawas and Muskingum Rivers, 3) Black-Killbuck and Muskingum Rivers, 4) Sandusky and Scioto Rivers, and 5) Maumee and Miami Rivers. During 1822 alone, Geddes surveyed out over 900 miles of potential canal routes. This tramping back and forth across the state, political bickering, and shameless community promotion went on for three years. Tired of all the public debate, some in Cleveland even yawned "Give it to Painesville or Black River (Lorain)." This certainly did not reflect Alfred Kelley's way of thinking.

When Ohio finally announced its decision on the canals in February 1825, the political considerations were obvious. There was much sentiment for a "diagonal route" from Lake Erie down through the capital of Columbus and on to the largest and most influential city in Ohio at the time, Cincinnati. But practical considerations, namely the lack of an adequate water supply, made this impossible so Ohio decided to build two canals. [...]

Most important to Cleveland was the selection of the northern route between Coshocton and the lake. This announcement was delayed for three months, likely to encourage property donation. Plus Cleveland had an "ace in the hole" in Commissioner Kelley. Finally in May 1825, a decision to construct along the Tuscarawas-Cuyahoga line was announced by the Canal Commissioners at a meeting in Wooster. But even then, was the canal coming into Cleveland? An 1824 plan placed the northern terminus at Newburgh near the mouth of Mill Creek with the remainder of the navigation coming down the Cuyahoga River. Another survey proposed a river crossing at this location with the final six miles of the canal along the west side of the river, terminating in Ohio City. Commissioner Kelley officially recused himself from this decision but the citizens of Cleveland were able to organize a land grant to the state of $5,000—much of the property belonged to Kelley!—and the canal was routed along the east side of the river into Cleveland. […]

A "grand dinner" was held in 1825 to celebrate the opening of the Erie Canal. Goods could now easily be imported into Cleveland from New York. Now that Clinton's dream had finally been realized, Irish and German immigrants began pouring into northern Ohio with at least 2,000 at work in the Cuyahoga Valley by the end of November. Work was hard, from sun up to sun down, six days a week for 30 cents a day and a jigger of whiskey. Except for some animal-powered stump pullers, all work was manual. Conditions were abysmal, men often laboring in muck up to their waist. Mosquitoes, malaria, fever, and ague were prevalent. But these were hardened, experienced men who were skilled with the shovel. They were put to work on the most difficult section in the entire Ohio canal system, a 38-mile stretch between Cleveland and the Portage Summit (now Akron, the town had just been laid out and only existed on paper in 1825) which would require 44 lift locks to overcome a 395' elevation difference between the lake and the summit. DeWitt Clinton himself visited Ohio to break ground for the Ohio Canal on July 4, 1825, at the Licking Summit near Newark but spades of dirt had already been thrown along Portage Summit by this time.

Progress was steady. Alfred Kelly supervised the whole affair from the saddle. Contractors were held to exacting standards as the canal bed and embankments were required to be absolutely water tight. By plunging an iron rod into the earth, Kelley was able to determine if a job had been "short cut" by overfilling with rubble such as stumps and underbrush instead of done properly with tamped earth and puddled clay. Finally, Canal Commissioner and Clevelander Kelley was able to write the following letter to Governor of Ohio Allen Trimble: "Coshocton 11 June 1827 Dear Sir: We expect that the canal will be in readiness for a boat to start from Akron Portage Summit on the third day of July in the morning, in season to reach Cleaveland in time to dine at that place on the 4th." […]

Governor Trimble and Commissioner Kelley, along with other assembled politicians and dignitaries, climbed aboard the *State of Ohio* at the appointed time and place. The *State of Ohio* was a product of the embryonic Akron shipyards. Animals hitched, the *State of Ohio* continued down the valley to Boston where it was met by the *Allen Trimble*. The *Trimble* was Boston's first boat. (The 1836 Boston Store, built by the Kelley brothers and now a National Park Service Visitors Center, houses a timber from what is believed to be from the *State of Ohio*.) Noble Merwin of Cleveland was able to commandeer a boat from the Erie Canal. Christening it the *Pioneer*, all of Cleveland's important citizens climbed aboard and headed up the canal to meet the governor's party about six miles south of town. This small fleet of three boats floated triumphantly into Cleveland on Independence Day, announcing to all that the first canal in the West was now open for business. Raucous celebrations were held all across town that evening. An interesting, if rather jaded, account of that historic day is given in Johnson's 1879 History of Cuyahoga County Ohio:

"Flags fluttered gayly in the breeze, cannon thundered their boisterous welcome, speeches full of roseate prophesy were made, and all were intensely enthusiastic over the great event of the day. Such enthusiasm over such a cause may seem overstrained in these fast times when railroads have absorbed nearly all the commerce of this region, and the canals are looked on as extremely old fogyish institutions. Nevertheless the Fourth day of July, 1827, was a great day for northern Ohio. An immense tract, previously almost entirely isolated, was provided with the means of transporting its produce to the markets of the East, and every kind of business showed an immediate and very marked improvement in consequence. It is doubtful if railroads would have been built as soon as they were, had not the wealth of the country first been largely increased by the construction of the canals." Keep in mind that this description of canals as "extremely old fogyish institutions" was written in 1879 and is generally reflective of the attitude toward canals during that era. The economic impact was almost immediate. An oft-quoted figure is that wheat purchased by Buffalo merchants in Cleveland increased from 1,000 to 250,000 bushels in one year. But the city itself did not immediately "take off" as population had only increased to 1,075 by 1830. Much of this was due to problems at the northern terminus. The final two locks, Locks #43 and #44, were not completed until late 1829. The soil here was extremely porous and as a result of so much marshy land being tossed about at the mouth of the canal, much sickness settled over the city. […]

When finally completed, there were two locks at the canal terminus along Merwin Street. Locks #43 and #44, these "Sloop Locks" were 100' long by 25' wide to accommodate schooners and other lake sailing vessels. All other locks on the Ohio Canal were 90' long by 15' wide. Between the two locks was a rectangular basin (about 200' x 150') known as Merwin's or the Lower Basin. Above Lock #43 was a long basin that stretched for about a quarter of a mile. This was called the Upper Basin and was the terminus during the 1827 celebrations. There were at least three dry docks along this basin for repair and maintenance of boats, likely more. The entire area was saturated with warehouses. A guard lock was installed at the foot of Seneca Street in 1851. Used to accurately determine cargo loads, it was the only weigh lock along the entire Ohio Canal.

Once the canal was finished, harbor improved, and sickness abated the anticipated boom began in earnest as unofficial census figures had the population quadrupling by 1834. […]

Cleveland had already developed into a major transportation hub by 1837. Advertisements declared "Daily Line of Ohio Canal Packets between Cleveland & Portsmouth, Distance 309 Miles— Through in 80 Hours". A southbound passenger boat left Cleveland every day at 4 p.m. along the canal and also carried mail. The "Pioneer Fast Stage Line" was claiming arrival within 30 hours at Pittsburgh as one of the three regular stage lines to that place also carried mail. There were also regular stages from Cleveland to Cincinnati via Columbus, Detroit, and Buffalo. In the fall of 1837, the passenger steamer *Cleveland* was open for lake traffic as steam was already beginning to surpass sail on the lake. Besides the growing passenger trade, lake and canal commerce had made Cleveland the undisputed king of the Western grain trade. But the economic Panic of 1837, which precipitated closing of the bank in Cleveland, brought a brief halt to the economic prosperity.

[…] The economic malaise would begin to lift in 1840 with the opening of the Pennsylvania & Ohio Canal which opened a water route between Cleveland and Pittsburgh via Akron. Although the first shipment of coal had arrived in 1828 from Tallmadge, hundreds of thousands of bushels began to arrive from the Mahoning Valley after the P&O Canal was completed. This signified the dawn of the industrial era. Population had increased to 6,071 by 1840 (Ohio City 1,577), a six fold increase in ten years. Just two decades earlier before the canal, Cleveland had only ranked 14th in population among villages on the Western Reserve. Now, in 1840, Cleveland was the second largest city in Ohio and 45th in the United States. […]

The 1840s were a good decade for Cleveland and the canal in general. […] The Ohio Canal remained prosperous. Except for an "off" year in 1845, receipts remained fairly steady at between $322,755 and $452,531 throughout the decade. (For comparison, receipts surpassed $100,000 for the first time in 1833, $200,000 in 1836, and $300,000 in 1838.) But an ominous sign for the canals appeared in Cleveland at the tail end of the decade on November 3, 1849. On that date, a locomotive from the Cleveland, Columbus & Cincinnati Railroad rolled into town.

Hailed as the decade of "Rails and Red Gold" in Cleveland, the period from 1850-59 marked the effective end of the canal era. This is apparent from a table of receipts for selected years during this time:

| Year | Receipts |
|------|----------|
| 1851 | $432,711 |
| 1853 | $258,793 |
| 1855 | $196,194 |
| 1857 | $155,598 |
| 1859 | $88,296 |

The cause of the decline is obvious. In 1851, the Cleveland, Columbus & Cincinnati RR opened to Columbus. Both the Cleveland & Pittsburgh Railroad and Cleveland, Painesville & Ashtabula RR (to Erie, PA) were open by 1852. (In what might be considered a traitorous act to a dedicated canaller, Alfred Kelley would become a railroad president.) Other rail lines would soon follow. A record 6.3 million bushels of coal still shipped by 1855 but this soon dried up as well when the Cleveland & Mahoning Railroad opened in 1857. […] Canals lost money for the first time in 1856. Realizing that the trend from the above table was irreversible, the state leased out its canal system to private interests in 1861. Nobody paid much attention then as troops were being raised to put down the Southern rebellion. Headlines were filled with items about Abraham Lincoln, Fort Sumter, the Confederate States, Bull Run, and so forth. The Ohio Canal continued to perform yeoman's work. Enough flour, oats, and gunpowder were shipped along the canal to make a significant contribution to the victorious Union war effort. Just four years later on April 28, 1865, the black draped funeral train of the martyred President rolled into Euclid Street Station and Abraham Lincoln's body would lie in state on Public Square.

By the 1870s, the canal was considered stagnant, disease filled, and "old fogyish". Industry chugged along. In addition to steel, chemical manufacturing and oil refining were thrown into the mix. (The biggest oilman of them all, John D. Rockefeller, had started his business career as a clerk for Hewitt & Tuttle on Merwin Street. Part of his responsibilities included logging canal transactions.) The city worked out a deal to purchase the northern 2½ miles of canal from the state for $125,000 with the condition that a new terminus would be constructed at what was then the southern edge of town at the foot of Dille Street. Lock #44 was obliterated when the Detroit-Superior Viaduct was constructed from 1875-78 and Lock #43 was wiped out by the necessary realignment of a railroad underneath the bridge. [...] The canal bed itself from Merwin Street to Dille Street was filled by the tracks of the Valley Railway in 1879-80.

**Dille Street Terminus with weight lock, *ca.* 1910**. From Harry Heidloff's photo history of the Ohio & Erie Canal in Cleveland, 1910-15. *From* Towpaths, *Vol. XXIX (1991), No. 1, p. 11.*

The canal retained some usefulness after the terminus was relocated to Dille Street in 1878 (the state retained control of the canal system from the lessees that same year) but was never again close to being profitable. Some local industries such as the Grasselli Chemical Company, which supplied acid to Rockefeller's refineries, and the Austin Powder Works still shipped and received goods by canal during this time and there was some limited Sunday picnic boat excursion trade. Harry Heidloff, who lived as a child in the lock tender's house at "new" Lock #42 from 1910-15 describes the Industrial Flats during the late canal era as being choked with "dirty red iron dust...fumes from sulfuric acid and zinc chloride manufacturing" but fondly recalls "fishing for minnows" in the weigh lock sluice and "playing baseball on the mud flats which were once part of the Cuyahoga River". Nothing remains of the canal at the Dille Street terminus either. There was one final gasp for the canals. Public sentiment was running in favor of saving these great public works at the beginning of the Twentieth Century so beginning in 1905, the state began appropriating millions of dollars to upgrade the system. [...] Funds ran out in 1909 and the project was not resumed. It did not matter. Devastating floods in March 1913 destroyed the Ohio canal system as an effective transportation network for all eternity. And that was that.

For years, the state generated a small revenue stream from its canals by selling water rights to local industries. The practice continues to this day. Now the canal is embraced as a cherished recreational resource, as evidenced by the Cleveland Metroparks Ohio & Erie Canal Reservation Visitor Center off East 49th Street and the exceedingly popular Ohio & Erie Canal Towpath Trail which runs through the park there. This is the newest jewel in Cleveland's famed Emerald Necklace. The Towpath Trail now ends at Harvard Road but will eventually be extended northward to the lake, meaning that after a 140 year hiatus the canal will return to downtown Cleveland. No doubt that George Washington, Moses Cleaveland, DeWitt Clinton, and Alfred Kelley would all be pleased.

§§§§§§§§§§§§§§§§§§§§§§§§§§§

*The first editor of* Towpaths, *L. W. "Lew" Richardson, produced this gem from the autobiography of John Malvin, an African-American canal boat captain from Cleveland.*

Volume IV (1966), No. 4, pp. 37-40

### JOHN MALVIN: CANAL BOAT CAPTAIN by L.W. Richardson

John Malvin was an exceptional man. He was preacher and church leader, carpenter, owner and master of a Lake Erie schooner and an Ohio & Erie canal boat. He was responsible for the establishment of a school system and was a successful business man. Such diversity was not unusual in the Ohio country of the early 1800's, the desire for self sufficiency and the abundant opportunities honed the talents of many men. Malvin's case was exceptional because he was a Negro.

Born in Prince William County, Virginia, in 1795, he was the son of a slave father and a free mother. Under existing laws, he inherited the status of his mother and was also a free person. This, however, made little difference in his early life and until slavery was abolished forever, he lived in the shadow of the restrictive Black Laws and with the constant danger of being kidnapped by roving fugitive slave hunters. Denied any formal schooling, he was secretly taught to read by an old slave. A Bible was his only text.

Determined to improve his lot and attracted by a state where slavery had been forever prohibited, Malvin came to Ohio in 1827. He first settled in Cincinnati but moved to Cleveland in 1831. Here he became active in the abolition movement and led in the establishment of the first schools for Negroes in the city.

At the time there were only a few Baptists in Cleveland. Melvin preached to this group and in 1833 he and his wife Harriet were two of the seventeen charter members of the First Baptist Church.

Very little is known of his life on the canal. The Western Reserve Historical Society has preserved a copy of his autobiography, a little pamphlet of 46 pages, published in 1874. In this he states that he bought the line boat AUBURN in 1840 from S. R. Hutchinson & Co., a Cleveland milling firm, and for a time hauled wheat, general merchandise and passengers. Later, Hutchinson & Co. bought back the boat but retained Malvin as captain. He then tells this story, which, not surprisingly, is more concerned with the problems of race relations than with canal operation.

"On one occasion while I was running the boat, after having loaded with merchandise, I was ordered to deliver the goods to Chillicothe. Leaving Cleveland about noon, we arrived at Niles (Ed. Note: Just north of present-day Botzum) about nine o'clock in the evening. At this place we were hailed by some person saying that a passenger wanted to get aboard to go south. We came alongside the dock and landed. Pretty soon after some baggage came on board and in a short time the owner of the baggage, who was a female, appeared."

"My crew consisted of one white steersman, one colored steersman, two white drivers, one colored bowman and one colored female cook. When the lady arrived, I stood aboard of the stern deck and assisted her aboard. When she went down into the cabin and saw the colored cook, she was taken completely by surprise. The colored steersman just then happened to go down into the cabin after something. The lady was sitting on the locker, and when she saw the colored steersman she immediately went to the other side of the boat. After the bowman had got his lines snugly curled, he went down into the cabin and she accosted him, saying that she would like to see the captain. Accordingly, I was called, and went down to see what she wanted. The light shone on my face so that she could easily see my features. The lady, after seeing me, suddenly sprang to her feet, and with great shortness of breath exclaimed, 'Well, I never! well, I never! well, I never!' I made a bow and left her, and ordered the cook to set her stateroom doors open, and to take off all the bedding from the middle berth, and supply clean bedding from the locker, so that she might see that the bedding was changed, and I requested the cook to tell the surprised lady to take the middle berth. She refused to go to bed, and sat up all night."

"We arrived at Lock 21, north end of the Akron locks at midnight. At nearly every lock there was a house or grocery, and I instructed the crew to keep the blinds on the boat closed, so that the lady should not know she was in a village; for seeing that she was afraid of colored people, I wanted to give her full opportunity of getting acquainted with them before she arrived at her home in Circleville. We arrived at Lock 1 a little after daylight; that brought us on the Wolf Creek level. On going into the Wolf Creek lock, seeing that the lock was ready, we ran the boat right into the lock and the hands divided, a part on one side of the boat and a part on the other side. I gave the driver the signal, and he opened the wicket, lowered the boat down, and the lady was prevented from getting off there, if she had felt disposed to do so. When we came to the Fulton lock, we pursued the same course as at the former lock. Before we had got to this point, and while we were yet in the Wolf Creek level, I invited the lady to breakfast, which she refused, saying that she did not feel very well. When we arrived at the Fulton lock it brought us to the Massillon level, and it being dinner time, I invited the lady to dinner. She still complained of not feeling very well, but took a piece of pie from where she stood. When we arrived at the Bethlehem level and when tea was ready I invited her to tea, and she took a cup of tea and a biscuit."

"Just about this time we passed through a strip of woods about a mile in length. The moon was full, and it was a beautiful evening. The cook, having got through with her cabin work, came on deck. While she was proceeding toward the deck, the lady passenger followed her in a hesitating manner. They promenaded the deck together and then retired. I suppose the lady had a good nights sleep for I did not hear anything from her until the next morning. When breakfast was ready, on receiving an invitation, she readily took a seat at the table, and ate a hearty meal, and from that time on she felt reconciled to her surroundings, and conversed freely with the cook and all on board. When we arrived at Circleville, she left us. I provided means for the conveyance of her baggage, and on leaving she thanked me, and said 'Captain, when I first came aboard your boat, not being accustomed to travel in this way, I suppose I must have acted quite awkward. Now, I must return my thanks to you and your crew, for the kind treatment I have received. I have never traveled so comfortably in all my life, and I expect to go north soon, and I will defer my journey until you are going north, even if I am obliged to wait two or three days.' I never saw the lady again after that."

There is no further reference in the autobiography to the canal or his experiences on it.

Captain Malvin died in 1879 and lies in an unmarked grave in the old Erie Cemetery in downtown Cleveland. A group sponsored by the Afro-American Historical Society is presently engaged in raising funds to erect a monument to his memory.

§§§§§§§§§§§§§§§§§§§§§§§§§§

*Here is another Cleveland canal story, a first person account told to J.G. Cowles by Captain Edward Ives in 1904. Captain Ives was born in 1832 and passed away in 1926 at the age of 94.*

Volume II (1964), No. 2, pp. 4-6

### THE BOILER THAT SETTLED WHEN THE CHAIN BROKE by J.G. Cowles

The logging season at Boston, Ohio, was good for many years prior to 1868 and for a short while there after. The sawyers had cut many thousand feet of logs and cord wood out of the woods surrounding Boston.

There being but one large saw mill at this place, it could handle logs in an efficient way. The head sawyer was the owner of the mill as well. He had heard of the wonderful opportunities of cutting timber in upper Michigan. So, before the closing of the season, in the year of 1871, the owner decided to move all the mill equipment up there. He made a contract with me, Edward Ives, owner of the boat JOHN

DAVIS. I lived in Bedford. The boat was built in Peninsula, Ohio, June 1864, by Mr. Crane and Mr. Cochran as recorded in the original bill of sale.

The contract was agreed on and signed for me to load and haul all the saw mill equipment to the north end of the canal at Merwin Street and the Cuyahoga River, where the canal emptied into the river at West and James Sts. in Cleveland.

According to the bill of sale, the JOHN DAVIS had a "burden" of 67 and 91/100 tons; length 78 feet 4/10"; breadth 18 feet; (NOTE: This would seem to be an error, canal locks in Ohio were, by law, 90 x 15 feet.) depth 7 feet; one deck, no masts. That was a mighty good load for a canal boat!

All of the mill stuff and boiler was loaded and stowed away and ready to start. I, as Captain, ordered the line loosed of the snubbing post and my son rode the lead horse north down the towpath in the early morning with twenty five miles ahead and many locks and several aqueducts to travel. This meant hard work at each end of the locks and a watchful eye for the Captain at the stick, or tiller, had to keep in midstream with a heavy load.

We came through the feeder lock at Alexander's where the grist mill was run by water power. (NOTE: This mill, built in 1851 by Mr. Alexander is still in operation. It is now owned by Mr. Thomas Wilson who has followed his father and grandfather in the business.)

Making the good time of about three miles an hour we passed the Palmer Brothers Organ Factory at Mill Creek Aqueduct and moved on down to the eight mile lock. A steam grist mill owned by Mr. Wood used to stand here but it burned down in 1870.

Just around the bend was the Hercules Powder Company at Independence Road and the canal. (NOTE: Now the site of an outdoor theatre.) Further on there was the pump house where the water is pumped to the mills of the American Steel and Wire Company. Several canal boats were unloading coal there. We locked through the five mile lock at Harvard Street and just above it was the Austin Powder Company on the east side of the canal. (NOTE: Austin Powder was incorporated in 1835 and occupied about 150 acres with some 40 buildings. It was in operation until 1913.)

We came to the Cleveland Paper Mills at Campbell Road and moved on past the Cleveland Rolling Mill Blast Furnace and under several small bridges and then to the weigh lock at the foot of South Water Street where we got the load weighed and paid the Customs Collector. Then we went through two locks into the river and were guided to the boat for transfer of the cargo to the lake vessel. After mooring alongside of the three masted schooner we had to wait until morning as darkness was on us. The next day meant work for all and from here on things commenced to shape up.

There was a large boom on this schooner and the Captain and the Mate looked over our cargo and ordered the crew to make ready and rig the boiler for the hold of their boat. So the crew of the schooner rigged the chains to lift the boiler a couple of feet off our deck to see if it was centered and equal on the lift. After a couple of adjustments and trials everything was ready, even the cribbing in the hold of the boat. The Captain warned everybody to stay in the clear and gave the signal to lift. Up goes the boiler over the gunwales or sides of the boat and over the hatchway it swings. The Captain orders "lower away" and down goes the boiler into the hold. And then – when it was within two feet of the crib prepared for it

– the CHAIN BROKE and down goes the boiler! Right on the timbers prepared for it, a perfect landing with no one hurt!

The rest of our cargo was transferred before the sun set and we went back through the twin basin, past the weigh lock and back to Boston for another load.

§§§§§§§§§§§§§§§§§§§§§§§§§§§

*Before the creation of Cuyahoga Valley National Recreation Area (CVNRA) in 1974—now Ohio's only national park—the canal through the valley did not appear as it does today. Thanks to restoration efforts, it is now a showpiece complete with visitor friendly amenities. One of the key projects was the Lock 38 rebuild at the Canal Visitor Center, as described in this two-part article by Rob Bobel, P.E. Technical Assistance & Professional Services, CVNRA.*

Volume XXXI (1993), No. 4, pp. 37-48
Volume XXXII (1994), No. 1, pp. 1-12

## THE 1991-1992 RESTORATION OF LOCK 38 OF THE OHIO & ERIE CANAL IN THE CUYAHOGA VALLEY NATIONAL RECREATION AREA BY THE NATIONAL PARK SERVICE by Robert W. Bobel

### BACKGROUND

All of the 44 locks between Cleveland and Akron were originally constructed of sandstone walls and wooden foundations, floors and gates. Experience quickly taught that repairs would be required on a regular basis. The wooden gates, for example, would require extensive repair or total replacement every 6 to 9 years. As early as 1864, it had been reported that the masonry in many of the locks was deteriorating and that the walls were being forced in by earth pressure. From then until 1904, many attempts were made to correct the problem. Finally the state legislature was pressured to appropriate funds for the improvements to the northern division, and from 1905 to 1909, a major rehabilitation of the locks along this segment was undertaken. Contracts were let for the removal of defective masonry and replacement with a relatively new construction material—concrete. Concrete was also pumped into portions of the interior rubble back-up which would otherwise have to be removed and rebuilt.

Although documentation is sketchy, some evidence exists to indicate the majority of concrete work on Lock 38 was done in 1906. From then until the abandonment of the Ohio and Erie Canal in 1913, there is no record of any repairs. From 1913 until 1992, the only repairs would have been those made by the holders of the hydraulic lease. Although there were obviously some changes made to the gates, balance beams and the spillway, there are no records of any other improvements being made to Lock 38's chamber.

## SUMMER 1991 - PLANNING

The desire to have Locks 37, 38 and 39 restored to operational condition, as spelled out in Cuyahoga Valley National Recreation Area's General Management Plan, was the guiding principle in the planning and restoration of Lock 38. The first step was to decide whether to take on the project in-house, as a day labor project, or to contract the work. Although the recreation area has a highly qualified maintenance staff, expert in restoration and rehabilitation of historic structures, the added work load ruled out this option. The sensitive nature of the work and the desired time frame ruled out the normal alternative of awarding to a private contractor. Park management then began discussing the project with the Williamsport Preservation Training Center.

The Williamsport Preservation Training Center (WPTC) is the National Park Service's facility for training crafts people and specialists in the skills needed to preserve and restore historic buildings and artifacts. In operation for over 15 years, WPTC is in Williamsport, Maryland, about 40 canal miles on the Chesapeake and Ohio Canal above Harpers Ferry, West Virginia. The work of these skilled professionals takes them throughout the entire National Park System. Working with the host park and the Regional Office, WPTC develops a task directive, clearly spelling out the responsibilities, scope of work, schedule and costs. In the case of Lock 38, WPTC requested the park's assistance in technical matters pertaining to concrete testing, analysis and design in addition to help with on-site logistics and government housing for workers staying in the park.

Once WPTC was selected to perform the work, discussion began in earnest as to the level of restoration. It was decided in order to minimize impairment of "original fabric", to convey a sense of evolution and to prolong the life of the structure, that the lock would be restored to its 1907 appearance. As this would involve some level of concrete repair, a petrographic study was ordered.

A private testing company was hired to remove twelve 2 3/4" diameter cores. The cores were used for observation and inspection of depth and composition of the historic concrete. One of the cores was also sampled using petrographic techniques. The results showed the aggregate to be a natural siliceous sand and gravel with top size of 1 1/2". Mixed in were a number of porous sandstone and shale particles, many with internal fractures. The original concrete contained about 4 1/2 sacks per cubic yard— rather lean by today's standards—with a top layer (2 1/2" in the core studied) severely deteriorated from, at least in part, freeze/thaw distress. Interestingly enough, the lack of present day quality control may have off-setting effects. According to the petrographic report:

> "Coarse aggregate like that contained in the core would most likely be rejected for use in concrete manufactured today due to its physical weakness, high porosity and its potential reactivity with cement alkalis. However, void space contained in the aggregate provided a place for deposition of silica gel. It appears that the porous nature of cementitious matrix in combination with the porous siliceous coarse and fine aggregate particles have provided space for deposition of expansive silica-gel that might otherwise have caused significantly more disruption of the concrete."

It was clear from this analysis, however, that surface patching would be inadequate and that total replacement of the entire surface layer would be required.

## FALL 1991 - DOCUMENTATION AND CATALOGING

During October, 1992, the WPTC Team took the first steps in the restoration by removing and cataloging all historic artifacts from in and around the lock chamber; all items were tagged and stored for further study. In addition to the wooden remains of the gates, a considerable amount of hardware was found—including an original set of gudgeons and pintels, cast iron reach rods and brackets, lock gate straps, wicket paddles, goon neck anchors and hinge straps, a wood frame and reach rod sleeve for the lock culvert, the lock culvert wicket paddle, timber quoin and lock flooring. In all, over 50 artifacts were found. Some were ultimately able to be refurbished and re-used. Most were badly deteriorated or corroded, but enough fabric was left to enable preservation specialists to replicate accurately. Detailed measurements of the chamber were recorded; all steps were carefully photographed.

## WINTER AND SPRING 1992 - START OF RESTORATION

During the winter, plans were drawn and details developed for the next phase of the project—de-watering of the lock chamber and fabrication of gates and hardware. By spring, a work plan had been finalized, vendors lined up and procúrement secured to insure a smooth flow of materials and supplies. In some cases, specialty sub-contractors were called upon to perform work that required unique equipment or unusual skills, such as scoring the concrete walls of the chamber with a track mounted cutting saw or forging and casting replacement hardware.

Soon after Memorial Day, site work began in earnest by damming up both ends of the lock, de-watering and cleaning out the chamber. After some trial and error, a combination of an earthen cofferdam topped with sand bags proved most effective in sealing the chamber ends. Two 1/2 hp sump pumps were used, with low and high water floats to keep the water level about 18" deep inside the chamber. This would insure the timber flooring and foundations would always be submerged. This premise was followed through the entire restoration process.

## SUMMER 1992 – RESTORATION OF THE CHAMBER & WING WALLS

The summer of 1992 was a busy time in and around the Canal Visitor Center. In addition to the lock restoration, a contract was underway for major re-grading and utility work around the building. This required careful coordination around Williamsport Preservation Training Center (WPTC), the private contractor, and park service staff to insure safe and clear access to the center at all times. In addition, the newly reconstructed Towpath Trail, which crossed between the lock and the visitor center, carried up to 100 bikers, hikers, and joggers an hour. Of course there was much natural curiosity about the lock work. The task of keeping the public informed fell primarily on the shoulders of the center's interpretive staff and volunteers. A mobile display board was set up to inform the curious about the progress of restoration.

WPTC in consultation with the park's technical staff, had decided to replace concrete to a level of 5 feet 6 inches below the coping on both walls. A horizontal six inch saw cut was made using a track mounted cutting saw. All deteriorated concrete was removed to a minimum of 6" deep. In some cases 12" to 14" was removed, with the average measuring about 8".

Most of the heavy removal was done with a hoe-mounted hydraulic ram. Finish work was accomplished by hand with jack hammers and chipping hammers. The removal exposed a considerable amount of rubble sandstone used in the original (sandstone) lock construction.

**West wall looking north**. Sections 1, 3, 5, 7 completed. Sections 2, 4, 6 in preparation. *Courtesy National Park Service.*

Once sound concrete or sandstone was reached, a way had to be found to bond new concrete to old. In contemporary concrete repairs this would mean the use of steel reinforcing bars drilled and grouted into place. Concrete is reinforced with steel to add missing qualities—that is, qualities not inherent in plain concrete such as ductility and tensile strength. A lock wall, however, is a simple gravity structure and these qualities are not called for. Steel in concrete, on the other hand, can have deleterious effects. If moisture (and air) are allowed access to the embedded steel, corrosion can result. This in turn can cause the surrounding concrete to crack, allowing additional moisture and air to enter, accelerating the corrosion and ultimately, if allowed to go unchecked, will cause the concrete to spall and fail completely. It became clear steel reinforcing may not be the solution.

What was needed was a simple mechanical bond to supplement the natural concrete-to-concrete bond and enough reinforcing to account for normal volumetric changes due to shrinkage of the fresh concrete and temperature variations. The solution was the use of fiberglass reinforcing. These rods which are formed into a twisted shape, were easily cut in the field, and drilled and epoxied into place. Although not always the answer in concrete repairs, here the use of fiberglass reinforcement turned out to be a high tech solution to an age old problem.

Form work was next considered. Close inspection of the historic concrete revealed subtle details in the original form work details that might be missed by casual observation. The walls were formed using 12" rough sawn planking. The outside corners of the gate pockets were formed of a segmented radius. This detail was replaced using an elaborate combination of 2 x 4's laid on edge.

Much discussion revolved around the concrete mix design. The petrographic analysis had clearly shown the original concrete mix to be lacking in qualities needed for durability—not surprising as experience with concrete was limited at the turn of the century.

Fortunately, there are no requirements in the Secretary of the Interior's Standards to duplicate poor materials or details. The design selected for the replacement concrete was a good quality mix using 564 lbs. (6 sacks) per cubic yard of medusa type I cement, #57 limestone and 6 oz. of air-entrainment admixture (5 to 7% air).

After comparing a number of test panels to the original concrete, 4 lbs. per cubic yard of buff tinting agent was added to soften the color and more closely match that of the original concrete. To minimize bug holes and aid in placement, a high-range water reducing agent (super-plasticizer) was used.

Both east and west walls were comprised of seven distinct sections of concrete separated by control joints. Concrete was placed in alternating sections allowing the forms to be used up to four times. Control joints were conventional with the exception of the use of lead wool in place of a caulking compound. Although difficult to install, this old-fashioned but low maintenance detail was used to preserve the integrity of these joints for years to come.

The final steps in the wall restoration were resetting, re-grouting, and re-pointing of the northeast wing wall (the only section of wall remaining entirely of stone). In all, seven courses of stone—twelve stones total—were removed, repositioned, and re-mortared. Other masonry features receiving attention included applying a small concrete patch to the northwest wing wall, filling the interior of the north end miter sill, placement of pads for the south lock gate hinge assemblies, and re-pointing of all open joints in the historic stonework and concrete. The lowest two courses of stone work were particularly interesting as they contained an amazing variety of mason's marks.

## LOCK FLOOR

After concrete placement and masonry work was completed, attention turned to the lock floor. All scaffolding and form work were removed from the chamber and the chamber pumped and thoroughly cleaned. About half of the original floor boards were missing. A few were deteriorated and required replacement, but the majority of the original boards still in place were sound and tight.

The original floor boards were fastened to the transverse timber foundation members by a combination of 60d metal spikes and 3 or 4 treenails laid in a random manner. New floor plank was attached using this detail. All foundation members were in good condition—many exhibited a lot of their original axe hewn tooling marks. Much of the original in-fill clay and stone puddling was in such good shape it could have easily passed for weathered concrete.

**Lock floor during restoration (left) and installing lower lock gates (right)**. Note timber foundations and floor boards. *Courtesy National Park Service.*

## LOCK GATES

Not all of the restoration activity was taking place at the lock. All summer, a separate crew in Williamsport, Maryland, had been working to rebuild the four lock gates. Using information obtained in the fall of 1991, the gates (less balance beams) and hollow quoins were reconstructed of southern yellow pine, milled and shaped, and test assembled with mortise and tenon joints. Much of this work was done using a chain mortise machine, but finish work was all done using hand tools. The gates were then completely disassembled and sent for CCA treatment (similar to pressure treating). Once returned, they were final assembled, strap hardware and wickets added and then prepared for shipping to the site.

The balance beams were constructed of untreated white oak. Each was fabricated from 12" by 12" solid stock. Conforming to the original (1905) drawings, they were tapered to 8" at the top post. The beams "balancing" the larger southern gates were two feet longer than those of the smaller northern gates. Both were fitted with a 3" thick cap plank of white oak.

On September 18th, the gates were unloaded and set in place. The refurbished goon neck anchors and hinge straps were drilled and bolted into place. Final mortising of the balance beams was done on site and they were attached to the heel and toe posts of the gates. The toe posts were then trimmed to insure proper fit. Finish work included painting of all hardware, removal of the earthen cofferdams, and final site grading and re-seeding. A small pedestrian bridge was added just downstream of the lower gates for ease of operation during demonstrations.

## FALL 1992 REDEDICATION

On a cloudy October 15, 1992, with the threat of rain in the air, one year after start of the restoration, the Governor of the State of Ohio (in 1827, that is), Allen Trimble, and his servant oarsman locked through Lock 38 to the applause of a large crowd of supportive well-wishers. Possibly someday, a full scale canal boat carrying a cargo of park visitors might lock through, thus putting into full service once again Lock 38 on the Ohio & Erie Canal.

§§§§§§§§§§§§§§§§§§§§§§§§§§§§§

*Larry Turner worked with the CVNRA Virginia Kendall Maintenance crew in 1992 and 1993. In addition to other duties he installed all of the fifty plus wayside exhibits. While doing so he covered the entire 20 mile length of the Towpath many times.*

Volume XXXVI (1998), No. 1, pp. 5-11

## CONSTRUCTION OF THE TOWPATH TRAIL WITHIN THE CUYAHOGA VALLEY NATIONAL RECREATION AREA by Larry Turner

The Towpath is a recently-constructed (1993), multipurpose, federally-funded trail following the alignment of the historic Ohio and Erie Canal. It is nearly 20 miles in length, and there are plans to extend it both north to Cleveland and south to Akron, with intent to go further south to Zoar and eventually link up again with the Ohio River, following the original route. It meanders through the boundaries of the CVNRA, from the Rockside Road-Canal Road intersection in Valley View (Lock 39) to Bath Road, passing through Cuyahoga Falls and ending at the Indian Mound Trailhead, within the boundaries of Akron.

The Towpath Trail today is similar to that of the past except it is engineered to carry people, bicycles, and sometimes horses and wheeled vehicles (for maintenance) where the path of 166 years ago carried only people and animals (wagons for maintenance). Mules and horses pulled canal boats capable of carrying up to 60-70 tons as well as passenger packets.

The old towpath was constructed of earth excavated from the canal prism which is still the base used today. In reconstruction, topsoil buildup was stripped a few inches, and old washouts were filled. The sub base was then compacted and covered with a waterproof plastic sheet that inhibits weeds from growing through. This was then covered with limestone of graded sizes, topped with screenings (a fine crushed limestone, almost of sand quality). When compacted, the path is hard as concrete and yet easily worked and repaired. Rakes and shovels are used with brooms to keep the surface smooth as new.

Jack Gieck, author of <u>A Photo Album of Ohio's Canal Era, 1825-1913</u>, quotes Harlan Hatcher's description of an army of about 2000 workers who filled the Cuyahoga Valley constructing the Canal between Akron and Cleveland. CVNRA's Virginia Kendall maintenance team redid their efforts with a squad of between 10 and 12 men and a few pieces of modern equipment. A 2.5 ton Ford dump truck took the place of hundreds of wheelbarrows and horse carts. A Caterpillar dozer and a John Deere grader replaced slip scrapers and hand tools. A steel roller replaced the tamping tools or animals used to compact the path. A modern crane replaced a windlass-powered derrick guyed to trees and deadmen to make the many heavy lifts. A Cat 931 Loader replaced hundreds of shovels.

Many things, however, did not change much. Picks and shovels, post hole diggers, and wheel barrows were used daily, just as in the old days, and the men's muscles and backs were just as sore. Hand raking was a daily activity, and fire rakes, pulaskies and sledge hammers were used regularly. Transits and levels to establish grades and slopes were not that different from 150 years ago. Problems of the past often remained the same—bugs, mud, rain, swamps, trees, sickness, and, of course, the threat of raging river water. The men had quite a job to reclaim what the Flood of 1913 and 80 years of weather since had tried to destroy.

Construction, under the leadership of John Debo and Bob Martin of the National Park Service, started on April 15, 1990 with a ribbon-cutting ceremony at Boston. The Virginia Kendall maintenance crew handled most of the towpath reconditioning.

At the beginning of the Towpath Project, a team of just four men was picked to cut the thousands of trees that had grown up too close to the towpath, almost an endless task. When the weather was freezing cold, the ground was solid and machinery could run over it. When winter thaws occurred, the vehicles sank and got stuck in the mud. Due to heavy rainfall that year, only 1.4 miles of Towpath were completed, with an additional 3 miles being cleared of brush and trees.

More manpower was added in 1991, an ideal construction year. Eleven miles of Towpath was completed and opened to the public between Boston and Lock 39, the northern end of the CVNRA. One of the toughest parts of this section was in the Pinery Narrows where the Cuyahoga River had changed course, washing away two sections of the original towpath and placing a third part of it on the west side of the new channel where it can still be found. Building a new towpath to replace the missing sections in this roadless area was a challenge. It and the bridge over the Cuyahoga at Peninsula were subcontracted.

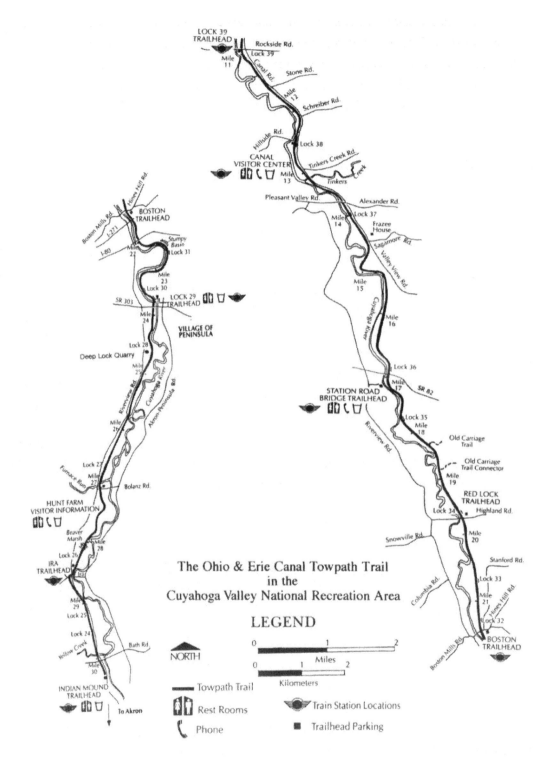

**Map of the Ohio & Erie Towpath Trail in the Cuyahoga Valley National Recreation Area**.
Now a national park, Lock 39 through Lock 24 may be visited along the trail here. Only Lock 36
is missing. *Courtesy National Park Service.*

The section from Boston to Peninsula was completed in 1992. During excavation for the bridge over the Cuyahoga at Peninsula a culvert noted on early canal maps, but long missing, was found. This four-foot diameter, cut-stone culvert over an unnamed run was apparently silted in, overflowed and buried when the Canton-to-Cleveland railroad built its own culvert upstream in 1880. A low-lying drydock site on the west side of the river south of the Peninsula bridge has been washed out several times by recent floods.

South of Peninsula, the Towpath enters Summit County's Metroparks land for 3.2 miles. In this stretch mule barn foundations were found south of Deep Run.

One and a half miles of Towpath was cleared between Bolanz Road and Ira. Scenic boardwalks near Stumpy Basin and Lonesome Lock (31) and at the Beaver Marsh near Pancake Lock (26) were subcontracted and also completed in 1992.

By mid season of 1993, most of the Towpath reconstruction was completed to CVNRA's southern boundary. No sooner had this section been laid down than hikers, bikers, and, on occasions, automobiles raced down its newly finished surface. Landscaping, grass seeding, raking, river stabilization and final touches were provided. Hundreds of sign posts were installed using powered and manual digging devices. Bollards were installed in the path to stop automobiles from driving down it. This happened occasionally, sometimes followed by rangers and even local police.

By the winter of 1993, the Peninsula Aqueduct bridge, all boardwalks, and most river bank stabilizations and the remaining 1.8 miles of Towpath were completed to the Indian Mound Trailhead. More than a dozen bridges, two tunnels under the historic, now very active Cuyahoga Valley Line Railroad, and numerous culverts were installed. Water-control devices were rebuilt for protection at some locks. Parking lots were added to accommodate the numerous visitors, and over 50 wayside exhibits were installed to tell the modern traveler about scenes from the past.

§§§§§§§§§§§§§§§§§§§§§§§§§§§§

*Newspaper writer Fred W. Bishop wrote many articles about the Ohio & Erie Canal in the Peninsula area that were reprinted in* Towpaths *during the late 1970s and early 1980s. This one is from the September 20, 1946, edition of the* Brecksville News.

Volume XXI (1983), No. 2, pp. 18-24

### PENINSULA LOCK AND AQUEDUCT by Fred W. Bishop

"With the possible exception of the twenty locks that lifted the Ohio Canal through Akron from the Cuyahoga Valley to the summit of the divide that separates the Great Lakes and Ohio Valley drainage systems there was likely no more picturesque section of the entire canal than that including the lock and aqueducts at Peninsula. The man-made waterway followed from Cleveland southward along the right bank of the river until it reached the village, but there it was forced to make a crossover to the left bank and the unusual occurrence of one stream of water passing over another was quite unique. The added features of an adjacent lock to give the canal sufficient height for the crossing, an aging mill nearby, steep shale cliffs along the river, tree-covered neighboring hills and the curious formation of the river-encircled peninsula with its connecting isthmus no further distant than young Jimmie Garfield might have thrown a stone as he drove his mules across the towpath part of the aqueduct, all combined to make the location intensely alluring.

AMW:

**Sketch of Peninsula Lock, 1883**. Drawn by A.M. Willard of "Spirit of '76" fame. This is the downstream end with change bridge crossing over the lower lock gates.

"Even in the later days of canal operation after the big loop of the river had been eliminated, the high dam that was built where the isthmus had formerly, added its visual charm to the picture, and the booming of its falling waters was joined by the sharper sound of leakage spurting from the lock gates, the spatter of overflow from the aqueduct as it struck the river underneath and the complaining of the river itself as it hustled away from this turmoil of waters in search of repose in the bosom of Lake Erie. Water and the roar of it seemed everywhere surrounding.

"The accompanying illustration shows the lower end of Peninsula – or Aqueduct – Lock as it was in 1883 and was sketched by A. M. Willard who painted that famous patriotic picture of the 'Spirit of '76'. With the exception of the Grocery which was toppled from its foundations by a flood only a few years after Willard visited the spot, this drawing shows the lower jaws of the lock exactly as they remained for a long time thereafter, even to the sloping timber (up which naked boy-bathers used to like to climb) by the towpath and the wooden sides of the lock approach. The timber probably had something to do with preventing the fouling of towlines as boats passed through.

"The heavy wooden gate-beam projecting at an angle over the towpath indicates that the lower gates are closed and the lock full of water awaiting the entrance of a boat from up-stream. A portion of one closed gate shows in the sketch. If the lower gates were open the sweeps would extend alongside the lock and parallel with it.

"Not only did the canal cross the river at this point but also the towpath crossed the canal, carried over by the small railed bridge above the jaw of the lock. It was necessary to detach the towline from a boat passing under this bridge and to re-attach it when the craft had cleared.

"For many years Daniel Peck kept the grocery store shown in the picture, catering to the canal trade. Similar stores were scattered along the entire length of the canal, particularly at locks or near a village or town as crew and passengers had opportunity of debarking for supplies or refreshments while their boat was locking through. Hank Monroe had a similar store at Boston and Alanson Swan, David Baxter and others at different times at Johnnycake. The demand was as apt to be for wet goods from a barrel as otherwise and such lock stores were usually stocked accordingly. Sort of a lock stock and barrel proposition, so to speak. Mr. Peck lived for many years in the house on Peninsula's Main Street just west of the stone building with 'H. V. Bronson' cut above its portal, but had sold his store at the lock to Andrew Stuart some time before the accompanying sketch was made. As a matter of fact the grocery was probably not in use when Willard made his drawing, canal trade having so diminished in volume that Mr. Stuart had deserted the lock site and purchased the Merrill Boodey store on Main Street by the railroad where his son Andrew and daughter Cora, with her husband Bert Stebbins, now continue the establishment.

"Back in the boat building days Johnson and Bouton had a dry-dock around the boat yard along the canal somewhat north of this lock and around the 1870s Harmon Bronson opened a brick yard close by. The latter enterprise was located between the lock and Pinnacle Hill, this hill being the source of the materials from which the bricks were made. Evidently the clay secured there was not good quality as the venture was not too successful and was abandoned within a comparatively short time.

"During the last few years that the old flour mill stood by the upper end of the aqueduct its water power was not sufficient for the milling capacity, particularly during periods of low water in the river. To supplement this power the milling company secured permission from the State of Ohio to tap energy from the canal. This was done by running a wooden flume from the lower end of the aqueduct and just outside of the towpath directly under where the old grocery used to stand, to an enclosed water power plant – probably a small turbine – at the lower jaw of the lock. To secure a sufficient fall of water this small installation was located close down to the lower level of the canal. The energy it created was transmitted by cogs and shafts to a large cast iron shive wheel above the plant and hence, by use of a heavy endless wire cable operated like a belt, across the river to a main shaft in the mill. This auxiliary was discontinued when a new mill with a larger power plant was erected and with its going all semblance of industrial activity was departed from Peninsula Lock.

"The aqueduct was merely a huge wooden trough through which the canal flowed above and across the Cuyahoga River. It was deep enough – probably five feet – to float a fully loaded canal boat and along its east side was a plank walk, elevated possibly three feet above canal level and maybe six feet wide which served as a towpath. A wooden railing clung along the outside of this runway which was an advantageous spot from which to fish in the river below.

"Massive stone abutments supported either end of this water bridge and a large stone pier rose from the middle of the river to the center of the double span. During a year of repairs to the canal in the late 1890s these abutments were at least partially rebuilt with concrete, Dayton Ely doing the work for the State. A few years later the owners of the neighboring mill complained that the center pier obstructed the clearance of ice after a cold winter, backing up both ice and water with damage to the plant. The old wooden aqueduct was then replaced by a single span steel structure and the impeding pier was removed from the river. This new aqueduct was destroyed, along with much of the canal between Akron and Brecksville, by the great flood of 1913…"

§§§§§§§§§§§§§§§§§§§§§§§§§§§§

*Several contributions to* Towpaths *were made by Arthur H. Blower in the late 1960s involving Summit County. This one explains the derivation of the common name for Lock 27.*

Volume VII (1969), No. 1, pp. 1-2

### JOHNNY CAKE LOCK by Arthur H. Blower

In the spring of 1828, a heavy rainfall caused so much sand to be washed into the Ohio Canal in Boston Township by the stream known as Furnace Run, that it stopped all traffic on the canal. Furnace Run was a feeder for the canal.

A number of boats, some going to Cleveland and some to Akron, were unable to travel for several days until the channel could be dredged and made passable.

This happened near the lock where there was a tavern and large stable owned and conducted by a man named Alonzon Swan. This was one of the largest supply centers along the canal.

Though the tavern was well supplied with food, it was not able to handle the heavy drain that was put upon it by the boat crews. The crews ate all the food on their own boats and then all the food in the tavern. They bought all the food that could be found in the sparsely settled neighborhood. Soon they were reduced to a diet of corn meal made into Johnny Cake.

This was their only food for breakfast, dinner and supper for about three days until the channel could be cleared enough to permit the boats to get through.

The penchant for naming locks prevailed here, and Lock 27 north of Akron Summit was known thereafter as "Johnny Cake Lock". A similar situation may have existed on the other side of the break, for the next lock south, Number 26, became known as "Pancake Lock" because of a slightly different diet enjoyed there. In the same township, Lock 28 was known as "Deep Lock". The 1926 edition of the Akron Quadrangle of the U. S. Geol. Survey still designated "Deep" and "Pancake" locks on the map.

§§§§§§§§§§§§§§§§§§§§§§§§§§§

*Along with Ted Findley and Lew Richardson, Ted Dettling was one of the founding fathers of the CSO. This story is priceless.*

Volume XI (1973), No. 2, pp. 21-22

### THE DAY THEY BLEW UP LOCK #8 by Ted Dettling

I remember the 1913 flood. It happened in late March of that year and I was in grade school at the time.

It had been raining steadily for a couple of days and all the streams in the area were over their banks. The Ohio & Erie Canal ran right through the center of town in those days and water was coming down the canal faster than the lock by-passes could handle. Each lock then became a dam and a large lake was formed behind it.

So many people were up-town looking at the flood waters, that I decided not to go to school, but to take the day off and look too. I finally joined a crowd on the Market Street canal bridge overlooking the pool backed up by Lock #8. The water was lapping at the foundations of the Alexander building and the crowd began to shout for someone to dynamite the lock gates, release the water pressure, and save the building.

Finally, some dynamite was obtained from somewhere and one of the men, a Mr. Madden, I believe, was picked to place the charge. A rope was tied around his waist and he was lowered into the lock chamber.

When Mr. Madden was safely returned to the bridge, the crowd took cover and the explosive was detonated. I don't know where the charge was placed or how many sticks of dynamite were used, but when they went off, everything seemed to dissolve!

Over the years, I've collected photos of old Akron. Two of my favorites are of Lock #8 on the Ohio & Erie Canal. One was taken during the height of the 1913 flood and clearly shows the crowd on the canal bridge, the high water, and the Alexander building. The second was taken a few days later, after the waters had receded. This photo was a clear one, and shows the deserted canal bridge, empty lock chamber with a gaping hole blown in the gates, and the ruins of the Alexander building.

The blast that tore out the lock gates also destroyed the Alexander building!

**Lock 8 in Akron during the 1913 flood**. Before (top) and after (bottom) dynamiting. *Photos by Ted Dettling.*

§§§§§§§§§§§§§§§§§§§§§§§§§§§

*Another Arthur H. Blower Summit County contribution, this one tells of the laying of the first lock stone on the Ohio Canal at Lock 3 in Akron. This location today is a downtown amphitheater park.*

Volume VI (1968), No. 3, p. 35

### DEDICATION OF A LOCK STONE by Arthur H. Blower

Reporting the ceremonies attending the laying of the "first Lock-Stone of the Ohio Canal", the Western Courier of September 17, 1825 stated that, at the conclusion of the ceremonies, a metallic plate was placed in the niche of the stone. The plate bore the following inscriptions:

(Obverse)

The First Lock-Stone of

THE OHIO CANAL

Laid in Masonic Form

September 10th A.L. 5825

N. Folsom, W.M. – E. Summer, S.W.

H. Rhodes, J.W. of Middlebury Lodge

No. 134

(Reverse)

A. Kelly Esq., Acting Commissioner

N. S. BATES, Chief Engineer

W. A. Price, Resident Engineer

| Truman Beacher, | Contractors |
| Calvin Hobart, | 4th & 5th |
| N. W. Wattson, | Sections |

THIRD LOCK

A. D. MDCCCXXV

Lock 3 was just north of Center Street, Akron, under O'Neils parking deck. It was rebuilt in 1906 at a cost of $5,400.64.

Perhaps it was the reporter's error, that Kelley's name was spelled without the final "e", and that Bates' first initial should have been "D" for David. In any case, these inscription plates would be fine historic souvenirs or museum pieces, if discovered.

§§§§§§§§§§§§§§§§§§§§§§§§§§§§

*The canal in downtown Akron has undergone a renaissance in the past 30 years. Lock II Park started it all. The site is now overlooked by the relocated Howe House and Canal Park baseball stadium.*

Volume XXII (1984), No. 1, pp. 1-4

### LOCK II PARK, AKRON, OHIO by Margot Y. Jackson

On October 26, 1983 the city of Akron dedicated a handsome bit of park holding a refurbished canal lock and the skeletal frame of a canal boat.

One hundred and ten years earlier, in 1873, William Payne had opened his own boatyard and dry dock at this same spot, Lock 2 of the Ohio and Erie Canal, just north of Exchange Street. He had previously been in business at Lock 3 and, before that, had built boats in Boston Township. He is credited with building a total of nearly 150 canal boats in his long life.

Now, the land on which he worked, the area that one time held brick or coal or wood or pottery for shipment and or storage, is the youngest of Akron's city parks, properly sodded and treed and with stone benches for pedestrians' pleasure. The background noise is not of the hooves of horses or the ring of hammers and anvils, but of squealing tires and screaming sirens.

Yet the sight of the water must be quite similar. Again it comes down from Lock 1, dividing at the southern tip of the dry dock site. Some water tumbles down the spillway while the rest narrows through the lock before exploding in a fast drop to the lower canal level. The newly-built walls are a fine, clean sandstone block from the Briar Cliff Quarry at Glenmont, Ohio just south of Millersburg in Holmes County; the skeletal frame of the pseudo-canal boat is of bars of solid steel. There are stone steps so that one may walk down between spillway and lock fall, feeling the mist of the churning water of seeing the droplets as diamond dust in the bright air.

Dedication speeches on that bright October day spoke of the financial and business hopes behind this restoration. Developers committed themselves to building condominiums alongside, so that Akron will be able to offer downtown residences of quality. This park of Lock 2 - now formally to be known by its Roman numeral as Lock II - will be a gracious focus. Bankers spoke of the transfusion of vitality into the dying downtown such residences would bring, thus justifying the government grant that paid for the design engineers, construction workers and landscapers who for more than two years had been fashioning the whole.

Present also were members of the Canal Society of Ohio and of The Summit County Historical Society. They knew there had been a dream years earlier. A newspaper of September 23, 1963 carried a sketch of a proposed park at Lock 2. Carl Pockrandt, then president of the Historical Society and a founding member of the Canal Society, wanted the State of Ohio to release this land at the lock rather than allowing a parking lot to jut in. "The lock will slip out of sight beneath rubble and old shrubbery," he prophesied as he spoke of Mr. Payne's work here and the fast-disappearing dry dock. The Historical Society could lead a proposed restoration, he suggested. Mr. Pockrandt had no success.

Years later, William V. Wallace, Jr., then director of The Summit County Historical Society and later president of the Canal Society of Ohio, carried the same engineer's sketch downtown to show Akron's planning engineer. "Interesting," the man said, "but not feasible now." Again the idea was pushed onto the furthest back burner.

Only when Akron followed the path of other cities, asking for out-of-town advice in re-designing its downtown, did Lock 2 reappear as a valuable and historic tool.

Today's version is not much different from that sketch Leonard Hiebel drew for Carl Pockrandt. Only the drydock is now completely missing; the shape of the canal boat appears on its site. The Kenmore Construction Company, successful bidders for the local work, removed much of the rubble that covered the drydock but then followed the orders of Design Nonpareil of Boston, Massachusetts, their supervisors. This was to stabilize the fill and pave over it, then place the steel framework of the boat.

William V. Wallace, Jr., one of whose hats is historical consultant for Akron, enjoyed being watchdog of the proceedings. He sent copies of *Towpaths* articles by Frank Trevorrow on lock construction to the Boston designers. He arranged and participated in a meeting with their agent, Peter Johnson, and the late Gale Hartel at Canal Fulton's Lock 4 so that the hardware of a lock could be examined, among other details.

Other Canal Society members somewhat involved were Jack Gieck and James and Margot Jackson, who were asked to review the wording of the plaques that will abstract the history of the place and of the canal's role in the growth of Akron. These panels are to be fitted into the canal boat structure, but - at this writing - have not yet been placed.

**Akron's Lock 2**. Prior to renovations in 1982. *Photo by Lew Stamp. Courtesy* Akron Beacon Journal.

No attempt was considered to make this a working lock with operable gates, yet a little imagination and knowledge offer this illusion. "I find it a spectacular sight," says Bill Wallace sincerely. "Only a rabid purist would object to the reconstruction."

And so again canal waters carry a hope for Akron just as they did so long ago - a hope for growth despite the fashionable fancy dress.

§§§§§§§§§§§§§§§§§§§§§§§§§§

*Resident Engineer Richard Howe's house now rests beside the canal in Akron and serves as headquarters for the Ohio & Erie Canalway Coalition (OECC). A brief biography of Howe appeared in the legendary Frank Trevorrow's "Ohio Canal Men" series, compiled from Summit County histories.*

Volume VIII (1970), No. 2, pp. 17-19

## OHIO CANAL MEN – RICHARD HOWE, 1799-1872 by F.W. Trevorrow

Richard Howe's association with Ohio's canals spanned a little over 25 years. During this time, he saw the beginning of the canal system, its peak operations and the onset of the decline. Beginning as an assistant engineer in the initial surveys when canal construction was authorized, he held the position of Resident Engineer of the Northern Division of the Ohio & Erie Canal for 21 years. His life was centered in and around Akron.

Howe was born in St. Mary's County, Maryland in 1799. Two years after his father's death in 1810, he moved with his widowed mother to Franklinton, opposite Columbus. Upon his mother's remarriage, Howe went to live with and was adopted by Lucas Sullivan. Sullivan provided the boy with a good education, and under his influence, Howe became proficient in surveying.

When surveys of the Ohio Canal routes were authorized in 1824, Howe secured an appointment as assistant engineer on the staff, of which David Bates, Samuel Forrer and William H. Price were the principal members. Francis Cleveland was appointed at the same time to a position corresponding to Howe's.

William H. Price, who came from the Erie Canal, took a liking to Richard Howe. Price recognized his ability and to aid and encourage him, gave him a sketch book of drawings of works on the

**Richard Howe.** *Courtesy Summit County Historical Society.*

Erie Canal. Price and Howe were associated in all the surveying and engineering of the Ohio & Erie Canal until 1839, when, upon the expiration of his term as Canal Commissioner, Price's name disappeared from Ohio canal reports. In 1829, Howe was appointed resident engineer of the Northern Division of the Ohio & Erie Canal, the position he held until his resignation in 1850.

William Case mentioned Howe and Leander Ransom in his account of his journey on the Ohio & Erie Canal in 1838. Case noted that Howe, the Engineer and Ransom, the Commissioner, paid the regular fare when they boarded the packet at Akron, and while they were on board, the crew's behavior improved remarkably.

Howe acquired considerable property in and around Akron. In 1825, he bought 400 acres near Ira and he also owned some land on Summit Lake. He is listed in an 1844 Report as having leased the surplus water of Yellow Creek taken into the canal at Lock 24. The lease involved a deed of land in payment, it was for a period of 99 years and was negotiated with Alfred Kelley.

Howe was married in 1827 to Roxana Jones. There were eight children born to the family, of whom five survived. An Akron school was named for him and his son Henry, in appreciation of their interest in the city's educational affairs. Richard Howe served at various times as village councilman.

In 1850, Howe resigned his position as Resident Engineer of the Ohio Canal to join the "Gold Rush" to California. It is said that he traveled with the horse and surrey he had used along the canal, and all arrived safely at Sacramento. After a short venture there, he disposed of his business and was appointed Deputy U. S. Surveyor. He returned to Ohio via Panama, in 1851 and resumed his business and survey interests until his death in 1872.

§§§§§§§§§§§§§§§§§§§§§§§§§§§§

*The floating section of the Towpath Trail south of downtown Akron was opened with much ado in 2009. Problems surrounding its original construction are highlighted below.*

Volume III (1965), No. 2, pp. 6-10

### THE FLOATING TOWPATH by L.W. Richardson

When construction began on the northern half of the Ohio & Erie Canal, the first concern of the Commission was to open that section from the Akron summit to Lake Erie. There were probably two reasons for this decision, an early connection with the port of Cleveland would allow the movement of considerable freight and begin to bring in much needed revenue and further, the completion of this section, with its staircase of locks ascending the rocky hill to the Akron summit level, would prove to the skeptics that the enterprise was feasible from an engineering standpoint. Whatever the cause, construction south from the summit was delayed. Although the engineers had, in August of 1828, arranged the passage of a boat from the summit level south, nine miles (*Towpaths* No. 4, 1963, page 7) this seems to have been chiefly for effect. The Commissioners reported this on October 18th of the same year.

"Of these sections, the one extending from the summit lake, to the Tuscarawas, is much the most backward, and indeed is the only one which is not susceptible of being finished by moderate exertions in a few weeks.

"The great delay in finishing this job has resulted from the difficulty of draining it, during the progress of the work. The difficulty was foreseen at the time of letting the first contract in 1825. In order to obviate it as far as possible, the contractors for the section extending north from the summit lake, toward Akron, were required so far to finish their work, as to draw off the waters of the lake nearly to the level of the bottom of the canal, as early as the winter of 1825-6. Had the stipulation of the contract been complied with, it would have afforded great facilities for draining the waters from the canal whilst in the

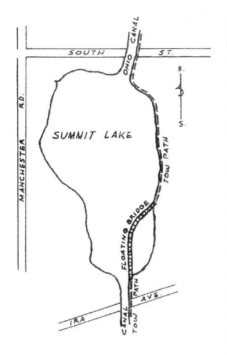

**Summit Lake**. With floating towpath.
*Map by Leonard B. Hiebel.*

progress of excavation through the swamp, which extends from the south end of the Lake to the Tuscarawas. The waters of the Lake were however not drawn down until the month of September, 1826; and until this period, the contractors for the job through the summit swamp were deprived of the privilege of draining their work in that direction."

The original contractor for Sections 1 and 8, south of the summit level, was Hiram Johnson of Middlebury. He was managing partner for a group consisting of Sheldon and Lyman Chapin, Jared Rathbone, John Pratt, James Simpson and Benjamin Sayer. As the report indicates, the syndicate failed to complete their contract. Johnson died in either 1828 or 1829 and his estate claimed damages from the Commissioners because of the alleged failure to lower the water level so that the work on these sections could be completed. In January, 1830, Alfred Kelley, Chief Engineer, his Assistants, William Price and Nathaniel Medbury, all made lengthy reports to the Commissioners, explaining that the claim had no merit. These letters make it clear that one of the major problems in the lake area was the absence of a firm subsoil. In many places, the weight of dikes built for towpaths and berms forced sand and muck to rise in the completed channel of the canal. And in spite of the surveyor's work, sounding for bottom "with long poles and rods of iron" there often was no bottom worthy of the name.

These problems not only delayed the completion of the whole project but explain the construction of one of the most unique features of the whole canal system, the "floating towpath". It was originally intended, as the Report of 1828 states, to run the line of the canal along the edge of the summit lake.

"The Portage or summit lake, along the margin of which the canal line passes, may either be used as a reservoir, by suffering its waters to remain at their present elevation, subject to be drawn into the canal as occasion may require; or the surface of its waters may be reduced to the level of the top water line in the canal; and by passing the canal line through it, and constructing a tow line along its margin, considerable excavation may be saved."

This idea was abandoned, presumably because of the difficulty of establishing a clear channel next to a firm embankment and a dike was built through a deeper part of the lake. This was only partly successful and the ultimate solution was described in the Report of January 22, 1833.

"One of these lakes, called the Summit Lake, near three fourths of a mile in length, forms part of the Canal. The towing path across it is constructed partly on floating bridges, made of light timber doweled together so as to form a perfect floor, secured in their proper positions by means of long piles driven into the bottom of the lake and rising above its surface; and partly by throwing up a bank along a projecting part of the shore between the bridges. The depth of the water and the marshy character of the shore and the bottom prevented the formation of a towing path of earth along those parts of the lake where the bridges are used."

The floating towpath continued in use until the canal was abandoned. Originally provided with a hand rail, in the last years this had disappeared. As the timbers on which it floated became old and water soaked, it was less buoyant and was usually just above the water level. This condition was well described in the bulletin of the Summit County Historical Society, Sept. 1958.

"An oddity of the bridge was the fact that it undulated under the weights of the horses and mules. The bridge floated on the surface of the water about hoof deep, and the bridge rose to the surface after the horses passed.

"A favorite trick played by the older boys on the 'new' boys was to have the 'new' boy sit on the edge and let their legs dangle in the water. When the mules came, the older boys would stand up, leaving the new boy sitting. When the bridge sank under the weight of the mules, the new boy would be immersed enough to get his pants wet, much to the merriment of the 'old timers'."

**Summit Lake by S.S. Dustin**. From *Frank Leslie's Popular Monthly*, 1890.

§§§§§§§§§§§§§§§§§§§§§§§§§§§

*When canal boats were being built across the state in the late 1960s and early 1970s, an effort heavily supported by the canal society, there were no plans. This dilemma is presented here by Carroll M. Gantz.*

Volume X (1972), No. 2, pp. 18-20

### DESIGNING THE *ST. HELENA II* by Carroll M. Gantz

The initial challenge seemed simple enough to a novice, develop a set of working plans to construct a sixty foot canal boat. The construction boss, Jim Cozy, assured me that he had authentic sketches prepared by an ex-boatman who recalled exact details. Furthermore, there were many boat models and photographs available. All I had to do was to develop a few overall dimensions and put the pieces together on paper. This was in April, 1967. Construction was to begin in May.

A few hours of study revealed the real problems. The sketches (taken from a State Maintenance Boat) were woefully inadequate. A few key details (like the stern) were obviously different from the photographs—mostly of freight boats, and these were all different, in detail, from each other. The models were little help as they, too, all differed from each other. If, for example, I took the height of the cabin structure, I found the models scaling from five to eight feet. What dimension was correct? The dilemma, in short, was to establish authenticity.

The solution to this dilemma, I felt, was to return to the only available source of authenticity—photographs. But one cannot scale dimensions from photos!

There is a procedure commonly used by Industrial Designers, known as mechanical perspective. It is used to convert 3-view mechanical drawings into a perspective image of the object through a system of space cubes. I decided to try this system, but in reverse. First, I used the photographs to prepare a perspective rendering of a freight boat so that it matched the photographs in appearance. Then, a three-dimensional cube grid was constructed over this drawing, and from this, a three-view mechanical drawing was plotted. Thus, the dimensions determined were a direct result of the photographs themselves, the only authentic physical evidence known.

This procedure, understandably, took time and by mid-May, 1967 the construction crew was getting impatient so preliminary drawings were released on the keel, ribs, stem, and stern post. There was one flaw in my system, however. There were no available photographs of the hull below the waterline, so I chose a shallow V-bottom shape to simplify the curvature and fitting of planks. (a procedure then totally unknown to any of us) As it turned out, this was an error, but construction was, at long last, under way.

Now that we had preliminary dimensions, I began checking them against models, particularly the model of *St. Helena*, constructed by W. J. McLaughlin around 1933. Mr. McLaughlin once worked in the old McLaughlin Dry-dock in Canal Fulton. Although prepared entirely independently, the preliminary dimensions coincided, within inches, to those of the scale model *St. Helena*. The overall length, width, depth, cabin heights, deck heights, curvature of rib rails—all were essentially identical. The discovery not only confirmed the development technique, it also verified the *St. Helena* model as sufficiently accurate and authentic to use as a detail reference.

The next few months were spent carefully taking dimensions and contours from the model. Mr. McLaughlin had spared no detail, even down to the tiny cabin furniture. These details were carefully incorporated into scale drawings with prime effort going into the hull and planking details. Ultimately, four full 36" by 48" detail sheets were produced.

Only a few deviations from the authentic model were permitted to adapt the boat to its job of transporting people. Since a freight boat had only three cabins with open holds between them, a deck and benches were added for passengers. And to permit passengers to walk from the foredeck to the aft deck (Canawlers walked "topside" on the catwalk), two doors were added to the center "stable cabin". Roll-down canvas awnings were added over the "holds" to protect passengers from rain and the hot sun. These were the only modifications permitted. Oh, yes—and one more—through ignorance. As mentioned earlier, the shallow V-bottom hull was proven to be in error by the model which has a flat bottom with rounded corners.

By the time the 1967 "building season" ended, the keel and ribs were in place along the canal bank in Canal Fulton. When construction resumed in the spring of 1968, the final hull and planking drawings were complete. They incorporated contour modifications so that the hull, where exposed to view at the stern, would look like an authentic rounded hull. This involved a series of planks which were tapered in shape yet tight fitting—a seemingly impossible task. Still, the photographs and model indicated they had to be this way. Suggestions to make the hull from plywood or fiberglass abounded, because people *knew* how to do that and *no one* knew how to plank a wooden boat without leaks.

No one, that is, except a professional boat-builder. My inquiries had led to a Mr. James Richardson, of Cambridge, Maryland, who is a well-known shipbuilder, still constructing boats with canal-era methods. He agreed to visit Canal Fulton, examine the hull frame, and review our plans on June 26, 1968. Mr. Richardson's keen eye and experience not only verified the correctness of our planking drawings, but contributed a wealth of construction tips and details which were incorporated into the plans. The summer was spent successfully planking 2/3 of the hull.

While a plastic "boathouse" was being constructed over the hull, my research continued via correspondence around the country, searching for authentic details to use on our Ohio & Erie Boat. This search did turn up drawings of a Chesapeake & Ohio Boat made in 1939 from the ruins of an old hulk, but these were, of course, uniquely different from Ohio Boats.

Mr. Howard Chapelle, Senior Historian of the Smithsonian, provided Erie Canal Packet and Barge lines—both of which are also quite different from Ohio boats. The Ohio Historical Society provided canal boat lines from the Public Works archives, but these were also of an Erie Canal Boat. Lines from an Illinois and Michigan Canal Boat and a Morris Canal Boat were also received. Not only were all of these inappropriate for the appearance of an Ohio & Erie Canal Boat, but, in most cases, they were simply external "lines" describing the general appearance of the boat, but not suitable for construction.

I hope someday to find the time to prepare a book describing the various canal boat designs so I'm continuing my search for authentic drawings or plans. Any information would be most welcome to me.

When I began work on the *St. Helena II*, I was dismayed by the "barges" being used for commercial purposes at New Hope, Pa. and Georgetown. Maryland. To my knowledge, the *St. Helena II* remains the first authentically designed reconstruction. Recently, I have provided plans of the *St. Helena II* to Rome, New York. Such a design, if built and operated there, will *not* be authentic as it represents an Ohio & Erie Boat.

I would suggest that regional Canal Societies, and particularly the newly formed American Canal Society, exert their influence on new boat constructions to insure authenticity. If nothing else, a small plaque could be awarded by the Society to mount on designs which meet the standards of authenticity.

Such a plaque could read something like…"The American Canal Society (or State Society) recognizes this reconstruction to be authentic in design and construction for this region". Otherwise, the new movement into canal restoration will be blighted by grotesque and commercialized boats which will mis-represent the character and beauty of the authentic boats to the general public.

In conclusion, I would like to convey my gratitude to those interested Canawlers who helped me in my research. Their enthusiasm, information, and knowledge made my work fascinating and created, for me, a lifelong interest in a most intriguing era of American History.

§§§§§§§§§§§§§§§§§§§§§§§§§§

*Massillon is a confusing place even for dedicated canallers as virtually nothing is left of the Ohio & Erie Canal there. So we turn yet again to Frank Trevorrow to straighten it out. Included is one of his wonderful maps, perhaps his most memorable contribution to* Towpaths.

Volume VII (1969), No. 1, pp. 5-9

## THE OHIO & ERIE CANAL AT MASSILLON by F.W. Trevorrow

### Sippo Reservoir.

The nearest thing to a Johnstown flood disaster on the Ohio & Erie Canal occurred in 1848 at Massillon. A deliberate break in the Sippo Reservoir dam sent water cascading through the town, just as festivities at the grand ball celebrating the opening of Tremont House hotel were at their height. No lives were lost but property damage was extensive.

The creation of Sippo Reservoir, to supply additional water power to mills along Sippo Creek and to Massillon Rolling Mills was proposed to the Board of Public Works in 1841 by James Duncan. Duncan was the then president of Massillon Rolling Mill Company. He was one of Massillon's leading citizens, having platted the town, built a section of the Ohio & Erie Canal north of the city and succeeded Mayhew

Folger to become the second toll collector at Massillon. Duncan had also acquired land along Sippo Creek where he erected a flour mill, saw mill and tannery.

When the line of the Ohio & Erie Canal was run through Massillon, the engineers saw no need to use water from Sippo Creek to feed the canal. The canal was supplied from the Portage Lake summit, but if the need developed, the engineers intended to build a feeder dam below Massillon on the Tuscarawas River.

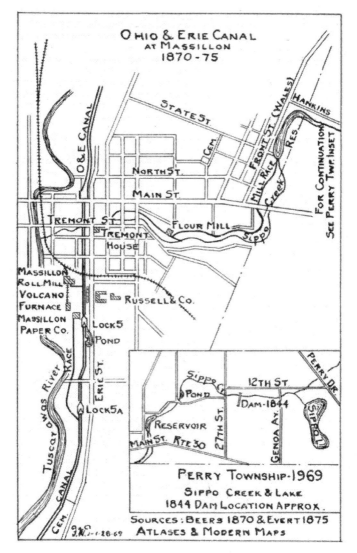

**The Ohio & Erie Canal and Sippo Feeder at Massillon.**
*Map by Frank W. Trevorrow, 1969.*

In 1841, Duncan informed the Commissioner of the Board of Public Works that he had in mind construction of a dam across the outlet of Sippo Lake which would raise the water 10 feet and create a 1,000 acre reservoir. A head of about 80 feet would then be available for water power at Massillon. Duncan proposed that the State share in the cost of the dam and reservoir on Sippo Creek by the amount it was estimated the Tuscarawas dam would cost. In return, the State would get exclusive use of the water from the reservoir, whenever needed for feeding the canal below Massillon. The value of Sippo Creek as a feeder to the canal was an open question. At one point the Board stated that the flow of the creek would not supply one quarter of the amount of water needed to supply the canal.

Perhaps because Duncan was an influential citizen, the Board of Public Works changed its mind, and on February 3, 1844, in a communication to the Legislature, intimated an "anticipated deficiency" in the water supply to the canal at Massillon. The Board recommended the construction of Sippo Reservoir as a cheap and certain means of supplying the alleged deficiency.

Action followed rapidly, for on March 11, 1844, the contract between the Massillon Rolling Mill Co. and the Board was signed. Duncan as president of the Rolling Mill Co. and Leander Ransom for the Board were the signers. The Rolling Mill Co. agreed to construct the dam and reservoir agreeable to instructions of the Commissioner and Resident Engineer. The contract conveyed all land covered by the reservoir and the channel for conveying the water to the canal to the State. The State agreed to pay $5,000 upon completion of the reservoir. The agreement provided that the water in the reservoir should be maintained so there was in readiness at all times, 500 cubic feet per minute for use in the canal.

The original contract remained in effect for slightly less than three years. In January 1847, the Board was authorized to dispose of Sippo Reservoir. By agreement with Wm. Wetmore, Amos Binney, and Richard Fay, assignees of Massillon Rolling Mills, the State surrendered title to all land acquired under the original contract. In return, the State was released from payment of the $5,000. Further, the reservoir and channel were considered part of the public works of Ohio and could not be disposed of without the consent of the Board of Public Works.

The Board was still answering questions of the Legislature about Sippo Reservoir in January 1848. Whether Sippo Reservoir was adequate to supply the needed amount of water in time of deficiency at the summit, or if the reservoir was the best method of supply that could have been adopted, the Board was "not prepared to state". Two able Commissioners made that cautious statement, C. Follett and Samuel Forrer.

All question of the value of the reservoir was resolved on the night of February 22, 1848 when the bank was cut and the entire volume of water flowed down Sippo Creek, through Massillon, across the canal and into the river. Vandalism was suspected, done by dissident residents in the vicinity of the dam.

Canal boats were thrown into the river when flood waters washed out the canal banks. Barrels and boxes of merchandise were washed out of warehouses, sections of which fell to the flood waters. The havoc wrought on the nerves and dispositions of the dancers at Tremont House was trivial by comparison. Richard Howe, resident engineer of the Ohio Canal, estimated the damage at more than $50,000.

## Locks 5 & 5A.

The construction of Sippo Reservoir may have been the sequel to another odd incident in the history of the canal at Massillon. Originally, the canal curved to the east, just below the railroad, and returned to the original Lock 5 in a distance of about one mile.

In 1838 or 1839, James Duncan induced the Board of Public Works to straighten the line so it ran through the Rolling Mill property. In so doing, the lift of the original lock was reduced from 11 or 12 feet to 6 feet and a new lock of 6 feet lift was built about one-half mile above the original. Construction of the new lock created a water power at the mill site and resulted in the oddity of lock numbers 5 and 5A.

The Rolling Mill Company assumed the cost, about $4000, for the new line of the canal and obtained the water power rights for $300 annual rental. The State bore the expense of altering the original lock and building the new one. The need for more water at the new lock may have led to the proposal to build Sippo Reservoir, some five years later.

In 1852, residents of Massillon complained of a nuisance created by a stagnant pond left when the canal was straightened. Dwight Jarvis, in a statement to the Board of Public Works, for the complainants, related the circumstances of the change in the line of the canal and the building of the new lock. The Board could find no record of the matter, other than mention in its 1839 report of building a new lock at Massillon.

§§§§§§§§§§§§§§§§§§§§§§§§§§§

*As the narrative stretches south into Tuscarawas County, we turn to a number of first person recollections of the canal. The first of these stories is told by Mrs. Ralph E. Detrich.*

Volume X (1972), No. 3, pp. 26-28

### BOLIVAR, OHIO by Mrs. Ralph E. Detrich

I remember Bolivar as it was before the beginning of this century—a quiet little town nestled among the Ohio hills, bounded on three sides by the Tuscarawas River, winding its erratic way between willow-fringed banks. First it flowed south, then veered east, then north, then east again, and finally settled down to flow south and empty its waters into the Muskingum, the Ohio, the Mississippi, and at last the sea. Lovely river! The hours spent following its sparkling waters in a canoe, the Blue Flower, were a never to be forgotten joy.

We could paddle down stream with the current as far as Zoar, make a short portage to the Ohio & Erie Canal, and paddle back on its still water. Several small islands in the river were welcome spots on which to beach our canoe and rest. One, Grape Vine Island, was so named because of the wild grape vines growing everywhere, looping from tree to tree. Have you ever swung on a grape vine swing?

North of Bolivar was a shallow space in the river we called "The Riffle." There, the water rippled and sparkled over the stones. It wasn't deep enough for our craft so off with the shoes to wade and carry her to deeper water.

Parallel to the river at the very edge of town, ran the Ohio Canal designed not as an avenue of commerce, but for the sole pleasure of the kids along its banks (or so we thought). At the intersection of Lawrence Street and Central Avenue, to the south, stood a lumber yard and planing mill. A dock was built there for loading and unloading lumber from the canal boats. The dock had a wooden floor and, at the water's edge, cribbing built of heavy timbers eighteen inches square stood just high enough to form a seat where we could perch and dangle our bare feet in the soft warm water.

The lumber sheds were filled with neat stacks of boards which had a delightful fragrance of new wood. The rather crusty individual who had charge of the mill had little use for the small army which left muddy, barefoot tracks on his clean lumber. But it was a lovely place to play "hide and seek", "house", and all the other children's games. South of the mill stood a huge sycamore tree—a landmark for many years and several generations.

On the east bank of the canal ran the towpath where the mules and their drivers plodded along, towing the canal boats with heavy ropes. This path was grassy and smooth—wide enough for a wagon. We often rode our bikes there to Zoar and back.

At the intersection of what is now Route No. 212 and Park Avenue, to the north of 212, was the First Basin, dipping back from the canal to where Park Avenue is now. South of 212 stood a creamery. At Fort Laurens, south of town, was Second Basin and south of that—Third Basin. Water lilies grew there, floating on the still water, and frogs croaked and splashed among the lily pads.

On to the south were the locks which raised or lowered the boats between the different levels; the lock tenders house stood near Lock No. 8. This house was later used by the Boy Scouts for camping. (only the foundation remains in 1972)

Getting back to Bolivar, a bridge crossed the canal, continuing Lawrence Avenue. The road from the bridge to the river was known as Tan Yard Hill. There, when we had snow during the winter, we could coast as far as the road bend at the river. That bridge has been torn away and Lawrence Avenue now ends where it once stood. Interstate 77 now crosses what used to be Tan Yard Hill.

North of the bridge, on the towpath side of the canal, was the drydock. It was built in the bed of the old Sandy & Beaver Canal between the Ohio Canal and the Tuscarawas River. The drydock could be filled with water from the Ohio & Erie Canal. A trough for the water had been cut through the towpath and the flow was controlled by opening and closing gates at its head. A boat was floated through this opening to a tressel-like framework. The gates to the canal were closed and the gates at the rear of the drydock opened, sending the water into the river. This left the boat high and dry for repairs to be made. When they were finished, the water was let in again and the boat floated back into the canal.

North of this were two more bridges. One, continuing Popular Street across the canal and the other, continuing Park Avenue at the northern edge of town.

Beyond this last bridge, the canal crossed the river on an aqueduct described in a report of the Canal Commissioners, dated Jan. 22nd, 1829, as a "structure believed to be the equal in strength and beauty to any work of its kind in the United States". It had a wooden trough resting on stone abutments and piers. The remains of these are still standing. The towpath always ran on the river side so there was a change bridge a short distance beyond the aqueduct.

This was the canal as it passed through Bolivar. The boats floated slowly along, drawn by the mules and steered by the Captain. It was a long ago world—peaceful summer sun—soft lapping water, bird songs, green fields, and grass. A place to swim, to fish, and in winter, to skate. The still canal often froze to a depth of eighteen inches and was smooth as glass.

All that is gone now; most of the canal bed has been filled in and Interstate 77 now follows the route of the canal through Bolivar.

§§§§§§§§§§§§§§§§§§§§§§§§§§§§

*Our next canal recollection from Tuscarawas County is told by former canal boatman "Wick" Lundenberger.*

Volume XI (1973), No. 4, pp. 37-38

### THE FIRST TIME I SAW SANTA CLAUS by "Wick" Lundenberger

Ben and "Wick" Lundenberger worked as "hands" on their father's boat, the BOLIVAR, just before and after the turn of this century. Both brothers have given us taped interviews. Since this is the Christmas season, one story that "Wick" told us seems particularly appropriate. He remembers being four or five at the time this story took place. He was born in 1892 so that would mean that it was in 1896 or 1897 that little "Wick" Lundenberger "First Saw Santa Claus".

"We got froze in one winter just this side of Canal Dover. We had about a half load of coal aboard so we decided to stay right where we were instead of trying to make it to Bolivar to winter at Granma's as we usually did.

"Christmas Eve came. There was snow on the ground and everything was froze up. A fellow by the name of Jim Steiner was there that winter, too. He had a daughter about 15 or 16 years old. Dad and old Jim had been to Dover on the team. I don't know if they got that Santy Claus suit while they were there or not, but the Steiner girl decided she was goin' to play Santa Claus for us kids in all those boats—there were six or seven boats froze up there with us. I must have been about four or five then because I don't think Ralph was born yet.

"We were all sitting in the aft cabin with Mom and Mrs. Steiner. I don't know where Dad and Jim was. There was a hatch on top of the cabin, the stern deck, and a step-ladder arrangement leading down into the cabin. I was sittin' on the bottom step, I suppose we were playin' some kind of game,—when, all of a sudden—that hatch flew open, AND THERE STOOD SANTA CLAUS! He throwed a bunch of candy and nuts down onto the floor. Us kids were scared to death and, back under the bunk we went. And that's the first time I saw Santy Claus.

"The reason I know it was the Steiner girl playin' Santy Claus was that, to top it all off—I don't know whatever made her go around on the outside of the boat. She could have gone along the cat-walk over the holds and then onto the bank from the bow deck, but she tried to walk around the outside of the boat instead. She must have missed her footing because she fell right into the canal! The ice wasn't very thick: she went right through it and there must have been six or seven feet of water where she went in.

"We all ran up on deck and Mom & Mrs. Steiner and some of the other adults from the nearby boats helped fish her out. With that Santy Claus suit on, they had a devil of a time getting her back on board. It's a wonder she didn't drown, but I don't think I'll ever forget that Christmas."

§§§§§§§§§§§§§§§§§§§§§§§§§§§§

*If the name sounds familiar, it should. Viona was the wife of CSO visionary and founding father Ted Findley. Her story tells of growing up along the canal in New Philadelphia's "Southside" neighborhood.*

Volume V (1967), No. 4, pp. 37-42

### MY LIFE ALONG THE OLD OHIO CANAL by Viona E. Findley

I was born, reared and have lived most of my life along the old Ohio Canal. Its waters flowed through our back yard. We were early warned to be careful as its waters were deep enough so that a child might easily drown in them. Few drownings took place as we had learned our lesson well.

I remember a close call of a younger playmate of mine. We went with a group bound for Zoar on a Sunday School picnic. The Latter Day, Saint's Church was the third building below us and the crowd gathered there at nine in the morning with well filled picnic baskets. The plan was to reach Zoar about noon, eat lunch, and return before nightfall. After reaching Zoar, the men left the boat to go to the town. The women and children stayed on the boat. My little friend leaned too far out the side of the boat and toppled over, un-noticed by anyone except my mother, who clutched at her long blond curls which floated on the water. Mother held on tightly against the strong current which was pulling my friend under the boat until help came and she was pulled back into the boat where she was soon revived and after dry clothes and a rest was able to resume her journey. All agreed that my friend's long curls helped to save her.

We always watched the big canal boats pass our house, sometimes several in a day and a favorite pastime of my sister and me, along with all the other neighborhood children was running to the old swing bridge at the corner and trying to hitch a ride. The caretaker would work the crank which turned the bridge to let the boat pass through. If he was in good humor he would let us sit on the edge of the bridge and ride back and forth. If too many crowded on, all were routed. No trip to the moon ever surpassed that ride for excellence.

Our home was close to the corner of Commercial Avenue and South Broadway, where stood my father's blacksmith shop, so my sister and I were usually there first with excellent chances for a ride. There was a small shanty for the bridge caretaker across the canal from father's blacksmith shop on the towpath side. His home was located on the same side, the first house down, in plain sight of his shanty. On busy days, his wife carried a hot lunch to him. When not busy, she called him home to lunch.

We used canal water for washing clothes, after boiling it, and on washdays my brother carried many buckets of water to fill the boiler before school time. We fished in the canal and caught many fish. Our methods were crude, some old fishing poles, home made lines, and worms for bait, so it is not surprising that many of our catch were small. Carp and catfish predominated. When the fish refused to bite we sometimes secured the pole with rocks at one end and watched from a distance. Many times a large fish carried the pole downstream. My sister was the better fisherman as she was not squeamish about putting the worm on the hook and taking the fish off. It was our task to clean the fish and prepare them for frying. My mother's many tasks left her little time for this chore.

We seldom swam in the canal as the bed was muddy and it was considered dangerous unless chaperoned. A few times our mothers joined us, well hid from view under some large weeping willow trees. But for the most part we had to content ourselves by sitting along the bank and letting our feet dangle in the water. Even that was blissful on a long, hot day when we often went barefoot. We had a small boat with oars which we were permitted to row between the swing bridge and the high bridge, a city block down the canal. We were not allowed to row to the mile bridge, one mile up the canal from our corner, unless accompanied.

In the winter, when the canal froze, we skated, but always close to home, as sometimes someone went through a hole in the ice and had to be pulled out. This was a thrilling time! There were many skaters and the boys were very gallant, always offering to put on our skates and adjust the straps tightly.

Many of the boys were excellent skaters and skated downstream to Stumpy Basin, a mile or so. The high bridge was a block below our house and we liked to stand on it and gaze into the water below. In winter it was an excellent place for sledding.

Farther down the canal was Lock 13, known also as Blake's Mills Lock, a very interesting place, with the old lime kiln nearby. It was an amazing sight to watch the boats approach the lock, see the gates part and the water attain the desired level, the boats glide through and continue their journey. When the gates were closed we often walked across them. This was a dangerous practice and finally forbidden, but miraculously no one was ever drowned.

We went to sleep to the tune of the frog's song, a rather monotonous, deep throated croaking but very conducive to sleep. Sleeping pills were unheard of and unnecessary. Early to bed and early to rise! We rose early, often to the deep swish of water as an early boat made its way past our house. They were pulled by horses or mules on the towpath with a man or boy trudging alongside. You could see how life was lived on the old canal boats which were home to many families.

The Tuscarawas River ran about a quarter mile north of our home and to get to New Philadelphia, we had to cross both the canal swing bridge and the Broadway bridge over the river. Our little village was first called Blake's Mills and then Lockport. When it was incorporated it became the south side of New Philadelphia. In the early days the river bridge was a covered bridge and my parents told tales of stumbling over animals while crossing it in the dark.

My mother lived on a canal boat in the summers as a child, as my grandfather, Benjamin Wells was a canal boat captain. We loved to listen to stories of her early life.

We usually had high water in the spring. Sometimes it would rise very high and cover the sidewalks. Everyone would then go to the river bridge to see how high the water was. In 1913 came the big flood and the river bridge was washed away. The canal waters came up into our back yard completely covering it. Our cistern overflowed and water came into our basement. We were entirely cut off from the town, with no gas or electricity. We got out our old oil lamps and candles and did what cooking we could on old cookstoves or any way possible. Neighbors helped one another. We stayed off the streets at night as the town was in complete darkness. No one had automobiles at that time, there were no street cars or buses and only a few horses and buggies.

The present day viaduct had not been built and the old sidewalk was a much longer way around. We walked a mile or more to the old Central School building in town. We were in high school at the time of the flood and for several weeks we were unable to get across the river. Finally, when the water receded a little, a home-made raft was built to ferry us across so we would not miss too much school. By then things began looking brighter. We had not been sure what might happen. Some men who had tried to cross in a boat were carried down stream by the strong current and drowned.

After the flood the canal was no longer used and an old time era had passed never to return. All of life is change and many are the changes that have been made here in the name of progress. My husband and I still live in my old home place and we see many changes that have taken place around us. A gas station now stands where father's blacksmith shop stood and a new super-market has replaced the old grocery store. The old canal bridges are gone and Lock 13 is now a ruin. A super-highway has destroyed a portion of the old canal and the jingle of the trace chains on the canal mule hitch has been replaced by the roar of modern traffic. Such is progress, but no modern improvement can wipe out the pleasant memories of my childhood days along the old canal.

§§§§§§§§§§§§§§§§§§§§§§§§§§

*The fourth installment of Tuscarawas County canal stories is by Ellis H. Shimp. Some of the structures described therein are in eastern Coshocton County.*

Volume XIV (1976), No. 2, pp. 22-24

### CANAL RECOLLECTIONS by Ellis H. Shimp

Although the flood of 1913 did extensive damage to the Ohio and Erie Canal in the Newcomerstown area, its useful days are still remembered.

Floyd A. "Boat" Rogers as a child helped to load canal boats with supplies from his father's store. He remembers well the locks east from Lock 21 at Newcomerstown. The Garfield, Lock 20, also called the Dougherty, not far distant from the turn-around basin which was along East Canal Street, Lock 19, the Hill, with much of its stonework remaining today. Lock 18, Bremer (Port Washington) was near the present location of Wickes Lumber, Lock 17, Lower Trenton, site of the present Wilson Roller Mill, once operated by water power from the canal.

"Boat" Rogers, recalls that the last canal boat to arrive with a payload in Newcomerstown was captained by Frank Lyons and carried a cargo of salt. Its mules were directed by Dave Wigfield. According to a Newcomerstown newspaper of 1943, "Ex-Canal boat captain, J. Frank Lyons, 78, died at home on Canal St."

Ernest Norris, retired blacksmith who died recently had lived his entire life in Orange, remembered when farmer's wagons were lined up from the warehouse there to the Tuscarawas River bridge awaiting their turn to unload wheat. Among his keepsakes was the large steelyard balance which was used in weighing the incoming wheat. Another contrivance used at the warehouse for unloading canal boats, was a simple hoisting winch, a revolving affair in which the center vertical barrel for coiling the rope was turned by a horse hitched to a long pole and driven at a walk round the axis clockwise.

The lock at Orange, number 24, he remembered as Felver and also Reed's. Lock 22 was called Sudam, also Sedam or Suydam's; Lock 23 was Mackey and Lock 25 was Wild Turkey.

**Wild Turkey Lock (#25)**. Between Newcomerstown and Coshocton, view looking east.

The repair of the lock at the south of Tuscarawas Village, completed in 1906 was criticised because of the excessive costs. In 1907, a new swing bridge was constructed across the 40 foot wide channel near Orange, not far from the aqueduct over Evan's Run. There were three structures spanning the canal in Newcomerstown. The bridges for River Street and Bridge Street were turn bridges using manpower by way of a long pole, a sort of walking beam with a center attachment which contained a square hole. A post card cancelled in 1910 shows the River Street iron bridge in a view of the canal eastward with a couple of line boats tied up close to the north side of the present Eureka Hardware building! The railroad bridge over the canal was a lift type.

There was a shallow spot in the canal in Newcomerstown where the present Goodrich Street is now. Old timers say this was a cattle crossing of which there were several on the canal.

Older members of the Jacops family of Newcomerstown have many stories to tell of the canal boat "Monroe" owned by Samuel Jacops. The "Monroe" traveled the Ohio and Erie Canal north to Cleveland, and south to Portsmouth. When Ohio coal mines were idled by a widespread strike in 1898, Captain Jacops filled his boat to its 60 to 70 ton capacity with undesirable slack from some of the local mines and transported it to the Akron area where it was sold without any discussion about the price to an out-of-fuel mill.

The "Monroe" was a family boat with forward and rear cabins, cargo space between and a stable cabin in the middle. During the fall months, Jacops would load the "Monroe" with quality screened coal. As he traveled the canal he bartered with farmers along the way, trading fuel for dressed hogs, beef quarters, potatoes, fruit and other eatables for the family's winter use. One cargo in particular which is remembered by the family, was a capacity load of wooden flour barrels which were delivered from the Akron vicinity to a buyer at Gnadenhutten. At one time there were five children and two adults living aboard. In winter, the "Monroe" tied up at Goshen where the children attended a two-room school.

The most unusual "cargo" came aboard the "Monroe" near the town of Goshen between New Philadelphia and Tuscarawas. The Samuel Jacops family was increased by one when a baby boy was born aboard the "Monroe" on a hot July day in 1905. The "Monroe" was sold by Jacops and eventually rotted in the canal near Goshen.

The canal was enjoyed by Newcomerstown residents all year round. There were always fish to catch, bullheads, carp, sunfish and snapping turtles. There were excursion parties in the summer to Blair's mill and beyond. In winter the Canal superintendent would give permission and provide for skating parties on the turn-around basins. In later days when the canal had been abandoned it was used for wooden washtub races during the town's summer street fairs.

§§§§§§§§§§§§§§§§§§§§§§§§§§§

*During America's bicentennial year in 1976, the former canal aqueduct over the Walhonding River at Coshocton was converted into a pedestrian footbridge as described by Roscoe Village historian Nancy Lonsinger.*

Volume XIV (1976), No. 3, pp. 25-27

### "AQUEDUCT" BRIDGE AT ROSCOE by Nancy Lowe Lonsinger

The "Aqueduct" Bridge spans the Walhonding River at the site of the Walhonding Aqueduct of the Ohio and Erie Canal. It is 326 feet long and 12 feet wide, built of timber using the Glulam process which gives it the strength and durability of steel and concrete, and was constructed by the Benton Bridge

Company of Wooster, Ohio.

The "Aqueduct" Bridge is part of the Coshocton Lake Park Recreation area of the Coshocton City Park Board which oversees the management of the "Monticello II," the swimming pool, campground and hiking areas.

The bridge, completed earlier this year, is supported by the original aqueduct abutments. In removing stone from the original aqueduct piers which had fallen into the Walhonding River, timbers 40 feet long, believed to be some of the original cribbing, were discovered. Samples of these are displayed at the Canal Museum at Roscoe Village and at the Johnson-Humrickhouse Museum in Coshocton. Also discovered during construction of the bridge was an iron bolt, six feet long, with a cast iron plate attached. The entire piece was hand-forged and weighs approximately 200 pounds.

Lock 26, damaged extensively by tree roots has been partially dismantled. The stones, to within a few feet of the bottom of the lock, had been pushed inward too far to be straightened and lack of sufficient funds prevented re-construction of the lock. The bridge was financed by local funds and should additional funds become available at a later time to rebuild the lock, the stones are nearby and can be replaced. Locks 26 and 27 had a total lift of 14 feet from the Lower (Roscoe) Basin. The Walhonding Canal which opened in 1841, also entered this Basin by triple locks.

Captain Pearl R. Nye, the canal balladeer, built his retirement home, using timbers of a canal boat for part of it, at the southwest corner of Lock 27 in later years. He named his home "Camp Charming." It was at this same site, but actually spanning the lock, that another home was built later. The walls of the lock were utilized for the basement and were painted green. This house has since been removed, but the section of Lock 27 used for the basement can be identified by the green paint still to be seen.

**The Walhonding Aqueduct**. Built before 1830. *Photo from Roscoe Village Foundation.*

The canal, river and village complex at Roscoe is an extensive, living chronicle of Ohio's canal era. The restored buildings and exhibits and photographs in the Canal Museum depict life in Roscoe Village in the canal days. At the north end of the Village at the parking lot, the tree-shaded towpath walk begins, passing along Roscoe Basin. The triple locks of the Walhonding Canal can be seen from here, also pilings in the water remaining from the Toledo, Walhonding Valley and Ohio Railroad Company which once crossed these locks using the walls for part of its foundation. The triple locks have been cleared of refuse and natural growth and are also easily accessible for inspection.

The towpath walk continues from Roscoe Basin beneath U.S. 36 by an underpass to Locks 27 and 26 which are being cleared of growth for easy viewing. The "Aqueduct" Bridge conducts the towpath across the Walhonding River to Middle Basin. An underpass beneath Ohio 83 is planned. This will enable towpath walkers to continue safely to the restored section of the Ohio and Erie Canal on which "Monticello II" is towed. From here they can either ride the boat or walk to Upper Basin.

§§§§§§§§§§§§§§§§§§§§§§§§§§§§

*Founded as Caldersburgh, renamed Roscoe, and now part of Coshocton, the effect of the canal on the community is described here by Nancy Lonsinger.*

Volume XI (1973), No. 4, pp. 46-48

### THE CANAL SPARKED BUSINESS by Nancy Lonsinger

"Business of every kind is very dull here; but we all hope to live on milk and honey and without labor when we get the canal." When a Portsmouth man wrote this in 1827, he believed that the Ohio & Erie Canal would provide tremendous opportunities and promised a great future for the people of Ohio. He was right but this goal was not achieved without labor and the milk and honey turned out to be flour and coal carried on canal boats.

Roscoe, a small canal port 135 miles south of Cleveland, experienced a typical canal-fostered business boom. According to Hill's History of Coshocton County, Roscoe was, prior to the opening of the Ohio & Erie Canal, "an ordinary little village with a tavern or two, a dry goods store, and the few little industrial shops common to every collection of home. But with the opening of this highway of commerce, and the water power facilities it afforded, an impulse was given to commerce, merchandising, and manufacturing which placed the village as a business center in the front rank in Coshocton County."

Before the canal came to Roscoe, area farmers had no ready market for their produce. When the canal finally reached the village in 1830, all this changed. With cash in the hands of farmers and canal workers, business sprung up to reap some of this "cash crop."

Initially, only basic needs were catered to and such artisans as shoemakers, tanners, carpenters, tailors, seamstresses, and lumber dealers opened their doors to the public. Then, after a few years of "canal prosperity," there came a need for additional taverns and hotels and doctors, bricklayers, stone masons, butchers, boatmen, lawyers, merchants, harness makers, etc.

As businesses flourished and people prospered, a few luxury-type industries were established. A barber came to town to set up shop and stayed. In 1858, a dancing school was held in a Roscoe saloon! Photographers came to town, bakeries were opened and hatters and jewelers were established. No longer did the old rule of "make it or do without" hold true. The time when a blacksmith had to pick up extra money by pulling teeth were over! It was almost a full time job to keep the animals shod that tramped the towpath. Then, too, iron fittings for the locks needed repairing or replacing from time to time. And as people became more affluent, they wanted more iron kettles & skillets and fancy hardware for their homes.

Nearly every business spawned by the canal begat businesses of its own which begat businesses of their own, etc. – a nearly unending chain of prosperity. The canal swelled Roscoe's population, for example. These new settlers required shoes. The need for shoes opened a market for beef hides which in turn created a demand for livestock and feed. This demand for grain to feed the livestock and increased population caused the country's corn and wheat production center to be located in Ohio. The center for corn production lay in southern Ohio (within easy reach of the canal) and the country's wheat center lay in Jackson Township, Coshocton County – Roscoe's location.

Coshocton County became, naturally enough, a center for the manufacture of farm machinery. Roscoe was the home of plowmakers; Warsaw on the Walhonding Canal, made wagons; and West Bedford, 10 miles over the hills from the canal, was noted for manufacturing threshers and hay rakes.

The canal provided power as well as transportation and mills loomed against the Coshocton County skyline. When one met the misfortune of fire, another took its place quickly as it could be built. Mills needed barrels and coopers made tight or "wet" barrels for liquids, slack, or "dry" barrels for flour, and piggins for home use.

In the 1800's the cooperage was one of Roscoe's most important industries. Barrels were needed to store products as well as for shipment on the canal. Winter work for many farmers was riving staves in exchange for finished barrels. It was reported in the *Coshocton Republican* of April 24, 1851 that Edwin Bailey, a cooper employed by Arnold Medbury, made a flour barrel in 27 minutes. Medbury owned one of the larger flour mills on the canal as well as a warehouse.

It was an avalanche! The canal created a need for mills, which in turn created a need for barrels, which in turn created a need for lumber, which in turn created a need for sawmills, which in turn created a need for the canal to carry rough timber to the sawmills. The canal was no more dependent upon these industries for cargo and tolls than the industries were upon the canal for an outlet for their products.

According to the *Farmer's Centennial History of Ohio*, "the advancement in the development of manufacturing in Ohio was not only due to the energy and industry of her sons...but also to the fact that she had Lake Erie on the north and the Ohio River on the south with canals and railways in between."

Coshocton County's business boom was equaled in the other canal counties. So great an impetus to business and industry were Ohio's canals, and later her railroads, that by the turn of the century Ohio ranked first in the nation in the manufacture of carriages and wagons, clay products, and metal working machinery. She ranked second in the manufacture of agricultural implements, bicycles and tricycles, and third in the manufacture of flour & grist mill products, in foundry products, in soap & candles, and in distilled liquors. No wonder early Roscoe residents were apt to call the Ohio & Erie, the "Grand Canal"!

§§§§§§§§§§§§§§§§§§§§§§§§§§§

*At almost any gathering of CSO members, the name Ted Kasper inevitably comes up. He was quite a character! Following is an article from a manuscript prepared for the 1986 spring tour, covering a section of the Ohio & Erie Canal from Roscoe to Frazeysburg.*

Volume XXIV (1986), No. 2, pp. 14-17

## THE OHIO AND ERIE CANAL IN COSHOCTON AND MUSKINGUM COUNTIES by Theobald W. Kasper

### Roscoe to Adams Mills

From Roscoe Village S.R. 16 West at times is parallel to the bed of the Ohio and Erie through Tyndall and Conesville where the canal was crossed by a covered bridge.

Eleven miles below Roscoe, the village of Adams Mills and Locks 28, 29 and 30 are located. At Lock 28 only a few rubble stones of the cut stone masonry lock and tumble remain. The lift was ten feet. This lock is in Coshocton County while Locks 29 and 30 are in Muskingum County.

In the 1830s brothers Edward and George Adams from Virginia settled here and built a flouring mill which operated on water power from Lock 29. In 1840 Edward Adams built a fine home now known as the Prescott Grey House, and in 1855 George Adams built Prospect Place, a stately home between Dresden and Trinway, both extant. *The Ohio Gazeteer and Traveller's Guide* of 1841 lists a post office, flouring mill, storehouse, "and a few other buildings..."

Locks 29 and 30, 1200 feet apart, each had a lift of ten feet, both with tumbles. Four hundred feet above Lock 30 there was a steel swing bridge across the canal.

There was something troublesome with these locks, as from the Board of Public Works Report of 1841, only 11 years after this section was open for navigation, the two locks at Adams Mills needed rebuilding. Again in the 1884 Annual Report, "Making preparations to rebuild locks at Adams Mills."

In the 1851 Annual Report, pay was issued to James Murphy, locktender here, $244.75 at $22 per month for 11 4/30 months. Also the report noted that a substantial tumble of cut stone masonry was built for the lower lock. This new tumble was built almost in line with the upper gate but 50 feet away from the main canal. Lock 29 has its tumble attached to the end of the lower right lock wall. The cut stones of the lift wall of No. 30 have been carried off and the remainder of the wall is now below ground level.

Little is known of the mill, but early in this century, Tom Corner, member of an old and well-situated Dresden family bought the Adams Mill, which was disassembled and shipped by wagons to Dresden. It was reconstructed at its present site at the canal bank and East Seventh Street. At that time, about 1906, the mill was probably run by steam as a flouring mill. In 1960 the mill was bought by the Eppley family of Dresden. Mrs. Eppley wrote, "A man named Ted Jamison who was then 63 years old, said that he got to ride the wagons loaded with the mill." She also wrote that her family had run the mill with a diesel engine and in later years the mill ground feed and grist.

## Adams Mills to Lock 16

A great expanse of swamp land is found here in the Muskingum River valley, the lowest level between the two summits of the Ohio and Erie Canal. From the Portage Summit at Akron, 395 feet above the level of Lake Erie, the canal descended 238 feet in 102 miles by means of 31 locks (Lock 5A at Massillon was added after the original numbering).

The canal builders made use of one big swamp for a canal basin. Monroe Basin is four tenths of a mile below Lock 30 on the south side of S.R. 16. Ice was cut there in the winter and just below it there were ice houses. Ice was supplied for railroad cars. The state charged a fee for ice cutting. A township road goes around the basin now much as the towpath did.

At S.R. 16 and Bottom Road at the Moore Equipment Company is the junction of the Ohio and Erie Canal and the Dresden Side Cut, referred to in reports of the Canal Commissioners as the Muskingum Side Cut.

Benjamin and Nathan Webb, sons of Dr. Benjamin Webb, the first doctor on record who served Dresden, operated a grain warehouse at the junction. They also gave their name to the settlement there and to the first two locks on the ascent to the Licking Summit. Edward and George Adams had a store at Adams Mills and later a store and grain warehouse at Webbsport, while Thomas Smith built the first tavern when the canal was completed in 1830.

Nothing remains of the canal junction except the depressions of the two canal prisms. The northern cut stone abutment of the Cleveland-Akron-Columbus Railroad which crossed the canal just east of the junction on an iron bridge, remains, while on the opposite side there is only the earthen embankment. The name of the settlement of Webbsport was changed to Trinway at the time the railroad was constructed in 1888.

From Webbsport the canal (and S.R. 16) climbs 160 feet to the Licking Summit by means of 19 locks in 32 miles. The numbering of the locks west of the junction of the Ohio and Erie and the side cut begins with No. 19, Lower Webb. The canal crossed Little Wakatomika Creek on a culvert. The ruins of Lock 19 are on the north side of the highway. The culvert gave way to the road. Lock No. 18, Upper Webb was on the south side of S.R. 16. Close to Frazeysburg on the south side of S.R. 16, the stone retaining wall of the railroad marks the route of the canal. No trace of Lock 17 has been found.

In 1827 the town of Knoxville was laid out by Clark Hollenbach who sold it in 1828 to Samuel Frazee. As there already was a Knoxville post office, the name was changed to Frazeysburgh and later Frazeysburg. Frazee was a harness maker, merchant and hotel keeper who built the Kirk Hotel.

When the canal was completed through Frazeysburg in 1830, the pleasure craft *Reindeer* made the first trip from Newark to Coshocton. The *Union of Dover* was the first freight boat. The Pittsburgh, Cincinnati and St. Louis Railroad, generally known as the "Pan Handle" was completed in 1855 through Jackson Township and Frazeysburg.

The Board of Public Works Report of 1859 shows payment of $244.75 to W.P. Prior, locktender at Frazeyburg at $22 per month for 11 4/30 months. From the Report of 1884: "During the season navigation was also suspended for some time, on the five-mile level [between Locks 18 and 17] on account of construction of a new bridge across the canal at Frazeyberg, and for which the P. C. & St. L. R'y Co. had a permit obtained from the board."

There are some old buildings and homes which may date to the early canal days. The canal prism is distinct in places along Canal Street. North and South Canal Streets were located on either side of the canal.

The remains of the aqueduct on which the canal crossed Wakatomika Creek can be seen upstream from the bridge on Canal Street which crosses the creek. The wooden trunk of the aqueduct was 120 feet long, supported by two abutments and two piers of cut stone masonry, resting on double platforms of timbers sunk deep into the bed of the creek and secured from undermining by a large quantity of stone. (Canal Commission Report 1833.)

Some loose cut stones from the piers remain in the shallow creek bed, about six inches above the water line. A part of the left wing wall curve is still on top of the stream bank. Drainage from the canal bed into the creek is provided through steel culverts.

Lock No. 16, just outside Frazeysburg, was named Vickers, after the property owner. Still today Vickers Hill Road ends at the old ditch where the lock used to be. Nothing has been found of the lock. The canal bed now serves as a drainage ditch.

§§§§§§§§§§§§§§§§§§§§§§§§§§§

*The following account with some editing appeared in* The Newark Daily Advocate *of August 7, 1914. A summary of the canal route appears at the end of the article.*

Volume XIV (1976), No. 4, pp. 42-47

### CANAL BOAT PICNIC AT BLACK HAND IN '57 by Joseph Simpson

"In the year 1857, or thereabouts, a coterie of swell folks in Newark decided upon a day's jollity, an excursion by boat to Black Hand. The canal packet (?) boat 'Coalport' had been chartered and put in prime condition from stem to stern for this eventful occasion, all the arrangements being under the supervision and command of Capt. Leonidas McDougal, late of the U.S. Navy, who had sailed the seas, and who had taken part in the bombardment of Vera Cruz and the capture of the City of Mexico in our former war with that nation. Also, later captain of the Third Ohio Volunteer Infantry, and the first man in his town to draw a sword for suppression of the great rebellion. He lost his life in the hard fought battle of Perryville, Ky. Hats off, boys! It was determined that the captain's past naval experience well fitted him as chief in command on this occasion.

"James Wiley's excellent bands—both brass and string—of which the writer was a member, were present. They added tone and excellence to the occasion. It was said also (*sub rosa*) that the gentlemen of the wind instruments and drums, in their forte passages, caused the welkin to ring loudly to the gratification of all on board and of the inhabitants of Licking's famous and fertile valley. Taking it all, everything proved to be quite "rick-a-shay", as Charles Underwood used to say.

"When the 'Coalport' was new she ranked way up. She was safe in transportation of coal, corn on the cob and human freight. She had speed, and frequently was likened unto Flora Temple, the Queen of the Turf. Across her bows was defiantly planted in bold black letters—CAN'T BE BEAT which meant something in canal boat parlance, especially when the right to enter a lock was in dispute and there were fighting crews aboard. Her midship had been profusely decorated and provided with two long seats, facing each other, leaving ample room between for dancing.

"The 'Coalport' rested securely at her dock, near the present county jail, at Third Street. There was no dallying, for time was precious and a long trip ahead. Amid waving handkerchiefs and joyous cheers the 'Coalport' cleared her moorings while the bank played that inspiring and appropriate air 'A Life on the Ocean Wave.' The rush of water while filling and emptying the town lock, was of great interest to the ladies, many being frightened as the boat gradually settled to the bottom. Dancing was in order, the midship was soon alive with eager dancers, and joy was unconfined. All went merry except when the boat would occasionally bump against an obstruction. This would partially dismay and mix up the dancers, and would cause more merriment. 'Low bridge' was a signal not to go unheeded. One member of the band was able to bear witness to this with a severely injured nose and the crushing of his instrument. In a newspaper report of the time, it was humorously stated that this bandman 'received as much brass in his face as would serve a Philadelphia lawyer for a year.'

"Bowling Green Spring was where we made our first stop. It was a noted place where boatmen slaked their thirst and replenished their water barrels with excellent water for cooking and drinking purposes. The next stop was at the upper Licking Lock, the head of slack-water navigation. There was a country store here, also a furniture repair shop conducted by Esquire Dowling. There was another feature here known as Rope Ferry. A long strong rope was stretched across the river and made fast to trees on either side. A scow boat that would safely carry two horses and a loaded wagon was ingeniously rigged with a rope, a windlass and pulleys which could be so adjusted that the force of the rushing waters of the river against the slanting side of the boat would drive or push it across from one shore to the other backwards or forwards as desired.

"Here we locked down into the river that we might enjoy sailing between the high frowning walls termed "The Narrows", where the river for centuries has been wearing a passage through the solid rock to lower grounds two miles further on in order to empty a lake or sea above that covered the broad Licking valley, including the territory now occupied by the city of Newark.

"The Licking Narrows has always been an interesting place to visit and has served the general public for many generations as a pleasure spot. Alas! the vandal has accomplished much in his efforts to destroy the beauties that once existed here. With its high pine covered tops. and over-hanging vines, its miniature dripping caves, palisades and moss covered boulders where one could sit and rest with comfort and watch the slow moving waters of the dam, it all made a picture worth seeing.

"After getting under way again the first object of interest was Cook's Rock, a solitary hindrance to navigation, resting in mid-channel and becoming dangerous at flood tide or when lost to sight by a heavy rain. Normally it stood about one foot out of water. The cook aboard a first-class boat, generally of the gentler sex was often a person of much importance. At times when cooks thought they were not fully appreciated or remunerated they went on strike, as cooks often do ashore. Once upon a time an unpleasantness of this kind occurred between the commander of the canal boat 'Northern Light' and his culinary assistant. Things did not please her ladyship and she became cross and obstreperous. To save words the captain gently slid his struggling helpmeet, baggage and all, fairly on top of this rock—and it raining, with the prospect of a sudden rise. The heartless skipper drew in his gang-plank and ordered the driver to go ahead, leaving the madam to the mercy of the elements, including the waters of Licking Dam. Luckily, it happened that the 'Aurora Borealis' a northbound craft loaded with hoop poles, hove to and rescued the garrulous, tearful but non-repentant sister, permitting her to ride extra to the next boat needing a cook. Thus 'Cook's Rock' became celebrated.

"The balance of the trip of the 'Coalport' was of continued interest and beauty and the famous Black Hand Rock soon appeared in view. Expressions of wonder, admiration and curiosity were heard from all quarters. Upon arrival they found a huge stone formation, as big as a good sized house—an island in fact, when there was plenty of water at hand. Everybody was ravenously hungry upon landing and the signal for dinner was a most welcome sound. The feast was to be celebrated on top of the rock, which was always the proper thing to do and there was a general scramble to get there. The trail was steep and much littered with stones and rough herbage. The climb was fun though, and the dinner was passed with good victuals and much laughter.

"Fishing was now in order, with plenty of bait and tackle. But there were no poles worth speaking of, and as a consequence those which appeared were of great variety. Fishing was poor and tiresome and after a short consultation those chief in command decided upon an early departure for home. The band played 'Home, Sweet Home', and all seemed ready and willing to go. And soon the 'Coalport' was buffeting the turbulent waters of Licking Dam.

"The light fantastic was again in order, but a different class from that on the way out—one that stirs old memories—not the quadrille, but the delightful, swinging old time 'Money Musk' where ladies and gents array themselves in lines facing each other, anxiously awaiting the director's commands: 'All ready. First couple swing once and a half round and go below one couple. Forward and back six and swing your partner, etc.'

"It is hardly necessary to continue the narrative when so near home and supper. We might dwell on the subject but forbear.

"Prof. Wiley thought it proper that after passing through the City's Gates (lock gates) and while the 'Coalport' was proudly swinging into her accustomed moorings the band should play that exquisite old time piratical melody

'The Rover

I'm afloat, I'm afloat

On the fierce rolling tide.'"

## ROUTE OF THE "COALPORT"

The canal boat "Coalport" would have passed through seven locks beginning at the "Town Lock" at First Street in Newark. This was Lock 9 on the Ohio and Erie Canal section from the Licking Summit in Licking County to Webbsport, the present Trinway in Muskingum County.

Newark was a thriving town when ground was broken for the Canal in 1825. One of the main streets was turned over to the State for the canal, which ran between the present Canal and Market Streets. This is one of the few instances when a canal replaced a street, as in later days streets and railroads replaced the canals.

On its journey of approximately ten miles to Black Hand Gorge, the "Coalport" would have crossed the North Fork of the Licking River on an aqueduct shortly after leaving Lock 9. The North Fork Aqueduct and Lock 9 no longer exist. The next lock was number 10, White Mill Lock. State Route 16 is close to the route of the canal from the "town lock" east to Rocky Fork.

Locks 11 and 12, called Upper Stadden and Lower Stadden were next on the trip. Beyond, the "Coalport" would have crossed Bowling Green Run on a culvert, in the vicinity of Bowling Green Spring where the first stop was made. Lock 13, three quarters of a mile further on and a half mile west of County Road 668, Brownsville Road, is in existence today.

The culvert which carried the canal across Rocky Fork on two stone arches is in good condition and is on private property. Rocky Fork Lock was number 14 and number 15 was the outlet lock. Toboso is now closest to the lower end of the Licking Narrows and Black Hand Gorge. The narrows was a slackwater section with the towpath partially cut from the rock face. Lock 15 at the upper end of the Narrows and the guard lock at the lower end remain and are in good condition.

The Narrows of the Licking is still picturesque and has remained a favorite spot for picnics as it was when the "Coalport" visited there in 1857, and when the Canal Commissioners reported in 1833 on the dam built to form the slackwater, commenting as follows:

"The high, overhanging ledges of rock, covered with laurel and evergreen timber, which form both banks of the river—the immense masses of rock, which in the course of time have fallen from the cliffs and now lie along the margin of the water—the beautiful cascades formed by the small streams which precipitate themselves from the brow of the ledges, and the calm sheet of water beneath, form together, a piece of scenery peculiarly interesting and romantic, and one which contrasts strongly with the broad, fertile and highly cultivated valley which opens immediately above the narrows and extends without interruption to Newark."

§§§§§§§§§§§§§§§§§§§§§§§§§§§

*This tour description was written by John Droege, an authority on the canals in Central Ohio. (Webbsport was spelled with only one "b" in the 1833 Canal Commissioner's Report.)*

Volume XXVI (1988), No. 2, pp. 13-14

### WEBSPORT TO THE RESERVOIR 1988 by John Droege

In crossing from one river valley to another, there were two major problems for the canal-builder: cutting through the ridge or ridges and finding enough water. In going from the valley of the Muskingum to that of the Scioto, the ridge problem required the Deep Cut at Millersport and the water problem led to the creation of the Licking Reservoir, both gigantic undertakings at the time. But both problems had also to be dealt with on the way up from the low point at Websport. Here the solution had been provided by the glacier some 10,000 years ago and we see it today at Black Hand Gorge, now a State Nature Preserve.

Websport, now long gone as a community, was at the junction of the Ohio and Erie Canal with the Dresden Sidecut. From here the Ohio and Erie climbed up in both directions. One of the Websport locks survives. There are also some remains of the aqueduct outside Frazeysburg. The lock here, now gone, was unusual in that it was above the aqueduct. Usually the extra height was needed to get enough clearance above the stream as at Roscoe and Circleville. In this case the extra height was needed to get over a slight rise beyond the stream, but not to clear the Wakatomaka. From this point the canal headed for Nashport, near the Licking River, now relocated away from the flood level of the Dillon Dam downstream. A proposed tunnel would have shortened this part of the canal, but the long way around was taken to save an estimated $77,000. There follows a beautiful five-mile off-road stretch along the river to the dam and guard lock at Toboso,

What shall we say about the Black Hand Gorge? First that the Licking here follows a passage through the hill originally cut by the glacier. So also does the railroad and so did the interurban line. And so today do many hikers and bike-riders. Secondly, that this has for years been a favorite picnic place for central Ohioans. Third, that it has lost none of the charm noted by the Canal Commissioners in their 1833 report. The guard lock at one end and the outlet lock at the other are still there. So also is the famous towpath section at Black Hand Rock. The outlet lock marks the end of an 11-mile level from Frazeysburg. Just beyond is the culvert over Rocky Fork, probably the best two-arch culvert left intact in Ohio. One lock survives in the plain outside Newark.

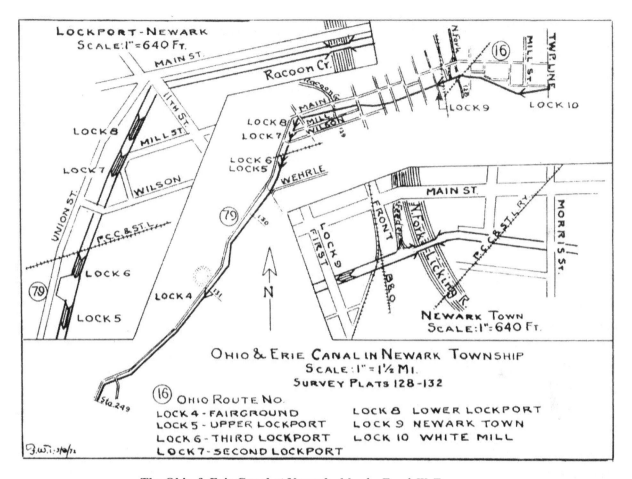

**The Ohio & Erie Canal at Newark**. *Map by Frank W. Trevorrow.*

Newark was a prominent community before the canal. The town gave one of its streets to the canal. The lock in downtown Newark, the two aqueducts, the four locks at Lockport just outside old Newark, the one lock at Moundbuilders' Park—all these are gone with hardly a trace. Of the three Taylors' Locks, only remnants of Lock 1, site of the 1825 ground-breaking ceremony, remain.

From here the summit level ran south to the reservoir where one final lock lifted boats into the lake. This level crossed the National Road at Hebron, making that place an important transfer point for passengers, who often took the canal from Cleveland, then changed to coach here for Columbus, Dayton and beyond.

In closing we need to mention, a little out of place, the one remaining piece of the Granville Feeder. Showman's Arch, which carries Cherry Valley road over Raccoon Creek, is said to be the stone aqueduct built in 1835 to replace the wooden one lost in a flood the preceding year.

§§§§§§§§§§§§§§§§§§§§§§§§§§

*There were two summits along the Ohio & Erie Canal, the Portage Summit at Akron and the Licking Summit south of Newark. This article by John W. Droege is the definitive article on the latter.*

Volume XIV (1976), No. 1, pp. 3-8

## THE LICKING SUMMIT by John W. Droege

Across the northern part of Ohio, a ridge separates the Lake Erie drainage area from the rest of the state, which drains into the Ohio River. Any north-south canal had to have a summit level as it crossed this ridge. The Ohio and Erie Canal, having climbed from Cleveland to Akron and begun the descent along the Tuscarawas, might well have continued down this river and the Muskingum to the Ohio at Marietta. But politics and economics dictated that it must pass along the Scioto. So another summit had to be crossed, to get from one river valley to the other.

The Problem: Water

The problem of the summit is the problem of water supply. Water has to be poured into the canal at its highest point, from which point the locks are supplied. But it is just at this highest point that water is hardest to come by. The problem was particularly severe at the Licking Summit. From its low point at Dresden up to Newark, the canal was supplied by the Licking River. But the 45 miles from Newark to Lockbourne had no natural supply except the Little Walnut, a pitifully small stream which sometimes dried up completely in the summer.

No other state made such extensive use of reservoirs for its canals as did Ohio. Since there was no considerable source of water at the Licking Summit, one had to be provided. If water were stored up during the rainy seasons, it could be used in the dry. So the Licking Reservoir, now Buckeye Lake, was created.

The demand for water from the reservoir was great, but the streams feeding the reservoir were small. The area draining directly into the reservoir was limited, although there were a few springs. The engineers had to husband their water carefully.

Reservoir Construction

When Elnathan Schofield surveyed the Refugee Lands in 1801, he found a marsh land known among the Indians as Big Swamp. It contained a pond about five miles long and 400 to 500 yards wide. The swamp drained into the South Fork of the Licking River in about the same place as the present outlet. When heavy rains caused the South Fork to flood, water would flow into the Big Swamp, to drain out again when the stream returned to normal. Water was to be impounded by building an embankment about two miles long along the north side and about two miles long on the west side of the reservoir. Low hills to the northeast, east and south completed the pool. The work was begun early in the construction period in 1825 and was completed in about two years.

The embankment along the west side served also as the towpath for the canal, which adjoined the reservoir. The spring rains filled the reservoir to six or eight feet above the canal summit level. A waste weir and flood gate was installed at its location, by which the reservoir could be emptied if desired. A feeder lock was installed in that part of the embankment which separated the reservoir from the canal. This allowed for regulation of the flow of water into the summit level of the canal.

Soon after its completion, the north bank failed, flooding the South Fork valley. It was determined to line the banks with stone. A few miles to the east not far from the present intersection of I-70 and Ohio Route 13, was a large stone Indian mound. It is said that the first settlers found it to be 183 feet in diameter at the base and 30 or 40 feet high. A considerable part of this mound was moved by wagon along the newly-built National Road to Hebron and from there by canal boat to the reservoir. Historic preservation was an idea whose time was yet to come! The stone was placed along the embankment to secure it against erosion.

The site of the Licking Reservoir was heavily wooded. Should the trees be cleared before impounding the water? A Canal Commission report of February 1828 estimated the cost of clearing to be $11,000. Evidently that was judged an unnecessary extravagance; the trees were not cut. As the reservoir filled, the trees died. In time they rotted at the water line and fell. The decomposing organic matter fouled the lake for years. The condition persisted until the 1870's. Even then submerged stumps remained to plague boat traffic. Finally during the winter of 1910-1911, the level of the lake was lowered and the stumps were cut back to ice level. Who knows how many boats came afoul of these stumps during canal days? The most famous surely was the *Black Diamond*, a coal barge down in 1850 off the north bank. The spot is still known as Black Diamond Bend.

Water Supply

Natural drainage is enough to keep Buckeye Lake full today, but Buckeye Lake doesn't have to provide water for a canal. A lock needed 8000 cubic feet of water when it lowered a boat six feet. A busy canal needed a lot of water. The drainage area of the reservoir would not provide enough. When the Licking Reservoir was being planned, consideration was given to bringing water from the North Fork of the Licking River and beyond. By 1824 this was deemed unnecessary, but the South Fork was used. The South Fork passes near the north bank of the reservoir, at which point it is perhaps 20 feet below the surface of the lake. Some miles upstream the level is above the level of the lake! At this point, just north of Kirkersville the stream was damned. A feeder, six and a half miles long was constructed in 1826 along the higher ground to the south. It joined the reservoir at its southwest corner, near the present Millersport.

When the canal was completed to this point and beyond, the feeder would have to pass over the canal by an aqueduct. The aqueduct was completed a few years later using the reservoir to transport stone from the hills near its western shore. Today the Kirkersville dam is in ruins but the feeder still carries some surface drainage water into Buckeye Lake. But the water problem, as we shall see, had not been solved. The summit level, but not the reservoir, received water from the Middle or Raccoon Fork of the Licking. Water was taken into a feeder near Granville and led south and east to a point near Fourmile Lock (No. 1), the site of the 1825 groundbreaking ceremonies. Except during dry weather the Granville Feeder provided water for lockage north of the reservoir, thus conserving reservoir water.

Deep Cut

The divide separating the drainage areas of the Licking, which flows into the Muskingum, from the Little Walnut, which flows into the Scioto, lies along a low ridge just south of the reservoir. The ridge had to be cut through. The canal builders knew the cut would be a tremendously difficult and expensive project. The only alternative was to raise the level of the reservoir. This would have meant an increase in the elevation at which water would have to be provided. So, the cut was made, about three miles long, as deep as 34 feet near the middle, plus the spoil bank. Nearly a million cubic yards of dirt were removed. The work was begun in 1826 and completed five years later.

The slope of the bank was one foot elevation for about one foot eight inches lateral distance. A bank so steep was likely to slip and wash until stabilized by vegetation. On each side, near the water level, a three-foot flat berm, a "catch channel" was provided to hold the earth washed from the bank. This accumulation could be removed by boat, thus preventing obstruction of the channel by silting. These measures were less than totally successful, however, as Deep Cut continued to cause navigation difficulties.

Deep Cut was the greatest single obstacle to be overcome in constructing the Ohio and Erie Canal. Delays in its completion, originally scheduled for October of 1828, held up the opening of the canal beyond the Licking Summit until the fall of 1831. When the digging was finally completed the canal was opened in September of that year to Columbus and Circleville, in October to Chillicothe and in the following year all the way to Portsmouth.

The New Reservoir

Navigation on the reservoir had not originally been intended, but channels were cleared of trees and boats were poled. There was no access to the canal, so local residents appealed to the legislature. An act instructed the Canal Commissioners to install a lock making possible passage from the canal to the reservoir. Some time later, 1835, the commissioners noted their failure to comply, explaining that a much more extensive project was about to make the special lock unnecessary. The reservoir, which already covered 2566 acres, was to be enlarged by building a 500 acre addition. A new embankment would be constructed to the west, but without removing the old. The reservoir would become a part of the canal and would be extended through Deep Cut, thereby raising the water level through the cut. Reasons given were these: The extra depth in Deep Cut would overcome the difficulty caused by sliding and washing of soil into the canal bed. The extra capacity would be needed to supply water to the canal. Finally, the second embankment would provide safety against accidental loss of the whole reservoir in case of failure of the embankment. There was one other reason not cited by the commissioners. The aqueduct carrying the South Fork feeder over the canal was made unnecessary. The clearance under the aqueduct must have been very low. Some have claimed that the aqueduct was never satisfactory.

The "New Reservoir" was located to the west and extended to the north of the old. At the northernmost point a lock was built to raise barges from the canal into the reservoir. The new lock was not numbered; the lock at the old groundbreaking site was still No.1. The new lock was called Minthorn's after the nearby Minthorn House. Thomas Minthorn was said to have contracted to feed canal workers during construction. In 1840 he built the Minthorn House, a part of which – or its successor – remains. The southern end of the new reservoir included the area of the cut, which now became a part of the reservoir. A second new lock was built at the southern extremity of Deep Cut. It became known as Pugh's Lock in honor of a nearby resident. The first stopping place south of Deep Cut, it became the scene of warehouses and other enterprises. The improvement in navigation through the cut did not last. In time the canal silted up toward the new level. Toward the end of summer, when the reservoir level was low, conditions in Deep Cut became critical. Loads were lightened at Millersport and Pugh's Lock. Extra teams were provided to pull barges through the mud. The State continued to dredge the channel.

As they passed through the reservoir, barges continued along the same course as before the new construction, but at a higher elevation. The old embankment remained and became a long causeway across the lake. At the northern end, where the outlet valves admitting water to the canal had been located a break in the old embankment provided passage into the original part of the reservoir. This spot came to be known as "hole in the wall". In later years a similar opening at the southern end was provided for the benefit of lake navigation.

In the 1860's, in an effort to solve the continuing problem of insufficient water, an attempt was made to maintain a satisfactory level in the new reservoir at the expense of the old. The openings in the old towpath were closed and high-capacity steam-driven pumps were used to pump water from the old reservoir into the new. The experiment failed; a lot of water was pumped but no change in level resulted. The blame was assigned to muskrats. The old causeway, firm enough on top, just wasn't sound enough below water. So the old dry-weather problems persisted.

When did it all end? Neither the Legislature nor the Department of Public Works ordered the canal closed. The canals were not sold to the railroad competition as in Pennsylvania. They just faded away. In 1881 it was reported that not more than one or two boats a week passed through Baltimore (Locks 3 to 6 south of the reservoir). In 1898 the spring floods washed out the North Fork aqueduct and the Black Hand dam to the north. In 1903 a last attempt was made to repair locks from Lock 8 at Newark to Pugh's Lock. By 1908 the canal was filled in at the street crossings in Newark, replacing the turn bridges. When the disastrous floods of 1913 came along it did not kill the canal. The railroads had already done that by slow strangulation and the State by prolonged malnutrition.

But the reservoir did not fall into disrepair. As canal use declined the level of the lake could be maintained constant through the year. The railroads, while taking away the freight business from the canal, brought vacationers and fishermen to the lake. In 1894 the Licking Reservoir became Buckeye

Lake, a state park maintained for recreation. With the building of the interurban traction lines in the early 1900's and even more after the arrival of Ford's Model T, the use of the lake expanded rapidly. The amusement park, the hotels, the summer resorts, the fishing and boating clubs – but that's another story. Let us note here that almost all of the canal reservoirs remain today, a continuing reminder of the canal legacy of Ohio.

§§§§§§§§§§§§§§§§§§§§§§§§§§§

*Early 20th century writer and newspaper reporter Joseph Simpson, author of the* Coalport *story, gives an account of the canal boat* Lady Jane *with an assist from* Towpaths *editor Brad Bond, who provides some clarification.*

Volume XXXIX (2001), No. 1, pp. 17-19

## THE BOAT TOO WIDE by Brad Bond

Edith McNally sent me a copy of "The Lady Jane", a story in a book by Joseph Simpson, published in 1912, which may be true except that he had the date and the name of the boat wrong. Edith also sent me a paragraph from a history of Licking County that describes what may be the same boat but with the right name and date. Joseph Simpson dates the launching of *Lady Jane* to July 4, 1836 and calls it "the first boat to run on the Ohio Canal".

There was a *Lady Jane.* She showed up in Columbus on October 5, 1831, and Chillicothe, 36 locks south of Buckeye Lake, on October 21, 1831, for the celebration of the opening of the Ohio Canal some five years before Simpson said she was launched. The *Columbus Monitor* reported:

"More welcome arrivals – On Monday, three canal freight boats arrived at this town, viz: the *Cincinnati, Red Rover* and *Lady Jane* from Cleveland. These were the first boats that passed the Licking Summit."

The Licking County history, published in 1881, offers the following version: "The first canal boat built in the county or that floated on the waters of the Ohio Canal within its border, was built by a joint stock company at Hebron, in 1827-8 and was called the *Licking Summit.* It was built under the supervision of Joshua Smith and made its first trip through the 'Deep Cut' on the Fourth of July, 1828, but it was built too large to pass the locks, and was so poorly constructed and drew so much water that it was not thought worth reconstructing, consequently it never left the summit level. It was laid up in the basin at Hebron, for a while used as a drinking saloon, then as a resort for the lewd, or a kind of house of ill fame, until it was destroyed, as a nuisance, or rotted down."

In any case Simpson's version is a good story and may be what truly happened to the *Licking Summit* on launch day.

### "THE LADY JANE" by Joseph Simpson

"About the time of first turning the water into the canal a large boat was built at Hebron. It was lengthy and wide, and supposed to be fit for future canal uses.

"Much controversy resulted as to what name the boat should bear. Many thought it should be called Hebron, when, with great opposition (the ladies included), and in accordance with the esthetic taste that always prevailed in Hebron, it was generously decided to name it the Lady Jane, in honor of the eldest daughter of Elnathan Schofield, then a popular member of the canal commission. Miss Schofield became the wife of Hon. John T. Brazee, of Lancaster, a man of great legal ability and distinction. The following notice was posted:

> Attention Washington Volunteers,
> You are hereby ordered to parade in front of Reeds Tavern in
> Hebron on July the fourth at 9 o'clock, 1836, for the purpose of
> saluting the Canal Boat - Lady Jane - which will be the first to run
> on the Ohio Canal.
>
> > By order of the Captain.
> > Jacob Bope, Orderly Sergeant

### "The Launching

"The builders of this great vessel took plenty of time for its completion, and set the time for its launching for the morning of the fourth, when great crowds gathered to see what a launching looked like. It was a gala day for Hebron. The people flocked to its shores from all quarters. Men came in home spun tow shirts and pants and home made platted straw hats, with no affected style whatever. Men came bare footed and on horse back. The only thought was to have a good time. The simple life was the fashion then.

"At a signal the props holding the Lady Jane were knocked away, when she slid down the well greased ways and took the water like a duck and sent an unexpected swell clean over the towpath, much to the inconvenience of the crowd that stood watching from that point, and laughter and great merriment among those that stood farther away.

"The boat had been provided with fore and aft cabins, with a wide and roomy midship, too wide in fact, as will be seen farther on. It was the nation's birthday. The old 1812 musket was brought into use early on this auspicious morn. And at times a louder boom rent the air, not unlike

'The cannon's opening roar.'

"It was Hebron's patriotic blacksmith's contribution of noise, in front of his shop, using his anvil and plenty of gun powder for the purpose.

## "The Excursion

"An excursion had been planned, to take place after the launching. The boat had been appropriately decorated. The steersman was the admiral of the hour. His authority no one could question. He busied himself preparing for the voyage. A gaudily trimmed paper soldier hat bedecked the head of the driver, and upon its sides it bore the legend

'Give me liberty, or give me death.'

"He felt proud of his job, and wore his hat with a smile and a rakish tilt. He also seemed confident of his ability to manage the motive power with the aid of a black snake whip and a long tow line.

"Ladies and children were helped aboard first, with the order that room be reserved for a committee of men, to insure safety. It was a royal occasion. Loaded to the guards almost, the joyful and impatient excursionists were anxious to be off for a ride on the first craft that rode the then turbid waters of the Ohio Canal. They were turbid from the fact that through the decay of the great quantity of vegetation that existed within the banks of the reservoir the water had almost assumed the color of ink. This condition, with a gradual improvement, lasted many years.

## "Wished for Event

This excursion was the culmination of a long wished for event. Amid hearty cheers, with flags waving amid drums beating, the Lady Jane stood ready. With hues cast off amid tiller in hand the steersman shouted 'let her go, Durb.' Durbin was the nickname applied to boat drivers. The team straightened up, and with a false pull or two the Lady Jane cleared for Taylor's Locks.

"One object in going north was to witness the intense force of the water while filling and emptying the locks. Another object was to visit the spot where Governor Clinton and others shoveled and wheeled out the first barrowful of earth, it being then the anniversary of that event. The big culvert was passed in safety. In places where the water widened the driver was able to increase the speed, which was greatly enjoyed.

## "Bumped

"All went well up to the time of nearing the Locks, when without warning and with poor steering the Lady Jane bumped against one of those tall fender posts usually found in front of canal locks. The impact was sufficient to create some consternation among the passengers but followed afterward with much laughter at the expense of the band who were quartered up on the bow deck, when all, including fife, fiddles and drums, in one scramble, nearly went overboard. The boat's speed was lessened, and upon attempting to enter the lock the Lady Jane 'wedged,' and to their dismay they discovered that her breadth was too great to enter. With force she was pulled back, when they all went ashore, and after exploring the region and witnessing the rush of waters through the locks they embarked and set sail for Hebron's port again, after which the day's festivities ended.

"The Lady Jane never got beyond the Hebron level."

§§§§§§§§§§§§§§§§§§§§§§§§§§§

*Generally acknowledged within the CSO as our resident expert on the canals in Southern Ohio, Dave Meyer has written books on both the Hocking Canal and the Ohio & Erie Canal in the Scioto Valley. Here, the topic is Lockville and the many canal structures located in that vicinity including 9 locks (8 lift & 1 guard) and a slackwater crossing of Little Walnut Creek.*

Volume XXXVI (1998), No. 4, pp. 49-59

## THE OHIO & ERIE CANAL THROUGH LOCKVILLE AND THE LITTLE WALNUT CREEK SLACKWATER by David A. Meyer

### Introduction

The 206 mile marker on the Ohio and Erie Canal was located in Lockville, Fairfield County. It was here that a series of locks were located that lowered the canal to the level of the Little Walnut Creek so that it could receive water from the stream, the first significant feeder water since the Licking Reservoir at the summit level.

Some of the best cut-stone locks to be seen by the modern day canal historian are still here. The slackwater pool for crossing the Little Walnut Creek was created by a rare cut-stone dam. The original Blackhand sandstone for these locks was quarried near Jefferson, a few miles from Lockville.

### Lock 11

The Ohio and Erie Canal arrives from the southeast at Lockville at the end of a two-mile level from Carroll's Lock 10. Here at the eastern edge of Lockville is the Upper or Grist Mill Lock (11). The towpath was on the northeast side of the canal until it reached this lock. The towpath change bridge required at this location utilized the county highway bridge which spanned the canal immediately below the lock and spillway. A grist mill stood just north of this lock along the right bank of the canal. A race feeding the mill from the canal supplied water power, and the tail race returned the water to the canal below Lock 13.

**Lock** 11. Looking east, showing the change bridge, lock and spillway.

The locktender's house was also located near this lock. This locktender and his family watched over all of the locks from 11 through 17. In 1852, a drought year, the Lockville locks were leaking excessively and the Canal Commissioners stationed a second locktender in Lockville to operate the locks and conserve as much water as possible. Each locktender worked a six hour shift around the clock. Even with this effort, the water flowing down the Deep Cut was only two feet deep in October of 1852

## Lock 12

Tenant lock was named after John Tenant and his brother who operated a general store near the lock before they sold it to the Mithoff family. This general store also held the town's Post office. After the Mithoff family purchased the store from the Tenants, they added a saloon to offer whisky which they had manufactured in a distillery nearer to Lock 13. The Mithoffs also built a whisky warehouse at the edge of the canal on the north side.

In the late 1840s, the Mithoffs built a larger distillery just east of Walnut Street on the north side of the canal. It was one of the largest distilleries in central Ohio in that time, using about 300 bushels of corn every day from which it could produce 1200 gallons of whisky at maximum capacity. The spent mash was moved through an open trough to a hog lot located on the south side of the canal. The hogs in this lot were fed the mash until they were big enough to slaughter, and then they provided food, leather, lard, and other valuable products to export to other markets.

Mithoff's sold the distillery about 1862 to the Becker family who operated it for a few years longer. Many distilleries in Ohio went out of business during the early part of the Civil War due to the federal government's taxation of whisky and the close control of whisky warehouses.

Lock 12 has some unique features. One is that the tumble is at a right angle to the canal's channel instead of parallel to it like most others. Another interesting feature is that there are indications of concrete egg-crate like structures in the lock chamber that were obviously added during one of the late rebuilding efforts of the lock. Exactly how those reinforcements were used is unclear.

## Lock 13

Rowe Lock (pronounced as if it were spelled Rau) had a store located near it on the south side which several people owned and operated over many years. One of the more famous was Sam Rowe. He ran boats on the Ohio and Erie Canal for many years both as a hired captain and as a boat owner. Seven of his ten children were born on canal boats. He had captained Jim Emmett's boat, *Lester*, and he had owned the *Rebecca* for some number of years. He was well known on the canal for practical jokes, and the canal men called him "Rowdy". Over the years, the Lockville locks received many different types of repairs from the crew of the state boat, the *Dick Gorham*, that tended this area. During the time that the State leased the canal to private operators other workers were involved as recording on a white marble plaque set in the lock (13) chamber wall stating:

BUILT JULY 1862

BY

THE LESSEES OF THE PUBLIC WORKS

SAMUEL DOYLE, CONTRACTOR

N. EBERLY, STONE MASON      H.E. BUTIN, FOREMAN

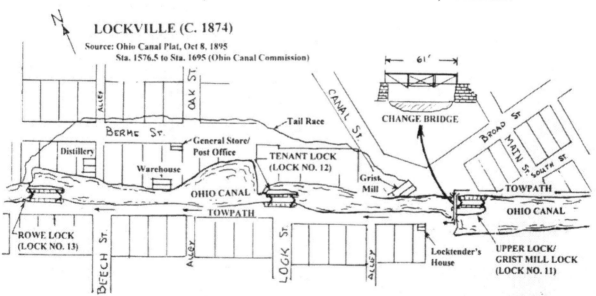

**Locks 11, 12 and 13**. Locks are in Lockville Park. *Map by Dave Meyer.*

In old photographs of this lock, this white plaque stands out against the darker color of the sandstone and is a flag as to the lock's identification.

Today these first three locks are in a Fairfield County Public Park and can easily be studied by the public. The park and lock remnants are well maintained to the southern edge of the towpath. An interesting aspect of the park is that most of the land forms are still in place so that a visitor can see where the basin water was during the canal era.

## Lock 14

The next three locks are on private property but they are too reasonably well maintained. Lock 14 was called Smallwood Lock after the owner of a small store and saloon located near the lock, just west of Walnut Street on the south side of the towpath.

## Lock 15

Only a short distance away is Fickle Mill Lock (Lock 15). It was named for a small grist mill that stood near this lock. No specific data could be located on when the mill was in operation, but it must have been removed prior to the 1870s since there is no indication of it on Evert's Atlas map of 1872 or on the Ohio Canal Plats of 1895.

Ohio Canal plats indicate that the small stream called Hog Run ran to the west parallel to the canal all the way to the slackwater of the Little Walnut Creek, but a farmer changed its course in post-canal days so that it now enters the creek close to Lockville's Pickerington Road entrance.

## Lock 16

Just a short distance west of Lock 15 is the stonework of Lock 16. It was called Short Level Lock for obvious reasons. As the modern day motorist enters Lockville from the northwest (from U.S. Route 33) this is the first lock visible, behind some modern homes.

## Lock 17

The last lock which the Canal Commission considered part of the Lockville Locks was Lock 17 which is also on private property, but is not visible from the roadway. It is in a grove of trees and is not maintained although it has survived the last century reasonably well. It was called Swimer's Lock (sometimes spelled Swimmer) after the owner of some adjacent property.

While this lock is actually outside of the platted portion of Lockville and is about halfway between the western edge of Lockville and the slackwater crossing of Little Walnut Creek, it was generally considered one of the Lockville Locks.

The citizens of Lockville considered the lift lock (18) at the Little Walnut Creek, the state dam and its slackwater, and the guard lock on the western side of the Little Walnut as part of their system also. This often causes confusion since sometimes a historian will read about the "seven locks of Lockville" and other times the "nine locks of Lockville".

In any case, about a mile from the western edge of Lockville, the Ohio and Erie Canal crossed the Little Walnut Creek for a second time in Fairfield County. It was first crossed by an aqueduct south of Baltimore, but here it was crossed by a slackwater which added water to the canal. This is the first significant addition of water since the Licking Reservoir.

**Little Walnut Creek Dam**

The slackwater was created by a rare cut-stone dam built some two hundred yards below the canal crossing. This dam was built by William Tong, early canal contractor and founder of the town of Carroll. While the dam was rebuilt numerous times over its life, it kept its essential elements and form until it was removed by the Board of Public Works in 1911 because of flooding that was caused along the canal to the west.

This dam worked reasonably well in conserving water to supply the western portions of the canal (to Lockbourne where it received additional water from the Big Walnut Creek) but it was damaged many times by spring freshets. There are many newspaper accounts of the water rushing over its top, stopping canal traffic afraid of the rapid waters at the slackwater crossing.

**Little Walnut Creek Crossing**. With Lock 18 on the far bank and the guard lock partially shown in the foreground. The towpath bridge has been removed indicating a date *ca.* 1900-1910. Locktender Benadum holds one of his children. *Photo from the collection of Dave Meyer.*

**Lock 18 and Guard Lock**

On the southeastern side of the creek, Lock 18 (Creek Lock) was the last in the series to lower the canal level to the water level of the creek. A guard lock on the western bank protected the canal and adjacent land for about four miles to the next lock, about a mile west of Canal Winchester.

Lock 18, the guard lock, and the state dam were all watched by a locktender who lived near the guard lock. The Benadum family served as locktenders here from 1866 until after the canal was closed at the turn of the century. The first road to the north of this location is named Benadum Road.

The road running north and south next to the slackwater is called Amanda Northern Road and it carried land traffic along the western edge of the slackwater over the guard lock. It is one of the oldest roadways in this area. In earlier days, it was called "Wheeling to the Lakes Road" or "War Road" since it was used in the War of 1812. During the late canal era, the roadway went over the guard lock via a covered bridge and then crossed over Little Walnut Creek by way of a larger covered bridge located a short distance south of the dam. The towpath was carried across the slackwater by a typical towpath bridge.

## Summary

Like so many other towns which grew exclusively out of the canal trade, Lockville stopped growing and actually declined when the canal trade left. For a person interested in canal architecture or just general history, a visit to this site can be fascinating since it preserves probably the best cut-stone lock remnants left in Ohio.

§§§§§§§§§§§§§§§§§§§§§§§§§§§§

*Famously credited with preserving the culture and way of life on the canals, Pearl Nye's verses describe the southern part of the Ohio & Erie Canal in great geographic detail.*

Volume V (1967), No. 1, pp. 3-4
Volume V (1967), No. 2, pp. 20-21

### "BARD OF THE OHIO CANAL"

**Pearl Nye**.

There were many people for whom the canals were an enchanting world of their own, which inspired them to poetry and songs. It was a world of beautiful scenery, action and interest. The hardships were a part of their exciting life on the canal.

Captain Gerald R. Nye was one of the well known canal poets. His poems, set to music by himself, have been published and recorded in collections of Folk Songs. Captain Nye, born on a canal boat at Chillicothe in 1872, spent a large part of his life on his family boats "Warren" and "Tom Marfield". About 1939 he built a cabin from pieces of the old State boat "Rosalie" on the lock just south of the Walhonding aqueduct. There he could again live on the canal and write poetry on the towpath.

"Towpaths" will publish, beginning with this issue, selected verses of Nye's untitled poem, from the manuscript in the possession of Mr. T. H. Findley. This poem is especially interesting for its reference to place names on the Ohio-Erie Canal. The manuscript itself is an exceptional document, in that it was written in pencil on any handy sheet of paper and the whole thing pasted together into a roll over ten feet long.

## CAPTAIN NYE'S POEM

Portsmouth was a junction with the Ohio River Craft
Up and down its silver water oft we'd go
But our "Levels" were most beautiful there, I was so content:
Famous bridges, basins, spots – I loved them so.

Union Mills, Paint Creek, Ghost Orchard, Powder Mills, Brush Creek,
Lucasville, Bear Creek and Piketon on the way –
Sunfish, Jasper, Cutler's, Sam Stutt's, McGowen's, Burkheimer's,
Jasper Basin, great when in their day!

Smilie Cutler's, Trimbler's Bridge and Pee Pee Locks were fine
Waverly and Aqueduct come fresh to mind
The Lock at Dillard's, Crooked Creek, Emmet's Tavern, dry dock, mills,
Stahler's Store – and all were busy you would find.

On every side was work and fun, as happy there were we
O, no tongue can tell the half of it dear Pal
For good times then were everywhere and nature seemed to smile
In those balmy days upon the old canal.

Creel's Bridge and four mile basin, State Bridge and Westfall's too,
Fishing in the old Scioto there was grand
The canal had great sufficiency but oft we loved a change
It was great there with our poles or nets on hand.

'Twas paradise in winter for the hunter, trapper too
Large and small game, fowl abundant, yes dear pal
The early days were wonderful – we bagged them from our decks
In those balmy days upon the old canal.

Three Lock Feeder, Lunebeck's turnbridge, Paint Creek Aqueduct
Still House straight and Chillicothe, O so grand
Snyder's Coal Yard, elevators on the tow path side
Water front and slaughter house at our command.

O many loads of wheat and corn to Marfield's Mill we took
It was like and endless chain, O yes dear pal
Poor House dock and old Deer Creek, Scioto Valley Mills
What a part they played along the old canal!

The tumbleway at Marfield's Mills was unique, unsurpassed
Overhanging trees so bowery like and fine
Those great tall elms, willows, shaking hands above our heads
As they mingle shading it all – it was sublime.

The Two Mile straight above it is so wonderful, grand
Can I e'er forget such beauties, dear old pal
While everything that had a voice would join the serenade
There's no life or picture like the old canal.

In Yellowbud were Shasteem's store, Pinto's corn crib, warehouse
Bill Nye's grocery, Evenhacks Dock, Davis' Bar
George Klein's Place – what watermelons – trips from hand to mouth!
We would make while enroute, be it near or far.

The Bluffs were near and famous rustic beauty O so rare
Water scenes enriching everything, dear pal
No other people e'r were known to have such times as we
In those balmy days upon the old canal.

Forman's Mills, Wide Water, Aqueduct in Circleville
Little Walnut Creek and Mills of Good Intent
Cowhorns, Swamp, Bug Island, Lockbourne's change and covered bridge
Thrills of joy and gratitude to me they sent.

My childhood scenes were always dear, no doubt will ever be
For no youngster had a better time dear pal
As trips were like excursions, singing, music, more or less
O such times and fun we had on the old canal.

The "Big Rope" across the creek we'd "overhand" from lock to lock
Then Columbus bound we'd make a flying trip
And everything along the way was named so you could tell
Where we met or passed the last boat with a clip.

The Straight and Soft Shell Turtle Bridge and Cemetery Bend
Crooked Bridge, Big Elm, High Bank, Shadeville, pal
The Slip and Seed's Mills, Warehouse and Weeker's Grocery gay
General Store – all catered to the old canal.

Little Willows, Kelley's Corn Cribs, Hay Stack Basin too
Big Beechnut and Nigger Cabin, Old Grape Vine
Simpson's Bridge and Old Mudhen, Muskrat Bend, Big Limb Tree
Deep Cut Bridge and Four Mile Lock, how bright they shine.

The Waste Way, Brick-House-on-the-Hill, Wild Onion Bend and Marsh
Cabbage Patch and Snapping Turtle Run dear pal
The Starch Factory, its stinking slip; what corn we boated them!
Sweetest memories of my life, the old canal!

Groveport, Canal Winchester, Lockville, Carroll, Havensport
Basil, Baltimore, Licking slackwater, see
Millersport and three mile Deep Cut, Cook's Rock and Black Hand
Granville-Hebron Feeder, famous Tow Path – gems to me.

The Island Bridge and thereabout with beauty sure was blest
White Mill Basin, Newark, Cemeteries pal
And solemn were the moments – often – when we said goodbye
To our dear old boats upon the old canal.

§§§§§§§§§§§§§§§§§§§§§§§§§§§

*Nye's verses were the inspiration for an article by Lloyd Manley and others in 1997. This excerpt describes the difficulties in navigating slackwater pools on the Columbus Feeder.*

Volume XXXV (1997), No. 1, pp. 6-7

### TRAVEL ON THE SIDECUT by Lloyd Manley
### with assistance from David Meyer, Barnett Golding, and Terry Woods

The Nye family boats, like many, did not reach Columbus on every trip through mid-Ohio. Some, as they passed through Lockbourne travelling in either direction, might be carrying only a partial load destined for the capital city. They might choose to discharge this at the transfer warehouse near the feeder's junction, then continue on in the main canal, allowing another boat to ship it later to Columbus.

Other boats might carry a large cargo directly to Columbus, but drop off a small portion at the same warehouse to be moved by another vessel further along the main canal.

Passenger travel was a little more complicated, but could be expedited with smaller transfers, canal passengers from Cleveland to Columbus might shorten the distance and save time by transferring to a stage coach (or, after 1853, to an omnibus) at Canal Winchester or Groveport.

As Nye's boat entered the feeder from the south end, it passed under a small towpath bridge and a little beyond entered the guard lock of the Big Walnut slackwater pool. During this time, the mules could be unhitched and led across a nearby bridge over the wide pond, but meanwhile the crew had to grasp a sagging rope and slowly pull the heavily laden craft more than two hundred feet to the lift lock on the opposite side. This must have been a demanding task when the river's level was a little high and the current swift. Long poles and perhaps some device for clamping firmly on to the rope would come into play, with much rapid hitching and unhitching. A mistake would cause a boat to be carried against the bridge piers or dam, a potential disaster.

The long slackwater offered one advantage put to use by Pearl Nye's family and other boat people. They navigated far up Big Walnut Creek to load grain shipments that might otherwise have traveled by wagon to a mill.

Another method of crossing the slackwater utilized rapid acceleration of the boat in one of the locks by means of mule power, followed by release of the tow line as the boat emerged from the lock. Momentum then moved the craft all or part way across. The towline was rove through a block attached to a ring bolt in the lock wall close to the river and hitched for instantaneous release near the stern of the boat. The mules, walking in the opposite direction, were prodded to maximum effort. The helmsman leaned on the rudder to keep the craft away from the lock walls, others poled it away as it gathered speed. Poling and use of the stationary rope completed the crossing if momentum alone did not.

Other navigation problems arose if a canal boat was required to enter the Scioto River pool at Columbus. High water causing swift currents would be the worst difficulty, but even when the pool was low and tranquil, moored boats at the long wharves interfered with normal towpath use. If boatmen needed to dock at the river's west bank, they faced the hard work of poling across. For these reasons most boats discharged or loaded cargo in the canal or its small basin south of the guard lock. The 800 foot long dike built in the river south of Town Street may have alleviated some of these problems. A long timber wharf was even built at one of its sides. In spite of all of this, canal boat navigation on the Scioto's pool was usually less troublesome than that on the Ohio River at Cincinnati or the Maumee River at Toledo.

§§§§§§§§§§§§§§§§§§§§§§§§§§§

*In June 1834 Alexander Phillip Maximillian, Prince of Wied in Rhenish Prussia traveled the length of the Ohio Canal. This account of his impression of the Circleville area is extracted from Vol. 24 of* Early Western Travels, *Arthur H. Clark Co., Cleveland, 1906.*

<u>Volume XII (1974), No. 1, p. 4</u>

## TRAVELS IN THE INTERIOR OF NORTH AMERICA by Prince Alexander Phillip Maximillian

"We now came to the considerable town of Circleville, which has many brick buildings, and must have increased greatly since it was visited by Duke Bernhard of Saxe Weimar. The Duke gives a detailed description of the remarkable ancient walls, in the interior of which this place was built; but they have been greatly demolished since that time. The courthouse stands in the center of the Indian circle wall, and the greater part of the town still lies within it. - - - Here, too, we see another deplorable instance of the love of destruction which animates the Americans, for, instead of preserving these interesting ancient remains with the greatest care, they have erected buildings exactly on the site of the leveled walls, respecting the former state and opening of which nothing now remains, except some scanty, superficial accounts given by Attwater and other American writers.

"After we left Circleville, we saw, on the canal, a great number of shells (*Unio*), of a greenish colour, with darker stripes, which are very frequent here; most of them were floating without the animal, which was, however, found dead in some of them. The canal traverses a country agreeably diversified with wood and meadows, which were formerly covered with uninterrupted primeval forests - - - -.

"After traversing a wooded country, with remarkably fine sugar maples and walnut trees, we came to Walnut Creek, which flows through a shady forest. Near the little town, Lockbourn, which was founded only three years ago, there are eight sluices close together, where the Columbia Feeder issues from the canal, which rises at this place about 100 feet, then runs along the eminence. The forest is not so lofty on the Summit, and the tops of many of the trees are withered. Thus we traversed by water the fine forest of the state of Ohio, and as it was Sunday, saw the inhabitants in their best dresses. It was a most agreeable journey, during which we sat quite at our ease on the deck."

*The line of the canal was originally supposed to by-pass Circleville but local citizens collected a fund to change that. This account and photo are from the very first issue of* Towpaths.

Volume I (1963), No. 1, p. 3

## A CHANGE IN THE LINE OF THE CANAL
### Report of the Canal Commissioners, Jan. 22, 1833

"After it was determined to cross the Scioto at or above Circleville, it was found about $7,000.00 cheaper to cross near a mile above, than to cross at that town. But such a location would probably have resulted in the serious injury, if not the ruin, of Circleville. One half of this difference, the inhabitants of that town agreed to refund to the state by subscription, upon condition that the canal shall be carried to that point before crossing. These considerations induced the Commissioners to adopt that location. The citizens of Circleville were, however, permitted by the General Assembly, to apply their subscription to another purpose, so that the whole additional expense of this location fell upon the canal fund."

**The Circleville Aqueduct, winter of 1868**. Traces of the piers can still be seen in the river bed at low water from the bridge on State Route 22 at the west end of Circleville. *Photo from the Findley Collection.*

§§§§§§§§§§§§§§§§§§§§§§§§§§

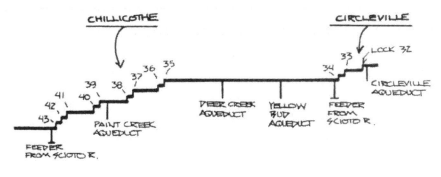

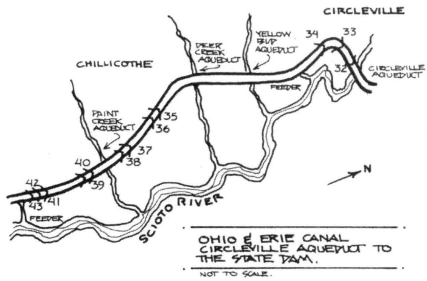

**Map of Ohio & Erie Canal from Circleville Aqueduct to State Dam below Chillicothe.** Section redrawn from original plan and profile by C.E. Gainey, C.E., 7-67. *From* Towpaths, *Vol. XXV (1987), No. 2, p. 15.*

*This article on the Ohio & Erie Canal in Ross County was put together by the editorial staff of* Towpaths *from period newspaper accounts and journal entries.*

Volume XXXV (1997), No. 2, pp. 5-9 & pp. 13-16

## THE OHIO & ERIE CANAL IN ROSS COUNTY

Scioto Gazette, November 23, 1831

"Among the many advantages which will result to the State and to the community generally, from the construction of the Ohio Canals the water power which they will create at almost every lock throughout their whole extent, is esteemed not to be the least valuable…" […]

"But the benefit from the creation of so much additional manufacturing power, in a country like ours, is not to be estimated by the dollars and cents which the use of it may throw into the public coffers of the State. Its advantages are to be valued by its usefulness to the community and by the multifarious human purposes to which it may be profitably applied. Scattered, as it is, along the line of three hundred and seventy miles of Canal, it will furnish sites, at convenient points, for the erection of every description of machinery which the wants of the country through which the Canals pass, may call for. This is one of the decided advantages which Canals possess over Rail Roads, in their passage through every country.

"Within the limits of this town, and at the locks two miles north of it, there will be a power to let, equivalent to eight runs of stone, at each place. This power, from the cheapness at which it may be improved, from its favorable local position and from the great facilities which the town, the country and the Canal offer for manufacturing extensively, creates two of the best sites on the Ohio Canal. To an enterprising company, who would erect extensive flouring mills, a paper and cotton mill, with a large woolen establishment, for the manufacture of the coarser fabrics of domestic wear, blankets, flannels &c. &c. - - which are much needed by the country - - the employment of this power would open a mine of wealth as inexhaustible to them as the fountain from which the power itself is supplied."

"Ten Days in Ohio; from the diary of a Naturalist" by Samuel P. Hildreth

[…] "We passed 8 locks between Circleville and Chillicothe[*], which are all built in a neat substantial manner, the top or coping stones being many of them 10 or 12 feet in length, 4 in breadth and a foot thick. We arrived at Chillicothe at nine o'clock a.m. This town is the seat of Justice for Ross County and was for many years also the seat of government for the State. It contains 3,000 inhabitants, and the whole county, 25,000. It takes its name from that of a celebrated Indian town, seated on the waters of Paint Creek, 12 miles northwest of here, which was probably the largest Indian village in the state of Ohio. Chillicothe has increased rapidly since the location of the canal, which passes directly through one of the principal streets, near the river. Water Street which fronts the river and along which the canal passes is 82 feet wide. Many fine warehouses are built along its borders and a great amount of business transacted. They have a beautiful market house and banking building. The other public buildings are not remarkable for beauty or taste."

<u>Scioto Gazette</u>, June 6, 1832

"PAINT CREEK AQUEDUCT. This splendid structure is now finished; and the water was let through it a few days ago. It is about two miles south of this place; and forms a part of the level which commences at the lower lock in town, and terminates in Lunebeck's plane. As a specimen of fine architectural masonry, it is, perhaps, not surpassed by any other work of the like description in this country; and promises to be as lasting as the ravages of time will permit any human edifice to endure.

---

[*] There were 4 locks between the Circleville Aqueduct and Chillicothe. Perhaps Hildreth counted each gate as a lock. Barney Golding pointed out a precedent for that.

Great credit is due to Messrs. Atherton & Price, the contractors under whose management it was erected. On Thursday last the *Union* of the Farmer's line – Captain Cash, commander – with about two hundred ladies and gentlemen on board, passed the Aqueduct and descended the Canal to a basin, one mile below it, being the first boat and the first party which have navigated that part of the Canal…"

"Mills on the Canal" by Towpaths Staff

For many years Chillicothe was a prominent grain and milling center. Three grinding mills (and a sawmill) were located in or near Chillicothe: David Adams (and others) leased water power for four runs of 4-1/2 foot stones at Lock 35 in 1832 for $500 a year, William McCague for three runs of 5' stones and land at Lock 37 in 1834 for $525 a year, and David Collins for 2 runs of stones and land at Lock 38 in 1836 for $338 a year. David Adams leased water power for two more runs at Lock 35 in 1836 for an additional $310.

David Adams ran the mill until the time of the Civil War and then sold it to Otho Marfield. In 1860 he congratulated T. J. Quin, superintendent of the division for some time, on the state of the canal: "[It] has been in better condition the past summer and fall than it has been for ten years. I have had a better supply of water and have ground double the quantity of wheat in the same length of time than any previous season for seven or eight years."

McCague's mill at the 4th Street Lock, the Frame Mill, was powered first by an overshot wheel and then in 1839 by a breast wheel. Ownership passed through many hands over the years. In 1881 when it was owned by George Ratcliff it was destroyed by fire and rebuilt. In 1889 Henry Keim bought it and installed a 40-horsepower Armstrong engine. No longer dependent on the whims of the canal, the mill produced "Sweet Violet" flour. In 1908 it burned again and was not rebuilt.

Millstones probably came from a flint-like deposit found along Raccoon Creek in Jackson or Vinton County, manufactured by Lantz & Richmond and sold by Thomas Orr & Co. in Chillicothe. In June, 1835, the Scioto Gazette reported tolls paid on seven pair of Raccoon Buhr Millstones.

Collins' mill at the 5th Street Lock was known as the Brick Mill by 1840 and also had a number of owners over the years: Atwood & Harvey, W. S. Sanford, Martin Schilder, Wm. Carson, Miles Ratcliff & Joseph Offutt in 1860, and Wells & Haynes.

Under the proprietorship of Martin S. Schilder and John J. Eichenlaub the Brick Mill ground all kinds of flour, corn meal and feed. Between November 25, 1874, and September 2, 1875, they bought 47 boatloads of corn from 17 area farmers. Boat names and captains, when listed in Schilder & Co's account books, were:

| | Captains | No Captains Listed | |
| --- | --- | --- | --- |
| *Companion* | J. Shaw | *M. K. Greene* | *N. L. Stockman* |
| *Wm. H. Reed* | Lewis and D. Pine | *D. E. Hill* | *Natural* |
| *Waltzer* | W. Dalzell | *Jennings* | *H. E. Ware* |

The corn was taken off the boat in a large tub and placed on a scale to be weighed. One boat, for example, unloaded 373 tubs for a total weight of 108,192 pounds; 1591 bushels, calculating at 68 pounds per bushel. Corn was bought by the bushel – 73¢ in this case – for a total of $1161.43.

George W. and Henry Renick leased sufficient water for a one-saw sawmill from the Canal near the crossing of Indian Creek just south of town in 1833 for $150 a year.

"Pork on the Canal" by Towpaths Staff

A great surplus was produced by farmers in the Scioto Valley, and much of it was fed to hogs and distilled into whiskey. The distillers also fed thousands of hogs their used mash. A good supply of salt for pork preservation was available from works at Zanesville and Jackson. Slaughtering of hogs could not begin until the cold weather had set in.

In early January 1850 three boats were sunk between Chillicothe and Portsmouth trying to deliver cargos of pork before the freeze. The *William Connell* sank two miles below Waverly after springing a leak. The *Arkansas* ran against the abutment of a bridge one and a half miles below Waverly and the *Rob Roy* sank near Lunebeck's mill on Indian Creek bottom.

§§§§§§§§§§§§§§§§§§§§§§§§§§§§

*Tomlinson's State Dam at "Three Locks" supplied the canal with water from a few miles below Chillicothe to its Portsmouth terminus.*

Volume XIX (1981), No. 3, pp. 33-34

### "THREE LOCKS" ON THE OHIO CANAL by Cecil S. Blair and Frank W. Trevorrow

The histories of Ross County supply information about Locks 41, 42, and 43 on the Ohio Canal in Franklin Township which are approximately 6 miles south of Chillicothe. *Pioneer Record and Reminiscences of the Early Settlers and Settlement of Ross County, Ohio* by Isaac J. Finley and Rufus Putnam (Robert Clarke & Co., Cincinnati, 1871) page 36 notes that "Richard Tomlinson, hotel-keeper at Three Locks or State dam was justice for several years, captain of militia, auctioneer…"

From the same source, "Joseph Hern was said to have been a soldier under Bonaparte…and keeps a grocery store on the Ohio Canal. Just below Mr. Hern's grocery store are the three locks and the State dam across the Scioto River. The dam is nearly one hundred yards in length, and is quite a resort for fishing parties, and Mr. Hern is always prepared to entertain guests on those occasions…Thomas Tomlinson was the first lock-tender, and Richard Tomlinson was the first grocer at these locks."

*History of Ross and Highland Counties, Ohio*, Williams Bros. (W. W. Williams, Cleveland, 1881) page 282, mentions that the State dam is "…one hundred yards in length, thrown across the Scioto…in 1832 as a feeder to the canal with three locks adjacent. The railroad station here, variously known as 'State Dam' or 'Three Locks'…and that there was no village in the township, but a post office at Higbys, Alma and on the Columbus and Portsmouth turnpike."

On page 283, it is mentioned that "…Thomas Tomlinson was the first lock-tender at the State dam, and his brother Richard the first grocer at the settlement here…" Joseph Hern or Hirn is not mentioned.

From the Board of Public Works Report of 1859, page 618 R.C. Philley is listed as lock tender at Tomlinson's dam Ohio Canal with wages of $16.66 per month, and had been employed for 12 months and had been paid $200.

The dam at Three Locks supplied water to the Canal as far as the terminus at Portsmouth. It was washed out during the 1913 flood. The trace of the Canal and remains of the locks can be seen by following "Three Locks Road" off US 23 south to Waverly. The Buckeye Trail Side Trail does not include the area of Three Locks.

**View of State Dam on the Scioto**. Including residence and store of Jos. Hirn & Brother. *From the Atlas of Ross County, 1875, p. 31.*

§§§§§§§§§§§§§§§§§§§§§§§§§§§

*The business activities of James Emmett, famed canal era entrepreneur of the Scioto Valley, are a primary area of emphasis in this 2008 article on Waverly by Dave Meyer.*

Volume XLVI (2008), No. 3, pp. 51-67

## WAVERLY AT THE 279 MILE MARKER by David Meyer

### A Canal Town is Founded

Mescheck Downing platted a town he called Uniontown in 1829 since he knew that the canal would run through the center of his land. A 23-year old named James Emmitt purchased the first lot and established the first business in the town. He continued to be a driving force in this town, Pike County and the Scioto valley for the next 60 years.

The Ohio Canal was opened in Waverly on September 6, 1832 with a large crowd gathering along the dry canal bed awaiting the water to flow into town. No water appeared. Finally about noon water trickled and then rushed through the canal prism and the crowd cheered loudly. It seems that the water that was added by the Scioto River at Three Locks in Ross County had to flow through some areas that were a gravel-type of soil and it just soaked up the water heading for Pike County until it was saturated. This caused a delay in the water reaching Uniontown.

A post office opened in Uniontown in 1830 with James Emmitt being the first postmaster. Mr. Emmitt kept a store and boarding house in his home and he placed the post office here too. Later, he constructed a large mansion on a different site. While boarding at Emmitt's boarding house, canal engineer Francis Cleveland realized that there was another Uniontown in Ohio and that the name of this location would have to change. Since he was reading Scott's *Waverly* novels at that time, he suggested the name Waverly and it was adopted and remained the same since.

Michael Miller and Martin Bowman of Chillicothe owned the first boat to arrive at Waverly and its name was the *Governor Worthington*. It carried cargo along with several passengers who were witnessing the opening day ceremonies. The boat carried a small cannon on the deck and it was fired at brief intervals with the sound echoing in the surrounding hills. A great public celebration was held at noon in honor of the canal's opening. Robert Lucas (of Waverly) and Duncan McArthur, both gubernatorial candidates, gave rousing speeches on the anticipated prosperity that the canal would bring to Pike County and the State of Ohio.

James Emmitt's life activities were intertwined with the canal and the Scioto Valley. When the first boat arrived in Waverly in the fall of 1832, James Emmitt was one of those standing on the bank and when he saw the little *Governor Worthington* glide by he decided he must own it. He discussed it with his friend Eli Harrison and they went into a partnership and bought the boat for $600. After Waverly's opening day celebration, James Emmitt steered his boat as far south as he could go with a load of cargo and several of his friends from Waverly. Since the canal was only open as far as Lock 49 at Bertha in Scioto County he probably stopped there. All along the canal banks, people gathered and yelled and waved at the passing boat and its passengers. Several years later James Emmitt traded the small *Governor Worthington* for a flat boat loaded with corn which he promptly sold for a sizable profit. The same boat came back to the Waverly area many years later and was moored at the State's boat facility. It still had the same brass and copper bell on it that James Emmitt had installed many years earlier. It remained in the basin for quite some time until it was finally stripped and sunk. The bell can still be seen in a museum in Waverly.

In 1837, pioneer citizens of Michigan depended on Cleveland (just a small town then) for supplies, and Cleveland imported from the canal ports of Ohio. Mr. Emmitt originally had a contract with McConathy & Taylor to buy corn at whatever price he could and sell to them for a relatively high profit. Soon he realized he could make even more money by shipping directly to Cleveland himself. He bought corn throughout the Scioto valley, shelled and weighed for 25 cents a bushel, loaded into his own freight boats, towed it to Cleveland and sold it for a dollar a bushel. He also bought flour from Newton Moore, who owned the "old river mill" south of Waverly for $3.37 a bushel and sold in Cleveland for ten dollars a bushel. In that year, Mr. Emmitt cleared $10,000 on his transactions which was a huge sum of money for any person in those days.

## A Tour Through Waverly

When an automobile travels south on Route 23 through the middle of the city, the occupants may look around to see if there are any remnants of the canal prism. It is difficult to see the canal prism because the automobile is traveling in the center of the canal. To try to recreate a trip on the canal through Waverly during the late canal era, we will begin at the northern edge of the Pike County city.

The canal entered Waverly from the northeast with a wide water area at the northern end of town which many local citizens used for washing their horses. The Kilgore covered bridge was just a bit south of the wide water area and it was a favorite loading place for local farmers since it had a trap door in the floor so that a wagon could be pulled over the open hole and the grain load be dropped directly onto the canal boat.

The next major feature along the canal was Gehres' Planing Mill and Lumber Yard which was located south of Water Street. Their equipment for planing lumber was powered by steam. Lumber was brought in by canal boat to their lumber yard on the southeast side of the canal and a scow was tied between the yard and the boat to bring the lumber for planing. Finished (dressed) lumber was sent to a canal boat in the same manner. Finished lumber was usually sent to Portsmouth for shipment up or down the Ohio River. Just west of the planing mill across North Street, the Waverly Public School grounds occupied a complete block between Clough and Mullen Streets. The James Emmitt mansion was built in 1861 on Walnut Street across from the school and still stands today. Prior to moving, Mr. Emmitt lived in the building which housed his general store on Market Street for many years. Mr. Emmitt's Wine House and Ice House were located nearby the mansion. Local legend says that there was an underground tunnel between the mansion and the wine house and ice house. His opera house was located at Walnut and East Street intersection.

As a canal boat came south, the first bridge over the canal was called "Third Bridge" locally and it crossed the canal at East Street. The 279 mile marker was located along the towpath just across from Best Slaughterhouse a few yards north of the bridge. This meant that the boat that was headed for Portsmouth had only another 29 miles to go until it reached its destination. There was a large cattle holding pen near the canal at Best's Slaughterhouse and the boatmen could smell the slaughterhouse aroma as they floated by the area.

Schooler's Tannery processed hides from the local slaughterhouses and used tanbark hauled in on canal boats to process the leather. It was just southeast of East Street. Later, Schooler's Tannery was moved south of Crooked Creek near the aqueduct.

Just one block from the canal on North Street, George Emmitt (James' brother) owned the Waverly Woolen Mill. The topography of Pike County was conducive to raising sheep and so this woolen mill was a busy place during sheep shearing times. The finished cloth was then shipped on the canal to clothing factories and other outlets.

At the High Street Bridge crossing the canal, a toll house was located at Emmitt's warehouse. This frame building was built by James Emmitt in 1837 for his shipping business and to operate his general store. A dance hall was operated on the second floor of the building for many years. Some of the toll collectors of Waverly were T.J. Graham (1860), W.C. Safford (1878–1880), Abisha Downing (1880–1883), Jonathan Sawyer (1883), William F. Taylor (1884–1886), H.R. Snyder (1886–1892), John Daily (1892–1894), George Barch (1894–1898), S.L., Patterson (1898–1900), James C. Voelker (1900–1906), and Charles W. Watkins (1907 until 1909). Many of these toll collectors carried on other businesses in Waverly so that the "collections" were only part time occupations. Charles Smith operated his hardware store near the bridge during the canal era and later in the warehouse building until it was torn down in 1978.

Gehres' Furniture Store and Undertakers was located at the corner of North Street and High Street. It was common for furniture builders of that time to also act as coffin builders and undertakers. The city park (often called Canal Park) was located along Water Street (now Emmitt Street) between High Street and Market Street. It was about 50 feet wide and all types of local festivities were held there.

Jim Emmitt's General Store was on the corner of the Market Street Bridge over the canal. Local citizens usually called this Emmitt's Bridge. This building was constructed in 1837 by James Emmitt and he used it to sell all types of merchandise. He also operated his shipping business from this location. Next door, he had a retail furniture store where he marketed the furniture constructed in his factory. Waverly Bentwood Company occupied this building later and they built spokes and rims for buggies and wagons. It was owned by J. Hoffman and George Ed Breece for many years. They often floated hickory logs lashed together to form a raft down the canal from the region around Three Locks in Ross County to their factory. The "raft" was captained by Waverly citizen Dan Blake. He maneuvered the logs to the mill where they were soaked before being sawed. A favorite past time of Waverly youngsters was to gather on the bridges and watch the log raft come down the canal and they would yell at the men maneuvering it. When timber was to be hauled from longer distances, Messrs. Breece and Hoffman used a small canal boat named *William Jennings Bryan*. After the Waverly Bentwood Company left the building, it was used by Greenbaum's as a furniture store.

Gehres' Sash and Door Company was located on the southeast side of the canal at Water and High Streets. Pine was shipped in on the canal from Michigan to manufacture doors, window sash and wood moldings. Pine was abundant in Michigan and was cut and shipped to ports on Lake Erie where it was transported to Cleveland by lake steamships. At Cleveland, canal boats were loaded with it and shipped it all over Ohio.

The Park Hotel was a large brick structure which faced the canal on the southeast side along Water Street. It provided room and board to many canal travelers who decided to stay a while at Waverly. Later, it became the Grand Hotel and it still stands today on Emmitt Street.

A two-story hotel building was built by Mescheck Downing in 1832 on a lot at the corner of Water and Market Street, but it was destroyed during a fire which burned much of Waverly in 1858. A second fire in the same year burned the original Emmitt House Hotel and Thomas Howard's Tannery which was above it. James Emmitt rebuilt his Emmitt House Hotel in 1861 and it is still in operation today. He built it in anticipation of the Pike County county seat being moved from Piketon to Waverly. One of the craftsmen who worked on the structure was Madison Hemings, son of Sally Hemings and allegedly Thomas Jefferson. He was generally considered to be a master carpenter. The Emmitt House was considered the finest hotel in the Scioto Valley. As the Scioto Valley Railroad and Ohio Southern Railroad entered the area in the late 1870s, the Emmitt House had a horse-drawn buggy shuttling

**Emmitt House in Waverly**. Photographed in 2004.

salesmen from the stations to the hotel. Special accommodations were made so that salesmen could show their "wares and samples" in a front room to local customers before they left to travel the country side to show rural Pike County store keepers their merchandise. The building is still being used as a restaurant.

On North Street was Bissell Port Hotel and Emmitt's Planing Mill. James Emmitt built this planing mill in 1863 to produce lumber for his furniture factory and his nearby lumber yard. Logs were often floated down the canal to his mill pond and then would be sawed into lumber. He leased the facility to others to operate.

In 1861, James Emmitt helped relocate the county government from Piketon to Waverly. The County Court House and Jail were located on Second Street just east of Market Street. When Mr. Emmitt wanted the county seat moved to Waverly the citizens of the county east of the Scioto River objected strongly at this proposal since there was no bridge or road across the river to reach Waverly and it would make their lives more difficult. To resolve the problem, Mr. Emmitt offered to pay for a turnpike and bridge over the river between Piketon and Waverly in addition to paying for the construction of a new courthouse building. The county voters approved the move.

After passing through the business district portion of Waverly, the canal approached the aqueduct to cross Crooked Creek. A roadway bridge was adjacent to the aqueduct. The roadway was called Towpath Road. Initially, a stone culvert originally was used to cross the creek but it was destroyed by flooding on January 19, 1862. An aqueduct was quickly constructed to replace the culvert. Just south of the aqueduct, there was a locktender's house in addition to Waverly Tannery.

Locktenders at Waverly tended Lock 44. It was called Waverly Lock. Some of the locktenders at Waverly were John Reiley (1859–1860), Thomas Davis (1878–1892), J. Swires (1892–1893), Ben Lewis (1893–1900), Hugh Scott (1900–1902), and Jacob Lewis (1902–1904). The remnants of Lock 44 are still in Canal Park at the southern end of Waverly.

South of Lock 44 was a large mill pond (basin) on the west side of the canal with several businesses clustered around it. Two mill races led to the west side of the canal. At the northwest end of the basin was James Emmitt's dry dock which was used to repair boats and build floating bridges during the late canal era. These were similar to pontoon bridges used by the military and could be moved aside when not in use.

**Waverly**. Celebration along the canal (left) and Crooked Creek Aqueduct (right). The aqueduct collapsed during the 1913 flood but the towpath bridge remained standing.

Just about fifty feet up the hill from the dry dock, Emmitt's cooper shop built barrels and kegs for shipping flour and whiskey. About 15 men usually worked at the cooperage. In addition to the commercial operations at the basin, the southern division's state boat used this area for its base of operations. Many of the men who worked on the Ohio Canal's Scioto Division lived in the Waverly area.

Waverly Mills, a flouring mill, was near the mill pond and had a mill race which emptied on the down side of the lock. There were four mill stones in the mill and it was built by John Howe, John F. Armstrong and Francis Campbell (all of Chillicothe) in 1836. James Emmitt bought a 1/3 interest in 1838 and he expanded it with two more stones so it could produce up to 100 barrels of flour a day.

Another mill race from the basin led to a stone saw mill. Originally built to card wool, Richard Waters leased hydraulic power for this mill from the state. Before the wool carding mill was completed,

Waters sold it to William and John Butt, who converted the first floor to saw stone while the second floor continued as a woolen mill and was operated by a Mr. Kemp. The stone saw mill was used to saw sand stone quarried from a hill south of Waverly near what is now Lake White. Its sawn sand stone was shipped to many locations for use as building material.

Pee Pee Mills was a large four story structure and it was built by George Emmitt, James' brother, in 1864. This mill used the canal's hydraulic power and steam power was added in the late canal days along with a roller mill. This mill could produce about 70 barrels of flour a day. In 1883, the mill advertised that it sold grain, flour, feed, Jackson Hill coal (from the Nelsonville area), lime, cement and calcine plaster.

Just beyond the stone saw mill was a short side cut from the canal. Jim Emmitt's Distillery (built in 1845) along with a malt house and a large brick warehouse was located on this side cut. The distillery was enlarged in 1850 to produce 100 barrels of whiskey a day using 1200 bushels of grain. Typically, the spent mash was fed to hogs kept nearby on the hillsides. Up to 5000 hogs were fed the mash from the distillery. When fattened, the hogs were butchered, smoked or salted, and then the pork products sold. Emmitt's canal boats were always searching canal ports for corn to use in his distillery. During the early days of the Civil War, James Emmitt estimated that he made $4,000 a day from his two distillery operations at Waverly and Chillicothe. By 1880, the whiskey tax had caused such a deterioration in the market that this distillery was down to 25 barrels a day.

The Bauersach's (sometimes spelled Bowersox) Brickyard was located on the southeast side of the canal and Columbus & Portsmouth Turnpike (now U. S. Route 23). The yard was located near the railroad bridge which carried the Springfield, Jackson and Pomeroy Railroad over the canal.

James Emmitt joined Ranson and McNair of Cleveland in 1836 to form the Eagle Line of freighter and passenger packets. The company owned twelve boats and 130 horses and operated between Portsmouth and Cleveland. Their competition was the Troy and Ohio Line and it was owned by Pease and Allen, The Farmer's Line operated by Chamberlain & Company and the Troy and Erie Line which was owned by Standard, Griffith and Company.

In the early canal days, horses were kept at "stations" along the canal and an animal tender maintained the animals until a boat arrived and then the team was changed. It was similar to pony express operations. Since the boat lines were very busy and operating 24 hours a day, the animals were soon overworked and became ill and underweight and could not continue to operate. This cost the lines severely. Someone finally got the idea of building a stable on the boat and then the animals could be carried with it and could be rested between "pulls." Before this change it cost the lines 26 cents per mile and after the change it was reduced to six cents a mile.

The Eagle Line was contracted to move the reservation Indians in Ohio so they could be moved to the west. Many of these peoples were moved on every boat through Waverly toward Portsmouth and the Ohio River. A story was told about one of the Indian transports that was sad for the natives on the boat. Just north of Waverly, an old squaw became injured and died while being transported on a boat. The Indians carried the dead squaw with them until the boat reached Camp Creek just below Waverly where there had been a break in the canal. The Indians were required to walk to Portsmouth with their goods being transported by wagon. Every time the group of Indians stopped for a short time, they would begin dancing around the corpse "while hooping and hollering." This practice continued for several days until at last they were compelled to bury the decaying and smelly corpse.

There has been speculation that James Emmitt owned more boats than any other person on the Ohio canal system. Some of the boats' names that he owned were *Select, Cooker, Buck, PP, Hunter, Maryland No. 1, Madam Roland, Marat, Corn, Robin, Cortes, Sethel Young, Noah's Ark, J.D. Mairs, Fulton, J.R. Harris, E.D. Jones, Q.R. Poston* and *Geo. A. Emmitt.* Some of the other boats of Waverly were *Waverly, James Davis, Young Napoleon* (scow), *Clipper No. 2, Elk, Grampus, Coaker, Hibernia No. 2, Buck* and *Newark.*

Today, Waverly is typical of many of the towns and cities along the canal's route. While it did have a railroad station, it has struggled economically to achieve the same glory it had in the 1800's.

§§§§§§§§§§§§§§§§§§§§§§§§§§§§

*The southern terminus of the Ohio & Erie Canal at Portsmouth is a difficult place to understand, even for die-hard canawlers. Thanks to Brad Bond for clearing up the confusion.*

Volume XXXVII (1999), No. 1, pp. 1-14

## THE SOUTHERN TERMINATION OF THE OHIO & ERIE CANAL by Brad Bond

### The Plan in 1828

"...it was decided that the canal be continued on the west side of the river, to a point immediately opposite the narrow isthmus, between the Scioto and the Ohio, at the lower end of the town of Portsmouth; and that a cut be made through the isthmus, so as to form a direct communication between the termination of the canal and the Ohio river...the canal will intersect the Ohio at a point presenting as deep water and as secure a shelter for steam boats, as any other on the river. It is believed that a convenient channel to admit the passage of steam boats from the Ohio into the Scioto river, at the point of terminating the canal, may easily be formed and secured. In this harbor steam and canal boats may meet and exchange their cargoes with perfect ease and safety, during much the greatest part of the year...the channel of the Scioto presents a harbor much more safe for the meeting...than can be found in the strong current of the Ohio."

Francis Cleveland, Grover's uncle, drew up a map showing the Scioto River snaking its way amongst old river beds on its way to a confluence with the Ohio about a mile downstream of Portsmouth. He sketched in a basin just north of Portsmouth on the east side of the Scioto with the canal locking in from the west side in the last and biggest loop before the Scioto headed west to join the Ohio. The map also shows a cut through the isthmus with a lock to the Ohio River and a dam in the Scioto. See the centerfold maps to follow the changes that followed (the 1828 plan is Stage 2). [Ed. Note: Centerfold maps have been reproduced on p. 182.]

Eads and McGregor had won the contract for the three locks at West Portsmouth in June, 1829. The section across the bottom lands had also been let. Bids for the three remaining locks - two on the west side and one in the cut - , the cut itself, and a dam on the Scioto for a slackwater crossing were solicited in November, 1829.

### "NOTICE TO CONTRACTORS

PROPOSALS will be received at PORTSMOUTH, on the

SEVENTH OF DECEMBER NEXT

for constructing two sections, embracing the Southern termination of the Ohio Canal.

THE PRINCIPAL ITEMS OF WORK ARE

*Three Locks and some Heavy Embankments,*

A DAM ACROSS THE SCIOTO,

And a Cut 40 feet in depth through the Isthmus into the Ohio river.

Nov. 25                                   M. T. WILLIAMS. Act. Com."

Lemuel Moss won the contract for the cut and the dam. What happened next and when is unrecorded, but Moss certainly would have worked on the cut before damming the river. As Frank Trevorrow put it, "The Scioto proved wholly uncooperative…it poured through the cut, forming for itself a new mouth." Lock, dam and east-side basin were probably never built. A toll bridge across the Scioto built over the cut was wiped out in a later flood.

The canal was declared finished December 1, 1832, except for a second outlet lock. The Annual Report was tight lipped about what happened.

> "The canal, at its southern extremity, terminates in the Scioto river on its western side, about 200 yards from its junction with the Ohio.

> "The Scioto formerly united with the Ohio one mile further west than the present point of junction, which is now immediately at the lower, or western end of the town of Portsmouth. A narrow isthmus of 140 yards in breadth, at top, and 154 yards at the level of low water, separated the two rivers at this place. Through an artificial cut across this neck of land, the Scioto now passes into the Ohio, having reduced its bed through this artificial cut, to the level of low water in the latter river."

A second lock was added at the outlet to reach the lower water level of the undammed Scioto in 1834.

### The Portsmouth Dry Dock and Steamboat Basin Co.

Francis Cleveland, in 1833, published a map illustrating a new proposal - a canal branch and basin on the west side of the Scioto River. This led to an 1839 authorization by the Legislature of the

Portsmouth Dry Dock & Steam Boat Basin Co. with capital stock of $200,000. Financing from New York City included John Jacob Astor.

Use of the locks on the Scioto proved to be troublesome as described by William Case who travelled by canal from Cleveland to Portsmouth in 1838.

"About 2 p.m. we arrived at Portsmouth. The manner of getting the packet from the end of the canal round to Portsmouth is very difficult and somewhat dangerous. The canal enters into the Scioto, and the boats have to be poled, or drawn by hand, down some 60 or 70 yards to the Ohio, then round a point of land and up the Ohio 80 or 100 yards to the dock. During high water, they sometimes struggle very hard, and one or two weeks before we arrived, a boat drifted down the Ohio nearly a mile."

Five years later the problems were the same:

"At the southern termination of this canal, some expense has been necessarily incurred the past season in removing the drift from the lower levels, which is brought down and deposited at every considerable rise in the Ohio and Scioto rivers, and, also, in removing deposits of sand and mud from the locks and entrances to them, and the cut connecting the two rivers. Additional protections have also been made to the west side of the channel leading to the Ohio, and to a point above, which are exposed to the action of the Scioto. At certain stages of the water at this point, either at the approach of low water in the Ohio, or when a rise takes place in the Scioto and not a corresponding one in the Ohio, very considerable difficulty is experienced in passing boats from the lower lock, around through the cut, to the landing in front of the town of Portsmouth."

But it appeared that the Dry Dock Co. plans might provide relief:

"The improvements now being made by the Portsmouth Dry Dock and Steamboat Basin Company, will, to some extent, remedy this difficulty; and when their plans are fully carried out, the facilities afforded by their works will, to a very great extent, if not wholly, remedy existing evils. The improvements already made by this company consist in the construction of a sidecut about one half mile in length, branching out on the west side of the canal, above the third lock, which is twenty-eight feet above low water in the Ohio, and terminating in a large basin on the bank of the Ohio river. In front of this basin, and on the immediate bank of the river, a gently sloping grade, well secured with stone protection and McAdamized, is constructed, and between the basin and grade several stone and brick warehouses have been erected, and they have already commenced doing a share of the forwarding and mercantile business. Their contemplated improvements consist of a steamboat basin and dry dock, with two locks of sufficient size to introduce the larger class of steamboats; also, the extending of their grade for additional warehouse facilities, and the construction of a bridge across the new channel of the Scioto, to connect Portsmouth proper and the company's improvements."

The Dry Dock Co. completed a toll bridge connecting the canal basin (Stage 4) to Portsmouth in 1849. It eventually met the same fate as its 1832 predecessor, wiped out in a flood. The locks, and dry docks were never built, but the stone "protection" along the Ohio river bank near the new mouth of the Scioto was still visible in 1998. The stones are massive; 8 to 10 feet long and 4 to 5 feet wide. The sidecut was used again in 1877 for the new outlet locks (Stage 5).

## Proposal for a Lateral Canal on the East Side

In response to a resolution of the General Assembly dated March 10, 1838, Alexander Bourne surveyed, leveled and estimated the cost of five routes for crossing the Scioto River to run the Ohio canal down the east bank of the Scioto River. There were two reasons for this; one was to include Piketon on the route, the other was to terminate in Portsmouth instead of in West Portsmouth.

After discussing the various options for crossing the Scioto upstream of Portsmouth and downstream of Circleville, Bourne commented as follows on access to the Ohio.

"There appears to be no necessity whatever, for locking the canal down to the Ohio river, which would cost about 40,000 dollars, and would be nearly useless.

"On this subject we have the benefit of experience on a large scale. The Miami canal was locked down to the Ohio river, about 120 feet, and according to the best information which I can obtain, not more than two or three boats have ever passed the locks. The Pennsylvania canal was also locked down to the river at Pittsburgh, but the locks are not used, and in both cases, the canal business is all done at the basins above the locks.

"...The best method of connecting the canal trade with the Steamboat trade of the Ohio river may be described as follows: Let the warehouses be built on the southside of the basin in Portsmouth. Then the steamboat freighted with goods for any port on the canal, or the lakes, or in New York, would discharge them on the river landing, and immediately pass on, up, or down, the river. The goods would be immediately drayed up to the warehouse of the commission merchant to whom they were consigned, to be forwarded by the first canal boat that was ready to take them. When goods come down the canal, they would be immediately stored in the warehouse of the commission merchant to whom they consigned to be drayed down to the river landing, when a steamboat arrived to take them.

"The Ohio canal is now locked down to the level of the Ohio river at low water, but nearly all the articles of transportation are stored and drayed twice, because the steamboat trade of the Ohio river is the *main* trade, and the steamboats cannot wait for some particular canal boat to arrive, that is bound for the port of destination of the goods, and of whose captain, and his responsibility, the steamboat captain knows nothing -- and who could not be designated by the original shipper of the goods -- but the commission merchants are generally known and trusted, and both owner and carrier know that they can safely deposit the goods with them, and I have no doubt but this method would be adopted by all the men of business who are connected with the Ohio river trade...

"Note. -- I admit that some cases may occur in which it should be convenient to pass a loaded canal boat, down to the Ohio, to be towed by a steamboat, a few miles up or down the river, particularly if the load was corn or grain in bulk. It would also be convenient to lock up boats from the river to the canal, if loaded with pig iron, coal or stone; but these cases would be so few in proportion to the whole canal business, as to form but small exceptions to a general rule, and the exception ought not to prevail against the rule. The locks would also be expensive, liable to obstruction and injury from the current of the river, and would form a bar in the river, which would probably injure the landing so much, as to render the locks a nuisance."

On March 16, 1839, the General Assembly authorized placing the route proposed by Bourne on the east side of the Scioto at or above Piketon under contract, but the Fund Commissioners failed to procure funds. The plan to run the canal down the east side was revived in 1846, but again it did not bear fruit.

## Where Did the Exchange of Goods Take Place?

When water was high, south-bound goods were dropped off as far up the canal as Cole's Basin, three miles north of Lock 51, and then carted to the bridge, if intact, or to the outlet lock (Stage 4, Lock 54) for ferrying across the river when the flood had receded. When low, they might be boated as far as the wharf at the outlet lock or even boated around the point to the Ohio River steamboat wharf.

According to H. A. Lorberg, Portsmouth historian, by 1844 there was a wharf at the canal terminal on the west side of the Scioto River. Canal boats unloaded their cargo on to flatboats there for shipment downriver.

"When the Ohio River was at a proper stage, a rope ferry across the Scioto enabled canal boats to come to the [Ohio River] wharf to discharge their freight, and it often happened that twenty or thirty boats were lying at the wharf awaiting return cargoes of sugar and molasses from the Sunny South for transportation toward the lakes."

Dr. Albert C. Koch, a fossil collector and museum founder in St. Louis, had another slant on the Portsmouth accommodations, arriving there in September, 1844, on his way to Maysville, famous for fossils:

"Last evening we came to the Ohio, but we could not cross the river [to Kentucky] because the night was too dark... We would have liked to stay on the boat until we could board a steamboat, and therefore offered to pay for breakfast, but the sailors and innkeepers here are in collusion so that we absolutely had to go to an inn. We had hardly taken our breakfast when a steamboat arrived from Cincinnati..."

The southern termination problem was reviewed again in 1854:

"...transhipments very difficult, and the termination of the canal on the side of the river opposite to Portsmouth, makes it almost impossible to reach the canal during high water. For several years past arrangements have been made with the New York Company [aka Dry Dock Co.] to keep a temporary bridge in times when the water is low, and a ferry boat when the water is high, for the purpose of facilitating the transhipment of freight".

A permanent bridge was recommended as a solution to the problem. The Portsmouth Bridge Co. was incorporated to build one connecting 2nd Street with the outlet of the canal. A road was authorized on the towpath between Union Mills and the outlet lock. The towpath was transferred to the other side of the canal. Built in 1858, the bridge was flooded out in 1859 and rebuilt in 1860. It was free to those engaged in canal navigation for annual payments of $600 by the Board of Public Works to the bridge company.

In 1858 the Board of Public Works greeted the first suspension bridge with the following comments which confirm the use of the Basin and warehouse on the west side of the Scioto to that date.

"In almost every year there have been times when boats could not pass into or out of the canal, and the cargoes have of late years been usually transferred by a short drayage between the side cut of the Portsmouth Dry Dock and Steamboat Basin Company and the Ohio River at the warehouse, a short distance below the mouth of the Scioto. On account of the better facilities offered by the new bridge for carrying cargoes to the Ohio at the Portsmouth landing, the discharging and receiving of canal freights will hereafter, at times of low water, be mostly done at the locks near the terminus of the canal..."

An undated sketch of one of these suspension bridges from the Portsmouth side shows the three-story National Hotel (built 1850s, razed 1880) in the foreground at the corner of Front and Scioto Streets and, in the background, a canal boat entering the Scioto River from the outlet lock just downstream from the bridge.

In 1866 there was a serious threat to the canal from the Scioto River's tendency to create new channels:

"During the past summer the Scioto River cut a new channel across the alluvial bottom, near its mouth, directing its course almost square against the canal bank. If permitted to continue in this new channel there would be imminent danger of its cutting directly through the canal; and not only would the canal be thus severed, but the important graveled county road leading to the Union Mills, and to the northward and westward from Portsmouth, would be cut through, and the Portsmouth suspension bridge would be isolated and rendered useless. In view, therefore, of the magnitude of the impending danger, an arrangement was entered into, in the latter part of October, between the Commissioners of Scioto County, the Portsmouth Bridge Company and the Lessees of the Public Works, by which a channel will be cut from the point where the present new channel makes its turn to the westward, in a straight line towards the suspension bridge. By throwing obstructions across the tortuous channel in which the river now flows and turning it into this new cut, it is hoped that the danger will be averted. The expense of the work will be borne by the parties above referred to."

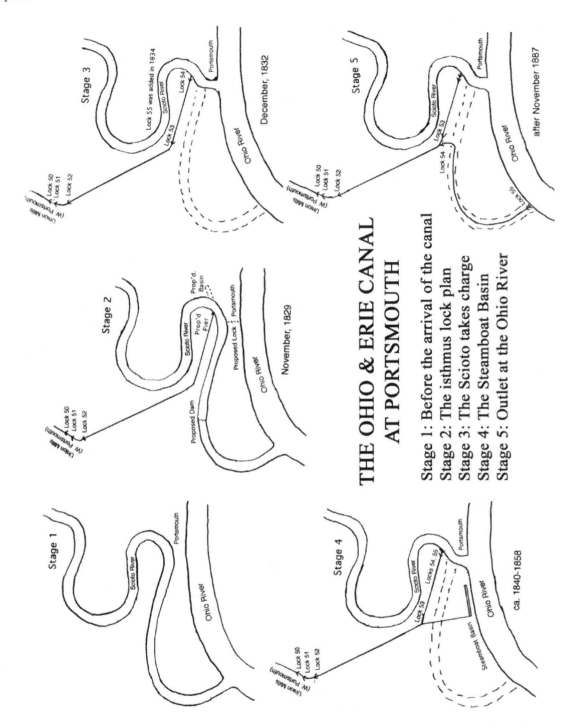

**THE OHIO & ERIE CANAL AT PORTSMOUTH**. The southern termination was plagued by frequent floods in both the Scioto and Ohio River watersheds. These tended to fill the outlet locks with debris and jeopardize the canal itself. Transfer of cargo and passengers took place at the Portsmouth wharf, Lock 51, further north at Cole's Basin, the Steamboat basin or at the mouth of the canal depending on water level and the year. Several stages in canal development at Portsmouth are illustrated in the maps shown here.

## Termination on the Ohio River

By 1879 there was a new problem:

"The Commissioners of Scioto County have, without compliance with the law, built a bridge for the crossing of a free turnpike road, over the Ohio Canal, near Portsmouth, and have built one of the abutments on top of and so near the face wall of the second lock [from] the Ohio River [Lock 54, Stage 4, aka Red Bridge Lock], as, by its extra weight, to push one side of the lock so far inward and to make it so narrow as to prevent the passage of ordinary freight boats through it.

"The evil was sought to be remedied by cutting off the face of the lock wall, and, for a time, it succeeded in preserving navigation, but the pressure still continues, and the lock is again so narrow as to prevent the passage of boats through it with safety."

Eight years later the two-lock termination on the Scioto River was abandoned for a double lock on the Ohio River (Stage 5). This turned out to be no more successful than the two locks on the Scioto River although the structures still stand. The timing was bad; the railroads had finally reached far enough into the Scioto valley to affect even local canal traffic. So why did they build them? The statement of the Board of Public Works in 1887 is not much help.

"During the present season there has been completed an improvement of greater value to the Ohio Canal than has been made probably during the past forty years. Terminal facilities have been provided and a connection made with deep water in the Ohio river. The improvements are of the most substantial and durable character. While providing this outlet by the way of the old Scioto river bed, the level below Elbow lock [Lock 53] has been raised and the Portsmouth wharf at the canal renewed.

"This improvement marks a new era in the history of the Ohio Canal. Boats can now enter the Ohio river, be towed to their destination, whether far or near, and discharge or receive cargoes. They are no longer confined to the limits of the Ohio Canal, but the products from or for other ports on the Ohio river now will add their tolls to the State revenues in proportion to the use of these increased terminal facilities."

There is no mention of this plan in the previous Annual Report. What changed to make this happen? There was a change in management. Board members in 1885 were all from the Miami & Erie area (Delphos, Defiance and Xenia). Frank Snyder (Dayton) as chief engineer in 1885 commenting on a plan for a ship canal similar in size to the enlarged Erie Canal for the Miami & Erie, the most viable Ohio canal, wrote:

"I am reluctantly compelled to confess my inability to see any inducement for the General Government to undertake such a work at the present time."

He was replaced by Samuel Bachtell, and the new Board member, Wells S. Jones, was from

Waverly. The District Superintendent, W. H. Jones, also from Waverly started work in the Spring of 1887, and The Portsmouth Times celebrated the result on November 5, 1887:

"FINISHED!
The Water to be Turned into the Canal Outlet in Ten Days
The Event will be Celebrated with Becoming Ceremonies

"Thursday afternoon in company with Capt. Len Wilson we drove over the line of the new canal outlet. The work is nearly completed. The gates of the lock where the side-cut leaves the main canal are about ready to be swung. This lock is 132 feet long and 20 feet deep, and one of the finest pieces of masonry in the State. The scrapers are at work below the lock and are about through. The trees are being cut off the right bank of the Old Bed, and a new towpath will be constructed. This will be the only change in the waterway of the Old Bed, save to scrape and dredge down to grade, which is already mostly done.

"The lock at the mouth is a double one, the upper section being 132 feet in length and 12 feet deep, and the lower one the same length and 13 feet deep. This brings the bottom of the canal on a level with the bottom of the river, so that a boat can go in or out at any stage of water.

"The old level between the elbow lock and the second lock will be raised about five feet, by a dam constructed at the old second lock, thus giving a deep and commodious basin.

"This work was done entirely by Kelley, Washon & Co., and these gentlemen are justly proud of their job…The engineer in charge of this work was R. A. Bryan."

The 1900 plat map of the new outlet justified the locks this way:

"A sand bar having formed in the Ohio River at the mouth of the Scioto River, rendering the outlet of the Ohio Canal useless, a new channel was constructed by the Board of Public Works in the summer of 1887. A considerable portion of the Canal was built through a pond that was at one time a part of the old channel of the Scioto River. The new channel has no well defined embankments for a considerable portion of its length. Two locks were constructed; one near its junction with the old channel, and the other, a double lock, near its outlet with the Ohio River."

The days of the southern canal were about over, and the new outlet locks were seldom used. The lower outlet lock, immersed by the high dams on the Ohio River, can now be seen only at low water levels.

# MIAMI & ERIE CANAL

*From one canal terminus on the Ohio River, we go 100 miles or so downriver to another. Like Portsmouth, these facilities were under-utilized. And few traces remain today.*

Volume IX (1971), No. 2, pp. 13-21

## THE MIAMI & ERIE IN CINCINNATI by L.W. Richardson

Cincinnati is known as a "river town" and certainly the mighty Ohio is responsible for most of its early growth and prosperity. It was also a "canal town". Important as the river was, farsighted Cincinnatians, led by Micajah Williams and Dr. Daniel Drake, as early as 1815 were agitating for a canal that would bring to the city the rich trade of the Miami Valley and Western Ohio.

The Miami Canal (it would not be known as the Miami & Erie until 1849) reached the outskirts of the city just a little over two years after the ground breaking ceremonies at Middletown, July 21, 1825. For the next seventy-five years, the canal influenced the lives of Cincinnatians, very possibly more than did the river. The canal wound its way through residential neighborhoods, along the back yards of city tenements and on to the wharves and basins of the business district. Generations of small-fry swam, fished, played and occasionally drowned along the busy canal.

In October, 1827 water was let into the finished section from Middletown to Howell's (later known as Hartwell's) Basin south of Lock 43. Two boats, the WASHINGTON and the CLINTON had been built and the first official trip was planned for the 4th of November. Before the big day arrived, an embankment gave way at White's Mill, near the Mill Creek Aqueduct, and it was Wednesday, November 28 before the two boat loads of dignitaries left for Hamilton and Middletown. Somewhere along the line, the SAMUEL FORRER joined the procession. The entire party returned safely on Friday.

A public "Excursion of Pleasure", from Howell's Basin through the four locks at Lockland, to return the same day, took place December 10th. Two days later, the CLINTON arrived from Middletown with a load of "flour, whiskey, pork and pork barrels" and the canal was in business.

By 1828 the section north to Dayton was complete, but for some reason, work on the "Twelve Mile Level" south of Lockland went slowly. It was 1829 before the way around the western slope of Cincinnati's hills and on across Main Street was open to traffic. In spite of the delays in opening the downtown section, business flourished. The last two miles of the canal, from the Plum street "Elbow" to the end of the level, were flanked by North and South Canal streets that were as much wharves as thoroughfares. For almost the entire distance, boat line offices, warehouses, forwarders, merchants and a variety of shops and factories fronted on the canal.

At the end of the level, just west of Sycamore and north of Court streets, was Lockport Basin. It was to provide additional docking and a turning pool, but soon proved inadequate. A larger basin, Cheapside, was built south of it, below Court and extending almost to 8th street. East and West Cheapside streets of today mark the limits of the basin.

Contracts were let for the extension of the canal to the Ohio River in 1828. The extension was to leave the level east of Broadway and descend to the river down present Eggleston avenue. Ten locks, each with a lift of eleven feet, were required. The river connection was completed in 1833 but seems to have been used very little. It was time consuming to traverse the twenty locks of the round trip and there was the expense of a steam tow on the river. It is also possible that most cargoes had to be broken on arrival for distribution to local merchants as well as to forwarders. Water power developed at the locks was important, however. At least one plant was still operating, using this power, when water was let out of the canal for the last time, three-quarters of a century later.

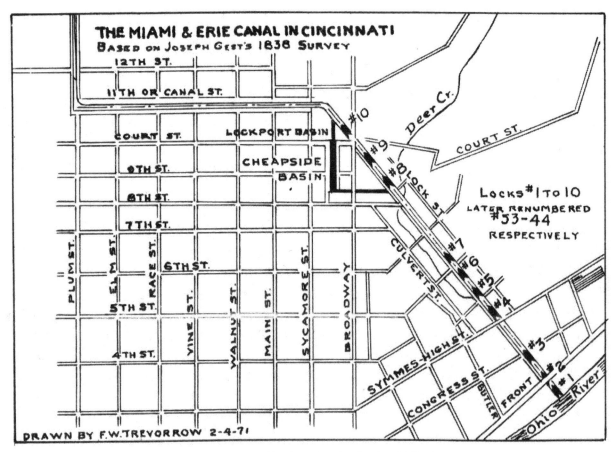

**Miami & Erie Canal at Cincinnati.** *Map by Frank W. Trevorrow.*

Little used, the river extension deteriorated, and an Act of the Legislature, March 24, 1863, authorized its abandonment and gave the city the use "…for a public highway and for sewerage purposes" all canal lands from Broadway to the river. Power rights were not affected and in 1870, when Eggleston was paved over the old locks, the water flowed through a large culvert under the street. A part of it is still there.

By an Ordinance of December 1, 1871, the city abandoned to the P. C. & St. L. R. R. the canal lands between Pearl street and the river for the site of a depot and in 1876 allowed the railroad to appropriate other canal property, obtained by the Act of 1863, between Pearl and Broadway. In the 1890's the State surveyed all canal property and contested these and numerous other encroachments and faulty titles. Space does not permit an account of the legal actions, certainly the lawyers had a field day.

Canal traffic in the area, as in other parts of Ohio, reached a peak in the two decades before the Civil War. In 1841, Cincinnati reported that 8,159 passengers, over 42,000 barrels of whiskey, 138,000 barrels of flour and 4 million pounds of pork had arrived and 8,500,000 pounds of merchandise, 7 million pounds of salt, and 3 million pounds of iron products had cleared via the canal, and this was only a partial listing.

After 1865, all canals began to decline, but local and specialized traffic in the Cincinnati region kept the Miami & Erie busy well into the Twentieth Century. Some phases of this business are worth notice. Although perhaps not entirely unique to this section, each contributed to the traditions and atmosphere of the "Queen City of the West".

The ice trade was one of these specialized operations. From lakes and wide waters on the edge of the city and far on up in western Ohio, ice was cut and stored each winter to be brought to Cincinnati via the canal during the summer. Before ice machinery became common, great quantities were shipped down river, often as far as New Orleans. One company alone could store 200,000 tons and operated a fleet of ten canal boats.

Then there was the daily whiskey boat - a large, heavy craft that held 350 to 450 barrels and required five horses on the towline. Three such boats were owned by the Clifton Springs Distillery in Carthage. They were usually unloaded at Plum street bend for re-shipment or warehousing. No doubt a greater quantity of the famous Cincinnati beer went north in the same way, but there is no record of the breweries owning their own fleet of boats.

The only "tankers" known to have operated on the Ohio canals were steel hulled craft that brought kerosene and petroleum products from the Allen County oil fields to the city. These were hauled by the usual mule teams, but in the last years, gasoline powered, steel hulled sand boats were common in the city area. Then, for a period after 1903, the "electric mules" whined along the towpath track on the way to Dayton. The "towpath Superintendents" were seldom bored.

Cincinnati must have been the only city in the country to utilize a section of an operating canal for an exposition. For the Centennial of 1888, Machinery Hall was built so that 1,250 feet of the canal, decorated in "Venetian Style" complete with gondolas, passed through the building. It is not known how commercial traffic overcame this obstacle on the towpath.

Possibly the citizens of no other city derived more pleasure from a canal. Each summer, thousands of the good "burghers" rode boats, cleaned and scrubbed for the occasion, on excursions to the many lakes and picnic groves in the northern suburbs. One contribution the canal made to local tradition became a nationally known expression. No visit to the city was thought complete without a visit "Over-the-Rhine". This meant crossing the canal from the central area to the variety halls and beer gardens in the

German district under the hill.

In 1913, the great floods in the Miami valley stopped the last of the dwindling through traffic. Some local business, largely sand and gravel haulers, persisted through the summer of 1917. In 1919, the water "went out" of the old ditch for the last time. Some of the serviceable boats were sold and served their remaining days on the Illinois and Michigan Canal, but most rotted away where they stopped.

After the first World War, a long section of the canal bed, from Broadway north, was further excavated and a double track subway, to be a part of the rapid transit system was built in the trench. To the sorrow of today's harassed commuters, this rail line was never finished. In 1928, Central Parkway, a spacious boulevard built over the old canal route, was dedicated. It remains an important central traffic artery. This was the end of a long, sometimes stormy but on the whole, a happy union of a great city and an inland waterway.

§§§§§§§§§§§§§§§§§§§§§§§§§§§§§

*A hundred years after the founding of Cincinnati, the Miami & Erie Canal was converted into an Italian scene. A park commemorating the canal was dedicated another century later. The events are linked here by George Crout.*

Volume XXX (1992), No. 3, pp. 32-33

### THE CINCINNATI CENTENNIAL EXPOSITION by George Crout

In 1888 the Centennial Exposition of the Ohio Valley and Central States was held in Cincinnati and the featured attraction of the show was the Miami & Erie Canal. To celebrate its 100th birthday, Cincinnati built what must have been one of the most unusual buildings in the history of Ohio.

Machinery Hall was a three-block-long building, from 12th to 15th streets built over the Miami & Erie Canal. Thus the actual canal ran through the middle of the building, whose twin towers marked its entrance. The Hall was 114 feet wide at the ends. At the center it was 150 feet wide and where it joined the Music Hall.

The aisles on each side of the real canal were filled with exhibits of new machinery. Four bridges were erected over the canal waters and arches supported the dome-like roof. This created a real Venetian scene, and the promoters of the celebration, which ran from July 4 to November 8, actually imported gondolas. The building was lighted with both electric and gas lamps. Regular canal boats brought visitors to the great exhibition hall where gondoliers guided their authentic craft on the flowing waters of the Miami & Erie Canal as musicians played for "The Carnival of Venice," one of the special programs.

Over one million people visited this extraordinary exposition, from all parts of Ohio. Honorary commissioners had been appointed by governors of the states of Kentucky, Missouri, Indiana, West Virginia, Illinois, Tennessee, Pennsylvania, Michigan, Iowa, Kansas as well as Ohio.

**The Cincinnati Centennial Exhibition**. Venetian Canal in Machinery Hall. *From* Harpers Weekly, *Vol. 33, # 1647, 1888. Drawn by H.F. Farny.*

## GREATER CINCINNATI BICENTENNIAL

Although Cincinnati's Music Hall survives and celebrated its 100th anniversary in 1978, Machinery Hall and the Miami & Erie Canal are long gone.

For Cincinnati's Bicentennial in 1988, the Cincinnati Gateway greeted visitors to the Bicentennial Commons. The entrance sculpture to the Commons included the history of Greater Cincinnati with a replica canal lock of the Miami & Erie Canal. The left wall of the lock shows the route of the canal from Toledo to Cincinnati.

The route of the Miami & Erie Canal to the Ohio River by the ten locks was commemorated by the "Canal Cut," a forty foot pool of water directly south of Eggleston Avenue.

§§§§§§§§§§§§§§§§§§§§§§§§§§

*George Crout teams with Nancy Gulick, chairperson of the CSO 50th anniversary committee, to provide this description of canal landmarks between Rialto and Port Union.*

Volume XXXV (1997), No. 4, pp. 49-55

## MIAMI AND ERIE CANAL IN SOUTHERN BUTLER COUNTY
### by Nancy Gulick and George Crout

### RIALTO AND LOCK 38

Only two locks remain standing between Middletown and Cincinnati: Excello Lock in a Middletown park and the Rialto lock. What's left of Rialto is a few miles north of Interstate 275 off Princeton-Glendale Road. Take the first interchange west of I-75 going north on State 747 and turn right on Rialto Road. Lock 38 south is on private property. Permission to view should be obtained from the owners, Mr. and Mrs. Bicknell.

Leased water from the canal was used to power a series of mills, and the town of Rialto grew up around the site of employment. Section 3 of Union Township had been purchased by Judge Jacob Burnet in 1790 from John Cleves Symmes. In 1842 William Burnett leased the right to enough water from the canal to power six runs of millstones at a rental of $822 a year. In 1849 the mill was sold to Taylor Webster. Then in 1866 the mill and rights to water power at the lock were sold to C. W. Friend and George F. Fox. They remodeled the grist mill into a paper mill, and the company purchased adjoining land for housing for employees.

In 1875 the Rialto Mill was reported to have four engines, and two papermaking machines produced paper for books and newspapers at the rate of 2-3 tons a day. The mill employed 50 men, operating 12-hour shifts. By 1905, the mill was described as "one of the leading industries of Butler County and an establishment in which people manifest an abiding interest and pride".

The 1913 flood destroyed the canal as a power source, and the mill converted to coal-powered steam. Rialto Road, which still runs along the site of the mill, was formerly known as Cinder Road, with cinders from the power plant being used to surface the roadway. Along the road were nine houses, including that of the mill superintendent and a boarding house—all had been erected by the paper company for employees.

Residents, however, were responsible for maintenance, and those who didn't keep up the property lost their jobs. Rialto was a clean, neat town.

The area was kept like a park. The island between the mill race and the canal was common property, the scene of many picnics and, in the winter, ice skating parties. There was no school or church at Rialto, these being in Port Union only a mile away. For a decade between 1880 and 1890 Rialto had its own post office before it was combined with that in Port Union. Rialto did have a general store, later converted to a residence, which is now the home of the Stewarts' daughter and family.

Richard and Helen Stewart grew up in Rialto. Their fathers, next door neighbors, worked for the Fox and Friend Paper Company. In late May 1932 two paper company employees observed smoke in the warehouse next to the mill. A fire had started in old paper and straw stored there. With no fire department near, it and the mill were soon in flames. With the mill gone, the village was to waste away.

Through a series of company mergers the John Manville Corporation had purchased the site. In 1988, when the Stewarts heard of a plan to use the site as a junkyard, they bought all 18 acres and remodeled one of the old buildings near the railroad as their home.

While much of the canal in Butler County became the base of new highways—Verity Parkway in Middletown, for example—the section in Union Township was spared. Between Port Union and Rialto the canal bed can still be traced along the west side of the road. The Stewarts have cleared brush from around the lock, and it is now on the National Register for Preservation of Historic Sites.

## CRESCENTVILLE AND LOCK 39

Crescentville Road, just north of Interstate 275 and running parallel to it, crosses the site of Lock 39 just west of the Norfolk and Western Railroad tracks.

Crescent Lock, just south of where the canal crossed from Butler County into Hamilton County, was the site of another Fox Paper Company mill. Built in 1888, the mill was located a scant mile from Rialto's Fox Paper Mill. The Crescentville Mill was state-of-the-art, "illuminated with electric lights and filled with the finest machinery made in the East". This mill manufactured roofing materials and wrapping paper and was also destroyed by fire, never to be rebuilt.

Crescentville's Post Office opened in July, 1888, to serve the small community that sprang up near the mill. Some original buildings still exist, including Crescentville School built in the 1900s. The post office closed February 15, 1911. The land previously occupied by the lock and mill, currently houses a cement plant whose access road passes directly over the lock site. Stone from the lock walls was crushed for use in the roadbed. A rise in the road is all that remains to mark the site.

## PORT UNION

Although Rialto is only a memory, nearby Port Union survives. In 1795 Joseph McMaken came into the area settling to the east of today's Port Union. A grist mill was built along Mill Creek as well as a log church. A son, William, set up a general store near the bridge over Mill Creek. The little hamlet on McMaken land became known as McMaken's Bridge.

Another son, Joseph, purchased a farm along the west side of the new trail which was to be called Princeton Road. When the canal was built this site near the bridge was chosen for a port, and a basin was built where boats could be loaded or unloaded and turned around. A swing bridge was built across the canal at the new road. In 1827, during the construction of the Miami-Erie Canal, William McMaken built the first frame house in the village, moving his grocery from the log structure into the front section of his new home.

During the canal's heyday, Port Union had a resident population of 80, with two grocery stores, a church, a shoemaker's shop, a blacksmith shop, a carriage shop, and the Port Union Tavern (Café), still in business, operated then as a hotel, with a bar, a sleeping loft for travelers and a dining room. An ice house located just west of the tavern provided ice to the saloon. Nearby ice ponds were operated by Cincinnati companies to provide ice to the city breweries and butchers. In 1878, an I.O.O.F. hall was built for public lectures as well as lodge meetings. Being in Union Township, the village was named Port Union, and from 1850 to 1915 it had its own post office.

PORT UNION AQUEDUCT

A few yards north of Port Union are the remains of a structure which carried the canal across an unnamed stream that flows northeast into Mill Creek. It appears in the early 1900s Board of Public Works' plat map in pencil as the Port Union Aqueduct, but is described in the 1907 Annual Report as both aqueduct and culvert: "The culverts at Bloody Run, Port Union, Hickenlooper Farm and Holwager were freed of debris." "Port Union aqueduct needs repair."

Upstream of the wing walls, the streambed is paved with rock slabs standing on end probably to reduce the force of flood water. What's left of the embankment could be envisioned as either washed out culvert or support for an aqueduct. Perhaps it was both at different times in its history.

§§§§§§§§§§§§§§§§§§§§§§§§§§§

*Although few traces remain, Hamilton was once a canal town. The basin in the middle of town, now covered by railroad tracks, was the center of activity as described in this article by James L. Blount.*

Volume VIII (1970), No. 2, pp. 20-23

### THE HAMILTON BASIN by James L. Blount

The Miami & Erie Canal had its start in Butler County near Middletown in July 1825. However, the canal missed Hamilton, the county seat, on its route to Cincinnati. The waterway was opened from Middletown to a point east of Hamilton in August 1827.

In anticipation of canal business, a new community developed east of Hamilton. Known as Debbsville, or Debbyville, it is now the area east of Erie Boulevard in Hamilton. Because of its position on the canal, Debbyville began to interest owners of Hamilton's small businesses and industries.

Hamilton's economy was saved by the concerted action of civic leaders in the small community of about 1,000 inhabitants. Leaders of Rossville, a community west of the Great Miami River, which was merged into Hamilton in 1855, offered support.

On December 22 and 29, 1827, four months after the canal opened to Debbyville, the Boards of Trustees of Hamilton and Rossville met to consider action on a canal connection for the villages. Three leading citizens, Robert B. Millikin, Thomas Blair and John Reily, were appointed to take the case to the Ohio Canal Commission. Jesse L. Williams, an engineer for the Miami & Erie Canal, was hired to survey possible routes for a side-cut from the canal to Hamilton.

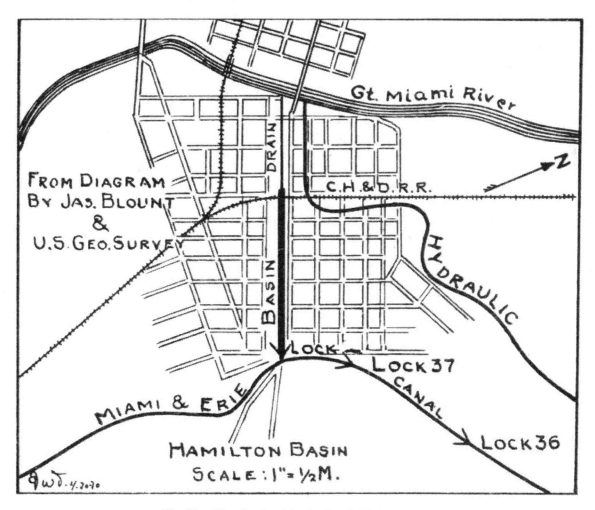

**The Hamilton Basin**. *Map by Frank W. Trevorrow.*

The leaders acted quickly. The Commission adopted a resolution January 15, 1828, approving a connection for Hamilton. It also authorized $2,000 in state funds for the project on the condition that Hamilton and Rossville raise the remainder of the money. The State Legislature added impetus by approving, on February 11, 1828, an enabling act for the ditch which became known as the Hamilton Basin.

The big problem at this point remained money. The $2,000 in state funds would have built about two-tenths of a mile of the basin. The side-cut would extend more than seven-tenths of a mile when completed. A public financial campaign netted funds which permitted the construction to begin. Andrew McCleary, a contractor, was awarded the work in an agreement concluded March 31, 1828.

The Basin extended west from the canal between the present High Street on the north and Maple Avenue on the south. The original western terminus was at a point between South Third and South Fourth streets in the center of the city. The Basin was much wider and deeper than the regular canal, which usually measured 40 feet wide and four feet deep with towpaths 10 feet wide for horses and mules. The Basin was 120 feet wide at the bottom, 148 feet wide at the surface, with an average depth of 18 feet. There were eight foot wide towpaths on each side. The Basin was connected to the canal by a lock. The water surface in the Basin was about four or five feet below the bottom of the canal.

Construction was started in the spring of 1828 and the waterway was completed December 13, 1828. However, problems delayed the use of the Basin until March 10, 1829. Serious leaks developed when water passed into the system causing flooding to three to four feet deep in some city streets, damaging several buildings. A drainage system was built from the western end of the Basin to the Great Miami River, four blocks west.

The contractor spent $7,503.02 in building the Basin and its drainage system, but was paid only $6,232 for 80,413 cubic yards of embankment. His loss was caused by the extra work required in patching leaks and building drainage ditches.

Soon after opening in March of 1829, the Basin thrived and its banks were lined with warehouses and wharves. According to an 1850 report, there were 40 or more canal packets arriving or leaving the Hamilton Basin each week. A total of 2,433 passengers paid the 75 cent fare, including board, for the 25 mile trip from Hamilton to Cincinnati, in April 1850.

The Basin experienced several changes during its history. In 1849, it was connected to the Hamilton Hydraulic along the present North Fifth and Market streets, providing a direct link with mills and factories along the hydraulic. In 1835, fire cisterns were created in Hamilton through a series of pipelines extending from the Basin, providing water for Hamilton fire protection for about 50 years.

There were the usual canal problems. The Basin was frozen from December 19, 1830 until March 4, 1831 offering a giant skating area, but stopping canal traffic for an extended period. Heavy spring rains caused flooding. Summer droughts reduced water to a point where traffic was stopped.

The demise of Hamilton Basin coincided with the decline of the Miami & Erie Canal in the 1860s. About 1870, the Basin became one of the dominant issues of Hamilton politics. The debate involved City Council, real estate developers, more than 40 property owners along the basin, numerous industries which used the waterway and many citizens concerned with health problems in the community.

A newspaper editorial summarized the problem this way: "The Basin is a Chinese Wall between two growing parts of the city…by reason of its leaks it is the prolific parent of much sickness and greatly depreciates contiguous property." However, the same newspaper said 9 out of 10 Hamilton manufacturers favored saving the Basin. It was estimated it would cost $20,000 a year in additional freight costs if the seven-tenths mile basin was filled in.

On April 27, 1872, the Ohio General Assembly passed legislation authorizing the city to close and fill the Basin if two-thirds of the voters in Hamilton approved. It also specified that Council must give 30 days of notice of its intention to cut off the Basin. An election was held May 18, 1875, and 1,516 out of the 1,918 persons voting favored closing the Basin. Despite the outcome, Council delayed announcing its intentions until June 14, 1877. It then announced it would meet June 20 "when the necessary steps will be initiated for cutting off the Basin."

The meeting wasn't necessary. At 9 p.m., June 19, 1877, about 100 men gathered at the eastern end of the Basin with wheelbarrows, picks, shovels and other tools. The vigilante group, led by City Street Commissioner Frank Krebs, emptied the Basin of water and filled a portion of it near the lock in about three hours. The debate ended and in a few years, the Basin embankment was leveled, streets were extended across its former course and a railroad was built through the center of the vacant land.

The filling of the Hamilton Basin precipitated an event of major importance, affecting the entire Ohio canal system. The Public Works had been leased to private operators since 1861. The Lessees appear to have been looking for an excuse to terminate the lease, perhaps because of dwindling revenues and the possible requirement of extensive repairs. They chose the filling of the Basin for their excuse and notified the Board of Public Works on June 23, 1877, four days after the vigilante attack, of their intention to abandon the lease.

The Lessees gave as the alleged reason that the filling up of the Basin amounted to an eviction from a valuable part of the leased property. On December 1, 1877, the Lessees ceased to pay rent and officially abandoned the Public Works. The State resumed full control of the canals on May 11, 1878.

§§§§§§§§§§§§§§§§§§§§§§§§§§§§

*Longtime curator of the Middletown Canal Museum, George Crout provided this humorous yarn about an Irish canal boat captain.*

Volume IX (1971), No. 3, pp. 39-40

### LEGENDS OF THE IRISH AT MIDDLETOWN by George Crout

They came to Middletown in 1825, swinging pick and shovel. They brought with them their love of the green shamrock and the traditional luck of the Irish. They added a dash of humor to the staid English and the matter-of-fact German settlers of the early Miami Valley.

They had heard that there was a canal to be built, and it was to start in Middletown. Official ceremonies marking the beginning of the Miami Canal were held on July 21, 1825 at the farm of pioneer Daniel Doty, leading citizen of the community, whose home would serve as headquarters for the distinguished party. After Governor DeWitt Clinton of New York and Governor Jeremiah Morrow of Ohio lifted the first sod from what was to become the Miami & Erie Canal, it was an Irishman who took the next dig into the earth, and then lifted his shovel, put it over his shoulder and led the parade of smiling Irishmen who had come to dig the big ditch.

Dig the canal they did, for the Irish were never a people to "shirk a bit of work". The very day after the ceremony, they started. Local farm boys with team and scraper also joined in; there was work enough for all. The Irish built shanties along the banks of the canal and for this reason were given the nickname of "Shanty Irish". As they prospered, many became boatmen and some Captains of their own boats. They built small homes. In Middletown, their section of town, centered around the Catholic Church and school, was called "Old Dublin".

With the canal built, many of the Irishmen stayed in Ohio and some became Captains of their own boats. One of the favorite stories still told in the Miami Valley is about Captain Bill. He was the toughest captain on the old Miami Canal. He fought whenever the opportunity presented itself, which was quite often around the canal locks. Few opposed his going through first. But Captain Bill was so quarrelsome and mean that he soon had difficulty finding any man who would work for him. One day when he arrived in Middletown, every man quit. Even poor Dunigan, the mule driver, who had been afraid to leave, hopped aboard a fast-moving canal boat on its way south.

Bill was tied up for several days at the Middletown wharf, because he couldn't get a driver for the tow path. At last, in desperation, he said to Mary Conners, his cook, the only crew he had left, "Mary, what do you say to our gettin' married?" Mary admired Bill, and while the proposal was unexpected, agreed, but she warned, "Now, I want you to understand that I am still your cook and no rough stuff goes". They went to a local magistrate, obtained the license and were married. Everyone around the canal laughed and waited to see what would happen.

Mary Connors was well-liked along the canal. Her kitchen cabin was the neatest and cleanest place one could imagine. When they returned to the boat after the ceremony, Mary went to her kitchen as usual, while Bill went to the stable cabin. In a short time he brought the mules out, harnessed them and attached the tow line. Then he yelled at Mary in a loud voice that was heard 500 feet along the canal, "Hey there Mary, get the 'ell out of that kitchen. We're partners now. You drive the damn mules and I'll steer the boat". So, Captain Bill was in business again!

§§§§§§§§§§§§§§§§§§§§§§§§§§§§

*We turn yet again to George Crout for an account of the dam at Middletown. Since this article appeared in* Towpaths *in 1984, the dam has been breached and no longer supplies water.*

Volume XXII (1984), No. 3, pp. 31-34

### MIDDLETOWN DAM by George C. Crout

In its Eleventh Annual Report to the General Assembly, January 22, 1833, the Board of Canal Commissioners described the nearly completed Miami Canal including the feeder and dam at Middletown:

"From Dick's Creek (ed. note: near Lock 34, Amanda Lock), the canal passes through Middletown, 42 miles from Cincinnati, to a point about two miles above that town, and 44 miles from its southern termination, where it receives a feeder from the Miami River. This feeder is 42 chains in length, and by means of a dam in the river five feet high, and 400 feet in length, gives this division of the canal command of an ample supply of water for all purposes of navigation, and furnishes in addition at Cincinnati, a surplus which is applied to hydraulic operations."

This is the story of that dam, known for most of its history as the State Dam, but now on official maps as the Middletown Dam. It is still accessible to the public being on land owned by the Miami Conservancy District. It is visited constantly by fishermen, who find the catch good.

It is a dam with a long history. It began as Abner Enoch's dam, which stood 600 feet north of the present dam site.

Abner Enoch had migrated from Virginia to Ohio in 1799. In 1802 he built a brush dam across the Great Miami River, which supplied a millrace leading to his sawmill, grist mill and woolen factory and later a distillery. These were valued at $2,000 in 1804. Enoch built a village there called Manchester, no longer existing.

When the Miami Canal was begun at Middletown July 21, 1825, a water supply was needed for that first section between Cincinnati and Dayton. A temporary canal feeder was found in Abner Enoch's millrace. The race was enlarged and a 1500-foot channel built between it and the new canal bed. However, this required a larger dam, for Enoch's mills had to continue to grind away. At that time, the State of Ohio agreed that Enoch should forever retain the right to all water from the dam that was in excess of that needed by the canal.

On June 2, 1826 a contract was made for the construction of the new dam across the Great Miami River with hewn timbers in place of the brush dam then in use. The cost of the dam and feeder was to be $15,000. Just as the dam was about completed in the fall of 1827 a heavy, constant rain began to fall, damaging the dam. The contractor gave up the contract. The next spring the state repaired the damage and completed the dam.

"...The dam is constructed with abutments of stone, and has its breast formed of hewn timber which projects below the breast of the dam about 30 feet, and forms an apron. Under the breast of the dam is driven a continuous row of heavy sheet piling, and a slope is formed on the lower side from the comb to the apron by means of hewn timbers secured at their upper end under the projecting ends of the rafters which cover the crib, and at their lower end to a plate of timber running lengthwise of and firmly secured to the apron. The feeder is secured at the upper end against the influx of floods, by headgates with abutments of wood upon a platform of hewn timber thoroughly sheet piled underneath the whole platform upon which the gates and abutments rest. It communicates with the canal by means of six square culverts of hewn timber, with an embankment of earth over them, which serves as a towing path bank; and with the gates at the upper end of the culverts, serves to secure the canal against the effects of floods from the river, which would be experienced in the event of a failure of the head gates at the upper end of the feeder."

Due to the increased demand for water by the building of a hydraulic at Middletown in 1852, Resident Engineer for the Miami and Erie Canal, John W. Erwin convinced the state to rebuild its dam. The new dam was of heavy timber construction, but 20 inches higher than the old one.

Then, after another 50 years, the deteriorating wooden State Dam was replaced by a modern concrete structure still standing and in use. Charles E. Perkins, Ohio's Chief Engineer of Public Works reported the new dam complete in 1908 at a cost of $61,057.30. In 1909 the old headgates, still in place, were repaired but are not now in use. A new set was constructed in 1975.

Before the 1913 flood the State Dam was 600 feet in length. After the deluge the dam was repaired and extended 400 feet, making it 1000 feet in length.

No governmental agency today seems to claim ownership of this dam. In the lease of water rights from Enoch in 1828 in a legal contract, the state agreed to "...continually maintain the dam." However in a letter from the Director of Public Works, State of Ohio in 1926, it was stated that since the State had no interest in retaining the water above the dam, the Middletown Hydraulic Company should repair the dam at its own expense. Now the State, the Middletown Hydraulic Company and the Miami Conservancy District are all involved in one way or another. The whole question of ownership and responsibility is in limbo, but will someday have to be resolved.

The State Dam stands today as a major engineering achievement and an historic landmark, still vital to Middletown's industrial interests.

**Middletown Dam, April 1984**. *Mahany photo. Courtesy* Middletown Journal.

§§§§§§§§§§§§§§§§§§§§§§§§§§

*Next to locks and aqueducts, structures such as tumbles and weirs are largely overlooked—even by canal historians. In this article, Edith McNally (a longtime and beloved CSO member) and Brad Bond take a closer look. Most of these structures were in Butler, Warren and Montgomery Counties.*

Volume XXXVII (1999), No. 3, pp. 46-49, 55, 60

## WEIRS AND TUMBLES by Edith McNally and Brad Bond

Surprisingly, this is a topic that was covered casually in the "Rules and Specifications relating to the Construction of Canals in the State of Ohio" issued in 1843 and not at all in the "Form of an Agreement" issued in 1825. Tumbles were covered in 1843 by one sentence: "A tumble to be built agreeably to a plan to be furnished shall also be built if required by the engineer or acting commissioner, to pass the water from the level above to that below the lock." Waste-weirs were treated similarly: "Both banks shall be so constructed as to remain at least two feet above top water line…except in such places as the acting commissioner or engineer having charge of the work may direct the bank to be left lower in order to serve as a waste weir or place for the escape of flood waters: and in such cases the contractor shall reduce of leave the bank at the height so required."

Tumbles maintained flow and prevented stagnant water in the canal as long as there was enough water to fill the locks. The tumbles were usually parallel to the lock, and the water was always passed back into the canal below the lock. Waste-weirs were usually placed between locks, and the water that flowed over them was not passed back into the canal. They were safety vents for the canal when there was too much water for the locks and tumbles to handle. A third kind of weir was installed to control the flow of water into a mill race. This water right was leased by the owner of the mill, and the rent became an important source of income for the canals especially in their declining years.

### Tumbles or Regulating Weirs

In their 11th Annual Report (1832) the Board of Canal Commissioners explained why the cost of the Ohio Canal exceeded the original estimate, a little over $3 million, by about $1 million. Part of the explanation was discovering the need for and installing regulating weirs. The additional cost was estimated at $26,800.

> "Regulating weirs - comprising a channel by which the water is passed around each lock from a higher level to a lower level, and a tumble of stone or wood erected to prevent the water in its descent from cutting away the earth and depositing it in the channel below, have been constructed on all the locks on the Ohio canal, with the exception of a few where the peculiar location prevented their erection, or rendered them unnecessary.
>
> These regulators are of great importance in preserving the equable flow of water from one level to another, and keeping it at a uniform height in each: at the same time greatly diminishing the

trouble and expense attendant upon passing water through the locks.

As the water flows freely over these tumbles from the surface of each level to the next below, the upper level is not liable to be too much exhausted, and no attention is required, except to keep the regulators clear from drift wood.

Of these tumbles, 67 are of cut stone masonry, resting on foundations similar to those of the locks; the walls, in most cases, connected with the lock walls - and 67 of the regulators have tumbles of wood, or arc constructed on either rock foundations, or on gradual slopes of earth, secured from abrasion by timber, brush and stone.

These regulators were not included in the original plan, or estimate of the canal; and we believe they were first adopted as a general appendage of locks on the canals of this State."

## Waste Weirs

Waste-weirs were built to prevent overflow of the towpath bank which would threaten washout. The 1909 profile and map of the Miami & Erie Canal shows there were an unusual number of waste gates in the section of the canal south of the Miamisburg Feeder. In order they were Lock 30, Greenland Waste Gate, Lock 29, Franklin Waste Gate, Lock 28, Clear Creek and Sunfish Waste Gates, Lock 27, Shepherd's Run Waste Gate, Lock 26.

Waste weirs were installed as needed after the original canal was built. Their construction was not specified and, in fact, varied from place to place. They were all gaps in the wall between the canal and whatever conduit, usually a stream, was used to carry away the overflow water. The gap was enough lower than the rest of the towpath wall to prevent overflow elsewhere, but tall enough to maintain a water depth adequate for boat flotation. The overflow gap was set into a concrete or cut-stone wall that rose to the height of the adjoining towpath bank to prevent erosion around the ends of the gap.

The simplest weir provided for no adjustment. It was simply a tumble perpendicular to the canal. A simple adjustable weir provided slots in the concrete or stone gap wall where boards could be inserted or removed to alter the height of the overflow. Under flood conditions the boards might be completely removed and still maintain canal depth because of the amount of water passing down the canal. A third variation was a fixed wooden wall with wicket gates which would leave the surface unaltered while removing water from the bottom of the canal. This method would tend to scour the bottom of the canal upstream of the wicket(s), perhaps reducing the need for dredging.

An example was installed on the Mad River Feeder in 1878:

"The waste gates on the Mad River feeder, near the Mad River lock, were built in a substantial manner, with rack and pinions for hoisting the gates, and the stone work connected therewith repaired."

Typically waste weirs were needed where the canal was in a trough and water tended to flow in over the berm bank in heavy rains. They were also used to drain the prism for repairs. A waste weir upstream of an aqueduct and flush with the prism bottom would permit diversion of the water to repair the aqueduct, for example. [...]

**Mill Race Weirs**

Weirs were also installed to supply mill owners the water promised by lease to run their mills. Rent was charged for the use of surplus water or the run of so many pairs of mill stones as long as water was available. Income from water leases became increasingly important as the canal use for shipping diminished. For example, water lease income, $17,643, provided only 6% of the Miami & Erie total in 1854, while in 1907 $32,045 accounted for 45% of the total. [...]

The weirs for mill races were placed upstream of a lock and the water returned to the canal below the lock. Samuel Bachtell, chief engineer, had this to say about leases and mills in 1887 (BPW Annual Report):

"All leases for water are carefully drawn and embrace the special clause that a weir shall be constructed and maintained under the supervision of the State employees at the expense of the lessee. The lessee is also required to guard and preserve the same.

But, upon examination along the M&E canal, I find many weirs out. In some cases they have been partially removed, and in others entirely destroyed, and no regard paid to the quantity of water called for in the leases. With a state of affairs like this existing, some levels are drawn down so low as to make boating difficult, while others, receiving this body of water are overflowed, and breaks are liable to be caused. A strict enforcement of all leases should be had, and the weirs in all cases replaced, and their maintenance strictly enforced."

§§§§§§§§§§§§§§§§§§§§§§§§§§§

*Sunfish Lock was constructed originally of stone in 1828, rebuilt with concrete in 1907 and restored in 1990. Miami Township deputy administrator James Foster tells of the restoration.*

Volume XXXVII (1999), No. 3, pp. 41-45

## THE RESTORATION OF LOCK 27 SOUTH (SUNFISH LOCK) ON THE MIAMI & ERIE CANAL by James A. Foster

On May 26, 1827, contracts were let for construction of the Miami & Erie Canal between Middletown and Dayton. Water was introduced in September, 1828, and the first boat passed through Sunfish Lock on December 17, 1828, on its way from Dayton south.

One of ten locks on this portion of the canal, it was originally constructed of locally quarried limestone blocks as were most structures on the Miami & Erie. Evidence on this site indicates it had the customary parallel bypass race for excess water. This was replaced around 1870 by iron culverts with beautiful stone abutments, necessary to carry that excess water under a new parallel railroad.

In 1907, as part of the upgrading of the canal system by the State, Lock 27 was one of those completely reconstructed in concrete. Presumably in this form it was used until functional abandonment after the 1913 flood.

Lock 27 was given to Miami Township in 1982 by Robert Steele, a developer of several adjacent residential tracts. The Miami Township Board of Trustees asked this writer in 1983 to see if it could be restored, so an initial application for Community Development Block Grant (CDBG) funds was made to Montgomery County during that year's funding cycle. Although CDBG funds are primarily, and rightly, intended to benefit low and moderate income citizens, they could also at the time be used for historic preservation, and it was in this context the request was made.

Although the restoration was not funded that year, an application during the 1988 cycle was finally successful and $55,000 was earmarked for a cosmetic reconstruction that would stabilize any further deterioration of the concrete. The Township's contribution was to be the clearing, grubbing, grading and final landscaping.

Architectural Reclamation, Inc., of Franklin, Ohio, a firm specializing in accurate restorations, was retained to do the job and began on August 24, 1989, after draining the bottom of the lock (just enough to dry it out so Architectural Reclamation could get in and work) and an initial clearing of brush and trees were completed by the Township Service Department. The outer four inches of concrete (of a total of about three feet in thickness) were removed under the direction of our structural engineer, establishing a "shelf" at approximately ground level on which a new concrete veneer would sit; a footer of sorts was therefore created.

This "shelf" was possible because the concrete below grade was in excellent condition and would structurally support the new veneer. About one foot of muck next to the walls was excavated by hand to facilitate this work, which still left about three and a half more feet of muck to protect what we think is a white oak foundation. That foundation was purposely not uncovered during the restoration. We at first found almost no artifacts, then the iron rods [...] were dug up plus one modern bottle, one insulator and lots of peach pits in the concrete.

The walls were tested for integrity by chipping away at them by hand. We determined that removing about four inches of concrete would provide a good base for the new veneer, although in places less was removed. The actual work was done with a 60-pound jackhammer that Architectural Reclamation hung from a temporary frame and rigged up with a counterbalance. As fearsome as this process sounds, it worked perfectly at a rate of 10-15 feet per day.

Reinforcing mesh was hung about two inches out from the "solid" concrete, so it would end up about two inches below the restored surface. The laborious process of building the wooden forms for pouring concrete then began. A beautiful curved wooden form for the gate pivot surfaces was built up in Architectural Reclamation's shop and trucked to the site; this form still exists and presumably could be made available to any other community rebuilding a concrete lock. The pours were a maximum depth of four feet, to keep the tremendous weight of the wet concrete from pushing out the bottoms of the forms. Many separate pours and an astounding quantity of concrete brought Lock 27 to essentially its present appearance by the end of 1990; the finishing touch was new red oak sills held down by the original bolts. The remaining grading and landscaping were completed over the next year or so by the Township Service Department. Total cost of the restoration was around $85,000.

Miami Township still contemplates, from time to time, building replica wooden gates, although there are no plans to rewater this portion of the canal. Rewatering would require rebuilding the low dam across the Great Miami River near West Carrollton and a hydraulic feeder, reconstructing the prism through Miamisburg (including Lock 26), rebuilding several culverts and ensuring the prism's structural integrity for several miles; there are many canal projects in Ohio that would be easier to accomplish.

Lock 27 is intended to be *the* major exhibit of the "transportation heritage corridor" theme for the expanded Crain's Run Reserve, a joint venture of the Township and Montgomery County Five Rivers MetroParks. Visitors are welcome; the lock is adjacent to Dayton-Cincinnati Pike (Dixie Highway) opposite the present terminus of Dayton's River Corridor Bikeway, just north of the Warren County line. A piece of an original gate unearthed during the restoration is also on display at the Township offices.

**Lock 27**. Canal Society of Ohio tour in October 1994, examines Sunfish Lock.

*Miami River, Miami Canal...and Miamisburg. The history of this community south of Dayton is summarized here quite neatly by Dave Neuhardt, an individual who has served the CSO in a wide variety of capacities throughout his membership.*

Volume XXXV (1997), No. 4, pp. 61-64

## MIAMISBURG, OHIO by David A. Neuhardt

Miamisburg was platted in 1818 on the east side of the Miami River at the site of a settlement known as "Hole's Station." Hole's Station was founded by Zachariah Hole and his family in the fall of 1795 and included a blockhouse constructed about 1798 in response to rumors of an Indian uprising. By 1811, the blockhouse was replaced by the two-story log Gebhart's Tavern, which still stands facing the Miami River ford (also the site of Yeazell's Ferry).

Present day Main Street follows the old River Road originally built by the military between Cincinnati and Dayton. It was not until 1840 (a dozen years after completion of the Miami Canal through town), however, that the road was improved as the Great Miami Turnpike. Two other early turnpikes connected Miamisburg to the towns of Centerville to the east (present-day Ohio 725) and Springboro to the southeast.

The first railroad, the Cincinnati, Hamilton and Dayton (later the B&O) was built along the west side of the river opposite the town in 1851. Two decades later the Cleveland, Columbus, Cincinnati and Indianapolis ("Big Four") railroad was built through town on the east bank. An interurban line connecting Dayton and Cincinnati was completed in 1896.

Miamisburg supported a number of industries that grew up along or near the canal, including: Shuey's Mill (1829) at Lock 26; a neighboring sawmill (also built at Lock 26 at about the same time—today's Peerless Mill Inn); Cassady & Strong's cotton mill (1830-1852); Cassady & Stewart's oil mill (1852-1874); Schultz & Manning's paper mill (on the hydraulic); and the Ohio Paper Company's mill (also on the hydraulic). Miamisburg was also known for its carriage builders and a company that built collapsible boats. The Market House that still stands in the center of town (with its original open arches bricked in) was built in 1851.

CANAL HISTORY

Construction on the initial portion of the Miami Canal from the Miami feeder at Middletown south to Cincinnati was already under way when contracts were closed on May 26, 1827, for the construction of the upper division from Middletown north through Franklin and Miamisburg to Dayton. Until the later construction of the Cincinnati river locks, the lower division of the Canal included twelve locks, five aqueducts, twenty stone culverts (3'-20'), one dam, a guard lock and a short feeder from the Miami River. The upper division contained ten locks, one aqueduct with a wooden trunk, three "aqueducts" of "heavy stone arches with embankments of earth over them", one dam and a feeder from the Mad River at Dayton. The length of the entire canal when completed was 66 miles.

Water was introduced into the upper division from the Mad River feeder at Dayton on September 27, 1828, but it was December before the canal was watered to Middletown. On December 17, 1828, the packet *Alpha* (the first boat built in Dayton) reached Miamisburg traveling south. By the next month, north-bound boats from Cincinnati also were passing through town.

**Structures.** The primary features on the canal from Miamisburg south to the Warren County line included the Miamisburg Aqueduct (originally a culvert) over Sycamore Creek in northern Miamisburg, Miamisburg Lock (Lock 26) in the southern part of town and, south of town, Shepherd's Run culvert and waste gate, Crain (or Cranes) Run (or Sunfish) Aqueduct and waste gate and Sunfish Lock (Lock 27). Of these features, significant remnants of only the Miamisburg Aqueduct, Shepherd's Run culvert and waste gate and Sunfish Lock remain.

Miamisburg Aqueduct was originally built as a culvert, and apparently was rebuilt as an aqueduct some time after 1880 (I have not yet checked all of the Commission and BPW reports). Miamisburg Lock was located in the rear parking lot of Peerless Mill Inn (on First Street near the end of Lock Street). Houses for locktenders were located at both Miamisburg Lock and Sunfish Lock.

**Lockkeepers.** The names of several lockkeepers survive in the histories of Miamisburg, including Conley Gebhart at Sunfish Lock (Lock 27) south of town and Jacob Ruegger at Miamisburg Lock in town (Lock 26). Ruegger had a one-story brick locktender's house built by the state in Miamisburg in 1834, and later added a second story and a frame addition at his own expense. The house, with space for boarders, reputedly included a ten-pin bowling alley that extended from the basement of the house to the tumble at the lock.

John Dreher of Miamisburg began boating about 1840 on the *Magnolia* under Capt. William Goudy between Miamisburg and Cincinnati. When he quit boating, he became a locktender and tended the "lower Miamisburg lock" (Sunfish Lock?) for "about 30 years."

**Reconstruction.** During the turn-of-the-century rebuilding of Ohio's canals, contracts were awarded to Fauver & Renich for the reconstruction of Sunfish Lock and Shepherd's Run waste gate in March of 1907 (the same firm also was given the contract for Lock 24, the Upper Carrollton Lock, north of Miamisburg in West Carrollton). John Snider got the contract for Sunfish Aqueduct (July, 1906), and a Snider partnership was awarded the Sunfish waste gate (June, 1908). The Miamisburg Lock reconstruction was done by Williams and Morse (June, 1909), while contracts for rebuilding the Miamisburg Aqueduct and the Lower Carrollton Lock (Lock 25) were given to B. Neihaus (June, 1909).

§§§§§§§§§§§§§§§§§§§§§§§§§§§§

*The famous (or infamous depending on how one views it) "electric mule" has been a favorite topic for* Towpaths *articles over the years. Here, Mark Renwick provides some interesting perspective.*

Volume XXXII (1994), No. 4, pp. 37-43

## THE ELECTRIC MULE ON THE MIAMI & ERIE CANAL – 1903 by Mark Renwick

The actual construction of the electric mule was well reported in issue #4 of *Towpaths* (by T.K. Woods).[*] The following is a time capsule look at newspaper articles in 1903 (*Dayton Daily News*) that show the people behind the scenes and what their intentions were.

1903 was a wondrous year for transportation. Panama's secession from Columbia cleared the way for the signing of the Hay Bunau-Varilla Treaty. This treaty would allow the United States to build the greatest canal of its time. Steam engines were joined by the fast growing interurbans. Automobiles, still a hand built novelty, would be humbled by the dawn of aviation. The gasoline engine, king of the 20th Century, begins to take hold. It was this "spirit of innovation" that produced the electric mule.

Although it was Thomas N. Fordyce who secured the franchise to build the electric mule, credit for its existence should probably go to William G. Wagenhals. News accounts of Wagenhals' legal suit against Fordyce tell of the events prior to the franchise. It was Mr. Wagenhals (former Superintendent of the Southern Ohio Traction Co.) who applied for the contract in 1898. The franchise was to be granted after proper demonstration of electric propulsion. Successful experiments were conducted in an area "South of Dayton". At this point, according to the suit, the contract entered into with the State Board of Public Works should have been in force. For reasons unknown, Governor Nash and Attorney General Sheets would not sign it.

Mr. Fordyce, along with Attorney S.A. Hoskins, Mr. W.G. Boerein, and Mr. Guy Huffman, entered into an agreement with Wagenhals. Fordyce was to take the place of Wagenhals and secure a contract with the State. It was agreed that Fordyce would have the right to use the knowledge gained by experiments made by Wagenhals. Fordyce then secured a franchise from the State and the Miami & Erie Canal Transportation Company (M&ECTC) was born. The original suit alleges that the other partners received "large sums of money and/or stock" and asked the court to appoint a receiver until a financial accounting could be made.

The annual report of the State Board of Public Works (1903) described in detail the agreement with Mr. Fordyce. No mention of Wagenhals occurred in the report, yet his suit against the M&ECTC was settled quickly. He agreed to drop the suit for a cash settlement of $51,000. This cash outlay was made at a time of serious financial hardship for the company. Two months after the settlement a Cincinnati Judge would appoint a receiver to represent the company. It would appear that Wagenhals had a solid claim against Fordyce and his company to warrant such a payment.

---

[*] Volume XII (1974), No. 4, pp. 42-46.

Controversy over the electric mule began almost immediately. In late January Mr. Harry Probasco (Cincinnati Hamilton and Dayton Railroad) complained to the Attorney General that freight hauled on the electric mule tracks was in violation of the franchise. The freight moved (while the canal was frozen) via the flat cars used for construction. This accusation was not mentioned by Fordyce in a letter to the paper but he does deny rumors of future track use by the Pennsylvania Railroad at Hamilton. The arrangement was expected to result in the transfer of 1,000,000 lbs of freight per month.

Other controversies with the M&ECTC involved encroachment suits. The franchise provided Fordyce with the legal right to build a network of poles, wires and track on the towpath. The exact location of the towpath became a point of contention whenever track was laid on it. Prior to track construction the towpath formed a vague boundary between State and private land. The tracks and poles created a distinct line that forced all concerned to ensure their property was protected. Miamisburg and Dayton were involved in a number of disputes.

**The Electric Mule**. Abandoned in front of the Sterns and Foster Company, Lockland, Ohio. This was the first use of a 3 phase alternating high tension transmission system in the country. It was operational in the Summer of 1903 between Middletown and Cincinnati.

Problems in Miamisburg centered around the area between Central Avenue and the lock (lock 26 South). At this location a large number of shade trees were removed along with "2 squares" of hitching racks. Despite a court injunction (mid-March) the M&ECTC continued laying track. On April 16th Judge

Kumler had 20 of the canal workers (all Negro) (*sic – Dayton Daily News* accounts of the period) brought into court along with Oscar Ellis (company foreman). The M&ECTC was ordered to remove the track and Sheriff Wright was assigned to observe the work. On April 18th Judge Kumler made the injunction perpetual. The decision of encroachment was based on personal testimony. According to local residents, a stone wall had once extended from Central Avenue to the lock but was destroyed as a result of dredging.

In Dayton, the Stomps-Burkhart Furniture Company filed a complaint involving the tracks and poles installed on Mill Street (between First and Monument). They contended the tracks were on a public street and they prevented normal business traffic. Another Dayton injunction was filed by Mr. H. Hollencamp for encroachment of his property near Jefferson Street. He claimed the towpath was dredged out in 1888 to allow more room for boats to turn while going through the bridge. The property line questions surfaced simply because the rails made it impossible to operate a vehicle on the towpath. Without tracks the problem did not exist.

Fordyce was also faced with the usual problems associated with a new business: labor disputes, cash flow, available resources, and competition. His labor problems were similar to those faced in the beginning of the canal. He faced the same difficulty recruiting workers because of the low pay and heavy labor aspects of the job. News articles repeatedly mentioned the "Negro workers" which would suggest an ethnic grouping much like the Irish workers in the earlier days of the canal. One article even mentions the recruitment of Negro laborers from Kentucky. The wages were probably recognized by the company as low because a strike by the "Negro laborers" was settled within 1 hour. It was a 20% increase from $1.25 to $1.50. An interesting note: the strike occurred 4 days after their court appearance for not obeying the Miamisburg injunction.

The cash flow problems of the M&ECTC were due to a number of events. There was an 8 month delay in the delivery of the electric engines. Without the engines they could not utilize their other resources (boats). This was followed by a 3 month period with no water in the canal. This was not fully explained in the paper except to mention the collapse of the 3 aqueducts. The Mad River Aqueduct collapsed on January 12th. The Lockington aqueduct collapsed on May 29th and the Great Miami River aqueduct collapsed in mid-July. The last one resulted in reconstruction from a covered wooden structure to an open steel design.

The lack of funds triggered a chain of events designed to forestall bankruptcy. In mid-June the M&ECTC canceled the track construction contract with the Cleveland Construction Company. They would try to complete the work themselves. On July 3rd, a Cincinnati judge appoints 2 people as receivers for the troubled Miami & Erie Canal Transportation Company. They are W. Kesley Schoepf (President and General Manager of the Cincinnati Traction Company) and Charles C. Richardson (County Commissioner of Hamilton County). By December all orders for new boats were cancelled. All boats currently under construction were to be completed. A large quantity of lumber was returned to M. B. Farrin Lumber Company (of Winton Place) at a price reduction.

Competition was always on the horizon. A number of companies showed a renewed interest in freight forwarding during 1903. The Cincinnati and Toledo Packet Company experimented with a gasoline powered paddle boat (16 horsepower). Their intentions were to move via self propulsion to Toledo and then be towed by tug to the Erie Canal. They would again move via self propulsion to the Hudson River and repeat the towing process to New York City. The Ohio Boat Company was formed in mid-December by partners all along the Miami and Erie Canal. Their stated purpose was the manufacturing, selling, leasing, and renting of water craft. Also, the transportation of passengers and freight cars via water craft. Daniel Ryan, Attorney for the M&ECTC, objected to the wording of the charter (transportation of freight cars). The CH&D Railroad also scrutinized the Ohio Boat Company but pronounced their intentions legitimate (not related to railroads).

So what does this all say? Did Fordyce really intend to build a canal transportation company or railroad? The original contract problems between Wagenhals and the State of Ohio are further muddled by the fact that Fordyce's Attorney (Daniel Ryan) was once the Attorney General for Ohio. That aside, the electric mule was built in good faith and it did operate between Cincinnati and Middletown. Adding to the puzzle is a legislative bill, penned by Ryan, that would give the M&ECTC authority to operate a steam railroad on the banks of the canal. This was introduced in December of 1903 and might be viewed as the act of a financially desperate company.

What can probably best answer the question is the actions of the Weldner-Elkins syndicate. They were an interurban oriented syndicate and had purchased an additional $200,000 of M&ECTC stock before any electric mules operated. This was a win/win opportunity for the stockholders. If the electric mule was successful they would realize a return. If the canal was abandoned entirely then they had an instant interurban railroad. If the M&ECTC went bankrupt then they would inherit the assets of an interurban railroad. Fordyce's actions mirrored the syndicate in that he always hedged his bets. He was not in the canal business and he was not in the railroad business. Fordyce was in the TRANSPORTATION business.

§§§§§§§§§§§§§§§§§§§§§§§§§§§§

*We go to the well once again with another Frank Trevorrow article, this one on Samuel Forrer from the "Ohio Canal Men" series. Forrer was the "Richard Howe of the Miami & Erie Canal." (Or was Howe the "Forrer of the Ohio & Erie"?) Only the opening paragraph from this long piece has been printed as the primary motivation for selection of this piece was the map of Dayton. Like most other urban areas in Ohio, these canals and locks have been erased.*

Volume VII (1969), Nos. 2 & 3, pp. 13-14 & 38-39

### OHIO CANAL MEN: SAMUEL FORRER by F.W. Trevorrow

Samuel Forrer holds the distinction of having had the longest association of any individual with the Ohio Canal system. For over fifty years, from the very beginning of Ohio's canals, he was variously engaged as a rodman, surveyor, engineer, contractor and Commissioner. Forrer, along with Alfred Kelley and Micajah Williams, rendered distinguished service to the State. His devoted wife Sarah shared the many vicissitudes entailed in such loyal services. […]

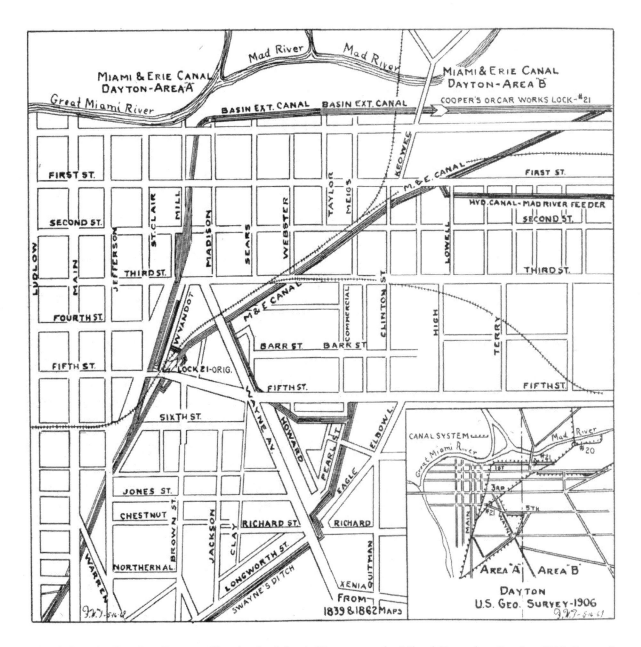

**Miami & Erie Canal at Dayton**. Showing both Lock 21s, one on the Miami Extension Canal at Fifth Street (just below the terminal basin of the original Miami Canal at Third Street) and the other on the Basin Extension Canal just east of Keowee Street. The Mad River Feeder is also depicted. *Map by Frank W. Trevorrow.*

§§§§§§§§§§§§§§§§§§§§§§§§§§§§

*Emerging as a frequent contributor to* Towpaths *of late, this photo article by Bill Oeters focuses on period canal structures from Dayton to Piqua. We revisit this article later for photos on the northern end of the Miami & Erie.*

Volume XLVII (2009), No. 1, pp. 1-10

## 1916 PHOTO SURVEY OF THE MIAMI & ERIE CANAL
## FROM DAYTON TO PIQUA by Bill Oeters

Among the many files requested during a recent visit to the Ohio Historical Society's archive library was a box of 1916 photographs taken by Howard R. Klepinger, Chief Engineer and Assistant Superintendent of the Department of Public Works. Planned goals for that day's research were quickly redirected. The following photographs, many with typewritten comments and recommendations by Mr. Klepinger, would indicate that the state did have the intention of maintaining portions of the canal system for water and pipe rental purposes. Nothing in the recommendations leads to the belief that navigation on the canal was in the Public Works Department plans. By the later stages of the Miami & Erie's life, prior to the 1913 flood, collected tolls often did not even cover the remaining locktenders salaries and expenses. On the other hand, collected water rentals generated a positive revenue stream. In 1916, the state of Ohio still, at least half-heartedly, considered honoring those rental contracts. Few, if any of Chief Engineers Klepinger's recommended repairs were ever executed. One can speculate that state accountants crunched the numbers and concluded that this would still be a money losing proposition. Perhaps the gathering storm clouds of a world war in Europe directed Ohio's political leaders toward other pressing needs. Regardless, the canal would eventually be officially terminated with much fanfare in 1929.

Although Mr. Klepinger's suggestions were largely ignored, he did leave future canawlers a photographic time capsule of the Ohio canal system. The focus of this article will be the Miami & Erie Canal and its associated feeders. Photos are arranged from south to north. A summary of the photographs is given in the table below. Some photos in the collection were either missing, duplicates, or not of interest so these were omitted from the article. Mileage is given from Cincinnati.

| Photo | Mile | Structure |
|-------|------|-----------|
| 7 | 66 | Bimm's Ice Pond, Dayton |
| 9 | 75 | Great Miami Aqueduct (Nine Mile Aqueduct) |
| 10 | 76 | Tadmore Sluice Gate |
| 11 | 84½ | Tippecanoe Spillway |
| 13 | 95 | Lock 9-S, Piqua |
| 15 | 96¾ | Piqua Aqueduct |
| 16, 17 | 97½ | Lock 8-S and State Dam |

*Bimms Ice Pond,*
*Dayton, O., July, 1916.*

**Photo 7**. Typical example of an early 20th Century ice pond. The brackish one shown above, called Bimm's, was just outside of Dayton. The city skyline, with its numerous smokestacks and industrial buildings, can be discerned in the distant background.

*East End - Nine Mile Aqueduct -*
*North of Dayton, Ohio, July 1916.*

**Photo 9**. Repaired from 1906-12, the partially submerged superstructure in the foreground is a testament to the destructive power of the 1913 flood. After its destruction, the canal between here and the Mad River crossing in Dayton was left high and dry. Klepinger indicated no plans to fix this section, which would have been costly. The Great Miami Aqueduct site is 9 miles above Dayton, hence the alternative name.

**Photo 10**. The concrete structure still exists, minus the iron gate, along the Tadmore spur of the Great Miami River Recreation Trail north of the Taylorsville Dam.

**Photo 11**. This weir north of Tipp City is an out of the ordinary example of a post-1913 repair, even more unusual because the improvement was not made by the state. Water was maintained through Tipp City to meet milling and power interests there. Crumbling concrete ruins of the weir may still be found. Note the car on the bridge at Frye Road (Tipp-Elizabeth Road).

Photo 13. Note Lock 9-S in the background, now a Piqua park.

**Photo 15**. This structure was almost certainly located where the Swift Run Lake overflow enters the Great Miami River.

*State Dam, North of Piqua, July 1916*

**Photo 17**. That the west abutment of this dam is sitting in the river attests to the severity of the breach here. The structure in the right foreground marks the spot where the feeder entered the canal. Besides the surviving west abutment, timbers from this dam are also still visible in the river bed.

**Photo 16**. A nice photo of Lock 8-S in the left foreground. Except for missing gates, this lock is almost unchanged after nearly a century. Lock 8-S is the turn around point for the *General Harrison of Piqua* canal boat ride, one of the featured attractions at the Piqua Historical Area State Memorial. The concrete feeder gate, in center background, is now blocked by both an earthen embankment and concrete bulkhead. This still-watered section of canal is now fed by a natural spring. The feeder entered the canal near the stone structure in the right foreground, also visible in Photo 17. The west abutment of the state dam is just outside of picture to the right. How water would have entered the canal above the lock from the Sidney Feeder is open to speculation, possibly by the construction of a relatively cheap narrow flume over the surviving abutments of the Loramie Creek Aqueduct (destroyed by 1913 flood) as was done at Delphos. See Photo 31 for an example. [Ed. Note: Photo of aqueduct at Delphos is on p. 252.]

*Canal boat fever was running rampant in Ohio during the late 1960s and early 1970s. Terry Woods recounts the inaugural ride on the* General Harrison. *Since replaced by the* General Harrison of Piqua, *the new boat, indeed, has adequate seating.*

Volume X (1972), No. 4, pp. 37-38

### FIRST RIDE ON THE *GENERAL HARRISON* by T.K. Woods

The christening and "first" ride of Ohio's newest canal boat replica was held on September 3rd, 1972. Now, with the help of a tape-recording made for the Canal Society of Ohio's library, let's go on that ride.

"We're now aboard the GENERAL HARRISON in Piqua, Ohio. Miss Shirley Carter Patterson, the great, great, great granddaughter of Colonel John Johnston whose homestead was dedicated today as part of the Piqua Historical Area, has just christened the boat. The crew is now poling our craft across the southern turn-around basin toward the twin mule-power waiting on the towpath. In the background, you can hear the Sidney Lehman High School Band as they strike up a lively tune to add a festive air to an already festive occasion..."

"Our motive power, Jack and Katy, are now being attached to a 150 foot long towline in the traditional tandem fashion...O.K. we're hitched up—the mules are moving up the towpath taking slack from the line. Soon we'll be under way...And, here we go!"

"Listen to that cheer go up from the crowd as the GENERAL HARRISON begins its initial voyage. Wait a minute!, now we've stopped. At least the mules have stopped. The canal boat continues to glide along...The harness has apparently slipped from the team and has to be tightened, but it will be just a temporary delay..."

"We're now lying still in the water after coasting nearly 50 yards. This was a good demonstration of how small the friction force is between the boat's hull and the water...The harness has been repaired and, once more, we're ready to go...The mule team is in motion once again taking up the slack. In a few seconds we'll once more be under way...A few more seconds will do it—just about—O.K., any second now, and—here we go, we're on our way, we're on our way."

"There is some jerking in our start. These mules appear to be somewhat inexperienced right now and don't give the GENERAL HARRISON as smooth a start as the ones experienced on the MONTICELLO II and the ST. HELENA II. A few days of work should eliminate any skittishness the mules now have, however, and allow the starts to be as smooth as the rest of the trip. And it is smooth! We're skimming along the canal at a rapid rate, about 3 to 4 miles an hour."

"Now would be a good time to describe our craft. It is painted much more colorfully than Ohio's other two replicas. The GENERAL HARRISON'S hull has yellow, blue, and brown striping while the cabins are painted yellow with blue trim. Its design is a composite of several standard types. Basically, its lines are quite similar to those of the familiar three-cabin freighter, but the GENERAL HARRISON has a full roof and the bow and stern decks are accessible from inside the boat via permanent wooden steps."

"Noticeable by their absence are the complete lack of seats. There are nearly 150 passengers aboard this inaugural trip and we're all standing! I don't know if this arrangement will persist in the future, but a lack of seats could bother some of the older potential travelers."

"We've just passed the regular loading area, about half way along this one mile stretch of restored canal. Here, paying passengers will be taken on either the northern or southern loop of the route. This ride will be about half as long as the ones given by the other two boats, but the price of the trip is about half as much."

"We've now completed our northern turn-around and are headed back down the canal. An original stone lock, Lock No. 8—or State Dam Lock, is clearly visible during the turn-around. The boat is now passing through a most picturesque portion of the canal. The towpath is smooth and well maintained. Both banks are tree-lined and back from the canal a bit stand some gigantic trees that could very well be part of Ohio's virgin timber."

"The boat dock is now in view and our trip will soon be over. A smoother, quieter ride can't be imagined. The GENERAL HARRISON is a well constructed, colorful boat and a ride on it is well worth the trip to Piqua and the Miami & Erie Canal."

**First ride of the *General Harrison*.** September 3, 1972. *Courtesy Ohio Historical Society.*

§§§§§§§§§§§§§§§§§§§§§§§§§§

*While the* General Harrison *is a well-known canal boat from the Piqua area, the* DeCamp Statler *might be more famous as it was the last boat along the Miami & Erie Canal in these parts. The following contribution was made by Leonard U. Hill.*

Volume IX (1971), No. 1, p. 12

### THE CANAL BOAT *De CAMP STATLER* by Leonard U. Hill

The story of the De CAMP STATLER, which made its last trip on the Miami & Erie Canal in 1912, was well reported in the Piqua region. It is recorded as the last boat to pass through the canal at Piqua, and the accompanying photograph is completely identified.

The photograph was taken in 1913 at Newport. In the foreground is Adam Conover, who commenced his canal career as a mule driver in 1837 and was captain of the packet boat ARROW in 1855. He was 94 years old at the time the picture was taken. The other man is either Eugene Pilliod of Newport or William Combs, Sr. William Combs, Jr. was the last owner and captain of the boat.

The De CAMP STATLER was named for the Statler family who owned and operated a stone quarry near Piqua. In its last years, the boat was mainly engaged in hauling stone from the quarry and gravel from Snipp gravel pit southeast of Newport.

**Canal boat *DeCamp Statler*.** Photographed in 1913 at Newport. *Courtesy Leonard U. Hill.*

*This snippet on Lockington appeared in the first issue of* Towpaths, *part of a short-lived series called "Places Worth Seeing." Strangely, little has appeared in the publication on Lockington since then.*

Volume I (1963), No. 1, p. 6

## PLACES WORTH SEEING...LOCKINGTON

Here the Shelby County Historical Society and the Ohio Society of Professional Engineers have erected a number of tablets which tell the story of the flight of six locks where the boats were lowered at the south end of the Loramie summit level on the Miami and Erie Canal.

The locks, the abutment of the aqueduct crossing Loramie Creek and the junction of the Sidney feeder are all to be found within a half mile stretch, readily accessible and kept clear of brush. The original mile stone, 100 from Cincinnati, is still in place on the towpath and the various tablets mark and explain the interesting features of this once busy spot.

Lockington is located north of Piqua and south of Sidney. A black top secondary road, east from State Route 66, will take you to the village.

§§§§§§§§§§§§§§§§§§§§§§§§§§§

*Dayton area resident Dave Neuhardt, an active and well-known CSO member, wrote this scholarly piece on the Miami & Erie Canal summit level water supply in 1985. His tour of that section is fondly remembered.*

Volume XXIII (1985), No. 2, pp. 13-22

## MIAMI AND ERIE CANAL WATERING THE SUMMIT: LEWISTOWN RESERVOIR AND THE SIDNEY FEEDER CANAL by David A. Neuhardt

When construction on the Miami Canal was authorized in 1825, the termination point was to be the Mad River just beyond Dayton. Nevertheless, the General Assembly intended for the canal eventually to be extended from Dayton to Lake Erie. Aside from financial and political considerations, the most significant hurdle to be overcome in any northward extension of the Miami Canal was the problem of providing an adequate supply of water in the summit area.

Midway between the valley of the Miami and Mad Rivers at Dayton and the valley of the Maumee River at Defiance, the Loramie summit encompasses the "divide" between the watershed of the Ohio River and the watershed of Lake Erie. This divide is about 400 feet above Lake Erie and 550 feet above the Ohio River and can be roughly traced by following Ohio Route 274 through Shelby and Auglaize counties. Although the summit area is the source of many streams, the small drainage area limits the water available from natural sources for canal purposes.

## Early Proposals

As early as 1822, canal engineer James Geddes reported that the summit probably could be supplied by a feeder from the Miami River at the mouth of Indian Creek (west of Bellefontaine) supplemented, if necessary, by a second feeder brought from the Mad River southwest of Urbana. Geddes believed that the amount of water needed from the Miami would require that the feeder be of navigable dimensions. The feeder was to be taken from the Miami at the mouth of Indian Creek, since this was the lowest point at which the river was on the same level as Geddes proposed summit crossing.

In May, 1824, the Canal Commissioners dispatched a locating party to propose a line from Dayton to the Loramie summit. Their proposed route followed the Mad River for about 17 miles above Dayton to the mouth of Jackson Creek, southwest of Springfield. In the Jackson Creek valley, the canal was to ascend 81 feet to reach the summit level. From Jackson Creek, the proposed route crossed back to the Miami River valley and proceeded up that valley on side-lying ground several miles to a crossing of the river. After crossing the Miami, the canal was to return back down the valley for several miles to the mouth of Loramie Creek and then along that stream north to Cynthian (near present day Newport). The proposed summit level, in total, was to be 62 1/2 miles long, with the natural summit "lowered" by means of a 12-foot deep cut in order to keep the whole length level.

The entire 160-mile extension, including the summit level, was to be supplied by a 10-mile feeder from the Miami River and Mosquito (Tawawa) Creek, introduced into the canal at the Miami crossing, and a 14-mile feeder from the Mad River, introduced into the canal at the Jackson Creek end of the summit. Canal engineer David Bates estimated that the Mad River feeder could supply 10,000 cu. ft./min. ("cfm") and the Miami River feeder 2,740 cfm. Bates warned that this would generate only 70-80 cfm/mile when 100 cfm/mile was generally considered the minimum necessary for canal operations. As a result, special efforts to seal the line would be necessary. He also proposed to "decline" the feeder to force water through at 3-4 mile/hour. Additionally, he believed that the proposed Mad River feeder would be costly to construction because of the necessity of much excavation and filling, including a 1-1/2 mile section to be built on the side of a perpendicular limestone ledge.

## A Change in Plans

In 1828, Congress granted public land to the state to aid in the extension of the Miami Canal. Two years later, the General Assembly authorized the Canal Commissioners to examine the practicability of extending the canal from the Mad River at Dayton to the mouth of Auglaize River at Defiance. Surveys and estimates were made in the summer of 1830. A drought during the summer had reduced the flow of the Mad River at the point of the proposed feeder to 4,000 cfm, substantially below the 10,000 cfm minimum which Bates had relied upon in his 1825 report. Also, another 1,000 cfm was being removed from the Mad River at Dayton to supply the canal there. As a result, in drought conditions, only 5,740 cfm might be available to supply the 160 mile extension -- clearly an insufficient amount.

In their 1831 report summarizing the studies made the previous summer, canal engineers Samuel Forrer, William H. Price and Jesse L. Williams, calculated that 17,000 cfm would be necessary to provide an adequate supply of water for the extension, based on the conventional wisdom of 100 cfm for each mile of canal, plus adequate lockage. Since only 5,740 cfm would be available from the two feeders, the engineers proposed that the deficiency be made up by the construction of artificial reservoirs. Expensive reservoirs, when added to the costly Mad River feeder, however would make the cost of the extension prohibitive.

The engineers solved the problem by suggesting a new route from Dayton to the summit. Instead of following the Mad River from Dayton, the canal would cross the Mad and follow the Miami to the mouth of Loramie Creek. After crossing Loramie Creek, the extension would rise by means of a flight of locks to the summit level. The Mad River feeder was deleted from the plans; however, the Miami River feeder was to be retained, receiving its water from the river 6 miles above Sidney and entering the main canal immediately above the flight of locks at the south end of the summit.

The engineers proposed that the additional water needed could be supplied by four or five reservoirs. Two or three related reservoirs were to be built on Loramie Creek and its branches to supply the northern end of the summit. Another reservoir at St. Marys would enter the canal 6 miles beyond the first lock north of the summit and would be large enough to supply all of the extension north of the summit to its junction with the Wabash and Erie.

The fifth reservoir was to be constructed at the head of the Miami River near Lewistown in northwest Logan County. The engineers estimated that a single embankment 105 chains (6,930 feet) long could enclose the north and south branches of the Miami without need for a separate feeder outlet. The reservoir would connect with an existing deep, 60-acre natural lake, Indian Lake, and would cover ground described as being so swampy as to be impassable at all times on horseback.

Water from the reservoir would be released into the Miami, which would transport it 23-3/4 miles downstream to the head of the feeder just above Port Jefferson. The Lewistown Reservoir was expected to cover 919 acres to an average depth of 11 1/2 feet. The banks were to be 10 feet thick at the top with a slope of 1.75 to 1, and were to be protected against "the ravages of muskrats and crawfish" by a two-inch plank wall in the center. The inner slope was to be protected from the surf by stones, gravel or timber and, especially, by a well-set growth of dwarf willow.

The engineers calculated under the new plan that the feeder would be required to supply 16 miles of the main canal from the mouth of Loramie Creek to the proposed Loramie reservoir(s) at Cynthian, together with the 14 miles of the feeder itself. Under the 100 cfm/mile formula, this would require 3,000 cfm from the Miami. Additionally, the engineers determined that the lockage up to the summit would require an additional 938 cfm (assuming 100 boats traversed the locks each 24 hours), for a total requirement of 3,938 cfm. The seasonal supply of water available from the Miami above Sidney was estimated as follows.

| | |
|---|---|
| 135 days each year | 11,500 cfm |
| 60 days each year | 5,000 cfm |
| 50 days each year | 4,000 cfm |
| 120 days each year | 2,500 cfm |

The capacity of the Lewistown reservoir was to compensate for the deficiency of the Miami during the 120 days each year when the river's natural flow would be insufficient for canal needs. Excess flow from the reservoir and from the Miami River, during the portion of the year when the natural flow was expected to exceed the needs of the feeder and southern end of the summit, would augment the otherwise barely sufficient flow from the Loramie reservoir on the northern part of the summit and the remainder of the extension.

Despite all of their studies, Forrer, Price and Williams admitted that such calculations were inexact and depended in part upon such variables as rainfall, drainage basin, evaporation and leakage, as well as the area and depth of the reservoir. The engineers also warned of the danger of relying upon reservoirs rather than natural streams since breaches in the walls of the reservoirs and their feeders could render the canal unusable for substantial lengths of time until the reservoirs were refilled. They added, "...there is no instance, it is believed, in any country, where this method of supply has been so extensively introduced as is now proposed for the Miami Canal." The costs were estimated as follows:

| | |
|---|---|
| Miami feeder | $152,681.21 |
| Miami reservoir (Lewistown) | 41,221.02 |
| Three Loramie Creek reservoirs* | 19,126.05 |
| St. Marys reservoir | 93,003.21 |

\* Includes 12 1/2 % added because of the "unimproved state of the country."

The estimated cost of the Miami extension in 1836 was $2,055,421.67. The total cost of the extension not including damage claims outstanding in 1845 was $3,195,100.

### Construction Begins

Disputes over funding for the extension of the Miami Canal delayed the commencement of actual construction. The first contracts were finally awarded in 1833, and construction was completed to the mouth of Loramie Creek by July of 1837. Contracts for the summit level, including the feeder from the Miami River, however, were not let until September of 1837. Contracts for the Lewistown reservoir were to be awarded in 1838; however, the growing financial difficulties faced by the state's canal program delayed any action.

The Board of Public Works reported in its Annual Report for 1838 that construction of the 14 1/2 mile long Sidney Feeder (as the Miami River feeder was now being referred to) was nearly complete, with completion expected in 1839. The Board also reported that the construction involved difficult and expensive excavation because the route for much of its distance ran along sidelying ground and heavy bluffs. Forrer, Price and Williams had warned of this difficulty in their 1831 report, stating that the ground was unfavorable to canal construction due to the high bluff clay banks, valleys and high points of land.

An additional difficulty arose when it was discovered that the quantity of water which could be depended upon from the Miami River was much less that previously anticipated. The Board felt that this deficiency could be remedied by expanding the proposed Lewistown reservoir to 5,000 acres, which recent surveys had shown was practical.

Despite the Board's predictions, the summit level and the Sidney feeder were not to be completed until 1843, six years after the contracts were let. Much of the delay resulted from Ohio's steadily worsening financial difficulties. The Board of Public Works was often unable to make regular payments under its contracts, with the result that construction was not carried out with much energy. For a period, payment was made only in checks redeemable for state bonds - which could be sold only at a discount. Construction came to a complete halt for a period in 1840.

In early 1842, the Board of Public Works once more estimated that the summit and feeder would be open for navigation early in the year. The Board cautioned that the extension of the Miami Canal from Loramie Creek to the north end of the deep cut twelve miles north of St. Marys (including the Mercer County Reservoir and the Sidney Feeder) was of such a character that it had necessarily cost much more than any other canal in Ohio of equal length.

Water was finally let into the Sidney Feeder in June of 1843. The result was almost immediate disaster. The high bluffs west of the Miami River along the side of which much of the canal south of Sidney was built are composed of clay, with occasional veins of fine sand through which water can pass with little obstruction. As a result, when water was let into the feeder, several heavy and extensive slides occurred, in some cases carrying the entire canal down the hill. Although the necessary repairs were completed with much delay and expense, numerous additional breaches continued to occur at short intervals. Navigation finally began on the feeder in September (and on the main summit level in November of 1843). The Board of Public Works warned that additional heavy breaches could be expected. The completed feeder cost was $392,258.

The year 1843 also saw the near-completion of the Mercer County Reservoir at St. Marys. Use of that facility, however, was delayed because dissatisfied residents of Celina had cut the embankment on several occasions. Construction of a single reservoir on Loramie Creek also began when P. W. Taylor & Co. of Granville was awarded the contract for the remaining work on the Miami Canal Extension. Construction of the reservoir on the Miami River at Lewistown was, however, years away from commencement.

## The Completed Sidney Feeder

As with the main line of the extension, the Sidney Feeder was constructed 50 feet wide at the surface and 30 feet wide at the bottom and 5 feet deep, 10 feet wider and 1 foot deeper than was standard on the Miami Canal. The canal was constructed of an even greater width where such could be done without additional cost.

A dam of timber with stone abutments diverted water to a bulkhead and headgates on the right bank of the Miami River approximately 1/2 mile east of the village of Port Jefferson in Shelby County. As described in 1867, this dam was 200 feet long and 6 feet high, although when rebuilt in 1884 it apparently was constructed 267 feet long and 9 feet high. A "locktender" was stationed by the state at this lockhead. The dam fell into disrepair after abandonment of the canals in the early twentieth century; however, in the early 1930s the WPA started, and then abandoned, a new dam at the site which would have rewatered several miles of the canal as a park.

From the bulkhead, the canal followed the right bank of the Miami River past a small basin into Port Jefferson. Just south of Port Jefferson, a 50-foot waste-weir was constructed to return excess water into the Miami. In the same area, a 6-foot by 8-foot arch culvert was constructed over a small stream. The canal was laid out through relatively flat bottom land southwest of the village, crossing Plum Creek four miles below Port Jefferson by means of a small timber aqueduct approximately 50 feet long. The towpath crossed the creek by a separate parallel bridge.

As with many of the other aqueducts on the Ohio canals, the Plum Creek aqueduct proved to be a constant source of trouble, requiring many repairs. As an example, in 1889 flood water caused the entire structure to fall into the creek. The same flood conditions caused a break in the towpath bank at the south end of the aqueduct which was 32 feet long, 80 feet wide at its base and 17 feet deep. A portion of the berm bank was also washed away. It is interesting to note the manner in which the damage was repaired. Two wing walls of timber 7 feet high and 35 feet long were constructed and fastened back with iron rods to ties "well anchored". The gap in the bed of the canal was then filled in and an apron with four floor timbers under it was put on.

Beyond Plum Creek, the river and canal turned south towards Sidney. Near this point, Dingman Pike (present day State Route 47) crossed the canal by means of a swing bridge. As the river turns south, it also skirts the side of the valley, squeezing the canal against the base of steep bluffs. As the river begins to descend from the level of Port Jefferson (and the summit), the canal maintained its level by rising along the bluffs until it entered Sidney at the level of the tableland on which the city is built. At the north edge of the city, the canal crossed Wells Creek on a small culvert with a 6-foot by 6-foot arch. Near this culvert a mill pond and flouring mill were built. Entering Sidney from the northeast, the canal passed through the northern section of the town in a southwesterly direction, turning south along the western edge of the tableland.

South of Sidney, a 150-foot waste weir and waste gates were located in the feeder near the line of the Dayton and Michigan railroad. The waste water may have helped to power two nearby mills. For the next 4 1/2 miles, the canal was constructed along the side, near the top, of the steep river bluffs.

Several ponds along this stretch of the canal resulted where the canal crossed, and dammed, ravines in the bluffs. Mill Branch (or Rumley Creek) was crossed by means of a stone, single-span culvert with a 10-foot by 12-foot arch. Because a local wagon road, as well as the streams, were routed under the canal by this culvert, early maps refer to the structure as the "tunnel bridge". It was also sometimes inaccurately referred to as the Kirkwood Aqueduct, after a nearby station on the railroad. The late Leonard Hill, canal historian and honorary trustee of the Canal Society of Ohio, estimated the culvert to be 200 feet long, with the canal banks about 60 feet above the stream. Hill recalled driving a horse and buggy and an automobile on the road that ran through the culvert.

About 1 mile south of the tunnel bridge, the feeder made a sharp turn west away from the Miami River valley to run approximately 1 more mile into the village of Lockport (Lockington) to unite with the main canal just above Lock No. 1. It has not yet been determined whether a guard lock or other structure was present at the entrance of the Sidney Feeder into the Miami Canal at Lockington, as the level of the Feeder and the summit level are the same. The total length of the Sidney Feeder was 14 1/2 miles.

## Lewistown Reservoir

Although the site of the Miami reservoir near Lewistown had been examined with a view to placing the work under contract in 1838, many delays occurred. The first embankment was finally completed, and the reservoir filled, in March, 1852. As constructed, the reservoir capacity was only about 1,000 acres. It was estimated, however, that construction of an additional embankment across several slashes, or bayous, by which water was escaping could increase the capacity to 5,000 acres.

The site of the reservoir was the low, marshy lands around Indian Lake through which the north and south forks of the Miami River flowed. In order to preserve the embankment from "wave action," timber in the reservoir was left standing. An early historian described the scene as follows:

> "Today one cannot well imagine anything more dismal and desolate than this spot, this vast submerged plain, thickly studded with the bare and darkly decaying trees, whose leafless branches spread abroad as if to warn the unwary of the dreadful miasma lurking below. Quinine ought certainly to be a premium in the locality surrounding this cesspool of pestilence."
>
> History of Logan County, p. 544.

The reservoir as initially constructed proved to be inadequate for its intended purposes. As a result, the water supply in the Sidney Feeder frequently failed to such an extent that insufficient water was available for the summit level of the main canal. Although a part of the deficiency could be made up from Loramie Reservoir, the small size of that reservoir limited the additional water which could be made available without exhausting the supply. It often became necessary late in the summer to provide "lighters" to help heavily-laden boats over the summit.

Expansion of Lewistown Reservoir was repeatedly delayed because of the expense and legal difficulties involved in condemning private land within its limits. Although construction of the second embankment had been all but completed prior to 1860, in that year 1,100 acres of necessary property still had not been acquired by the state. Negotiations to purchase, and efforts to condemn, the remaining lands were then suspended because of the exorbitant prices being asked by the landowners. As a result, the summit level continued to experience repeated periods of low water throughout the early 1860s. It was not until 1863 that most of the claims were settled to the point where the reservoir could be filled.

Another recurrent problem involved intentional destruction of the embankments, presumably by disgruntled citizens. The first breach cost $10,000 to repair. Subsequent cuts were made in May, 1863 and April, 1864 and were repaired by the canal lessees at a cost of $3,000 and $3,500, respectively. At the time of the 1864 breach, the reservoir had been filled for the first time to within 6 feet of the top. The escaping water cut a hole in the bank 140 feet wide and 8 feet deep. It took ten days for the reservoir to drain through the gap. The breach was repaired by driving piles and putting brush and timber in the cut.

As finally completed, the top of the 600 foot long waste weir was 12.1 feet above the base of the discharge gate at the bulkhead, with the top water line of the reservoir being 2 feet higher. In the late 1860s or early 1870s the waste weir was lowered by 1 foot to reduce the pressure on the reservoir embankments, although a later canal engineer complained that this also had the effect of eliminating one month's supply of water from the summit level. When filled, Lewistown Reservoir covered in excess of 6,300 acres, even with the reduced capacity resulting from the lowered waste weir. The surface of the impoundment was approximately 50 feet higher than the summit level at Port Jefferson.

In 1877 and 1878 the flow of water from the reservoir to Port Jefferson was greatly improved by removing obstructions in the Miami River. Previously, these obstructions had caused severe flooding problems whenever water was released from the reservoir.

By the mid 1880s the reservoir's several miles of embankment had seriously deteriorated, in part because of its use as a roadway. Repairs, which were commenced in 1884, included the addition of 5,000 feet of timber facing and 3,000 feet of stone facing to the banks. The timber facing consisted of a skeleton frame in the embankment of 8 x 8 square timbers, securely tied back to the cross-ties and back-sills. The face was covered with two courses of solid white oak plank (the inner course 1-inch thick and the outer 2-inches thick), so placed as to break joints and to extend into the solid earth in front of the bank 2 feet, in a trench. The trench was filled with puddle on both sides of the plank, and the remainder on the inside next to the bank was filled with gravel. Stone facing was laid 3 feet high.

With the decline of the canal system in the early twentieth century, Lewistown Reservoir began a new life as Indian Lake State Park.

§§§§§§§§§§§§§§§§§§§§§§§§§§§

*Port Jefferson, a sleepy village at the head of the Sidney Feeder, once had visions of grandeur. This article is reprinted from the June 26-July 1, 1976, special bicentennial editions of the* Sidney Daily News.

Volume XXIII (1985), No. 2, pp. 23-24

## PORT JEFFERSON THE LITTLE CHICAGO OF THE MIDWEST by Pat Flinn

Driving west on Ohio Route 47 a few miles east of Sidney, one comes upon a roadside park at the outskirts of Port Jefferson, a community of approximately 450 souls. Here behind the picnic tables, the odd stone and cement work, the stagnant pond and the nearby dam on the Great Miami River is the beginning of the Sidney Feeder of the Miami and Erie Canal which winds along the west bank of the river 14 miles from Lockington.

Now to refer to Port Jefferson as "Little Chicago" is to give a new meaning to the word "little" but a hundred years or so ago this community of so much promise was believed by some residents to be destined to eclipse the Windy City.

Settled in 1814 by one John Hathaway and "a man named Gilbert," Port Jefferson, known as Pratt, Ohio prior to 1820, was platted as a village in 1836 and incorporated in 1842. The feeder canal was completed in 1841 and a boom was at hand for the new village. Construction of the Lewistown Reservoir (Indian Lake), 1851-1860, at the headwaters of the Miami River, which helped regulate the water supply, also raised the hopes of the towns upstream from Port Jefferson (such as Quincy) that they would one day become the terminus of the feeder. This proved futile. "As the highest point of traffic on the feeder canal…Port Jefferson attracted all the grain and lumber shipping from a large and rich district to the north and east of it," wrote Judge Joseph D. Barnes in *Memoirs of the Miami Valley*, (Robert O. Law Co., Chicago, 1919).

In time five warehouses clustered on the canal bank, and a grist mill, cooper and stave shops (employing about 150 men) and four blacksmiths were all kept busy.

Two or three canal boats were built there and the feeder was a busy thoroughfare for packet and freight boats. A man named George Gump (*ca.* 1831-1920), known as the hack man or Port Jeff Hack, worked the canal boats from Port Jefferson to Dayton as a boy before beginning, at the age of 23, his delivery service (by mule and later by spring wagon) to Sidney in direct competition with the canal. This service he maintained for just over 60 years, retiring, crippled with rheumatism, at the age of 83.

Business was brisk and the streets thronged with people. Port Jefferson boasted three physicians, three dry goods stores, three groceries, a shoe shop, a stove and tinware business and two taverns "filled with wayfarers," according to an unidentified visitor to the community in 1876.

It was at this time that Samuel Rice (or Wright), traveling from Buffalo to Chicago on horseback, decided to look the village over as a possible investment site. He ventured on to Chicago and soon after returned to Port Jefferson, a location he saw, not altogether sagaciously, "as having far more promise than the settlement at Fort Dearborn." But the dream envisioned by Rice for Port Jefferson was doomed, and as historians noted, once the Dayton and Michigan Railroad and the Bellefontaine and Indiana intersected at Sidney, "a cloud came over the business sky of Port Jefferson which has never lifted." In concluding his record of Port Jefferson, in 1919, Judge Barnes wrote, "One no longer hears the sound of hammer or wheel save when some automobile needs repair." There were no taverns left and "…the wayfarer who hungers must go away empty." The canal was but a waterlily pond, being entirely disused.

The feeder, however, had one more chance for life. A new dam was built across the river with funds furnished by the WPA in 1935-36. (My father and uncle Red Zimpher took part in this.) It was intended to divert waters back into the canal feeder with the gates at the old bulkhead to be utilized (thus explaining the "modern" work here post-dating the original by almost 100 years). Two and a half miles of the feeder were cleaned out with the project to be extended to the waterworks in Sidney, and a new aqueduct was to span Plum Creek at the site of the old one. Boating, fishing and fire protection for Port Jefferson were hoped-for results, but this canal-related project died as did so many others when flood waters destroyed the new dam. The remnants can still be seen at the roadside park east of Port Jefferson, the beginning and now the end of our visit to the Little Chicago of the midwest.

§§§§§§§§§§§§§§§§§§§§§§§§§§§

*Former CSO president Mike Morthorst led a tour of the Miami & Erie Canal along the summit level north to Delphos in the fall of 2006. Here, we shorten it a bit in order to draw the line at St. Marys.*

Volume XLIV (2006), No. 4, pp. 61-77

### THE MIAMI AND ERIE CANAL: NEWPORT TO ST. MARYS by Michael E. Morthorst

The stretch of the Miami and Erie Canal which parallels Ohio Route 66 from Newport to just beyond Delphos contains many of the most interesting artifacts remaining of this particular canal. Our nominal beginning point is the town of Newport, although a wide water located approximately a mile south of town, and a culvert situated three and one half miles away in the same direction merit some comment.

The culvert is over **Painter Creek** on the summit level. It is situated approximately two and one half miles southeast of where the canal intersects with State Route 47 along the canal right-of-way. This structure is somewhat difficult to reach, due to its location on private property. It is not the culvert identified as Painter Creek Culvert in the 1997 Spring Tour Book. That culvert is six miles further east on the canal and slightly smaller (a fifteen foot span). The Miami and Erie Canal Corridor (MECCA) has identified this misnamed culvert as the "Little Painter Creek Culvert," which is as good a name as anyone can come up with for now. The culvert that actually spans the real Painter Creek features a sixteen foot span, which makes it the largest existing culvert on the summit level. Only the spans of the double arches of the destroyed Turtle Creek Culvert were larger at 22 feet. The Painter Creek Culvert is similar to the Mill Creek Culvert in that the downstream side is intact. However, damage from erosion to the upstream side has occurred. Indications are that erosion of this culvert is almost as severe as the damage to the Mill Creek Culvert (by comparison, a 13 foot span). This stretch of canal, including the Painter Creek Culvert is to be a future walking trail developed by Shelby County Parks. At the moment, however, there are reportedly some landowners hostile to that idea, so visits in this area may

**Painter Creek Culvert**. On the summit in rural Shelby County. *Courtesy Bill Oeters.*

not be a good idea.

The wide water is presently known as **Leighty Lake**. Located on the north side of Ohio Route 47 just east of Ohio Route 66, this body of water has an interesting history. Originally it was a wide water on the canal, as the canal flooded a natural ravine. Since there were no locks nearby, there was little practical use for a wide water in that area. After the canal was abandoned in 1913, the area was left fallow for about 50 years. During that time there were two developments. The body of water became even wider and deeper, due to the accumulation of runoff water. Also Loramie Creek, located just to the west at a level twenty feet or so below the canal began to erode into the wall of the lake. In the 1940's a control structure was built to retard the erosion process. This structure can still be viewed today. Subsequently the erosion began to occur just north of the control structure. In 1968, the lake was drained to avoid a catastrophic failure. Between 1968 and the present, the lake has refilled and again presents the risk of failing, placing in peril a gas station and a number of houses at the intersection of Ohio Routes 66 and 47. Meetings have been held in the last three years seeking a solution. Latest plans center around moving the route of Loramie Creek away from the earthen canal wall on the western side of the lake. Leighty Lake can be viewed from State Route 47, or can be hiked to from the town of Newport.

The small town of **Newport** is the first settlement found on Route 66 as it parallels the canal. Originally known as Cynthian, it was plotted by Nicholas Wyant in 1839. The first businesses were a hotel and grocery store. Later steam and grist mills were established. A flax mill was built in 1881. This settlement marked the southern boundary of the area of intense German settlement, centered at Minster and New Bremen, which began in 1832. These German immigrant communities usually featured a large (and usually) Catholic Church. Newport is no exception. […] Newport did not become a large community, as its population never exceeded 150 at any time in the nineteenth century. Presently, two canal era buildings can be found where the canal crosses Route 66.

Two miles to the north on Route 66 is the much larger town of **Fort Loramie**. Originally known as Berlin, its great landmark is the massive St. Michael's Catholic Church situated in the center of the community. St. Michael's is one of the more prominent German immigrant Catholic Churches, also called the "Land of the Cross Tipped Churches." This is a remarkable concentration of approximately 42 churches in a 20 by 20 mile area. Most were founded by Father Francis Brunner, a Passionist priest, in the mid to late nineteenth century. The Passionists were so successful in this area that the religious order ran the public schools in the area up until the 1960's. If one travels to the west of Route 66 in this area four to twelve steeples can be seen on the horizon at any time. […]

Fort Loramie is located on the western end of the Native-American portage between the Ohio River and Lake Erie. It was a crossroads long before the white man arrived. In 1769 Peter Loramie, a French Canadian former priest, established a trading post at the site of the present town which was then a large Native American village. Loramie was suspected of inciting Native-American hostility toward the arriving settlers. George Rogers Clark burned Loramie's outpost in 1782 and Loramie left the area. In 1795 Anthony Wayne built a blockhouse and supply depot on this site and called it Fort Loramie. Settlement began after the War of 1812 and the community was incorporated in 1837. Just north of town is the **Greenville Treaty Line**. This boundary line marked the demarcation zone for land that the Native Americans ceded to the settlers (south of the line). From those lands the Native Americans were to hold in perpetuity (north of the line and consisting of the northwest corner of the state). "Perpetuity" turned out to be less than twenty five years, as the Native-Americans were under pressure to cede the remaining territory to the white man, and did so in a series of treaties executed in 1805, 1807, 1808, and 1818.

North of Fort Loramie, almost opposite the historic marker along the road for the Greenville Treaty Line, the **Loramie Creek Aqueduct** can be viewed from a distance. This is the northern crossing of the canal over Loramie Creek. This aqueduct crosses Loramie Creek just as the creek exits the Loramie Reservoir of the canal system. The reservoir dammed a narrow ravine and provided a water supply to the summit level of the canal. The lake encompasses over 1,500 surface acres and thirty miles of shoreline. This was the cheapest reservoir to build, costing approximately $25,400. It is currently an Ohio state park. The aqueduct abutments still exist, and are easily viewable. Just north of the aqueduct is the feeder channel to Loramie Reservoir. It is a short channel, less than 2 miles long. Along the route of the feeder is an early twentieth century control structure. This regulated the flow of water to the canal.

The next large settlement along the Miami and Erie Canal is **Minster**. It was settled by Francis Joseph Stallo in 1832. Francis Stallo was a printer by trade who emigrated from Oldenburg, Germany in 1831. He initially settled in Cincinnati, where he worked in a printing shop and befriended William H. McGuffey, who later published his famous series of readers. Stallo used his printing background to flood his former neighborhoods in Germany with information about the wonderful opportunities in America. By 1832 a significant number of his countrymen began to arrive in Cincinnati. Soon there was a backlash, as the Cincinnati residents resented the influx of "Dutch" Catholics. The more extreme elements believed the immigration was part of a plot to seize the Mississippi Valley and create a Papal domain in the New World. The new residents, disappointed with Cincinnati, asked Stallo what they should do. Stallo proposed founding a town or colony. A tract of 1200 acres in Mercer and Shelby Counties was purchased from the U.S. Government from lands north of the Greenville Treaty Line along a Native-American portage between the Auglaize and Miami Rivers. The cost was $1.25 an acre. The purchase was finalized in October, 1832. The settlers began to drift north almost immediately.

The original name of the settlement was Stallostown. When it was incorporated as a village in 1839 it was renamed Muenster, which was later simplified to Minster. Minster is another of the remarkable German settlements which built large Catholic churches. […]

The canal is located on the western side of Minster and is still watered, although the canal is used for the local water waste treatment facility. There are no locks, culverts, or aqueducts in the town, but there is a three mile walking path located on the towpath which has become a focal point for the area. […]

Located three miles north of Minster on the Loramie Summit, the next locality on the canal is **New Bremen**. This town was founded by 33 German immigrants from Hanover and Bavaria in 1832. Scouts were employed and a site midway between Toledo and Cincinnati was chosen. As it was situated on the edge of the Black Swamp, it was believed to be very fertile. In this region New Bremen is distinct in that it is not a Catholic community—its original founders were Protestants. It was platted on June 11,

1833 as Bremen. However, the original name, Bremen, was changed to New Bremen in 1835 to avoid confusion with the Bremen located in Fairfield County. New Bremen was the first of five communities in the immediate area that developed along the canal. Amsterdam, located to the south of modern New Bremen, was at the intersection of the west side of the canal with the present Amsterdam Road, and was founded in 1837. It was decimated in the 1849 cholera epidemic and little remains. Mohrmansville, settled in 1838, was located along the present Lock Two Road northeast of central New Bremen. With the opening of the canal in 1845, the original New Bremen settlement divided into two communities with the canal as the boundary. New Bremen was to the west and Ober (Upper) Bremen was to the east. Ober Bremen was platted in 1853 and was settled by people from all over Germany, in contrast to New Bremen which continued to attract Germans from the Hanover area. Ober Bremen developed into the business center, but each community had its own town hall, mayor, fire department and school. New Bremen and Ober Bremen finally merged in 1876. The distinction between the two areas has continued long after the merger, as the neighborhood east of the canal is sometimes referred to as "Frogtown" which is a reference to large frogs that lived in a canal pond located in town. The area west of the canal was nicknamed "Cheesequarters," a reference to the dairy farms located there. Vogelsangtown, the last of the communities, was founded on the west side of the canal to the south of New Bremen and west of Ober Bremen. It was primarily a residential area and was annexed by New Bremen in 1865.

New Bremen is the highest point on the canal—512 feet above Cincinnati and 396 feet above Toledo. In the center of town is Lock 1n. Originally a wooden structure, this lock provided water power, and commerce generated by boats passing through the area. Additionally gristmills, woolen mills, sawmills, warehouses, and pork packing plants developed along the canal. The wooden structure was rebuilt in concrete in 1910, as part of the canal improvement scheme of that time. Lock 1n is presently located in a park next to the library along Ohio 66. It is presently being rebuilt in concrete by the Division of Water of the Ohio Department of Natural Resources. Part of this redevelopment will be a more faithful reconstruction of the lock to resemble its original appearance. There was a lockkeeper's house, which was unfortunately burned down as a local fire department exercise approximately forty years ago. The right of way of the canal located north across Monroe Street was flumed in 1968 and developed into parkland. [...]

The canal and Ohio 66 separate just north of New Bremen. The canal veers eastward a few miles to the little community of **Lock Two**. Lock Two Road follows the canal to that locality. As late as 1859, the town was also known as "New Paris." It was never officially platted. This was the location of a wooden lock, whose superstructure has been removed, of which nothing remains except for the change of elevation in the earthworks that can be observed at the former site of the lock. Wooden locks were the most inexpensive construction available, and were used when lack of money was an issue or when building stone was unavailable. This town was originally called New Paris. It contained a combination sawmill/lumberyard, a gristmill, a pork packing plant, a warehouse, a grocery and a general store. Today the town square remains and features large brick buildings surrounding it, these being the former mills and stores. On the former mill building, the west wall features shoots where canal boats were moored.

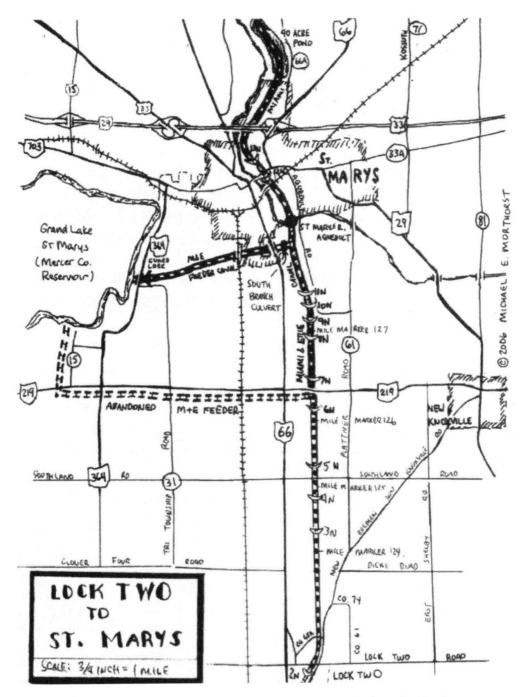

**Miami & Erie Canal from Lock Two to St. Marys.** *Map by Mike Morthorst.*

The canal now heads due north, one half mile east of Ohio 66. In this stretch were nine locks. As eight were constructed of wood, little remains of them. Lock 8n, located on private property, is in excellent condition, and features a spillway, and the stones have a distinctive design. It was originally a wooden lock, but is believed to have been rebuilt in stone in the early twentieth century. Another attraction on this stretch of canal are four stone mileposts numbered from 124 to 127 (the distance from Cincinnati). This stretch of canal is located on the Buckeye Trail, and is available for hiking. On the third Sunday of October each year, the local area has a **"Walk with Nature"** which features a supervised hike from Lock Two to Forty Acre Pond north of St. Marys. During this hike, there is bus service and numerous stops along the route to aid and accommodate visitors. The St. Marys Chamber of Commerce can be contacted to supply additional information.

The final large canal town along Ohio 66 is **St. Marys**. This part of Ohio has long been a heavily traveled area by various groups of humanity. Originally, the Native-Americans in the area used the portage between the St. Marys and Auglaize Rivers to facilitate travel from the Great Lakes to the Gulf of Mexico. French fur traders were active in this area as early as the 1600's. There was a Shawnee village called Kettle Town located in this area, which was later renamed by Europeans as Girtystown.

In 1794 General Anthony Wayne established Fort St. Marys as a supply post for his army as it moved north to Fallen Timbers. In 1812 Colonel John Johnston, of Johnston Farm fame, negotiated the Treaty of St. Marys, which made the area safe for further American settlement. What became the modern City of St. Marys was established in 1823, several years before construction of the Miami and Erie Canal began. Once the canal opened, the usual trappings of wealth developed, such as various mills, stores and other industries. […]

This community is located on the eastern end of Lake St. Marys, originally constructed as the **Mercer County Reservoir** to provide a water supply to the canal. Before the construction of Hoover Dam and Lake Meade in Arizona, Lake St. Marys had a long run as the largest man-made lake in the country. A feeder canal exits the lake toward the south of town and intersects with the main canal on the east side of town three and one half miles distant. At the lake is a bulkhead lock. This is part of the control system regulating the release of water from the lake. The water provided fed water to the lake heading north to Toledo. The feeder canal was navigable as it was possible for boats to transit through the lock and into the lake. The lock remains much as it looked when built, with some concrete modifications constructed on the top of the structure.

Back at the intersection of the canal and the active feeder canal it is possible to get across the canal carefully on a low rise crossing structure from Aqueduct Road. About one thousand feet west on the feeder canal is found a large culvert. This is known as the **South Branch Culvert**. This structure is a triple stone arch affair, the arches approximately six feet in diameter. It was constructed in 1859. Presently this can be best viewed on the south side of the feeder canal. The structure is in fair to poor condition. Liners of corrugated steel have been inserted into the arches to keep them from collapsing. A supplemental large block culvert has been built on the western side to accommodate the shifting of the stream in that direction.

As part of the extended plumbing system for the lake, a second feeder canal was constructed further to the south. This is known as the **Dry Feeder**. It was situated at an elevation higher than that of the Mercer Reservoir. The plan was that it would take a theoretical excess water supply which was to accumulate during the rainy season from the Loramie and Lewistown Reservoirs, and store it in the

**Wooden Lock 13, Downtown St. Marys**. This lock was under the woolen mill.

Mercer Reservoir, to be used when needed. The dry feeder left the main canal near Lock 7n. The ditch can still be viewed on the south side of Ohio 219 going westward from the canal. As matters turned out, it fell out of use rather quickly once the enlargement of the Lewistown Reservoir was completed.

Just north of the intersection of the Mercer County Reservoir Feeder Canal along Aqueduct Road, is found the location of the **St. Marys River Aqueduct**. This was originally a wood and stone structure, which collapsed in 1943. It was replaced with an elaborate steel and concrete replacement, built on the stone foundations of the old aqueduct. The replacement structure carries the watered canal over the river in a series of pipes. It is now used to supply water to industries in the city. The canal runs behind the stores on the south side of Spring Street. East of Chestnut Street, the large municipal parking lot was a turning basin. Where Chestnut Street crossed the canal, Lock 12n was situated just to the east. It was partially destroyed and buried in 1980. Plans are now being considered to restore this structure. Just east of the lock, was the junction of the canal with a hydraulic waterway, known as the St. Marys Upper Canal. This waterway paralleled the canal for approximately a half mile and supplied water to a number of mills, and now cools water in the municipal electric plant. A watered section of the canal exists west of Chestnut Street. In this remnant of the canal is located the "Belle of St. Marys" replica canal boat. It was a project of the local Miami and Erie Canal Society and the late Ray Zunk. It was dedicated in 1990, but being a wooden boat, it soon deteriorated. It was removed from the water in 2002 and repaired. It now rests on an underwater mooring cradle and no longer actually floats. The hope is that it will last much longer with this arrangement.

The canal passes under Spring Street under an extended bridge. In recent times the canal and Lock 13n were underground for the next block going north. A large retail store faced Spring Street and a woolen mill was behind the store that faced High Street. The store was destroyed in a fire in 2002 and the ruins were demolished. As of this writing the woolen mill is being razed. The plan is to develop the woolen mill site into a park centered on the lock. It is hoped that the former store site can be redeveloped into some sort of retail development.

From Chestnut Street north for approximately five blocks the canal and the millrace run parallel together. At about the halfway point of the Upper Canal's length there is a structure known as **The Tumbles**. This structure dates from canal times and was restored in 2003. It allows excess water from the Upper Canal to flow into the main canal. From High Street it is possible to hike along the improved towpath to Forty Acre Pond. It is a very scenic walk. This author has taken this particular walk during a "Walk with Nature" and can vouch for its beauty. One of the highlights of the trip is the bridge under the US 33 expressway, which allows safe passage for pedestrians. [...]

§§§§§§§§§§§§§§§§§§§§§§§§§§§

*Bridges are a favorite* Towpaths *topic. This short piece from 1969 by Ralph May explains how swing or bump bridges worked.*

Volume VII (1969), No. 4, p. 50

### THE SWINGING BRIDGES OVER THE MIAMI & ERIE CANAL by Ralph May

I was one of those fortunate lads to be brought up within a half block from a swing bridge in New Bremen. There were three of these bridges in the town and one lift bridge over the main street, and boats were still coming through when I was a boy.

Seeing a boat coming round the bend south of town, it was not long until a group of boys and girls would gather on the bridge, leaning over the railing and waiting for the boat and the mule team as it drew closer and closer until the bow would gently bump the bridge open, being guided to the one side by a stretch of timbers extending out into the water from the bridge. You see, the bridge had to be bumped from the one end in order to properly swing it round on its track midway to let the boat pass through.

There was a circular track on which castor-like wheels moved in turning the bridge from one side to the other. The track was located to the one side and that end of the bridge was weighted down with heavy limestones to give it the proper pitch in swinging around.

The approach to the bridge from the highway was in a curved pattern to match with the curved structure of the bridge platform, with an opening of several inches to permit the bridge to move freely.

It was quite a thrill in those days, to get the bump of the bridge when the bow of the slow-moving boat hit the heavy timber on the outer side of the bridge. Sometimes after the boat had passed through, the bridge might only swing back part way, and then the lock tender or whoever might be near-by would have to push the bridge back in place so the children could get off and traffic be resumed.

These bridges were convenient for the old threshing machine outfits to take on water, when tractors were steam-operated, a water tank was coupled on behind and on crossing the bridge, it was such an easy task to throw over the large intake hose and by a hand-pump draw water from the canal before going on to the next threshing operation.

*Recognized by the selection committee as a* Towpaths *"classic," this 2-parter on Grand Lake St. Marys was written by C. Ernest Robison in 1965.*

Volume III (1965), No. 3, pp. 7-12
Volume III (1965), No. 4, pp. 10-12

## THE GRAND RESERVOIR by C. Ernest Robison

Begun in 1837 and completed in 1845, for many years this reservoir was proudly hailed as "The greatest artificial body of water in the world" - - and it was; until Gatun Lake was created during the building of the Panama Canal. Some nine miles east and west, two to four miles north and south, containing 17,000 acres, this reservoir was an achievement to be proud of, especially so at the time and under the conditions then existing.

Like all the canal reservoirs, it was somewhat of an anomaly, being located on a summit in order to be above the canals, yet in a valley, in which to confine the needed water. The valley in which this reservoir was to be built sloped gradually to the west and the lake was made by building an embankment across the east end of this valley, some two miles in length and another some four miles across the west end. This latter was finished in 1845. These embankments were from ten to twenty feet high. Originally this area was about half prairie and the rest forest, with some of the prairie already being farmed. After the valley was enclosed by the two embankments, it began to fill with water flowing into it from the south shore from various small streams, including branches of the Wabash and St. Marys Rivers. As there was no great amount of water flowing, the newly finished reservoir filled very slowly, gradually spreading from west to east, with a great area of very shallow and almost stagnant water advancing ahead of the main body.

When construction began a contract was let for deadening and removing the timber in the bed of the reservoir but for some reason this was not done. The trees died when the water covered their lower trunks and together with the stagnant and foul smelling water, it is said to have been a very dismal place indeed.

And now we come to the aftermath of this situation; the State had seized the farms from their owners, promising to pay them a just compensation. Instead they had been paid nothing. Their fields were under the waters of the reservoir and they were becoming desperate for a means of livelihood.

In 1917, the *Spencerville Journal News* and *Celina Standard* published this account of the ensuing events, "…water…submerged the farm of Mr. Coate, with thirty-four acres of wheat, fifteen for Mrs.

**Grand Reservoir**. As it looked
to Henry Howe in 1843.

Crockett, the whole of Thomas Coate's land, nineteen acres for Judge Linzee and forty acres for Abraham Pratt, together with others. This outrage on the part of the officers of the State was too much to be borne by the people of Mercer County...On May 3, 1843, the inhabitants of Celina held a mass meeting and Benjamin Linzee, late judge of Auglaize County, was sent to Piqua to lay the peoples' grievances before the Board of Public Works. These gentlemen sent back the response: 'Help yourself if you can.' Again the messenger went back to say, if the land was not paid for the banks would be cut. The reply came; 'The Piqua Guards will be with you and rout you on that day.'"

Under these conditions they acted; some one hundred and fifty of the inhabitants of Celina and vicinity turned out with spades and shovels and after a period of intense labor, cut a channel through the west embankment into the old channel of Beaver Creek, a tributary of the Wabash, making a cut of some six feet below the bottom of the reservoir.

A great hue and cry arose from Columbus. Warrants were issued for all suspected parties, including all the county officials, but oddly enough, the grand jury failed to indict one single person. This damage cost the State $17,000 to repair, canal traffic was held up for months while the break was being repaired and the reservoir refilled. In fact the damage cost the State almost as much as the total cost of building the Loramie Reservoir, just finished, at a cost of $20,000.

When completed, the Grand Reservoir fed sixty miles of canal and, according to J. W. Erwin, carried to the Maumee River about 3,000 cubic feet of water per minute.

There were two feeders built to connect the reservoir with the canal. One led from the center of the "Bulkhead", on the eastern side, east and a little north to the canal. This was navigable and there was a lock at the bulkhead to lift boats to the lake level. It still supplies water to the canal. The other feeder, long ago abandoned, ran south from the south shore of the lake then east along the Montezuma Turnpike to the canal. There has been considerable confusion as to the purpose of the two feeders and we are indebted to Mr. Wilbur Coil of Spencerville for the following information.

The two feeders are the result of some very creative engineering. Concerned as always about the water supply available from even as large a source as Grand Lake, the engineers tapped the canal far enough to the south so that the canal could supply water <u>to</u> the lake! This is from the Report of the Board of Public Works, 1864.

"The side cut, or feeder, to the Mercer County Reservoir...is not yet entirely completed, but will be an a short time...In the winter and spring months when the Miami River has a large supply of water, a portion of it may be conveyed through the canal from Port Jefferson into the summit level, and then from thence through this side cut (or feeder, from near Lock No. 7, north of the summit) into the reservoir...for storage."

Is it not strange that water from the Great Miami River could eventually flow into Lake Erie?

One of the causes of the confusion before mentioned is the plate on the present feeder lock. Mr. Coil has called attention to the Report of the Board of Public Works, 1853, which explains the later date.

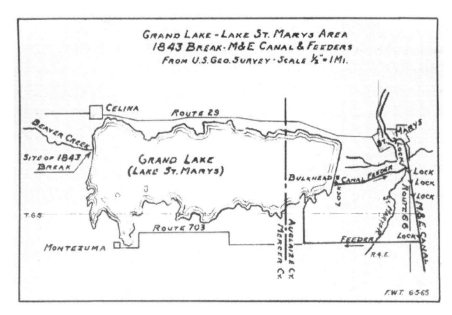

**The Grand Reservoir**. *Map by F.W. Trevorrow.*

PLATE ON THE FEEDER LOCK.
Col. A. P. Miller, Comm., Board of Public Works.
John W. Erwin, Resident Engineer.
Michael Haviland, Asst.
Sam'l Doyle & R. R. Dickey, Cont's.
Jon't Spilman, Mason. 1852.

"The outlet lock and bulkhead at the Mercer County Reservoir was so much decayed that it was almost impossible to pass a boat through the lock…Under these circumstances it was deemed necessary to rebuild both immediately…it was determined to build the lock of Dayton stone and the bulkhead of iron, and the work was advertised accordingly. These works have both been completed."

It seems strange that canal boats came up this feeder, locked through to the reservoir and by one means of another crossed the lake to Celina, a thriving industrial town. We find various stories as to how the boats crossed the lake.

In 1916, the *Weekly Herald,* Tippecanoe City, interviewed an old boatman; "S. S. W.", who stated, "Celina, Mercer County is located on the opposite side of the reservoir from the canal and ten miles from the feeder lock. Push poles or sails were used in crossing from Celina to the lock and if the wind was blowing in the opposite direction from the way the boat was going, they were compelled to await a favorable wind to make the voyage across the reservoir."

"Celina was a town of some importance at that time…Flour, staves, hoop poles and railroad ties, constituted shipments from Celina…and the canal furnished the means of transportation, after the ten mile trip across the reservoir…In the early sixties the screw propeller came into use and the propelling of canal boats was solved. Y. M. Davidson, owning a boat bearing his name, was the first to use steam. Other boatmen followed Capt. Davidson and before long "Jimmy" Johnson minced the PILGRIM under steam, followed by Christopher Schunck's CLIPPER."

Was the writer referring to steamboats on the reservoir only, or on both canal and reservoir?

Bronson H. Gilberg, in the *Celina Daily Standard*, 1962, wrote this; "Through Mercer County, freight and passengers found their way…to Celina, which, although ten miles west of the canal, became an important shipping terminal from where cargoes were either boated or poled across Grand Reservoir to the feeder canal lock on the east side, from there transported to the canal. Canal freight and passenger packets plied through the feeder canal to and from Celina. Incoming boats upon reaching the lock at the Reservoir, took their tow mules or horses on board. From that point, crew members poled the boat the remaining nine miles to Celina."

"Two members worked at the task, one at each side of the boat. Starting at the bow or front of the boat and with back to the stern, the long pole was thrust to the bottom and rushed, propelling the boat forward."

"In addition to the canal boat traffic, many thousands of dollars worth of virgin timber was cut in Mercer County, hauled to Celina and stacked in huge piles along the west bank…These were lashed together, forming a huge raft which was poled across the Reservoir, loaded on a canal boat at the feeder lock and shipped to Toledo and other Lake Erie shipbuilding yards."

No mention of steamboats here.

Ralph May, in the *St. Marys Evening Leader*, 1963; "The feeder lock at St. Marys was no doubt constructed so that boats could enter the reservoir from the canal. On their way to Celina, they would have to be propelled by huge oars operated from the stern, for there was no tow path along which the mules could tread. I wonder how often they got stuck on some of the submerged stumps."

This problem of submerged stumps has long been a sore one to any form of boating on the reservoir. The faithless contractor mentioned above left the trees standing to be submerged and later the State had them sawed off at the water line and the trunks and limbs removed. Unfortunately, this left the stumps completely covered during periods of high water when they were unseen and very dangerous.

While unsightly and a menace to navigation, the timber in the lake provided the villagers of Celina their winter supply of fuel for many years and helped establish the lake as an ideal fishing ground. In May, 1897 the Celina Democrat observed that "Fish seems to be a drug on the market. Bass weighing from two to three pounds each were offered at three and four cents a pound last week. The big pond seems to be alive with fish this year and everybody who goes after them gets more than they can use." In later years began the long struggle to remove these submerged timbers. This work has continued until now high-speed motor boats dash hither and yon with perfect safety.

But to return to the question about how canal boats crossed the reservoir; in the *Mercer County Standard*, April, 1871, has been preserved the following: "A few years since, we are informed a steamer twenty-five feet in length, under command of Captain Gustavus Dornell, with a boiler of seventy-five gallons capacity and four feet in length, moved upon its waters (Grand Reservoir.) In 1850-51, Mr. Doyle, of Dayton, owned a steamboat, which ran between Celina and St. Marys, on the canal and the Grand Reservoir."

In 1933, John J. Hauss, St. Marys, who was the last canal boat captain on this section of the Miami & Erie, wrote; "In those days they would take a boat loaded with merchandise to Celina across the reservoir and back again. The reservoir was full of trees those days. It took four men with long pike poles, two on each side, to pole the ten miles over and the ten miles back."

Mr. May, mentioned above, has in his collection a sketch of the feeder lock, drawn by Fred Magill, of St. Marys, in 1885. On the embankment itself to the south of the lock, may be seen the old Sweigert Hotel, to the north, a saloon and moored at the foot of the lock is a houseboat. Nothing now remains but the lock.

An unusual feature about this body of water is that the overflow from the west embankment runs to the Gulf of Mexico and that from the east embankment flows to the Gulf of St. Lawrence. The reservoir has had many names; The Grand Reservoir, Mercer County Reservoir, Lake St. Marys and Lake Mercer.

During the oil boom of the early 1890's considerable oil was discovered under the reservoir and soon it was almost covered with oil derricks. From the *Celina Standard*, Aug. 20, 1896; "Lake Mercer presents a grand sight these days. It is dotted over with derricks and it looks like business to see the number of men at work everywhere on its placid surface." In a few years the oil was gone and it again looked as of old. This was quite likely the first "off shore drilling" in the world!

Coming down to modern times, the reservoir has always been a Mecca for duck and geese hunters and fishermen without number. The State has made every effort to beautify and improve the area by building breakwaters, improving roads, dredging channels, everything possible to please vacationers and they have certainly responded. Summer cottages, motels, camping grounds and permanent homes now surround a greater part of the lake. Many visitors come from other states to this resort.

So, we have come from the dank and dismal "dead tree forest" of the 1840's to the vacation resort of today.

**More views of the Grand Reservoir**. Sketch of bulkhead lock (left) drawn by Fred Magill in 1885. Photograph of oil derricks (right). *Courtesy Ralph May and Ray Zunk from* Towpaths *Vol. XXVIII (1990), No. 4, p. 43.*

*Navigating a laden canal boat along a wide basin, or pond as they were called on the Miami & Erie, was hazardous duty as recalled by old boatmen.*

Volume VI (1968), No. 1, p. 12

## FORTY ACRE POND ON THE MIAMI & ERIE CANAL by C. Ernest Robison

From the old pioneers I have learned two bits of information about Forty Acre Pond, which is located a few miles south of Spencerville: (1) Its west bank was constructed from soil excavated at Deep Cut and hauled to the site in ox carts, (2) No boat captain would ever attempt a passage of the pond when a strong westerly wind was blowing, because pressure on the full length of the boat would blow it out into the pond and draw the horses or mules towing the boat to their death by drowning.

## §§§§§§§§§§§§§§§§§§§§§§§§§§§§

*Just as there was a village of "Lock Two, Ohio," there was also a "Lock Fourteen" which met its demise around 1865. The story is from the John J. Hauss scrapbooks, courtesy the Allen County Historical Society Museum.*

Volume IV (1966), No. 3, pp. 33-34

## THE END OF A CANAL TOWN by John J. Hauss

I knew Lock 14 when it was a thriving little village and employed a lot of men. There was a railroad back of the Bosche land, about three miles east of the village, and by its use they would bring logs to the mill at Lock 14 on little cars. The Osborn Company built a dozen new houses in the village, and it had a bright future until the fire came, about 1865, and wiped out the mill. This is a newspaper account of the fire.

### GREAT DESTRUCTION OF PROPERTY BY FIRE AT LOCK 14

Between two and three weeks ago, two large sheds at Lock 14 containing about 22 hundred thousand staves and a lot of hoop poles were set on fire by an incendiary and entirely destroyed. These sheds belonging to and near the large steam saw mill at that place, and it seems to have been the intention to destroy that also, for on Thursday evening last, two more sheds, containing a large amount of heading, were set on fire and the flames communicating to the mill, barn and other buildings, they were all burnt to the ground. Every thing was destroyed. The conflagration could be plainly seen from our place, a distance of about fourteen miles. Besides the other property destroyed, a valuable horse – estimated to be worth

$600 – was burnt up, with 15 sets of harnesses. The loss is estimated at about $75,000 – insured for only about $40,000. Lock 14 is in Noble Township, this county, six miles north of St. Marys. The property destroyed was owned by a firm named Osborn. The loss will be great to the people of that portion of our County, as it is not probable that the mills will be rebuilt. Every possible effort should be made to ferret out the incendiaries and properly punish them.

§§§§§§§§§§§§§§§§§§§§§§§§§§§

*The following newspaper article from the* Spencerville Journal News *was written by C.E. Robison and contributed to* Towpaths *by John Vanderlip. It tells the legendary "Bloody Bridge" story.*

Volume XI (1973), No. 4, pp. 38-39

### THE STORY OF THE "BLOODY BRIDGE" by C. Ernest Robison
Copied from the JOURNAL NEWS, Spencerville, Ohio, contributed by John Vanderlip

There is scarcely a person in northwestern Ohio who hasn't heard of "Bloody Bridge". It is located seven miles south of Spencerville and crosses the Miami & Erie Canal three miles south of Kossuth, at a point where the general terrain is level. In 1854 it was a high bridge. It was built on high earthen and stone abutments so that boats could pass under it in safety. In the 120 years or so that have passed since the bridge acquired its name many legends have been built around the murder that occurred there.

Some of the old timers claimed that they knew where Jack Billings and Minnie were buried. They say that during the last week in June of each year the graves of the two sweethearts are covered with wild roses - the only deep red wild roses found in the state. Others say that if you stop your car on the bridge during the month of June when there is a full moon and look into the waters of the canal, you will see the face of Minnie Warren in the moon's reflection.

No matter what particular legend you subscribe to, the true story of the murder is interesting enough; - In the early 1850's Bill Jones and Jack Billings were employed as drivers on two of the many boats that plied the Miami & Erie Canal in those days.

Bill handled the mules on the MINNIE WARREN, named after the Captain's daughter who also presided over the culinary department of the boat. Jack was employed in the same capacity on the DAISY. Both Bill and Jack fell head over heels in love with the pretty cook, but her affections were all bestowed upon the big-hearted Jack Billings.

A rivalry sprang up between the two men. At first it was friendly, but an intense hatred for each other soon developed. On each trip, as the two boats passed each other and exchanged greetings, the two rivals became more and more aware of each other's hatred, although they remained on "speaking terms". As the mules passed on the towpath the drivers would each wield an extra crack of their long whips as

**Bloody Bridge**. As it appeared in 1990. *Courtesy Ray Zunk from Towpaths, Vol. XXVIII (1990), No. 4, p. 48.*

though the poor animals were the cause of their rivalry. Jack would exchange greetings with his sweetheart and throw her a kiss with his great brawny hands.

During the month of June of 1854 both boats received orders for a cargo of lumber which was being taken from the large timberlands adjacent to the fatal bridge. It required several days for the boats to load and the young people became pretty well acquainted with the lads and lassies of the neighborhood.

Jack and Minnie received an invitation to a party being given by one of the local girls. It was to be the social event of that rural district and Bill was fairly crazed with anger at not having received a "bid". He was morose and at supper time never spoke a word all through the meal. Jack, who had consented to remain and eat supper with his sweetheart, chatted gaily and cast triumphant glances in the direction of poor Bill.

The hour for the frolic arrived and the young people started off in high spirits at the thought of being in each other's company for an entire evening. After the games were over, the front room, or parlor, was cleared of furniture and the dancing began.

The party didn't break up until the "wee hours of the morning", but as Jack and Minnie started across the bridge to reach the boats on the heel path side, they were startled to see Bill Jones standing in the shadow of the far abutment with an axe in his hands.

"Ho! ho! my pretty pair, you have played it fine tonight," said Bill, "but my turn comes now!" So saying, he shouldered the axe and delivered a well-aimed roundhouse swing that completely severed the head from Jack Billings' body. For a moment, poor Minnie stood as if in a dream, then with one wild shriek she swooned away, falling to the floor of the bridge. Her unconscious body rolled to the edge, then over into a watery grave below. The whole neighborhood was aroused by the shriek, but they were too late to save the girl. They recovered her body and laid the two lovers side by side.

Bill Jones disappeared and no trace of him was ever found, though a human skeleton was found in a near-by well some years later and the general belief was that Bill Jones had committed suicide.

For 40 years the blood stains on that bridge defied the rain and weather. Then, in 1904, a new bridge was built and the old one became a victim of relic hunters. Nearly everyone for miles around secured a piece of the blood-stained timber as a memento of one of the most horrible crimes ever committed.

§§§§§§§§§§§§§§§§§§§§§§§§§§

*Readers paying attention may have noticed a string of articles by C.E. Robison, an expert on the M & E Canal in the St. Marys-Spencerville-Delphos area. The editorial paragraph reviews his accomplishments.*

Volume XVII (1979), No. 4, pp. 43-48

## THE STORY OF THE DEEP CUT by Charles Ernest Robison

A Canal Society member of long standing, and an honorary trustee, the late Charles Ernest Robison's interest in the history of Ohio and its canals led him to search out much forgotten information. "The Story of Deep Cut" first appeared in The Allen County Reporter, Vol. XVII, No. 1, 1961, pages 5-17, quarterly publication of The Allen County Historical Society, 620 West Market Street, Lima Ohio 45701, from whom permission has been obtained for its reprinting. The Allen County Historical Society has Mr. Robison's collection of canal photos and historical information about Spencerville.

A short distance north of the village of Kossuth, the north-bound traveler on State Route 66, which here parallels the old Miami and Erie Canal, will notice that the old waterway suddenly changes its northerly course and flows almost due west for about a half mile, where it again turns and resumes its northward course.

What, one would wonder, could be the reason for such a change in course through this perfectly flat section? But chief engineer, Samuel Forrer, knew only too well the reason. Ahead lay the St. Mary moraine, a formidable east and west ridge through which the canal must be cut, and Forrer was aiming for the most narrow part of this barrier and the shortest cut through it.

This tremendous labor was begun in late 1841 and completed late in 1844. This difficult portion of the canal was termed Section 71, which section, according to the canal commission's annual report for 1844, was 100 chains (6600 feet) in length and the cutting ranged from 5 to 52 feet in depth "and is composed entirely of hard blue clay."

Strangely, we have a conflict in figures as to the depth. In 1888 the canal commission reported its depth as 39 feet, including the excavated soil piled on the banks. But, again in 1901, the depth was given as 44 feet, including about ten feet of fill on top. It is not clear where the last two measurements were made, but, if at the county line, where the canal crosses from Auglaize County to Allen County, this point is not at the greatest depth. The deepest part of the cut is about a half mile in length.

The excavating was done by hand with pick and shovel, and legend has it that the soil was brought to the top of the banks by wheelbarrows. This implement was used in the less difficult portions of the construction, but to anyone who has ever pushed a wheelbarrow full of soil, gazing at the steep, high banks of this cut it seems utterly impossible for a man to scale these banks once with a loaded barrow, much less doing it all day.

It seems more likely that a device such as was used in making deep cuts in the construction of the Erie Canal in New York was used. This consisted of a tall mast, or "gin pole" equipped with a long boom at the outer end, to which was attached a wooden bucket or cage. The bucket would be lowered to the bottom of the cut, filled with excavated soil, the boom raised with ropes and pulleys, and then swung to the tops of the banks and emptied.

Between four and five hundred men (not 1700, as has been so often stated) worked for nearly four years on this—at that time—gigantic undertaking. On this section the contractor paid them, if they boarded themselves, one dollar per day in what was called contractor's scrip, or state scrip, which was good only in exchange at state or contractor stores and was not legal tender. Some boarded at the contractor's boarding house, known as the "big shanty," and these received fifteen dollars per month and their board. Those who boarded themselves lived in scattered "canal shanties."

Sanitation did not exist. Mrs. Mary Decker states in her recollections that her father had the contract for furnishing meat to the camp, and she would accompany him carrying butter and eggs, which the men also purchased. Freshly killed beef, she stated, when delivered was never covered but left exposed to the flies.

All in all, this was a sizable settlement, and, in order to extend mail service to it, the post office department established a post office here on March 11, 1840, with E.N. Martin as postmaster.

When a boy, the writer was told by an old pioneer settler that the soil for constructing Forty Acre Pond, some seven miles distant from the cut, had been hauled to that point by ox carts from the cut. This account may have been apocryphal, but, be that as it may, it is known that a wooden tramway was built from the cut to the low ground south of present day Kossuth and a fill constructed across this swampy region and over Prairie Creek. This fill is said to have been 24 feet high and over a mile long. It is quite possible that the tramway was extended to Forty Acre Pond and used to make that fill also. If the immense amount of soil in these fills had been piled on the banks of the cut, in addition to that already there, it would be hard to imagine just how high these banks would have been.

On the milestone which stood beside the towpath in the deepest part of the cut were carved the numerals "142." This meant that the cut was exactly 142 miles north of Cincinnati.

After the Deep Cut was completed and the canal constructed to a point where Spencerville now stands, the waterway was open for traffic from Deep Cut to Cincinnati. An east and west road was established on the backbone of the moraine and called the "ridge" road. Because this ridge was much higher than the swampy land to the north and south, and because the canal served as an outlet for farm products, this ridge was quickly settled, so quickly, in fact, that when the government called for volunteers at the outbreak of the Civil War, the "ridge" from Deep Cut to some six miles west furnished a full company—Company E, 118th O.V.I.

At the cut, the contractor's commissary vanished to make way for a general store and grain storage building (which also served as a post office), a fine residence for the store proprietor, and, last but not least, a saloon. Deep Cut was in business!

A flourishing trading point was established, which for many years served a wide community extending westward for some miles beyond the present village of Monticello. The writer's grandparents, who resided north and west from Monticello, did their trading and received their mail at Deep Cut during the period of the Civil War.

From 1844 to 1882 history is vague as to when, and by whom, the first store was established, but, from the latter date on, it is possible to glean a fairly complete history.

The earliest record we have is contained in the obituary of Isam B. Robbins (1838-1890). "When fourteen years of age (1852)," it reads, "he was employed as a clerk in the dry goods store of Kelsey and Howe at Deep Cut, remaining in their employ until he was 21 years of age (1859), when he and Jackson Pickerell purchased the store of his old employers. The new firm carried on the business together until 1862, when Mr. Robbins enlisted in Co. E, 118th O.V.I."

"…At the close of the war, he returned to Deep Cut and again resumed his business, which, in his absence, had been conducted by Mr. Pickerell alone… He moved to Spencerville in 1866."

The obituary of Simon Robbins (1841-1909) also states: "He with his brother, Isam, conducted a store at Deep Cut." After his brother withdrew in 1866, Simon conducted the business in connection with Calvin E. Riley until about 1870 when he, in turn, withdrew and moved to Spencerville.

Here is an excerpt from an undated newspaper article signed by "Old Pioneer." "We now come to old Deep Cut, where most of the produce and timber were sold for miles around. The canal was the only means of conveyence we had for many years, and, I expect, more grain and timber were shipped from Deep Cut than from any point between Toledo and Cincinnati. The Store was owned and managed by Jack Pickerell, and I used to think he would buy anything from a horse to a jack knife. My wife bought her wedding clothes there."

A letter to a St. Mary's newspaper, signed "Salem," reads: "Deep Cut, December 10, 1868…There are two post offices in Salem Township, one at Kossuth and one at Deep Cut…At the Deep Cut, Riley and Robbins have a fine dry goods store and a large warehouse and are doing quite a business in the produce and goods line and also timber, buying and shipping large quantities every season. McClure, Lawrence and Company have a fine portable sawmill in operation at Deep Cut."

The account book of Dr. J.C. Cambell (1827-1888), pioneer Spencerville physician, reads: "Account of Bernard Fitzpatrick, November, 1870, settled at Robbins' store. Account of Simon Robbins, June 3, 1868, credit by molasses, $.25 credited by store goods, $11.25."

The Deep Cut "Business Directory," found in Robert Sutton's *Atlas of Auglaize County, Ohio* (1880) lists: John W. Arnold, editor, *Spencerville Journal*, general agent Ohio Farmers' Insurance Co., and notary public; J.H. Dunathan, dealer in grain, timber, dry goods, groceries, and family supplies, warehouse and store; ("J.H. Dunathan (1836-1899) moved to Deep Cut about 1837, where he conducted a grain and general merchandise business for nine years, then moved to Spencerville."—Obituary). A.C. Cisco, notary public and associate with J.H. Dunathan in general merchandise business; and J.C. Stayner, justice of the peace and farmer.

Thus we have a fairly accurate picture of the business men at Deep Cut from 1852 until 1882.

As the post office was in connection with the store, the majority of the postmasters, after the late 1840s either owned or were connected with the store. (*A complete list of post-masters and date of appointment in original article.*)

The large building housing the store and grain storage was on the east bank of the canal, north of the bridge. The owner's residence was directly across the road (Route 66) from the store, and the saloon was on the west side of the canal at the southwest corner of the junction of the ridge road and the canal road. These were the only buildings until an I.O.O.F. Lodge was established here May 10, 1870, and a lodge hall was built on the east side of the canal road just south of the residence.

A picture in the Sutton *Atlas* shows Deep Cut as it appeared sometime between 1873 and 1882, the viewer is looking toward the northeast from the west side of the canal. A boat owned by James Rider is loading grain from the storage building. The saloon is not shown, having ceased to exist previous to this period.

James S. Rider (1846-1933) one of the last living canal boat captains, owner, at different times of five boats, married at Deep Cut on September 17, 1870 when "Deep Cut was larger than Spencerville." He tells of the days when "wheat could be loaded at Deep Cut on Saturday afternoon and in three days be in the elevators at Toledo."

Deep Cut and Spencerville were founded about the same time and, naturally, were business rivals. But Deep Cut was easily in the lead for some years. Even Prine DeHart, Spencerville's pioneer blacksmith, was compelled to go to Deep Cut to obtain coal for his forge. It is said that a tremendous flat rock, lying on the west bank of the canal and south of the bridge, was used as a wharf on which to unload shipments consigned to individuals and not the store.

But, in spite of the little settlement's early success, time eventually ran out on it. Its rival village to the north, though platted in 1844, did not attain the popularity of Deep Cut as a trading point for many years. So slow was its growth that it was not granted a post office until March 29, 1854, fourteen years after Deep Cut was given an office.

However, as the years passed, Spencer, as it was then called slowly forged ahead, aided principally by the two canal locks within the village limits. The upper, with 10½ feet of fall and the lower with 7.75 feet furnished ample water power for the village's grist mill and saw mills and numerous small wood-working factories. Then, when a narrow gauge railroad came through the village in 1878, and the present Erie and Lackawanna in 1882, the fate of Deep Cut as a trading point was sealed.

The saloon had long since disappeared, leaving only a depression in the ground where the cellar had been. And, in the spring of 1882, J. H. Dunathan, last proprietor of the store, abandoned the building, moved to Spencerville, and started anew at the southeast corner of Broadway and Fourth Streets.

The founding of the village of Kossuth in 1858, two miles south of Deep Cut, hastened the demise of the latter by absorbing its trading area to the south.

In March, 1886, the Deep Cut Odd Fellows Lodge disbanded, also moving to Spencerville. They abandoned their hall and left Deep Cut, a locality of scenic beauty and a visible reminder of what the undismayed pioneer spirit could accomplish, to dream of its past glories. As a commercial point, it has long since vanished, but nothing can subtract from the impressiveness of this truly "handmade" canyon.

The State has created a beautiful roadside park at this point, and, more recently, the Allen County Historical Society and the Anthony Wayne Parkway Board placed here a marker reciting the history of the "deep cut". In 1963, the Department of the Interior cited it as one of the seven historical spots in Ohio to be noted.

And, to end on a humorous note: In the *Spencerville Journal* of January 11, 1889, appeared an account of a local couple's marriage. In the groom's horse and buggy, they journeyed to Lima where they were married. In returning to Spencerville, they seemed to have taken a roundabout course, coming past Deep Cut—a honeymoon journey, in a way of speaking. At this point the editor, with tongue in cheek, waxed lyrical in his description of their Deep Cut saga: "…returning over the cloud capped hills of Deep Cut, where among the beautiful and picturesque scenery they could view the 'raging canal' meandering its serpentine course among the rose embowered clay cliffs of that remote locality."

§§§§§§§§§§§§§§§§§§§§§§§§§§

*Who ever heard of a fish plugging a hole in a boat? This reprint of a 1941 article from the* Lima News *appears courtesy of the Allen County Historical Society.*

Volume V (1967), No. 1, pp. 9-11

## CAPTAIN MANDERY

When this was written, Captain Mandery was 87 and a resident of Delphos. He worked on the Miami and Erie Canal from the time he was 16 until the waterway went out of use, first as a hired hand on the boats and later as owner of two, altogether 35 years. He was described as active, healthy and mentally alert. His memories of the canal were vivid and factual.

"Mandery was born at Ottoville when it was known as Lock Sixteen, a stopping and transfer point on the canal. After working on boats as he grew to manhood, it became a proud moment for him when he became owner of his own - the EMPIRE - the motive power of which was two teams of horses. He hired four hands, also his sister as cook, and then for years transported lumber between Ottoville and Cincinnati."

"The distance was 169 miles, the round trip of 338 miles taking seven days. This was the routine - traveling day and night, the 24 hours were divided into four six-hour shifts. At 1 A.M., a driver and team and a helmsman would start work and remain until 7 A.M. The animals were led across a drawbridge into the boat as shifts were changed. With the new team came another driver, another steersman took the helm and the new workers remained until 1 P.M. and the process was repeated."

"After his marriage, Mrs. Mandery became cook. The Mandery's home was in the stern. The help slept in the fore part of the boat and the stables were in the center. Another boat owned by Mandery was named REYNOLDS."

"After some years spent in the transportation of lumber, Captain Mandery had his boat made over so it could carry wheat, its capacity being 2,500 bushels. There were some trips on which Mandery carried both grain and lumber simultaneously, making trips both to Toledo and Cincinnati."

"The first trip Mandery made with grain, the boat sank near Napoleon. It was foggy and a water feeder for the canal near that location caused a swell against a boat behind the EMPIRE and the crew of the former boat, unable to see the EMPIRE owing to the fog crashed into its side. Pumping went on for hours, but the workers were unable to save the boat. The cargo was a total loss, but the boat was raised and after repairs, went again into commission."

"Another time one of Mandery's boats was stuck in a lock at Piqua. Carrying grain, the sides had swollen and become jammed in the lock. The water in the lock moved but the boat did not. Over a period of hours, with other boats waiting to travel north and south, there was a string of them waiting. Workers of these boats gave advice, but finally with the help from so many, the boat was moved out of the lock into the water-way, the team in the stable rescued and some equipment salvaged before the boat sank. It was near enough to the bank that traffic was resumed."

"The most peculiar accident that Mandery recalls was when his boat sprung a leak near Toledo and the leak was plugged by a catfish. Water began to seep into the boat and hand pumps went to work when the water stopped as quickly as it started. About 200 bushels of grain were spoiled. At Toledo, Mandery had the boat placed in dry dock and investigation showed a hole in the side and into the hole the tail of a catfish had been sucked with the flow of water until the thicker portion of the fish had become wedged."

"In those days the canal averaged a width of 60 to 70 feet. It is believed throughout this section that Mandery is about the last survivor of canal workers. When the canal was frozen during the winter, Mr. and Mrs. Mandery remained on their boat home until the ice left the canal, and transportation was resumed."

§§§§§§§§§§§§§§§§§§§§§§§§§§§§

*Delphos was the first Ohio community to hold a "Canal Days" festival. One wonders how the 1968 canoe trip was managed.*

Volume VI (1968), No. 4, p. 43

### DELPHOS CANAL DAYS FESTIVAL by C. Ernest Robison

An old fashioned "Canal Days Festival" was held at Delphos September 13 and 14, 1968. Sponsored by the Delphos Chamber of Commerce, the festival was the first annual statewide observance of Old Fashioned Canal Days.

The feature of the celebration was the canoe trip from Cincinnati to Delphos made by Dan Harpster and Marvin Brennaman. Of necessity, they paddled up the Great Miami River to Piqua, and then on the Miami & Erie Canal to Delphos. The trip evoked memories from a man in Cincinnati who had canoed all the way to Defiance in 1908, camping, fishing and hunting along the way. It was found, too, that there is still one drawbridge intact across the canal in Delphos.

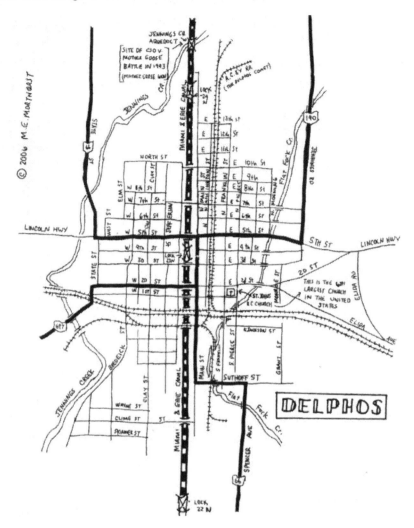

**Miami & Erie Canal at Delphos**. *Map by Mike Morthorst from* Towpaths, *Vol. XLIV (2006), No 4, p. 82.*

§§§§§§§§§§§§§§§§§§§§§§§§§§§§§

*Oil tankers once ran along the Miami & Erie Canal. These 1887 newspaper accounts from the* Toledo Blade *and* Delphos Courant *describe the shipments. Both clips were contributed by C.E. Robison.*

Volume VIII (1970), No. 2, pp. 24-25

### MIAMI & ERIE TANKERS by C. Ernest Robison

*Toledo Blade*, October 21, 1887. - "Oil Boats for the Canal. - The propeller ROANOKE is expected here this afternoon or tomorrow, towing two iron boats that will be pioneers of a revolution in the cheap fuel question. The boats are consigned to William St. Johns of this city. Mr. St. Johns said this morning that they were probably detained somewhere between here and Buffalo, on account of the late heavy blow."

"The boats were built in Buffalo by George Netter, the well known boat builder, and, on their arrival here will be taken by the canal to Delphos, where they will be loaded with crude oil and then towed to Lockland, near Cincinnati, where the oil will be burned for fuel. They were built at the order of A. C. Halderman, the great paper maker at Lockland, who has determined to utilize oil for fuel. This oil will be taken from the Lima field to Delphos on the Miami and Erie Canal, loaded on these boats, which were constructed especially for this trade, and by them taken to the factory. This is the first step of the plan that has been long contemplated of getting a portion, at least, of the Lima oil field out of the hands of Standard. It is probable that the two boats will be but forerunners of a large fleet that will supply southwestern Ohio with cheap fuel."

The *Delphos Courant*, November 4, 1887. "The iron boats came through last Saturday from Toledo on their way to Lockland. They were loaded with corn and will for a while carry coal. In the spring they will carry oil from this field for fuel purposes."

§§§§§§§§§§§§§§§§§§§§§§§§§§§§

*Returning to the Bill Oeters photo article, we fill in some missing gaps along the canal from Delphos to Defiance.*

Volume XLVII (2009), No. 1, pp. 1-2, 17-20

## 1916 PHOTO SURVEY OF THE MIAMI & ERIE CANAL
## FROM DELPHOS TO DEFIANCE by Bill Oeters

[…] Although Mr. Klepinger's suggestions were largely ignored, he did leave future canawlers a photographic time capsule of the Ohio canal system. The focus of this article will be the Miami & Erie Canal and its associated feeders. Photos are arranged from south to north. A summary of the photographs is given in the table below. Some photos in the collection were either missing, duplicates, or not of interest so these were omitted from the article. Mileage is given from Cincinnati.

| Photo | Mile | Structure |
|---|---|---|
| 33 | 153 | Lock 23-N, Delphos |
| 31 | 154¼ | Delphos Aqueduct (Jennings Creek) |
| 35 | 170½ | Little Auglaize Aqueduct |
| 36 | 174 | Blue Creek Aqueduct |
| 39, 40 | 189 | Locks 36-N to 39-N, Defiance |

**Photo 33**. This is the site of Lock 23-N in Delphos. It was later replaced by an ugly concrete water control structure. In addition to the gate and some concrete walls, a locktender's house and relocated mile marker may be found here today.

**Photo 31**. Photo shows the Jennings Creek Aqueduct. Only a canoe sized vessel could navigate through this aqueduct in 1916. A portion of this structure's north abutment is still extant. […]

*Aqueduct Spanning Little Auglaize River, July, 1916.*

**Photos 35 (top) and 36 (bottom).** The wooden flumes in these two aqueduct photos do not exhibit the excessive water leakage that is usually seen from these structures. The southern abutment of the Little Auglaize Aqueduct at Melrose and the northern abutment of the Blue Creek Aqueduct near Charloe are still extant. Both are impressive ruins. The photo of the Little Auglaize structure was featured in Mr. Gieck's book on page 25. What appears to be the same man in a white hat and shirt is standing atop both structures. Most of the 1916 Klepinger photographs include people in order to provide scale.

*Aqueduct Spanning Blue Creek, Paulding Co, O.*

*House Boat at Defiance, O., July, 1916.*

**Photo 39**. View looking south towards Lock 37-N and 36-N, probably taken from the Second Street Bridge, also seen in the background of Photo 40 below. Lock 37-N behind city hall is the only surviving lock in downtown Defiance.

*Old Timber Wall at Defiance Outlet Lock, July, 1916*

**Photo 40**. An excellent money shot showing the downstream gates of Lock 38-N and the upper section of a rotting Lock 39-N at the outlet into the Maumee slackwater at Defiance. Neither structure has survived. The First Street Bridge crossed over the canal between the two locks.

*Grover Hipp's recollections of Lock 31 in Paulding County were told when he was 95 years old and represent a first person account of the canal era.*

Volume XVIII (1980), No. 3, pp. 33-35

### HIPP'S LOCK, No. 31 TIMBERVILLE, PAULDING COUNTY by Grover Hipp

At ninety-five years of age, I am probably one of the very few persons yet living who rode as a passenger on the Miami and Erie Canal while it was still a mode of transportation for people and merchandise.

I was born at Lock No. 31, which was about eight miles north of Ottoville, Ohio; and since the year 1863, it has been known as "Hipp's Lock." My father came to the lock from St. Marys, Ohio in 1863 and erected a mill for the grinding of wheat into flour. This was perhaps the first flouring mill in Paulding County. There were numerous small mills along the streams for grinding corn, but none for the manufacture of flour.

No photograph of the lock or the grist and flour mill of John J. Hipp at Timberville has been found. This reproduction of an artist's sketch, drawn in 1958 by Murray Woods of Grover Hill, shows the installation as recalled from memory by Grover Hipp. Reprinted with permission of Laurence R. Hipp, from THE HISTORY OF GROVER HILL.

**Installation at Hipp's Lock**. *Sketch by Murray Woods, 1958.*

A grocery store was conducted by my father, John J. Hipp, in conjunction with the mill. The mill, which also ground corn, was on the east side of the canal and since the towing path was on the west side, a floating bridge supported by coal oil barrels was in place above the lock and was poled to the east bank when a boat approached. The bridge was not anchored at all. When not in use it lodged against the two sides of the embankment for the dam that backed up the water for the mill race.

A small hamlet grew up around the lock and took the name of Timberville by reason of the vast quantities of ship timber and logs brought to the site to go downstream to Melrose, Defiance and Toledo.

The ship timbers were of massive oak 30 to 40 feet long and 2 to 3 feet square. They were cut and hewn from the forest trees by French-Canadian and Scots-Canadian woodsmen. Some of the woodsmen boarded with my parents and others made their domicile near the lock. I recall Joseph and Peter Antoine (French) and Kenneth "Sandy" McDonald, Phillip and Angus Grant (Scots). The ship timber period ended about the late '80s, to be succeeded by the logging economy.

The logs were cut mainly by local timbermen and farmers and brought to the canal in the winter season and when the ice went out, were rafted to Melrose and Defiance to be made into barrel staves and lumber. Among the raftsmen I recall—Vern Shirley, who later became sheriff and probate judge of Paulding County, John and William Sherman, Marion and Cal Ayers, Sam Swihart and Francis Miller.

A Mr. Robert Harvester had a mill about three quarters of a mile east of the canal where the smaller trees were sawn into bolts and four-foot lengths of wood and hauled to the canal on a wooden tramway for shipment by boat.

A "bolt" was what the timbermen called the smaller logs and large limbs that were cut into lengths approximately the length of a barrel stave. You will recall that before the advent of fiber containers, much merchandise was shipped in wooden barrels. Sugar, salt, flour, crackers (you have no doubt heard the expression "cracker barrel philosopher"); vinegar and coal oil were also shipped in barrels made of heavier staves—usually of oak; elm being mostly used for the other merchandise. At the stave factories which dotted northwestern Ohio (Paulding County had as many as 12 or 13) the larger logs were also cut into barrel lengths and quartered into bolts before being manufactured into staves. I worked at the factory in Grover Hill at fifty cents per ten hour day when I was seventeen years old.

As a lad of five or six years of age, I was taken along on a trip to Ottoville (Putnam County) by my mother. The boat was captained by a Mr. Wise. The State boat captained by Mr. Spencer was used for maintenance of the locks and canal banks.

The boat captains were, I believe, generally the owners, and among them I recall Chris Booth, Charles Medary, Ira Green, Dave Shively, DeLarm Cattel, Jack Gleason. I believe the last boat to use the canal in the vicinity of Hipp's Lock was in the year 1908 or 1909.

There was always good fishing below the dam that diverted the water for the mill race, and folks would come for miles to seine in the deep water below the lock. I recall one time when my older brothers were fishing below the dam when an eel was caught. So I learned early what "slippery as an eel" meant when the boys had extreme difficulty in holding it to extract the hook.

I recall also quite vividly the time when I was watching Mr. Wes Coley (lock tender at Hipp's Lock) dipping fish with a net and I fell into the deep water of the canal. Mr. Coley made a quick grab for me, otherwise this would not be written.

I believe in the early days of the canal the bridges were all built high over the water so the boats could pass under. By my day they had been replaced by "bump" or "swing" bridges, which were on the level of the roadway. A boat would press or bump against the bridge and it would swing open to allow the boat to pass. It would then swing back into place.

There was a high bridge at Hamer, a small hamlet in Paulding County near the Putnam County line, while at Mandale to the north and just north of Hipp's Lock, the bridges were of the bump type.

I left the lock when my parents moved to Grover Hill, Ohio in 1892.

§§§§§§§§§§§§§§§§§§§§§§§§§§§§§

*The 1988 CSO fall tour was centered at Junction, Ohio, named appropriately enough as the junction of the Miami Extension and Wabash & Erie Canals.*

Volume XXVI (1988), No. 4, pp. 37-44

## THE JUNCTION OF TWO HISTORIC WATERWAYS IN THE EARLY HISTORY OF OHIO AND INDIANA by Albert F. Celley and Daniel F. Perch

This significant junction and its surrounding areas are to be toured jointly in the Fall of 1988 by the canal societies of Ohio and Indiana.

The Wabash and Erie Canal from Indiana joined the Miami and Erie Canal at Junction, Ohio in 1843, thus opening canal boat traffic between Toledo, Ohio and Fort Wayne, Indiana and points west. The canal connection south to Cincinnati was not open until 1845.

The Wabash and Erie Canal was constructed between 1832 and 1853 and cost over $8 million. Extending from Evansville, Indiana on the Ohio River to Toledo on Lake Erie, it was 462 miles long -- the longest canal in the United States and the second longest in the world at that time. The Ohio section, 18 miles in length, was begun in 1837 and completed in 1843, and remained in use until 1887 when it was destroyed. Construction of the Miami and Erie Canal was started in 1825 and was fully opened between Toledo and Cincinnati in 1845. This construction cost over $6 million. The canal was 249 miles long, required 105 locks, several major aqueducts, numerous culverts and was in use until approximately 1913 when large areas of it were destroyed during the great flood.

The M&E and W&E canals used the same canal prism between Manhattan near the mouth of the Maumee River and Junction, Ohio, a distance of 68 miles. At this point the W&E turned west toward Fort Wayne, Indiana and the M&E continued south to Cincinnati.

The following description of these man-made waterways can be uniquely appreciated as related in the Sixth Annual Report of the Board of Public Works, January 2, 1843, Public Document No. 36 (41st General Assembly).

"From the dam at Independence, the river is used as slack water navigation, to a point opposite the town of Defiance, a distance of four miles. At this point the river is crossed on a towing path bridge to the opposite side. At Defiance the canal leaves the river again and overcomes an ascent of thirty five feet by means of four locks numbers 14, 15, 16 and 17.

"From Defiance to the contemplated junction with the Miami Extension Canal, is a distance of eight and a half miles, and the ascent of twenty two feet is overcome by means of three locks, numbers 18, 19 and 20. From the junction to the lower side of the reservoir, is a distance of eleven miles, and an ascent of fifteen and three fourth feet, is overcome by means of three locks, numbers 21, 22 and 23. From the lower side of the reservoir to the Indiana State line, is a distance of seven and two thirds miles, in which an ascent of thirteen feet is overcome by means of three locks, numbers 24, 25 and 26.

"The canal from Defiance to the State line, is to be supplied with water from the Indiana Canal, and from a reservoir located six miles on this side of the State line.

"This reservoir covers an area of two thousand five hundred acres of land, all of which has been cleared of a heavy body of timber, excepting a belt of a few rods in width, which has been left near the banks for the purpose of protecting them, for the present, against the action of the water that may be put in motion by the winds.

"The embankment around this reservoir is ten and a half miles in length, and in height varying from five to fourteen feet. To prevent the crawfish and water rats from cutting through and breaching the banks, there is a two inch plank fence constructed in the centre of the embankment as high as the top water line on the reservoir. There are two sources from which this reservoir can be filled; the one is by means of Six Mile Creek, on which the reservoir is located. The drainage of the country into this creek will, in ordinary seasons, fill the reservoir; and, should this source prove inadequate, the Little St. Joseph's can be used through the Indiana Canal, and passed into the reservoir during the winter and spring seasons of the year, when it is not wanted for navigation.

"The Wabash and Erie Canal, from Manhattan to the contemplated junction with the Miami Extension, a distance of sixty eight miles, is sixty feet wide at the top water line and six feet deep, and from the junction to the State line it is fifty feet wide and five feet deep. All of the locks on the main line, thirteen in number from Manhattan to Independence, the two locks on the side cut at Toledo, and the six locks on the Maumee side cut are of cut stone masonry. The streams on this portion of the line are crossed by means of culverts of cut stone masonry, except Swan Creek, which is crossed by an aqueduct similar in construction to the aqueduct at Circleville. These locks and culverts are so substantially built, and of such durable material, that, it is believed they will last a long time without rebuilding."

The authors note; little did these canal engineers and contractors realize that 150 years later many hundreds of heavy loaded semi-trailers would cross over these same culverts every day as they support U.S. 24 between Toledo and Fort Wayne.

"From Defiance to the State line, the locks, thirteen in number, are constructed of wood, and appear to answer the purposes for which they were intended. The expense of obtaining proper material for constructing these locks of masonry was such, that as a matter of economy, wooden locks were adopted, believing they would answer for several years without rebuilding, and if it then should be thought advisable to rebuilt them of stone, they could, by means of the canal, be rebuilt at a much less expense.

"On this part of the canal there are three streams crossed by means of culverts of cut stone masonry, and one by a wooden trunk. This canal is of larger dimensions and it is believed to be as substantially constructed as any other canal in Ohio, and when the banks have become settled, it is presumed, will cost less for repairs."

In 1870 after a useful life of approximately thirty years, the State of Indiana abolished the entire length of the Wabash and Erie Canal that lay within the State. As with the Ohio canals and those throughout the rest of the United States, canal operation became uneconomical -- that is, if it ever had been economical for the majority of them -- as post Civil War railroad technology and growth spurted rapidly ahead.

Following the demise of the W&E Canal the State of Ohio constructed a dam across the canal at Antwerp so that the eighteen miles could be used in Ohio by lumbermen to freight their logs to the saw mills in Defiance. Also located in Antwerp were charcoal kilns and iron furnaces which employed as many as 250 choppers, sawyers and furnacemen. This reduced (pig) iron was shipped by canal and lake steamer to Cleveland and Pittsburgh.

A further note of economic interest was that Toledo had expected a large volume of corn and grain products to flow through it from northern Indiana. However, when the canal hook-up was made to the Miami Extension in 1845, these agricultural products by-passed Toledo and flowed south to Cincinnati to support the hog feeding requirements of Cincinnati, the "Porkopolis" of the mid-west.

A final significant note of canal history along our tour route took place at the Six Mile Reservoir in 1887 when the embankment and several locks were blown up by disgruntled local farmers and citizens to rid the area of a noisome, mosquito-ridden nuisance that could be better used for crops.

The destruction of the reservoir and locks is described by Otto E. Ehrhart, an Antwerp, Ohio local historian, in *A Century of Progress, Antwerp, Ohio, 1841-1941*:

"In the early '80s when shipping by canal had all but ceased, the citizens of Antwerp looked out over this gloomy and impenetrable swamp that was no longer a source of revenue, and decided it was time to abandon the canal and reservoir and reclaim the flooded land for farming purposes.

"In 1886 a petition which stated the grievances of the reservoir and asked for the abandonment of the canal from the Indiana State line to the junction of the Miami and also Six Mile Reservoir, was sent to Columbus to be considered by the House of Representatives. It was passed.

"The bill was fought bitterly by a large delegation from Defiance which still depended on the canal for rafting logs to its manufacturing plants in that city.

"In March 1887 the bill was defeated in the Senate by a vote of 26 to 8. The defeat of this bill brought out the fighting spirit of the citizens of Antwerp. Small groups began to gather under cover of darkness. Secret meetings were held and sworn to secrecy, plans were made to drain the reservoir.

"In their first try an attempt was made to float a bucket filled with dynamite with a long fuse attached into the feeder from the reservoir side.

"The damage caused by this explosion and also several others at different points was promptly repaired by men from Defiance.

"Finally on the night of April 25, 1887, a large force of men, numbering between 200 and 300 gathered, carrying large amounts of dynamite. All were masked and carrying guns…

"People living along the canal between Junction and Antwerp were warned to vacate.

"Another delegation went to Tate's Landing part way between Antwerp and Junction. Others went to the lock at the lower end of the reservoir and still others began digging through the reservoir bank in several places to within a few feet of the water. Large charges of dynamite were then placed in the remaining bank.

"The other delegations having arrived at their scenes of operation, saturated the wooden locks with kerosene and placed two 50 pound charges of dynamite in each end of the locks.

"The hour of midnight was the signal.

"At the set time the mighty roar of the explosion of 100 pounds of dynamite echoed through the night from the direction of Junction. Hardly had the din died when a similar blast shook the earth at Tate's Landing where another lock was blown.

"Before the rumbling had ceased the sky was lighted by the explosion of several hundred pounds of dynamite placed in the lock at the lower point of the reservoir and in the bank separating the water from the canal.

"With a rush the water poured out into the canal and over the country-side. All again was quiet except the rushing of the water as it poured through the breaks made by the dynamite.

"About a month later Governor Foraker (of Ohio) made a personal visit to Antwerp.

"He was met by a group of citizens (many of them dynamiters) and escorted to the scenes of the late destruction where he saw the dilapidated condition of the reservoir and canal and the swampy conditions of the surrounding country.

"In May 1888 a second bill was passed by both houses which then became law -- and the final chapter of the reservoir and canal."

No real effort was ever made by the State -- even though many of the names of the dynamiters were common knowledge -- to bring these individuals to justice for destroying state property. Such was the nature of life in this part of Northwest Ohio 100 years ago.

It is of interest to observe that the locks in Defiance originally constructed of wood were rebuilt of poured concrete in the first decade of the twentieth century with the hope that this would breed new life into the canal. Several of these remaining locks will be examined on the tour, along with several culverts and a remaining section of the pier that supported the Mule Bridge over the Maumee River in Defiance.

§§§§§§§§§§§§§§§§§§§§§§§§§§§

*In addition to Grover Hipp's boyhood stories, another first person account of the canal in Paulding County is recorded here by Mrs. Walter S. Stevenson as told to L.W. "Lew" Richardson in 1973. Stevenson's grandmother tended one of the locks along the Wabash & Erie Canal in the vicinity of Antwerp.*

<u>Volume XI (1973), No. 3, p. 30</u>

## MY GRANDMOTHER WAS A LOCKTENDER
### by Mrs. Walter S. Stevenson

Yes, I well remember the old Wabash & Erie Canal – it has a very special meaning for me. Of course, in my childhood, it had been many years since there had been any boat traffic and most of the canal bed was dry and overgrown with weeds and bushes. In places there were pools, possibly caused by springs or small streams draining into the old canal. In cold weather these little ponds provided us children with convenient skating rinks. I don't remember any fishing, although there could have been some of that, too.

My family were pioneer residents of Paulding County. When I was very young, we moved to the old McGuire place on the canal, east of Antwerp. As Merrie Luella Hughes, I attended Murphy School, a one room institution that was also on the banks of the canal. The old towpath was a playground for us, both at home and at recess.

However, I feel a personal attachment to the canal that just living alongside it could not give me. The fact is – my Grandmother was a lock tender on the Wabash & Erie – so far as I know the only girl on the canal with that responsibility. It happened this way: Grandmother Mary Coffelt was an orphan and, as it so often happened back in that day, worked for her "keep" with a family whose head was an official lock keeper. The man was also a farmer and could not be in constant attendance to his canal job. This chore then fell to Grandmother's lot and she became well known to the boat crews traveling the canal.

This was in the 1850's, when she was in her early teens, she was born in 1840. There at the lock, my Grandfather first met her, although he was not a boatman. In 1860, when she was twenty, she married Jasper Newton Hughes, my Grandfather, and left the canal. She died in 1909.

When I was a little girl, Grandmother would tell me of her experiences on the canal, it was all very exciting to me. She was a little woman, not quite five feet tall and weighing less than a hundred pounds. I wondered how she could have moved the heavy balance beams of the lock gates, but she said that she "managed". No doubt she had help from the boatmen. She was a remarkable woman and of course I am proud of the fact that "Grandmother was a lock tender".

§§§§§§§§§§§§§§§§§§§§§§§§§§§

*The two concurrent running canals remain a source of confusion, especially regarding lock numbering. Frank Trevorrow straightens it out here.*

Volume XXX (1992), No. 3, p. 29

## RENUMBERING LOCKS ON THE WABASH & ERIE AND MIAMI & ERIE CANALS
### by F.W. Trevorrow

The confusion about lock numbers of the Miami & Erie Canal arises from the original designation of the western canal into three parts, the Miami Canal from Cincinnati to Dayton, the first section constructed, the Miami Extension Canal from Dayton to Junction and the Wabash & Erie from the Indiana State line to Toledo.

The Wabash & Erie locks were numbered from No. 1 at Manhattan to the Indiana line. The original numbers 1 and 2 were retained for the locks at Manhattan.

When the whole line was consolidated into the Miami & Erie, the locks were renumbered according to the system then in use, numbering from the summit down. The relation of numbers is then as follows:

### NUMBERS AND NAMES OF THE LOCKS
### WABASH & ERIE AND MIAMI & ERIE CANALS

| Wabash & Erie | Miami & Erie | Name |
| --- | --- | --- |
| 1 | 1 | Manhattan, River [Maumee River] |
| 2 | 2 | Manhattan |
| 3-8 | 50-45 | Toledo to Port Miami |
| 9 | 44 | Providence (The marker at this point has No. 9 for this lock.) |
| 10 | 43 | Bucklin's |
| 11 | 42 | Rice's |
| 12 | 41 | Texas |
| 13 | 40 | Independence |
| 14 | 39 | River [Maumee River] |
| 15-17 | 38-36 | Defiance |
| 18 | 35 | Palamo/Erie Mill |
| 19 | 34 | Paper Mill |
| 20 | 33 | Schooley's |

§§§§§§§§§§§§§§§§§§§§§§§§§

*The Paulding County "Dynamiters" are part of Ohio canal lore, although most true canawlers regard them as common vandals. This excerpt from an article on wood lock construction by Scott Bieszczad concludes with an interesting irony.*

Volume XXXI (1993), No. 2, p. 23

### WABASH AND ERIE CANAL IN OHIO by Scott Bieszczad

The Wabash & Erie Canal, from the Indiana state line, originally ran to Toledo before the completion of the Miami Extension in 1845. Like the work from New Bremen north, all the locks on the Wabash & Erie through Defiance were made of wood. All were eventually replaced by concrete, except for Lock 39, the River Lock, which allowed boats to enter the Maumee River for their slackwater navigation of the four miles to the second guard lock at Independence Dam.

Like the wooden locks on the Miami Extension, the W&E locks were dilapidated and by 1887 the line there was really only used for rafting logs to mills in Defiance. The Six Mile Reservoir near Antwerp was a constant source of irritation for the local residents and eventually became the target of a group of dissidents who banded together under the banner 'No Compromise - The Reservoir Must Go' and named themselves 'The Dynamiters'.

Demolition charges made quick work of the aging wooden locks and reservoir gates. What took the state years to build of wood was destroyed in seconds when 'Three hundred determined men, went out at midnight last night and overpowered the few guards who were stationed at the reservoir and locks. The guards were securely bound and then the mob scattered and then went up and down the canal. The aqueduct was blown up, one lock blown up and another burned…After this had been done, the men returned to town and quietly dispersed to their several homes.'

Ironically, the wooden locks were destroyed because they'd become useful only for transporting wood to market.

§§§§§§§§§§§§§§§§§§§§§§§§§§§§

*During the waning days of the canal era, Defiance was a timbering town as described in these late 19th century newspaper accounts provided by C.E. Robison.*

Volume VI (1968), No. 2, p. 24

### RAFTING TIMBER ON THE MIAMI AND ERIE CANAL by C. Ernest Robison

From the *Delphos Courant*, April 15, 1897. "Jesse Suprise, the Defiance ship timber man, went to Vendocia with his gang of men, Monday to get out some ship timber. Mr. Suprise has over 900 fine looking sticks distributed along the canal banks between Ottoville and St. Marys. He expects to raise the number to 1,000 before the timber is floated."

From the *Spencerville Journal*, October 19, 1893. "James Rider rafted 40,000 feet of elm from Lock 14, for the Cooperage Company, Wednesday."

It is of interest, in view of the tremendous volume of timber rafted along the Miami & Erie in the later years of the canal, to note that such shipments were originally prohibited. In the rates of Toll, published Feb. 21, 1833, by order of the Commissioners, it is stated, "On each cubic foot of hewed timber transported in rafts, (round timber in rafts prohibited), for each mile…3 cts." Large amounts of logs were being shipped through Defiance at the turn of the century as evidenced by these returns of the Collector; 121,764,000 feet in 1900 and 391,396,700 feet in 1901 cleared that point.

§§§§§§§§§§§§§§§§§§§§§§§§§§§

*More on the Defiance timber industry. These memoirs of Edwin Phelps first appeared in* Northwest Ohio Quarterly, *Vol. 17, No. 4, October 1945, pp. 72-124.*

Volume XXX (1992), No. 3, pp. 25-29

### DEFIANCE JUNCTION ENTREPRENEUR "Memoirs of Edwin Phelps"
### by Francis P. Weisenberger

Edwin Phelps, a resident of Defiance, Ohio had studied law for two years when, in 1839, he was appointed Clerk of Courts for Williams County, Ohio and, in the fall of that year he was elected justice of the peace of Defiance Township. While continuing his law studies, he practiced law and dabbled in other enterprises some of which were related to the Miami & Erie Canal as in the following selections from his memoirs.

"The canal was being constructed at that time, [1839] which made considerable legal business. In the month of September, William Semans, my preceptor, at the instigation of his client had three stalwart Irishmen arrested for riot and for some reason they employed me to defend them, which I did and got them clear, for which they paid me $10, which rather nettled Mr. Semans, as his client failed to pay him anything or very little. I think he got $1 or perhaps $2. I was proud of earning this $10.

"I also practiced law and earned about a hundred dollars attending petty cases in the vicinity of Defiance. I was farming and raised over two hundred bushels of potatoes which I sold at 37 1/2 cents per bushel. I was also a contractor on the Wabash & Erie Canal, Section 103…and did several hundred dollars worth of work at a great disadvantage as Ohio State checks were worth only 50 cents on the dollar. The contract commenced about six miles from Defiance and I was up there considerably and frequently left there after the men quit work and came home. I was justice of the peace which required considerable time and I had quite a large collection of canal claims. Together with my law practice I was a pretty busy man. I finished up my contract on the canal during this year and got the checks but it was a pretty hard time to get the money. Checks sold as low as 45 cents on the dollar the last of the year...

"...in 1850...I went to Columbus to see about leasing the water for a sawmill at the 6th lock above Defiance...Maria Welles, daughter of Woolsey Welles, went with me to visit Alfred Kelley, one of the canal commissioners. I see it cost then to go to Columbus $8.12 and it took about three days. We went by canal to Dayton, R.R. Dayton to Xenia and by rail from there to Columbus. I had taken a contract to saw the timber to rebuild locks 5 & 6 at Defiance. Although they were originally built in 1840 they had to be rebuilt in the winter of 1850 & 1851 and I built the sawmill and sawed the timber and plank for the locks and I had to get the most out of the logs myself and I went into the woods above Junction on the Miami canal between the canal and river and got most of the logs working with the men until I got enough to raft, then rafted them and a boy and I brought them down to the mill. I got the mill in operation and sawed the timber and plank before the close of navigation, as the water had to be drawn off the canal to put in the locks. It kept me pretty busy all the summer and fall getting the logs and attending to the sawing of them. I built a basin at the mill in which to run the logs and I had considerable trouble to get the banks to stand and had a good many breaks which caused me considerable hard work.

"In the winter of 1850 & 1851 I went to Columbus and I spent considerable time there trying to get appointed collector of canal tolls at the Junction, a pretty important office the salary of which was about $800 per year with an allowance of $600 for clerk hire, making over $1400 per year of about 8 months. I succeeded in getting the appointment and at the opening of navigation in the spring of 1851 I took charge of the office and went to the junction.

"While in charge of the collector's office I dabbled considerably in other matters. I had to keep a clerk and in company with Dana Columbia, who kept a hotel at the Junction and with whom I boarded. I made a contract with R.R. Dickey of Dayton, Ohio to furnish stone on the bank of the canal. Dickey had his own boats and we quarried the stone during low water in the bed of the Auglaize River and worked quite a number of men and made a little money.

"The Cincinnati, Hamilton & Dayton Railroad was in process of construction during this year and I purchased of Taylor Webster, near Springdale in Butler County, and eighth interest in what was then called the Beeswax farm and agreed to pay him in ties delivered at Hamilton, Ohio. They were to be sawed ties, 7 1/2 feet long and six inches square, and I sawed them at the mill at what was called the Jones lock. I had purchased 229 acres of what was called the Beeswax farm and in sawing the ties I took off a good many inch boards, 6 inches wide and 15 feet long, as I sawed the ties all 15 feet long and then sawed them in two, and in about every log there were four three-cornered pieces and these I sawed in two and used for fence posts and although the fence posts were all sap and not considered lasting timber in the ground, the fence remained standing pretty good for fifteen years and it was a very cheap fence for me. I shipped these ties to Hamilton to Doolittle & Chamberlain, for which I got 26 cents a tie. I furnished them 6,157 ties amounting to $1600.82, a net of about 18 cents per tie. I sold the mill to Weisenburger & —— about July 15/51 for $2800.00.

"This was a very good year for the canal, the receipts at the Junction office amounting to about $105,000. I cleared boats in the fall of 1851 up to the 4th day of December, 1851, and was glad when the season was over. It was slavish work, as I was compelled to get up at all the time in the night to clear boats and sometimes in the case of a break in the canal west of Junction I would have to be up all night. On the 20th day of November, 1851, I had on hand $13,000 and my bond was only $10,000. Still it was no temptation for me to run away.

"In the winter of 1852 & 1853 I spent some time in Columbus and while there I got a contract with R.R. Dickey of Dayton, to furnish stone on the bank of the canal near the Junction in Paulding County, Ohio. Dana Columbia who claimed to own some land on the Auglaize river just below the present bridge across the Auglaize and I got out the stone in partnership. He furnished the stone and during the summer of 1852 we expended over a thousand dollars; wages were 50 cents per day and board for men and $2 per day for men and teams and board.

"February, 1853 I made a contract with Findlay, Gilboa & Defiance Plank Road Company to build a plank road for them from the corner of Fifth street and Clinton street in the town of Defiance to Ayersville, 5 miles and 134 rods at $1600 per mile, of $5 per rod. I received $5000 Defiance Township bonds at 75 cents on the dollar and the balance was to be received when it was collected of the stockholders. I bought about 250 acres of timber land of James Cheney in Paulding county and contracted with Nick Guiot to cut the logs and raft them up to my sawmill at the 6th lock from the river, where I sawed the plank and stringers, and I would have made pretty well on the contract if I had received my pay, but the soil from here to Ayersville was clay soil and when wet very slippery and it was hard work to keep the planks in place and there was a great deal of dissatisfaction with the road and the stockholders refused to pay and I lost about $2500…

"In the year 1853 the contract for building the Wabash Railroad, then called the Toledo & Illinois Railroad, was let and…Gilson & Co. took the contract of tieing the grading of the road from the Maumee river to the Indiana State line, and they sublet two miles from the Maumee river to Timothy Fitzpatrick, and to Freeman & Gardner five miles west of Fitzpatrick's, and in the fall of 1853 I purchased the interest of Moses Gardner and Freeman and I worked through the winter of 1853 and 1854, and finally my cousin Edward H. Phelps bought out Freeman and in the fall of 1854 the company failed to raise money to pay their contractors and gave the contractors the privilege of quitting or going on with the understanding that if they went, the railroad company would pay whenever they were able to raise the money. We concluded that we had the shanties built and tools and bedding, etc., all of which would be a total loss if we abandoned the work and the men needed the work as they would have nothing to do through the winter, and we went on with the work, paying the men 75 cents per day and charging them $2.25 per week for board, which if they put in full time left them $2.25 per week for their work or 37 1/2 cents per day. We had to pay as high as 3% a month interest for money and when the work was completed there was due us about $20,000 and we completed the work so far as to get the engine over our work and to the state line of Indiana. July, 1855, there was considerable work still to be done, fencing, clearing up the old logs and stumps. I finished up the work and in the fall was appointed agent for the railroad at Defiance and commenced work for them in October.

"…There was no depot, not even a freight car, and I boxed up a little place under the water tank and kept my office there. It was nearly a year before the telegraph line was completed. I tended the office night and day, with only one man to pump the water…

"I contracted with the R.R. Co. to furnish the telegraph poles from the Maumee river to the Indiana State line. The first poles were either white or burr oak and had to have the bark taken off and were to be 30 feet long and not less than 6 inches at the top. I got them delivered at 25 cents a piece and received 30. My wages were $50 per month and I managed by trading one way and another to get about $75 per month…While engaged in the building of a railroad…in every shanty along the line we had to keep a barrel of whiskey, as the men would not work without it…"

§§§§§§§§§§§§§§§§§§§§§§§§§§§§§

*To Ohio canal buffs, Florida is not a state in the south but a canal village in Henry County. These early 20th century recollections by Harriet Long describe the canal at that place.*

Volume XVII (1979), No. 1, pp. 11-12

### RECOLLECTIONS OF CANAL BOAT DAYS by Harriet Long

In 1904 or 1905, I stood on a bridge and saw a canal boat for the first time. I was seven or eight years of age and lived in the small town of Florida, Ohio and the canal was the Miami and Erie.

To recapture the feeling of excitement and pleasure I experienced, one needs to recall that in a small Ohio town at that time, the only means of travel was by horse and buggy. And here before my eyes was a fascinating mode of transportation.

Having seen nothing previously any larger than a rowboat, the canal boat looked very large to me. It seemed to be propelled by magic as it quietly glided along. What intrigued me, too, was that people were actually living on it. There was a woman at a tub washing clothes on a washboard, while on a line stretched across the deck the clean clothes were drying in the sun. A young child with a rope around her waist was running about, the rope tied to a post to keep her from falling from the deck. I daresay the husband and father was walking along the towpath behind the horse that pulled the boat, but I do not recall seeing man or horse.

The towpath, which was between the canal and the Maumee River, was very narrow. When the ice broke up in the river in early spring, sometimes there was a flood as the ice jam broke through the towpath and into the canal, and homes, shops and stores were flooded. To me, this was an exciting occasion, unaware as I was of its consequences to the people who lived in its path.

Other things I know of only from family stories of earlier days before I was born. Father at one time had a general store, and the produce for that store which was stocked with everything from boots and shoes and yard goods to groceries, came by canal boat and was easily unloaded into the store on the canal bank. Meals were served to the canal boat crews and they were prepared by a woman known as the best cook in town. Sometimes the crews were a rough lot, or so father said.

The fertile land in that part of northwestern Ohio was farmed by thrifty Germans, so next door to the store father built a grain elevator, There the farmers brought their grain to sell, and there it was stored and later shipped to Toledo by canal boat.

The summer when I recall seeing a canal boat for the first time was long after father had stopped shipping by canal. The building of the Wabash Railroad provided more rapid transportation. However, it meant that the larger elevators were in towns where the trains stopped, and Florida was not on a railroad at all, so father went by horse and buggy from one to another when it was necessary.

§§§§§§§§§§§§§§§§§§§§§§§§§§

*James Durbin was a famed canal contractor who placed a monument to himself atop the Bad Creek Culvert in Texas, Ohio. This account by his brother is from* The Village: A documentary of a rural Ohio Village from its earliest beginnings to the present day *by Marilyn Stevens with a 1961 copyright by William A. Kuhlman. Reprinted with permission. The postscript was provided by the* Towpaths *editorial staff.*

Volume XXI (1983), No. 1, pp. 1-3

### WILLIAM DURBIN TELLS OF THE BUILDING OF THE CANAL by William Durbin

"I was born in Carrol County, Maryland, September 22, 1814. In 1837 I sought a new home in the wilds of the Northwest, and in the spring of that year I found myself located fifteen miles west of Detroit, Wayne County, Michigan, then nothing more than a wilderness. During this time a brother of mine, James Durbin became quite an extensive contractor in excavating the Miami and Erie Canal, then in the course of construction. In the spring of '39 I left Michigan for the purpose of joining him in the labor, but I landed at Sandusky and found employment on the old Mad River Railroad, then running up through Bellevue, where I remained the whole summer, and did not reach the Maumee River, where Texas now is, until November of the same year—'39. My brother had contracted for four miles of the work - Section 49, 53, 56, and 57. (Ed note: Section 49 is in what is now Lucas County, sections 53, 56 and 57 in Henry County.) Section 49 commenced with the lock at the head of this slackwater. Section 53 commenced a short distance above Texas and extended three quarters of a mile below, including the culverting of Bad Creek, etc. Sections 56 and 57 commenced three miles further up. The ground excavated from the high bluff at Texas and above, was carried in wagons to form the heel and toe-paths (*sic*) through the low ground below. No scrapers were used, nothing but shovels and wheelbarrows; and wagons when it was necessary to convey the dirt any distance.

In the year 1839 the canal was finished up from Toledo to the slackwater at Providence, and the water let in. This proved to be a great help to the transportation of stone for the building of the locks and culverts required in my brother's contracts: He built three locks and four culverts. The stones used in these were quarried in the river at Providence for the first four feet of the wall which was supposed would always be covered by water; but the river stone was not thought durable enough to stand exposure, so the bulk of the stone for the work was brought up the canal from Marblehead. I was a mason by trade, and built most of the stone work on the locks and culverts at Texas.

If I remember right there were about 300 men working on the section at Texas, though I think there were more on the other sections. The men were mostly Irish, and the contractors kept large supplies of whiskey on hand in compliance with the demand for that drink. Whiskey was drunk in as great quantities as water would be now. Morning and evening the stuff was tolled out to them, besides 'jigger' boys passed around to each man during the day, carring a pail of whiskey with a tin cup attached. My brother was quite strict in adhering to the rules of drink he had laid down, and the result was few rows or drunks while in the camp.

The canal was completed and water let in, in the spring of 1843, and all put in shape for the transportation of boats to Lafayette, Indiana. Afterward, when the canal was in its balmiest days, I saw at more than one time a line of boats as much as a mile and a quarter long, extending up the river, awaiting their turn to pass through the lock. All boats, though, had to give way to the packets; every other vessel was switched, and the packet boat went through the locks first. There were two lines of packets each way daily, and an extensive business was done, and Texas soon became a town among others.

In 1840 there were no towns or settlements along the river this side of Defiance, except for a few stragglers, and everything was a wild dense forest clear up the river, and but one house where Texas now stands. The road to the up-river country was a trail cut out of the wood, which wound along the river, many times going far inland to avoid gullies and bayous lying nearer the river.

The only building in Texas was a double log house, used as a public house; also where was kept a kind of general supply store—tobacco, whiskey, etc. This was located near where the M.E. Church now stands. Two miles further up the trail from Texas, stood another tavern, close to the river bank where still stands an old orchard to mark the place. All of the houses were double log buildings, and were run as general stores and as accommodation stopping places for travelers: they were the only habitations close to the river, and continued within a few miles of each other on up the river. Where Napoleon now is was nothing but heavy timber, although on the south side of the river resided a number of settlers."

NOTE: William Durbin's are the only canal-related recollections reprinted in the section "Voices from the Past," in *The Village*. They are attributed to the publication *The Maumee Pioneer*, by A.J. Friess of Grand Rapids of 1886. The original publication has not been located.

## THE DURBIN CULVERTS AND LOCKS

The four culverts referred to by William Durbin in his reminiscences are still standing and in good condition in the Texas area of Washington Township, Henry County, Ohio under U.S. 24. While the culverts originally were constructed to take the Miami and Erie Canal over the creeks which emptied into the Maumee River, they have served the present day purpose of taking U.S. 24 across the streams.

Three of the culverts were viewed by Canal Society members on a tour of the Wabash and Erie-Miami and Erie canals from Maumee to Defiance, conducted by Canal Society trustee John Vanderlip of Toledo April 28-29, 1973. These were the culverts over Bad, Dry and Turkeyfoot creeks.

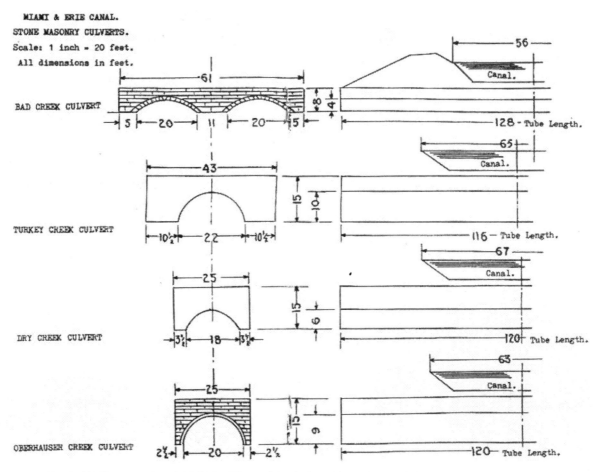

**Henry County Canal Culverts**. Showing dimensions. *Drawing by Frank W. Trevorrow.*

The fourth culvert was not known to exist at that time. The search for it began with the decision to reprint the reminiscences of William Durbin. This culvert was eventually located by John Vanderlip in 1981 about 100 yards from Bad Creek, the site of another Durbin culvert. Vic Verity of Cincinnati had located the fourth culvert on a plat map of the area at The Ohio Historical Society in late 1980, which led to the eventual location of the unknown culvert. From the map he noted that the culvert was 7 feet wide and that the stone work extended 12 feet.

The creek over which the culvert was constructed is not named on the plat map. However, after John Vanderlip discovered the missing culvert, he learned from Mr. Artz of Liberty Center, whose farm's south boundary is the creek, that he knew it as "Belly Creek" and that it is about 3 miles long.

The *Gazetteer of Ohio Streams* compiled by J.C. Krolczyk, Columbus, 1954, Ohio Department of Natural Resources, Division of Water, on page 34 lists creeks emptying into the Maumee River in Henry County, their lengths and other statistics. Among those listed are Bad, Dry and (North) Turkeyfoot creeks, all of which are noted also on a map of Henry County, copyright 1978 by *The National Survey*, Chester, Vermont.

The name "Belly Creek" however, is not listed in the *Gazetteer* or noted on the 1978 map. There are, of course, other un-named creeks thereon.

Until another name is discovered, the fourth Durbin culvert will be identified as the culvert over "Belly Creek" as designated by Mr. Artz.

The three Durbin locks were: No. 41 (Texas Lock), No. 42 (Rice's or Rees Lock) and No. 43 (Bucklin, Bucklands or Bulkhead Lock). All were rebuilt in concrete during the canal reconstruction program of 1904-1911. Lock No. 43 as rebuilt in concrete is still standing.

§§§§§§§§§§§§§§§§§§§§§§§§§§§

*All told there are 8 canal culverts along the Miami & Erie/Wabash & Erie Canal in Henry County which still carry modern highways across Maumee River tributaries. As indicated in Scott Bieszczad's article, these are in comparatively good shape.*

Volume XLVI (2008), No. 1, pp. 13-15

## ADDITIONAL CULVERTS ON THE MIAMI EXTENSION AND WABASH & ERIE CANALS by Scott Bieszczad

Not all canal era culverts have suffered as badly as those on the Loramie Summit. Others have survived and look almost untouched after 166 years of daily use. For example, there are eight stone culverts in Henry County which are in daily use to carry the modern highway traffic of Ohio Route 424 and US Route 24 over the creeks originally spanned by the Wabash & Erie Canal in 1842.

Of the eight original stone canal culverts in that area, Benien Creek, Wayne Park, Garrett Creek and Oberhaus in Napoleon and North Turkeyfoot, Dry, Bad and Belly Creeks near Texas, O., only one, Garrett Creek has been rebuilt. According to Jim Bradley, the District 2 Bridge Engineer for the Ohio Department of Transportation, the culverts receive an annual inspection but little maintenance is necessary.

**Bad Creek Culvert**. Under U.S. Route 24 in Texas, Ohio. *Courtesy Boone Triplett.*

The Shelby County Engineer, Robert Geuy, suggests that time, nature, and no maintenance have contributed to the failing of the Loramie Summit culverts when he said "Mother nature and age will eventually destroy anything because the freeze and thaw cycle affects materials and the integrity of structures." The effects of nature and a lack of maintenance will eventually lead to the loss of any structure.

Other canal culvert changes made after the original construction include the March 1868 legislation which authorized funds to construct a culvert one and a half miles west of Antwerp, at the Wabash Valley Railroad crossing of the canal, to eliminate flooding and allowing that water to flow to the nearby Maumee River. This being only a few years before Indiana abandoned the Wabash & Erie Canal to their state line.

Similarly, in 1871 another culvert was to be built below Lock 28 in Ottoville to allow drainage of farm fields near the canal into the Little Auglaize River.

Finally, in 1886 a joint resolution of the Legislature *recommended* building an additional five culverts in Paulding County to further control the flooding of adjoining agricultural property. Apparently no action was taken because on May 1, 1891 the state passed legislation stating "Nearly five years have elapsed and the state board of public works has failed to perform the recommendations of said resolution, therefore... that the state board of public works are hereby *instructed* to build culverts of sufficient capacity to permit the proper drainage of the lands affected..." Later, the 1891 B.P.W. Annual Report tersely states "The culverts authorized by the adjourned session of the legislature to be constructed on the Miami & Erie will be constructed after navigation."

§§§§§§§§§§§§§§§§§§§§§§§§§§§

*Prepared for the CSO's October 18, 1986, tour of the Lower Maumee Valley by former* Towpaths *editor Albert Celley, this article describes landmarks along that section. References to photographs which accompanied the article have been deleted.*

<u>Volume XXIV (1986), No. 4, pp. 40-45</u>

### TWIN CANAL – MAUMEE TO PROVIDENCE PARK by Albert F. Celley

### Canal Society of Ohio Fall Tour 1986

The tour will cover approximately fifteen miles of the Miami and Erie-Wabash and Erie Canal between Maumee and Providence Metropark, starting in the City of Maumee and proceeding as follows:

**Maumee**. Maumee Woolen Mills, between the Side Cut Canal [...] and the Maumee River. [...] Stone piers remain. [...] The Sally Klewer Towpath Park now runs along the canal in this area.

The Wolcott House, built in 1827 by Judge James Wolcott a leading citizen of Maumee, faces the Maumee River; the rear faced the Miami and Erie Canal. Now the Wolcott House Museum, it is the headquarters of the Maumee Valley Historical Society.

Just across from the Wolcott House is the Toledo Edison Club, originally built as a hydroelectric plant using water from the canal, by the Defiance Gas and Electric Company. Much of the electricity supplied power to the sprouting interurban rail lines.

A log cabin which originally stood near the canal has been restored and stands on the grounds of the Wolcott House Museum.

**Side Cut Metropark**. Six locks originally allowed canal boats to descend sixty-three feet from the level of the Miami and Erie Canal to the Maumee River, to allow Perrysburg on the other side of the river to have access to the canal and all its commercial benefits. The Side Cut Canal was in use scarcely five years and was abandoned about 1865.

**Waterville**. Our tour now moves on approximately five miles west along the old canal. Pekin Mill, built in 1846, was located at the north end of Mill Street, now Third Street. The mill, four and one half stories in height, represented Waterville as the grain center of the mid-west before such rapidly thriving centers as Chicago and Minneapolis took over that function. The towpath is [...] between the mill and the canal. [...] The Pekin Mill was partially destroyed just after the turn of the century because of a grain dust explosion and following fire. Water to power the mill flowed under the drive wheel house [...] and then on to the Maumee River. [...]

The historic Columbian House, a Waterville landmark, was built in 1828 by John Pray founder of the town in 1831. It served as an inn for weary land and canal travelers and will be the lunch stop for the tour.

Located in Waterville is a towpath bridge, the only remaining canal appurtenance within the village. [...] Excess canal water drained under this little bridge and down into the Maumee River. [...]

**Providence**. Our tour continues, following the canal route about ten miles to the former village of Providence which disappeared in the 1850s due to flooding and cholera epidemics. The Isaac Ludwig Mill adjacent to Lock 44 was built by Peter Manor in 1846 using the canal water to drive the milling machinery. As part of Providence Metropark, the mill has been restored and demonstrations of a working sawmill and exhibits of grain milling equipment and tools can be seen.

At Providence Metropark a roller dam stretches 1700 feet across the Maumee to a mid-river island. Originally a wood structure, it was built in 1836 to divert water for the canal and for the many mills alongside the canal down to Toledo. The slack water above the dam served as the canal itself for approximately one and one half miles with the canal again entering the river bank through a guard lock and continuing on atop the river bank.

(The bridge) in Providence Metropark is an excellent example of where one would hear the cry "low bridge" while traveling aboard a canal boat a century or longer ago.

The eclipse of the canal along our tour route started with the coming of the railroads which first reached Waterville in the 1870s. The twin canal was officially abandoned about 1922 and existed as "that stinking ditch" until 1929, when the towpath bank was dynamited by disgruntled farmers between Waterville and Providence which drained off most of the stagnant water.

§§§§§§§§§§§§§§§§§§§§§§§§§§§§

*The creation of the "canal experience" at Providence Metropark in Grand Rapids is told by Ron Studer, retired park manager and ranger for the facility.*

Volume XXXIII (1995), No. 4, pp. 41-51

**REBUILDING THE MIAMI & ERIE CANAL AT PROVIDENCE METROPARK by Ron Studer**

## Providence Metropark

When the Toledo Metropark District first conceived *The Volunteer,* their canal boat reproduction at Providence Metropark, they envisioned it as both an educational tool to demonstrate what canal operation was like and also as a means to move people to visitor attractions in the park.

The park provides a unique opportunity to study canals and canal operation in what might best be described as a "one stop" lesson in canal history. While other sites have operating boats, none has the combination of a boat and restored canal, a ride through a lock, a mill operating on canal water power along with a canal era town for shopping and recreation. The park also demonstrates the difference between a canal prism and slackwater operation in the river as a substitute for a canal channel. Additionally visitors can see the construction differences between a stone lock, Lock 44, and one made of poured concrete, Lock 43.

Providence Metropark is situated in the southeastern edge of Lucas County and consists of a 160 acre long strip of land which is centered on the Miami & Erie Canal and parallels the Maumee River and US-24. The park extends east from Lock 44, and follows an easterly path along the highway, canal and river to where it joins Bend View Park and later Farnsworth Park at Waterville, seven miles east of Grand Rapids. The three parks maintain the eight mile hiking trail along the towpath which provides easy access to the entire length of the canal. The canal here demonstrates how canal builders needed to build only a raised towpath which allowed the canal water to back-up against hills of the Maumee River valley. There are several places where the canal is over 400 feet wide between Grand Rapids and Waterville because the natural topography was allowed to become the berm bank.

## Grand Rapids and Providence Metropark Area

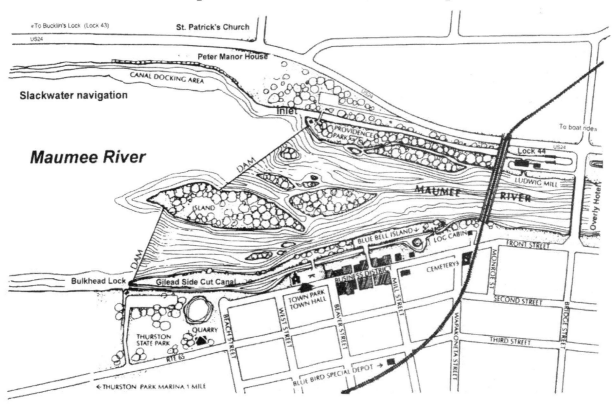

**Providence Metropark Map.** Showing Lock 44 on the Miami & Erie Canal, the Providence Dam, and Gilead Side Cut Canal across the river. *Courtesy Toledo Metroparks.*

## Same Places, Different Names

When originally settled, the town of Providence was on the northern side of the Maumee River, with Grand Rapids directly across the river on the southern shore. Grand Rapids was known earlier as Gilead, but that name was changed because of postal confusion with Mount Gilead, located in Morrow

County. The name Gilead did stay with the side cut canal there which provided water power to the town's industries. The town of Providence was ravaged by cholera and what population remained in the area centered itself in Grand Rapids.

Today, the area on both sides of the river is generally known as Grand Rapids, even though that municipality is technically located only on the southern, Wood County side of the River.

The canal which is located here also experienced a name change from Wabash & Erie to Miami & Erie when the state wanted to use a common name for the entire canal system on the western side of Ohio. The change to Miami & Erie eliminated the name Wabash & Erie, from Toledo to Junction to Evansville, Ind.; Miami Extension Canal, from Dayton to Junction; and Miami Canal for the original section from Cincinnati to Dayton.

## Used Until 1929

The Providence-Maumee section of the Miami & Erie Canal continued to be used until 1929 mainly because the Toledo Edison Company was generating power at a 1500 k.w. capacity generator in Maumee. This single use made the Miami & Erie Canal little more than a millrace supplied by the Providence slackwater.

The question of closing the canal continued for several years because the state's efforts to end the canal were delayed by continued litigation by both Toledo Edison and the Providence Milling Company. The U.S. Supreme Court finally held that the state could close the canal because the contracts held by the plaintiffs stated they had rights to water which was surplus from the canal's operation. The court said that because the canal was no longer used for navigation there could be no surplus water from navigation.

On Wednesday, July 3, 1929 the canal was dynamited 2½ miles below the dam which put the canal and the Edison generating plant out of commission. It took until July 5 for the canal water level to become too low for power generation at the plant. This demolition was probably done by over-anxious residents because the state had already planned celebrations to officially close the canal the following Saturday. News reports say the officials could do little more than make the gesture of closing the gates to end the canal era there because there was no water to stop.

Lock 44 was subsequently blocked by an earthen dike which dried-up the canal below, but maintained a water supply upstream for Heising's Mill (Ludwig Mill) which operated for another 30 years on water power. The canal below the lock flooded in the spring and became a swamp at other times. In 1935 the highway bridge (Ohio 578 today) over the canal was replaced by an earthen embankment. The canal rested for half a century.

## Rebuilding A Canal

In 1985 it became apparent that something had to be done about the parking situation at the restored Isaac Ludwig Mill. The 18 car parking lot was inadequately serving the needs of several hundred mill visitors per week. The Metropark District owned property suitable for parking on the opposite side of the busy Ohio 578 highway, but it was too dangerous for pedestrians to cross over to the mill. It was decided to build a pedestrian tunnel beneath the highway where the old canal bridge once stood and soon this plan blossomed into a full-sized bridge which allowed the canal to once more flow beneath the highway. This plan was further expanded into a mule-drawn replica canal boat to haul visitors from the parking lot to the mill.

Due to towpath elevation differences, it became necessary to put the lock back into operating condition before the boat could pass past the mill. A survey showed the walls were sound and square indicating the lock was still in perfect condition. Upon excavation it was discovered the reason for the lock's condition was that Lock 44 wasn't built upon timber as was customary, but upon solid bedrock. The stone walls rose to a height of 20 feet from the floor of the lock.

In April 1993 a timber framing workshop was sponsored by the Park District to construct new lock gates. A class of 20 students working five days built the gate frames and installed them on the sixth day.

Original wickets were salvaged from Lock 40 at Independence Dam State Park near Defiance along with some that were buried in the remains of the gates which were excavated from Lock 44. The best eight wickets were reinstalled in the new gates. Providence Lock was once more operational after 65 years.

Again a canal boat locks through twice per hour each Wednesday through Sunday, May through October.

## Boat Design

Several boat designs were studied but it was decided the "state boat" configuration best met the needs of providing shelter during bad weather and an open deck for clear visibility during good weather operations. The traditional state boat design was compromised somewhat by the addition of an overhead walkway, giving *The Volunteer* a freight boat appearance. This overhead walkway has proven advantageous since the crew of three must move about frequently during docking, locking, and turning maneuvers. The normal compliment of three is sometimes supplemented during hot weather to reduce crew fatigue.

After the design was set, an architect was hired to design the hull and superstructure. Due to the high cost of construction it was decided to build the boat of the most durable and easily maintained materials possible. This resulted in a steel hull which could be easily repaired, along with a wooden superstructure which lends an air of authenticity while being easy to clean and paint. This double material construction allowed the best quality at the best price.

A construction contract was awarded to a Toledo firm which sublet the steel construction to a fabrication shop in Grand Rapids. As it turned out, *The Volunteer* was built a half mile from its present home.

## Mules And Crews

Originally a crew of two was thought to be adequate. However, experience has shown that operation of a canal boat is quite demanding and a crew of three is necessary. The three are necessary because they must turn the boat around twice each trip using only poles, navigate through a narrow, crooked area under the highway bridge and then lock-through a hand operated lock. The return trip doubles the work which must be done, all in under an hour!

Since Metropark Rangers have had little opportunity to become experts in mule husbandry, other options were explored to find animals to tow the new boat. A contract was awarded to supply two teams of two mules five days a week from May through October. This has worked extremely well during the shake-down period of seven weeks during the fall of 1994. *The Volunteer,* then unnamed, began operations on September 9, 1994. The mules and visitors have treated each other well and no problems have been experienced. The spring of 1995 marks the beginning of *The Volunteer's* first full season of operation.

## After-Season Storage

About 90% of Providence Park floods occasionally when the Maumee River rises after the spring thaw and rains. These floods have demonstrated the need to move the boat to dry ground when the river passes its banks. Hauling a 14 foot by 60 foot boat out of a canal is no easy task unless you employ the canal's mortal enemy --- a railroad. A nine foot gauge railway was built with steel railroad rails along with a boat cradle. The boat is simply positioned over the cradle. While the canal is drained the boat settles onto the cradle and the boat is easily towed up and out of the canal.

## Water Supply At Providence Park

All canals must have an ample supply of water at the summit level. Without enough water boats cannot cross from one river system (drainage basin) to another using water transport only.

Additional water sources must be fed into the canal system whenever practical to compensate for losses due to evaporation, leakage and the development of water powered mills.

Northwestern Ohio has a relatively flat topography that offered few opportunities for water powered industries during the early industrial revolution. When the canals were being planned it became apparent that if enough excess water could be introduced into the canals, numerous mills could be powered without affecting navigation.

The Maumee River is the largest river emptying into the Great Lakes and therefore provided nearly limitless water to the Miami (Wabash) & Erie Canal from Defiance to Toledo. Many saw mills, flour mills, hydro-electric plants, woolen mills and paper mills lined this section of the canal.

The Ludwig Mill at Providence Park is the only canal mill still operating on water power in northwest Ohio today.

***The Volunteer* canal boat**. Locking through Lock 44 at Providence Metropark. It is the only place in Ohio where one may "lock through" on a canal boat.

Other mills in the area included the Vocke Flour Mill, Napoleon; Napoleon Power Plant; Edison Power Plant, Maumee; Purdy's Mill, Grand Rapids; Grand Rapids Planing Mill, Grand Rapids; Otsego Sawmill, Waterville; Perkin's Flower Mill, Waterville; Armada Mill, Toledo; Maumee Woolen Mill, Maumee Side Cut; a Paper Mill at Grand Rapids and many more.

### Lock 44, Providence Lock

Lock 44, Providence Lock, at the park was originally part of the Wabash & Erie Canal and was known for a time as Lock 9 using the numbering system which started at the river lock of the Manhattan Extension. Lock 44 is at the western end of the 20 mile level, Lock 45 being in Maumee, O. at Scott Street. The lower courses of Lock 44's limestone blocks were quarried in the adjacent Maumee River, while the upper, exposed layers were hauled in from the Marblehead Peninsula near Sandusky. The stone from Marblehead was employed because of its superior ability to resist weather. Not only was Lock 44 a lift lock with a 3½ foot lift, it was also a guard lock which was necessary since the river was canalized above the Providence/Grand Rapids Dams. These 6 foot high dams totaled 1858 feet in length and impounded water for 2 miles to the town of Florida, Ohio and provided water to operate the canal and its industries for the final 30 miles to Toledo and Lake Erie. The canal ran in the slackwater created by the dams for 1½ miles westward to the Bucklin outlet Lock 43 where the canal and river once more separated.

The Toledo Park District has been unable to locate any maintenance records for Providence Lock, but it is known that the upper wing walls, gates and a new concrete by-pass weir were constructed in 1908. Additionally, both dams at Grand Rapids were replaced in the same year by contractor John Weckerly of Whitehouse, O.

## Conclusion

Providence Metropark has seen many changes and improvements since the Works Progress Administration built shelter houses and made improvements to the area during the depression. Continued improvements such as the restoration of the Ludwig Mill, the rewatering of the canal and the launching of *The Volunteer* will ensure its continued popularity with the general public as well as with canal enthusiasts.

§§§§§§§§§§§§§§§§§§§§§§§§§§§§§

*The scene recollected here is now decidedly urban and difficult to imagine today. Editor Frank Trevorrow informs us that the setting for this account was the Lenk Street (now City Park Avenue) drawbridge and the Lock was Number 47, old number 6.*

Volume XVI (1978), No. 2, p. 23

## TOLEDO CANAL MEMORIES by Genevieve Linden Bell

In the early 1890's my brother and our friends, another brother and sister, and I attended St. Peters Catholic School on South St. Clair Street in Toledo. It was an elementary school and we were of varying ages from six to ten. On the way to and from school, we crossed a bridge over the Miami and Erie Canal.

From time to time on the way home we would hear a whistle, the signal that the bridge would turn. We would run as fast as we could to beg Mr. Schmidt, the bridge keeper—and a very firm but kind man he was—if we might stay on the bridge as it turned. He invariably said, "No kids on the bridge tonight." Then we would beg, promising to stay in the middle where it was safe and Mr. Schmidt always relented.

We could see the canal boat waiting to enter the lock. The two mules that walked on the towpath and pulled the boat along had been taken on the boat over a gangplank.

We could hear the water rush into the lock and watch the boat rise higher and higher like magic. Then the gates would open and the boat would be in the canal again but at a higher level.

We would call to the people on the boat. There was usually a woman on the deck, washing clothes or emptying dish water, and two or three men standing about. We would ask where they had come from and where they were going and when they would get to their destination.

In the early winter or spring, Mr. Schmidt stayed in the bridge shanty, a small place with a little stove to keep warm. On the way home from school, we would beg to come into the shanty to warm our hands. He would say, "No, no kids in here tonight." "But our hands are so cold," we begged. "You got mittens, put them on." Then he would relent and the four of us crowded into the shanty. After a time he would shout, "Now your hands are warm. Go on home. Your mother's waiting for you!"

Many years later when visiting my childhood home with a nephew. I said I would like to see the canal. He replied that we were driving on it right now, for it had become a highway.

§§§§§§§§§§§§§§§§§§§§§§§§§§§

*Due to compromises, there were actually three separate termini to the Miami & Erie Canal: at Maumee, Toledo and Manhattan. These are described in this article by John C. Vanderlip.*

Volume III (1965), No. 1, pp. 4-7

### THE NORTHERN TERMINUS OF THE MIAMI & ERIE CANAL by John C. Vanderlip

The contracts for the northern section of the canal were let in May 1837, over 12 years after the contracts were let on the southern division. The delay was due in part to the difficulties encountered in the Toledo War.

Heated rivalry also existed between Toledo and its up-river neighbors, Maumee and Perrysburg, and its down-river neighbor, Manhattan, to be the northern end of the canal. The rivalry for the northern terminus of the canal was so keen that, on the 23rd of August, 1836, the canal commissioners met in Perrysburg to hear the various arguments presented by the rival factions. The different claims were so well asserted that the commissioners granted each place a canal connection with the Maumee River. This brought to a harmonious end a bitter point of contention. The decision was confirmed by Governor Lucas on his visit to these places in Nov., 1836.

The Maumee connection, known as the Maumee Side Cut, was 2½ miles long. It consisted of six locks with a fall of 63 feet. The side cut left the canal just southwest of town and locked into the river at the "Point", in the lowlands directly across the river from Perrysburg. The stone lock walls are preserved in Side Cut Canal Park.

The Toledo Side Cut left the canal proper just south of the Swan Creek crossing. It entered the creek about 0.4 of a mile further east, downstream, with a fall of 15 feet in two locks.

The Manhattan extension crossed Swan Creek on a wooden aqueduct. The course of the canal ran in a northeasterly direction through the present downtown section of Toledo. At the Manhattan town line it turned to lock into the Maumee River between Lapier and LaSalle streets with a drop of 15 feet, overcome by two locks near the outlet. Manhattan is now a part of north Toledo.

On or about March 26, 1864, both the Maumee Side Cut and the two locks at Manhattan were officially abandoned by an act of the Legislature. The remaining portion of the Manhattan extension was abandoned by an act of the 31st of January, 1871. The Swan Creek Side Cut was then the only connection with the lower Maumee River.

A rock bar, allowing only boats of shallow draft to navigate up-river to Maumee and Perrysburg, hastened the early decision to abandon this connection while the location of the natural river channel was very detrimental to Manhattan. The large lake boats had to by-pass Manhattan for Toledo where the channel was much more favorable. Considering these two natural hazards, it makes one wonder if the State money was not spent a little too freely constructing these short lived connections.

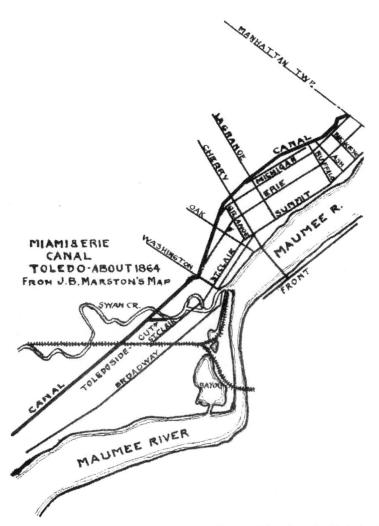

**Northern Terminus of the Miami & Erie Canal**. Showing the Toledo Side Cut and Manhattan Extension through downtown Toledo. *Map by Frank W. Trevorrow.*

# BRANCH CANALS

*Part of a larger article on the Pennsylvania & Ohio Canal by Earl J. Heydinger, the section selected here highlights the brief canal career of "Towpath Jim" Garfield, 20th President of the United States.*

Volume V (1967), No. 3, p. 25

## FUTURE PRESIDENT A P & O DRIVER by Earl J. Heydinger

Future-president James A. Garfield, by driving a towing team on the P & O in 1847 became its most famous personage. At 16, failing to get a job on Lake Erie, Garfield walked from Cleveland to Pittsburgh driving the team towing the canal boat "Evening Star", loaded with 50 tons of copper ore and owned by his cousin, Captain Amos Letcher. On the return trip, the "Evening Star" loaded 60 tons of coal from future-governor David Tod's Brier Hill mine. On a Sunday visit to his loading dock, Tod recalled all crewmen playing cards except the driver who was reading history. With ten days experience, (the time for the round trip to and from Pittsburgh) Garfield became bowsman at $14 a month and board. He later illustrated his strength by dispatching a canal "bully" and his character by refusing to abuse his beaten opponent. Malaria ended Garfield's P & O Canal career.

§§§§§§§§§§§§§§§§§§§§§§§§§§§§

*Youngstown was a canal town. Hard to believe today as almost all traces of it are gone (see Cleveland, Massillon, Cincinnati, Dayton, etc.), but the city owes its early growth to the Pennsylvania & Ohio Canal as detailed in this Ron Reid article.*

Volume XX (1982), No. 1, pp. 1-12

## THE CANAL HERITAGE OF YOUNGSTOWN, OHIO by Ronald D. Reid

On the Federal Plaza in downtown Youngstown stands a stone sculpture known as the Soldiers' Monument. A 110 year old visible link with the city's past, this "Man on the Monument" represents the community's determination not to forget its heritage. If one looks closely at the marble pedestal under the figure, a not-so-familiar image is to be seen, the weatherworn outline of a canal boat. Except for that faint image, no other trace remains today of the time when Youngstown was a thriving "port" on the Pennsylvania and Ohio Canal.

*Early History*

The story of this largely unknown period was one of inestimable importance to the early industrial development of the city. George Washington first conceived the idea of this canal as result of his extensive surveying experiences in the 1700s. Agitation to expedite the utilization of the region's agricultural and industrial potential led to detailed route surveys and the creation of the Pennsylvania and Ohio Canal Company in 1827.

Among the elected delegates from Trumbull County (which then included Youngstown) to a three-day canal convention held in Warren during November of 1833, were canal visionaries William Rayen and David Tod of Youngstown. Favorable findings by this convention led to the implementation of the enterprise, with the opening of stock books in 1835.

*Canal Engineers*

Several Youngstown area engineers contributed their capable efforts toward the technical design, surveying and construction supervision for sections of the canal.

Joseph Barclay was one who started reading textbooks on civil engineering while working as a clerk. In 1836 this self-made man obtained the position of engineer on a section of the channel, and in 1837 assisted in building a wooden bridge at Spring Common and drew the plans for the Mahoning River slackwater dam at Lowellville. Traces of this dam may be discerned today.

Barclay was assisted by James McEwen, whose son, J. Harris McEwen later served as superintendent for one portion of the waterway. A future mayor of Youngstown, J. D. Raney was a contractor for one and a half miles of the canal. Cabinet maker William Fitch became a canal toll collector at Youngstown and in later years went into the banking business.

*Proposed P & O Canal Routes*

The engineering survey of 1828 by Lt. Colonel James Kearney of the U.S. Topographic Engineers intended for the canal to pass through Youngstown parallel and to the north of Federal Street, along what is now Commerce Street. This would have required an earth cut up to 14 feet deep. An alternate alignment was calculated by Kearney that would have taken the canal south of Federal Street near the present location of Boardman Street.

Both of these preliminary routes were rejected by the engineers of the P & O Canal Company in 1835 in favor of a curved alignment closer to the Mahoning River. The primary advantages of this accepted canal route were: less earth work, the need for fewer bridges and proximity to the village's fledgling iron furnaces.

As early as 1803 the smelting of iron had been practiced in the Mahoning Valley, utilizing the ample deposits of bog ore, limestone and hardwood. All of these early furnaces used charcoal produced from the extensive forests of the region.

*Final Route*

The final route survey selected a waterway 83 miles in length, of which 73 miles were in Ohio. Primarily the canal consisted of an artificial excavation from Akron to Warren, but the eight mile reach south of Warren, through Niles, and down to Girard was provided by slackwater in the Mahoning River. Leaving the river in downtown Girard, the P & O route passed through the Youngstown area via an artificial channel running to the north of the river. Except for a two-mile stretch of slackwater above Lowellville, the remainder of the waterway was by canal to New Castle, where it tied into the Beaver and Erie Canal of western Pennsylvania.

*Opening of the P&O Through Youngstown*

The section of canal from Newcastle in Pennsylvania running through Youngstown was completed as far west as Warren in May of 1839. The local significance of the work was manifested in the joyous celebration which greeted the arrival of the first boat from Beaver.

On May 23, 1839, the packet *Ontario,* commanded by a Captain Bronson and carrying a merry Pennsylvania delegation, floated into Warren "...in gallant style, amid the roar of cannon and the shouts and hearty cheers of our citizens." On the return trip to Beaver the next day, the vessel carried about 40 prominent citizens of Youngstown "... who were highly delighted with the excursion." Among the spirited elocutions presented along the route were the following toasts: "The Pennsylvania & Ohio canal—a new link in the chain of sisterhood between two states whose interests can never be severed," and "Pennsylvania & Ohio—Pennsylvania, the keystone of the arch, and Ohio the stone which supports the arch."

*Early Youngstown Industry*

In 1840 a Welsh coal miner, Thomas Davis, came to Youngstown and leased a coal bank owned by Peter Werts. Mr. Davis sent the first coal shipment from Youngstown via canal barge to Ravenna. During the autumn of 1841, he was credited with the discovery of coal under a region of vine-covered land now known as Brier Hill, owned by David Tod. The future Civil War governor of Ohio and perhaps the most illustrious native son of Youngstown, David Tod (1805-1868) had been one of the original stockholders of the Pennsylvania and Ohio Canal Company. Tod, with the assistance of Davis, William Rayen and Jeremiah Stambaugh established a mine and built a short railroad down to the canal, thus launching the thriving coal industry in the Youngstown area in the 19th century. By the mid-1840s it was found that the native "block coal" was suitable in its raw, uncoked state for the smelting of iron ore in blast furnaces. Local deposits of quality coal, ore and limestone supplemented by the *fortuitous availability of waterborne transportation* for the economical assembly of those materials, were essentially responsible for the early development of the iron and steel industry in the Mahoning Valley.

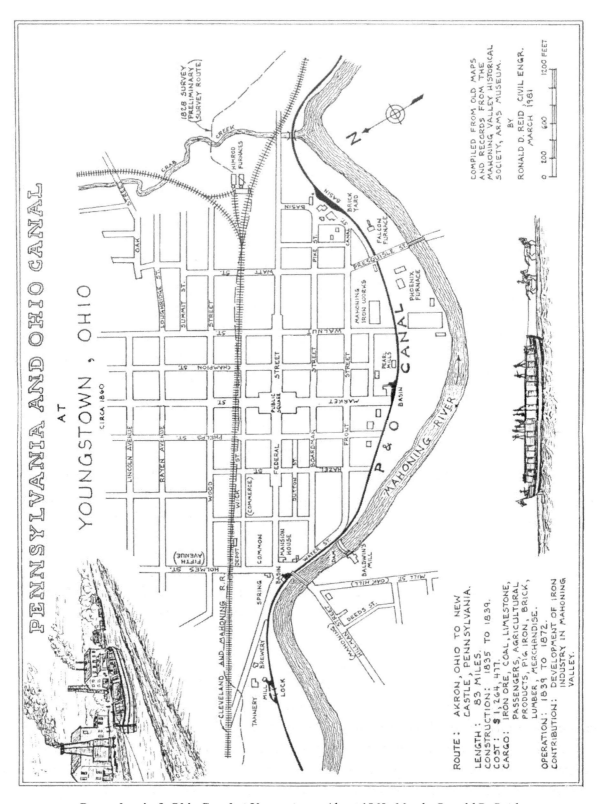

**Pennsylvania & Ohio Canal at Youngstown.** About 1860. *Map by Ronald D. Reid.*

*Youngstown in 1846*

The year 1846 saw the creation of Mahoning County from sections of Trumbull and Columbiana counties. A contemporary image of Youngstown is given here by Henry Howe in his *Historical Collections of Ohio*:

"Youngstown is the largest and most flourishing town in Mahoning county, beautifully situated on the north bank of the Mahoning river...It contains about 1,200 inhabitants, has 12 mercantile stores, 3 warehouses for receiving and forwarding goods and produce on the canal; 4 churches...The Pennsylvania and Ohio Canal passes through the village, and the products of the surrounding country are sent here for shipment. Few places in Ohio are more fully situated; few have greater facilities for manufacturing, or bid fairer to become places of wealth and importance. Bituminous coal and iron ore abound in the immediate vicinity of the village and along the line of the canal, adequate, it is believed, to the wants of a large manufacturing place...three furnaces similar to the English and Scotch furnaces, each capable of producing from sixty to one hundred tons of pigiron per week, have been erected in the township, and the village, at which is made the various sizes of bar, rod and hoop iron; also sheet iron, nails and spikes."

Officially the waterway bore the title, "Pennsylvania and Ohio Canal," but usually was nicknamed "Mahoning Canal," or "Cross Cut." To the citizens of Youngstown this vital ribbon of water was a source of pride and commonly referred to as "our canal."

*Canal Boat Line*

A prominent line of canal freighters running cargoes to and from Cleveland, Youngstown and Pittsburgh was operated by the Clark & Co.'s Line, for which R.G. Parks & Co. was the local agency. This company ran the following advertisement in the March 22, 1844 issue of the *Olive Branch*:

"YOUNGSTOWN & CLEVELAND

The Boat 'Youngstown' will commence her trips to Cleveland on the 29th instant. Merchants having Freight to ship, will find it an object to ship by her, as she runs regularly, and they may depend upon having their freight put through without delay and at the lowest prices."

*Through Youngstown by Canal Boat*

Approaching the city by canal boat from the west in the late 1850s, a traveler would pass along a wide curve through Riverview. This old community, now vanished under industrial sites was located north of the confluence of Mill Creek with the Mahoning River. Within ten minutes our boat would be entering the lift lock near what would now be the old Pennsylvania Railroad Station site. For many years a tannery, an old grist mill, a dry dock and later the Youngstown Brewery utilized the water available along the lock's mill race. Inside this stone masonry "hydraulic elevator," the boat would slowly settle about eight feet, blocking off the view until the large oak gates at the lower end were opened.

Under way in the lower reach, the thriving hive of commercial activity at Spring Common would be passed. Here a wide section of the canal known as a basin was provided for loading and unloading the many freight barges which supplied the adjacent warehouses. Most passengers boarded packet boats at this location. A covered wooden bridge spanned the river and canal near this spot until replaced by an iron arch structure in 1869. In places the canal towpath was a scant 30 feet north of the river bank.

The next half mile of canal curved through the flat terrace above the bend in the river. Records of early surveys indicate that the top water width averaged 42 feet, with a 15 foot wide towpath on the south bank of the canal. Initially the crescent of land between the canal and river was farmed, but the city's growing iron industry eventually transformed this waterfront into the industrialized area that remains today.

A bridge and trestle crossed over the canal at South Avenue (then known as Presquisle St.). Additional impressive mill works would appear on the right amidst the scene of several barges being unloaded of their vital cargoes of coal, ore and limestone.

The third and largest basin in the city was located adjacent to—appropriately enough—Canal and Basin streets. Several machine shops, planing mills and a bolt factory lined the 500 foot long by 130 foot wide basin, and here a warehouse was kept by A.D. Jacobs. Within minutes our canal boat would have floated over a culvert on Crab Creek, passing further developing industrial sites on its way out of the city.

*Canal Packet Boats*

An article in the June 6, 1851 edition of *The Ohio Republican* speaks of packet boats frequented by Youngstowners:

> "THE BEAVER PACKETS
>
> Are running full at the present time, carrying as many as they can well accommodate. This route from Cleveland to Pittsburgh is becoming the route for the travelling community. Captains Hoffman and Tiuby are rendering themselves more popular every trip, by their attention, and efforts to make travelers happy and comfortable. No better men travel on fresh water."

Captain Hoffman commanded the packet *Pennsylvania* and Captain Tiuby, the *Niagara*. A Captain Brown commanded another boat named *Mayflower,* and all three packets were operated by the Clark Parks & Co.

Undoubtedly this article was an attempt by anxious canal operators to hold onto their passenger business in the face of a new form of competition. In 1851 tracks had been laid south of Cleveland by the Cleveland and Pittsburgh Railroad, reaching to Ravenna on the canal in 1852. Canal passenger traffic soon dwindled.

*P & O Canal Men and the Railroad*

Many of the prominent Mahoning Valley leaders who had been instrumental in early efforts to charter the canal, now turned their attentions toward this latest method of public improvement and enterprise. William Rayen a stockholder and director of the P & O Company, aided in obtaining the charter for the Cleveland and Mahoning Railroad Company in 1848. It was perceived that although the canal provided cheap transportation of bulky materials such as coal, ore and limestone, it was too slow for the quickly growing iron and manufacturing industries.

In 1847 David Tod had been appointed U.S. minister to Brazil under the administration of President Polk. Accompanied by Dr. Timothy Woodbridge (who previously had been an engineer during the construction of the P & O) Tod started the first leg of his voyage to Brazil by boarding a packet at Spring Common. After five years of effective service, Tod returned to Youngstown in 1851. Joining forces with Jacob Perkins of Warren, he immediately became an outspoken advocate for the proposed C & M Railroad. In 1855 the first canal barge loaded with rails arrived at Niles. The arrival of the first train to Youngstown on November 12, 1856 was a major event for the city and the beginning of a slow decline for the canal.

*Early Railroads, Industry and the Canal*

The railroad acquired a modest but steady income, and the greater share of passenger travel. Soon railroad stock was traded for canal stock until the C & M Railroad had control of both the railroad and the canal. Across the state other canals experienced a similar decline in tolls as the result of railroad competition, and by the late 1850s a few voices were heard (especially from the railroads) suggesting closing the P & O.

By 1859 Youngstown's population was near 3,000. On the skyline were four large blast furnaces constantly in operation, each employing about 30 men and producing 80 tons of iron each week. The names of these furnaces were: Phoenix, Eagle, Falcon and Brier Hill. Locally, iron ore was consumed in the proportion of 66 parts Lake Superior to 34 parts of native ore mined in the Mahoning Valley. Heavily laden canal barges continued to haul large tonnages of coal, ore, pig iron, gravel, limestone, fireclay brick and lumber.

The directors of the C & M Railroad experimented with a policy of higher freight rates. Although they controlled both the canal and the railroad the directors were compelled to go back to lower rates, for the local coal and iron industries were faced with being priced out of the market.

In a transfer of questionable motives, the State Board of Public Works of Ohio in 1863 sold all of its P & O stock to the railroad for only $35,000, which was essentially less than nothing.

*Decline of the Canal*

The canal continued in operation during the Civil War years although insufficient funds for proper maintenance gradually led to structural and operational deficiencies. It was not uncommon in the mid-1860s for a canal boat to be delayed at a lock for a day or two waiting for water supply or for gravel deposits to be cleaned out in order to make the lock gates close.

By the late 1860s the track of the Ashtabula, Youngstown and Pittsburgh Railroad had been laid over the berm bank of the canal near Spring Common. Although the entire waterway was still navigable and continued to transport a modest tonnage of bulk materials for the rapidly expanding iron industry, its eventual fate became apparent.

During late 1868 and in the spring of 1869, the summit and parts of the eastern and western divisions of the P & O Canal fell into disuse and disrepair, leading to destruction of feeder dams and reservoirs near Ravenna essential for maintaining adequate water supply. It became impossible to navigate any further west from Youngstown than into Niles, and occasional low water hampered navigation eastward to the New Castle junction.

## Last Boats

According to some sources the last boat to navigate the canal section between New Castle and Youngstown was the barge *Telegraph* on December 17, 1868. An inspection of the last toll collector book shows receipt listings for a few boats having Pennsylvania registrations from as late as 1870. During 1871 only boats of Youngstown and Lowellville registration are noted, their cargoes consisting of limestone, fire clay brick, lumber and gravel.

Under the pressure of railroad competition the neighboring Beaver and Erie Canal of western Pennsylvania was abandoned in 1871. This left the isolated section of P & O Canal from Youngstown to the state line still in use during 1872, to the last few shabby boats struggling for life hauling limestone for the local iron industries. The last entry in the faded toll books is that for the *J. C. Heenan* carrying limestone from Lowellville to Youngstown on November 8, 1872. A search of old newspapers from 1872 and 1873 would lead one to believe that the old canal died almost unnoticed in the valley's bustle of the industrial growth that it made possible.

## Canal Route Abandonment

As might be expected, the strategic route of the canal with its convenient level grades was soon "appropriated" by railroads and industrial interests. An amusing account of one such event was related in 1924 by Mrs. J. H. Bulla in *Romance of the Canal*:

> "There was an understanding that property used by the canal here was to revert to its former owners in the event of the canal's failure. The strip of land running from Market to Basin used by the canal should have come back to the owners of the iron mill located where the present Brown-Bonnell mills of the Republic Steel Co. now stand. On the abandonment of the canal, the new railroad wanted the old canal bed and decided to appropriate it. To accomplish this the rails would have to be laid in the night. Preparations for this were supposed to be secretly made, but the men in the mill heard of it and when the railroad people came to start work they were accorded a warm

reception in the shape of red hot iron bars wielded by brawny arms. The would-be army of occupation beat a hasty but ignominious retreat."

With the abandonment of navigation certain, the railroads lost no time insuring that the canal was laid to rest for good. Maps from 1874 indicate virtual erasement of the canal near Basin Street by an extensive ladder track yard of the Erie Railroad. By the 1880s a main city sewer had been laid in the center of the canal bed near Spring Common, the remainder filled over and railroad spurs laid directly across the old bed and towpath.

And so the iron horse inherited the promising iron producing, coal mining and manufacturing industries developed and nurtured by the old waterway. Along the valley stretched a landscape of industrialization which would soon become virtually contiguous with the Mahoning River.

§§§§§§§§§§§§§§§§§§§§§§§§§§§§

*It has become somewhat of a myth that nothing of the Pennsylvania & Ohio Canal remains. While little stone is left, much of the ditch may be found in Portage County if one knows where to look. This article by local historian Dudley Weaver, which was submitted by Terry K. Woods, describes the effect of the canal in this area.*

Volume XXXVII (1999), No. 4, pp. 76-79

## THE PENNSYLVANIA & OHIO CANAL IN PORTAGE COUNTY, OHIO by Dudley Weaver

[…] One effect of the canal was reflected in the small towns that sprang up along the route. In Portage County, these boom towns enjoyed a brief period of prosperity then dwindled to insignificant villages, or died out completely. McClintocksburgh and Newport (now Wayland) established about 1836 in Paris Township, are fair examples. The former disappeared when the canal was abandoned only to reappear in the 1920's. The latter was kept alive by the establishment there of a station on the Pittsburgh & Western Railroad. Campbellsport, southeast of Ravenna, was once considered a dangerous rival of the County Seat. The town appeared to be about to experience quite a boom as it was on the canal and served by several good roads, plus having a good waterpower potential from the Mahoning River. But the shining rails stunted its growth, and it is just managing today to maintain its identity.

Over in Franklin Mills (Kent), a group composed largely of Cleveland men, purchased the water rights in both the lower and upper village. About 400 acres was included. They organized the Franklin Land Company and undertook a remarkable program of development and speculation. Everything went well until the Panic of 1837 nearly prostrated the country. The Land Company collapsed, but Franklin Mills stood forth as a village which had possibilities.

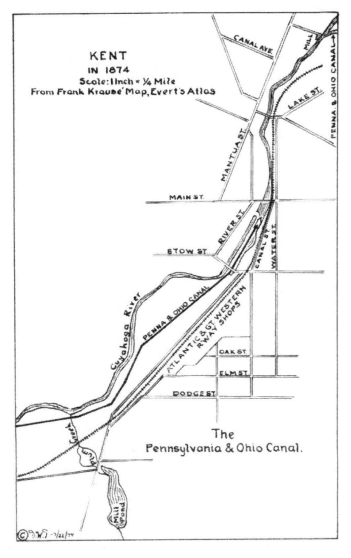

KENT
IN 1874
Scale: 1 inch = ¼ Mile
From Frank Krause' Map, Evert's Atlas

The
Pennsylvania & Ohio Canal.

**Pennsylvania & Ohio Canal at Kent**. *Map by Frank W. Trevorrow from* Towpaths, *Vol. XV (1977), No. 1, p. 6.*

With the inherent prosperity brought on by the canal came new enterprises, and banks to dispense the capital. All this tended to pave the way for the new industrial prosperity ushered in by the advent of the railroad. The whistle of the Iron Horse, first heard in Ravenna on March 7, 1851, announced the slow death of the P. & O. Canal. By the following summer, all passenger traffic had ceased on the canal. However, much heavy shipments, such as coal, lumber, ore, and stone continued to be made by the fading waterway. In 1857, the Cleveland & Mahoning Valley Railroad reached Youngstown via Warren, opening the Mahoning Valley coal fields to Cleveland and other Lake ports. This dealt the killing blow to commerce on the P. & O. Canal.

The start of the Civil War saw the canal cease to be of any use as a carrier, however some revenue was received for water used out of the canal to power mills. The State of Ohio sold the State-owned stock, once valued at $450,000, to the Cleveland & Mahoning Railroad for $30,000! In 1867, the railroad leased the western division to the Akron Hydraulic Company, which wanted it as a future water source for Akron. Because the Hydraulic Company neglected the canal, the water became stagnant. Franklin Township pleaded for its abandonment. May 7, 1869, saw complete abandonment north of Old Forge (north-east Akron) to the summit at Ravenna. Shortly after this, the huge (19' lift) upper lock north of Kent was destroyed. This permitted water to drain out of the Brady & Pippen Lake Reservoirs. Likewise went the famous Feeder Dam across the Cuyahoga River which supplied water to the summit. Farmers living near Feeder Dam and the two-lake reservoir gained back much valuable land.

With the canal abandoned, the boats stranded in the eastern section of the county were either salvaged for lumber or taken to a widewater on a farm about a mile northeast of Campbellsport. Here they were allowed to decay away in a sort of burial ground for old canal boats.

In 1877, the P. & O. Canal Company was disenfranchised by action of the State Supreme Court, and all its property, consisting of locks, wharves, boats, etc. was sold at public auction by order of the Court at Warren.

The old right of way of the P. & O. Canal was yet to serve a useful part of a different means of transportation. Between the years 1884 and 1905, the towpath acted as a bed for the Pittsburgh & Western Railroad, then the Baltimore & Ohio Railroad. With the turn of the century, the B. & O. Railroad disregarded the original route of the canal and straightened the roadbed wherever necessary.

So passed into history the Pennsylvania & Ohio Canal. The people of Portage County, in their enthusiasm for the steam railroads, were quite willing to treat the canal which they had aided to build, with much effort, as expendable on the upward curve of County prosperity.

§§§§§§§§§§§§§§§§§§§§§§§§§§§§§

*A Photo Album of Ohio's Canal Era, 1825-1913 by Jack Gieck is regarded as the "Bible" on the topic by Buckeye State canawlers. This Gieck article is from "Death of a Fantasy," published in the Summit County Historical Society's Old Portage Trail Review, November 1982. Sorry to say, the pristine Pennsylvania & Ohio Canal was not found buried under Akron.*

Volume XXXIV (1996), No 4, pp. 60-63

### EXPLORING UNDERGROUND AKRON by Jack Gieck

The Fantasy

The recent (in 1982) partial dismantling of the Portage Hotel at Main and Market Streets, now totally gone, has laid to rest a long-cherished personal theory, but has also yielded some fascinating new (to me at least) historical information. The fantasy was that there might be an Akron underground, where the city's downtown was rebuilt one story higher on the ruins left by a disastrous fire in 1889.

Why should there have been an Akron underground? The clues were fascinating:

One; When the Pennsylvania & Ohio Canal, which ran down the center of Main Street from 1840 until 1873, was later covered over, it could not merely be filled in. Something had to be done with the water, which flowed in from the Lower Basin -- where the P & O Canal had joined with the Ohio & Erie south of Exchange Street. Indeed, one can still see a flowing stream of water abruptly disappearing as it dives underground behind the Civic Theater. This water flows north, underneath Main Street, before eventually pouring into the Little Cuyahoga River.

Two; When the Portage Hotel was built in 1911-12, it was erected on the site, if not upon the actual foundation, of the old Empire House -- which dated from 1847.

Three; I was in the Portage Hotel in 1975, while filming "City at the Summit", and was surprised to see the inside of plate-glass store windows at the basement level.

Four; When one walked down either of the two former stairways off the Main Street sidewalk in front of the hotel (which provided access to a barber shop at the basement level), one passed by the mystery of painted-shut windows on the east or street side of the stairway!

Ergo: If one got permission to break through those windows, would one find oneself on the bank of the Pennsylvania & Ohio Canal, frozen in time for more than a century -- with the original first floor of the Academy of Music (now the People's Federal Building, on the northeast corner of Main and Market) reflected in the water before him, just waiting to be photographed? I fervently hoped so.

Alas: The deep trench excavated in front of the Portage (which wiped out the painted-shut windows) revealed a 16-foot wall of concrete running the length of the east edge of the trench. This wall is apparently one side of an enclosed concrete channel in which water now flows. With a flashlight I explored some subterranean labyrinths at the south edge of the property; and, although these passageways do run beneath West Market Street for a short distance, I was disappointed to discover that the Main Street wall was impenetrable.

Concrete had been a commercial building material in the United States for barely 40 years in 1911, and even its basic ingredient, Portland cement, was still experimental. There were some 98 different formulations extant at the time -- until the U.S. Bureau of Standards finally addressed the material in 1917. Nevertheless, this vintage concrete wall remains uncracked and uncrumbled after 71 years -- a substantially better track record than that of several Akron bridges, which have expired in less than half that time.

Further, poking around with my flashlight at the basement level revealed a foundation made of huge rectangular blocks of sandstone, beautifully sawed with a precision beyond the call of such humble structural duty -- unless, after all, they were the original east facade of the Empire House, studded with that row of store-front shop windows, now broken out and gutted. Stonecutters in Akron-area quarries had had lots of practice providing similar sandstone blocks for literally scores of locks in the area by 1847.

One floor above, the gloomy scene in the bare, unlit lobby was less of a joy for a romantic to behold. There, the faded, peeling plaster and unrelieved universal decay carried not a hint of the exuberance of the *Akron Times* on June 11, 1912, when it celebrated "...the completion of one of the finest hostelries in the State of Ohio. The beautiful women gowned in the height of fashion, with the men who had made Akron known throughout the world for its industrial and commercial progress mingled in the spacious lobby which was a bower of beauty with its rich furnishings and complimentary floral pieces...".

The Reality

Since my 1982 "Akron Underground" adventure (in which I avoided being arrested for climbing the Portage Hotel's fire escape to the fifth floor level in order to explore the building's subterranean passageways) I have learned that water from the vestigial Pennsylvania & Ohio Canal apparently finds its way into the surviving segment of the Cascade Mill Race -- which actually still exists in the valley of the Ohio & Erie.

P & O aficionados will be familiar with the fact that the northern Akron portion of that canal was constructed by widening and expanding "Crosby's Ditch." By 1832 physician-entrepreneur Dr. Eliakim Crosby had completed a mill race from a dam on the Little Cuyahoga River at Case and Bank Streets in Middlebury (near today's Goodyear headquarters) flowing into downtown Akron at the head of Main Street and turning left at Mill Street -- delivering its torrent of water to his five-story Old Stone Mill at Lock 5. Crosby's mill stood on the site of today's Cascade Plaza Holiday Inn.

After turning Crosby's four French-made buhrstones, the effluent water flowed north, plunging down the Cascade Race to power a string of mills and factories (and even a distillery) during its precipitous descent down the valley of the Ohio & Erie -- and incidentally giving birth to the town of "Cascade," centered at Howard and West Market Streets. Later called North Akron, the village's population had surpassed that of South Akron by 1835. In 1836 the two Akrons became one.

The Cascade Race is easy to find in the O & E valley north of Market Street. It runs along the east side of the valley, parallel to the canal, but at a substantially higher level. Ace Rubber Products (built on the site of Aetna Mills) used its water for many years to cool its rubber mills -- until a tank car accident doused the channel with sulfuric acid, eating up Ace Rubber's pipes!

Just south of North Street the water today disappears into a 150-year-old arched stone tunnel which once delivered the stream to a 40-foot overshot waterwheel in the Cascade Mill. Today the tunnel is clogged with old tires, scrap refrigerators and other unfortunate debris. The water reenters the Little Cuyahoga River below Mustill's Store at Lock 15 as it has for a century.

By 1840, the Middlebury-to-Akron segment of Crosby's Ditch had been widened to the specifications laid down for the Pennsylvania & Ohio Canal, and the channel was extended south down Akron's Main Street to the Lower Basin near Lock One at Exchange Street to join the Ohio & Erie Canal at the Summit level. A single lock was constructed just south of Mill Street, helping to divert the water down the remaining short section of the Cascade Mill Race from Main Street down to Crosby's Mill at Lock Five. The effluent water continued down the remainder of the race as before, to power the mills in the valley to the north, until their waterpower was replaced by steam in mid-century.

In August, 1840, when a flotilla of brightly decorated passenger packets arrived from New Castle to celebrate completion of the Pennsylvania & Ohio Canal to Akron, the boats carried, in addition to Pennsylvania Governor David Whittenhouse Porter and other distinguished dignitaries, a cargo of sherry and Madeira wines as well as imported champagne. The ensuing celebration is said to have paralyzed Akron business for several days.

§§§§§§§§§§§§§§§§§§§§§§§§§§

*Erection of this historical marker (which still stands beside U.S. Route 30 near Hanoverton) commemorating the two tunnels on the Sandy & Beaver Canal was one of the CSO's earliest projects.*

Volume III (1965), No. 1, pp. 1-3

## NEW HISTORICAL MARKER DEDICATED

Over fifty people attended the dedication of a roadside marker on Route 30, one mile east of Hanoverton in Columbiana County on the afternoon of Oct. 24, 1964. The marker commemorates the Sandy and Beaver Canal tunnels.

Speakers at the ceremony were, left to right in the photo, R. Max Gard, Lisbon, Co-author of "The Sandy and Beaver Canal"; Wm. E. Vodrey, Jr., East Liverpool, Vice-President and Trustee of the Ohio Historical Society; T. H. Findley, President of the Canal Society and Daniel R. Porter, Administrative Head and Associate Director of the Ohio Historical Society.

**Canal Tunnels Marker Dedication on October 24, 1964**. Pictured from left to right: Max Gard, William Vodrey, Ted Findley, and Daniel Porter. *Courtesy Al Simpson of the* Canton Repository.

The marker bears this inscription:

CANAL TUNNELS
Southeast of this point are the Big and Little
Tunnels. They were links in the 73-mile Sandy
and Beaver Canal which connected the Ohio River
with the Ohio and Erie Canal. Shifts of Irish
laborers worked day and night with hand drills
and blasting powder to cut the 1,000-yard Big
Tunnel which opened for commercial use in 1850
and was abandoned 2 years later, a victim of
the railroad.
The Ohio Historical Society
with
The Columbiana County Historical Association
and
Canal Society of Ohio
1964

The Canal Society is honored to have been so recognized and is grateful to those who made it possible.

## THE SANDY & BEAVER CANAL TUNNELS

The contracts for the construction of the Big Tunnel were first let in November 1835. Actual work proceeded slowly and with only excavation of the approach cuts partially completed the contractor failed, necessitating the re-letting of the job in February 1836. The crash of 1837 and the subsequent halt of all construction on the canal, left the tunnel project with the open cuts excavated but with only 500 feet of the bore completed. In August 1845, with capital again available, drilling began anew and the third contractor finished the work. The Big Tunnel was drilled through solid rock and was left unlined. It was 17 to 18 feet high and only wide enough for one way passage. No towpath was provided, boats were hauled through by a horse-powered, endless chain device. At the highest point the hill was 80 ft. above the bore.

The contract for the Little Tunnel was not let until 1845 and it was completed in three years. Because of the loose rock and shale encountered the tunnel was lined with cut stone. Veins of coal and hydraulic limestone, both utilized in the canal construction, were uncovered in the Little Tunnel.

§§§§§§§§§§§§§§§§§§§§§§§§§§§

*The builder of the Brooklyn Bridge actually cut his engineering teeth as a canal builder with Ohio connections as explained in this piece by Terry Woods, reprinted from* The Blade.

Volume XI (1973), No. 1, pp. 1-5

## MASTER BUILDER by T.K. Woods

The Brooklyn Bridge stands as a fitting memorial to its designer, John A. Roebling. Except for an obscure Ohio canal, though, this engineering genius might have remained a fairly prosperous and totally unknown Pennsylvania farmer.

John Roebling was born in 1806, the fifth child of a middle-class shopkeeper, in Muhlhausen (now a town in Germany). As he grew up in the tiny village with its high protective walls, his temperament was alternately influenced by his father, an extremely content and pragmatic man, and his mother, an ambitious woman who hated the isolation and monotony of her life.

Largely through his mother's efforts, Roebling was sent to the Royal Polytechnic Institute in Berlin where he received an engineering degree in 1826. He immediately went to work building roads for the Prussian Government. However, that part of his temperament acquired from his mother refused to allow him to be happy using outmoded engineering techniques and attempting to surmount vast reams of governmental red tape. His natural enthusiasm for life also refused to allow him to be happy at the thought of military conscription. The Napoleonic Wars had raged throughout Europe during Roebling's boyhood and gave him a hatred for soldiering and war. By 1830, a second French Revolution was threatening to again ignite Europe, and young John Roebling began to think of moving elsewhere.

About that time, an acquaintance returned from America with glowing accounts. John and his older brother Carl began making plans to form a German colony in the United States.

The story of the Roebling's departure reads like a piece of fiction. The French upheaval evoked severe restrictions and it became illegal for an engineer to leave the country. One by one, Roebling and his followers secretly made their way to the coast where they chartered a ship and escaped to America.

The group purchased 1,600 acres north of Pittsburgh and set up a farming community that eventually became known as Saxonburg. For a while, that part of Roebling's temperament inherited from his father seemed to assert itself. He appeared to be quite content in the role of a farmer. He married the daughter of the village tailor in 1836 and a year later she bore him a son, Washington Augustus Roebling.

Since he now had a family to support, Roebling began to think about his future and American engineering. This was a new land, hungry for fresh ideas, and anxious for clever men to teach them to her. Roebling knew that he wanted to practice engineering in the United States, but how should he go about getting started? His command of the English language was mediocre at best and he knew no one in America who could provide him with references. His rekindled enthusiasm for engineering might have faded, but then a letter arrived that, for pure good timing, couldn't be equaled.

A private stock company in eastern Ohio was attempting to build a connecting link between the Ohio and Pennsylvania canal systems. Their chief engineer, a European named E .H. Gill, was hiring foreign-born engineers in spite of their language handicap. One of these, Edward Thierry, had been a classmate of Roebling. When asked by Gill if he knew of any other German engineers who might like employment, Thierry immediately thought of his classmate and wrote to him.

The letter stated, in part, that Gill would soon be visiting Pittsburgh. Roebling could meet with him there and talk about a job. On the way to Pittsburgh, Roebling stopped at the Butler County Courthouse to take a very important oath, his oath of citizenship. A European farmer left Saxonburgh; an American engineer arrived in Pittsburgh.

Roebling met with Gill; and the Sandy & Beaver Canal Company had a new engineering aid. Roebling came to Ohio and began assisting in laying out the levels and line of the eastern division and the proposed extension to Beaver, Penn. The 1837 financial panic forced the canal company to suspend operations just two months after Roebling was hired, but he had his taste of American engineering and remained an engineer for the rest of his life.

**John A. Roebling**. *Contributed by the Pennsylvania Canal Society.*

State-financed projects were still operating despite the panic so, after a winter of perfecting his English, Roebling sent a letter to the Pennsylvania canal commissioners requesting a position. This letter, plus favorable references from Gill, made Roebling an assistant engineer on the Beaver & Erie Canal in Pennsylvania.

This project, too, soon fell victim to the financial conditions of the day and he was transferred to the Portage Railway. Freight, passengers, and entire canal boats were carried over the Allegheny Mountains on a series of inclined planes. Stationary steam engines hauled their cargo up and down the planes at the end of huge hemp cables, nine inches and more in diameter, which often failed with disastrous results.

One day, Roebling witnessed an accident caused by a cable failure that resulted in two men being crushed to death. He was haunted by the sight when he returned to his room that night. Surely, he thought, there must be a stronger material for the cables than hemp.

A vaguely remembered article from a Prussian engineering journal came to mind, one that mentioned twisting iron filaments into rope. Roebling didn't remember all the details, but if someone else could do it, so could he.

He experimented all winter in Saxonburg and had a 600-foot length of braided wire cable to show the canal commissioners in the spring. Even Roebling was surprised at the test results and his fame as an inventor was established.

Roebling saw other applications for his cable. He remembered once seeing a suspension bridge of chain construction while he was a student and he began to consider ways of substituting his wire cable for the chain.

When the canal commissioners wanted to replace an ageing aqueduct in Pittsburgh, Roebling was ready with a design that called for the center span to be suspended on wire cables from two end-towers. It is to the everlasting credit of the commissioners that they were far-sighted enough to accept this novel design. When the waters of the canal slowly filled the aqueduct trough, subjecting the design to a 4 million-pound load, and the cables held, the future of wire cable suspension bridges was assured.

John Roebling's future was also assured. Many bridges followed, including the two aqueducts over the Lackawaxen on the D. & H. Canal. His crowning design, however, was to be the 1,400-foot Brooklyn Bridge. The building of this bridge could be a complete story in itself!

John Roebling died in 1869 of injuries received in an accident while locating the Brooklyn end of the bridge. His son, Washington, took over and, when an attack of the bends made him an invalid, his wife studied engineering to be able to carry his orders to the workmen.

The Brooklyn Bridge was completed in 1883 and stands as a tribute to Roebling's engineering genius. And deep in the valleys of eastern Ohio, the stone locks of the Sandy & Beaver Canal stand as a reminder of the turning point in the career of John A. Roebling, master builder.

§§§§§§§§§§§§§§§§§§§§§§§§§§§

*The society has always been supportive of community lock restoration projects as evidenced by Lock 38 in Cuyahoga Valley National Park, Lock II Park in Akron and Sunfish Lock 27 near Miamisburg. Lock 36 at Gaston's Mill on the Sandy & Beaver Canal is another example.*

Volume XXIII (1985), No. 3, pp. 30-33

## LOCK 36, SANDY AND BEAVER CANAL PARTIAL
## RESTORATION PROJECT by Floyd Lower

Early in 1982 the Columbiana County Forests and Parks Council in co-operation with the Columbiana Historical Association began the planning for a partial restoration of Lock No. 36 on the Sandy and Beaver Canal. The lock is part of the historical complex of buildings in Beaver Creek State Park.

The Council was formed November 21, 1960 at the time that the 1830s Gaston's Mill, which had operated until the late 1920s, had deteriorated and was about to be torn down by the Ohio Department of Natural Resources which owns the land and Beaver Creek State Park.

Gaston's Mill was restored by the Council and now operates as a stone buhr grist mill. The dam walls for the mill pond have replaced the upper gate of Lock 36. Both the mill and the lock are listed on the National Register of Historic Places.

Both walls of the lock remain, but the lower end must be rebuilt. "The plan is to restore the walls on the lower part of the lock and to build and put in place the lower gate. Visitors can then see how a canal lock operates. No water will be used but the lower gate would be operational."

### "Work Proposed for the Partial Restoration of Lock 36

"Excavate and remove silt in lower half of lock to original depth, extending to mill tail race.

Install basin and drain to relieve seepage from mill dam. Excavate and expose stone at lower end of lock for necessary resetting.

Rebuild stone wall now missing at lower end to conform with original appearance.

Repoint walls to extend approximately six feet beyond quoin (recess in wall for gate to open).

Treated sills and floor to be installed at least four feet beyond quoin.

Install missing iron anchors in walls.

Install wall planking a short distance beyond quoin.

Construct operable gate as in original, including valve.

Install protective viewing fence to surround dangerous area above the walls."

### "Budget for the Restoration Work, Materials, Equipment, etc.

| | |
|---|---:|
| "Excavation and equipment required to handle the stones. | $4,850.00 |
| Oak timber and plank. | 5,000.00 |
| Iron fittings, bolts, etc. | 900.00 |
| Clay, mortar, etc. | 875.00 |
| Removal and resetting of present stones in the deteriorated lock walls. | 2,000.00 |
| Treatment of timbers and wood used. | 600.00 |
| Safety fence around the top of the walls after completion of wall restoration. | 1,000.00 |
| | $15,225.00 |
| Contingencies. | 1,700.00 |
| Labor. | 19.850.00 |
| | $36,775.00 |
| Value of donated cut stone. | 3,000.00 |
| Estimated dollar value of project. | $39,775.00" |

"No operating costs for the lock will be involved after restoration. The small amount needed for maintenance can be provided by the Council."

The Columbiana County Forests and Parks Council is a Columbiana County citizens' non-profit corporation organized in 1960 consisting of about 100 members of which 30 to 40 are local organizations of all kinds. In addition to Gaston's Mill, the Council has also built a log cabin and a log school house near the mill with logs and building materials donated from nine different old buildings in the county. These were completed about 1971. A covered bridge originally built in the 1870s and no longer in use near Elkton, was moved to the park and built over the tail race just below the mill.

The Council also acquired an abandoned church near the campground built in 1869 and abandoned in 1952. It was restored to its original condition and summer services have been held each year since 1964. With the help of the Columbiana County Historical Association, the Council is now restoring the Williams Farm house to its original condition. In the late 1970s a log church and a log blacksmith shop were erected near the mill with funds provided by William H. Vodrey, Jr., now deceased, of East Liverpool, Ohio. Restoration of Lock No. 36 would complete this complex of historic structures in Beaver Creek State Park.

A fifteen year written agreement with a renewal option with the State of Ohio allows the Columbiana County Forests and Parks Council to operate the complex. If a change in the future should be needed, the Ohio Department of Natural Resources (which owns the land) or The Ohio Historical Society, is expected to maintain the historical complex and operate the mill.

Most of the funds for all of this restoration work were raised locally. The Ohio Department of Natural Resources provided water for the mill operation with the main expenditure being a pump one-fourth mile upstream to supply the mill pond, and a payment of $16,300 was made to complete work on the mill, log cabin and log school. The total investment in cash, not including donated materials and labor is approximately $75,000. This does not include the two Vodrey buildings, which would approximate $15,000.

Of the $75,000, the Ohio Department of Natural Resources contributed about 21 per cent, the Columbiana County Commissioners with small annual appropriations to the County Historical Association for the park work about 29 percent, and the remaining 50 percent was raised by local donations from citizens and organizations. Receipts above expenses for (the sale of) meal (from the mill) and souvenirs have been used for operation and maintenance expense.

To date, the largest donation received from requests to many foundations for funding is $500 from the Firestone Foundation. State Senator Robert Burch (D-3) and State Representative John Shivers (D-30) have been asked to assist in obtaining the necessary funds.

Donations of any amount may be sent to: Canal Lock 36 Fund, Columbiana County Forest and Parks Council, Floyd Lower, Chairman, 373 East Chestnut Street, Lisbon, Ohio 44432.

§§§§§§§§§§§§§§§§§§§§§§§§§§

*The late Baird Steward of Salem is fondly remembered as a Sandy & Beaver Canal expert. Not an easy canal to decipher, no less than six different interpretations are presented below. The parcels published in the* Ohio Patriot *are generally considered most correct.*

Volume XXXVI (1998), No. 3, pp. 33-37

## WILL THE REAL SANDY AND BEAVER CANAL PLEASE STAND UP by R. Baird Stewart

Is it any wonder that so many questions are unanswered when today's canal historians get together? Six different accounts by as many authors describe what made up the Sandy and Beaver and how it came to be.

W. F. Gilmore said it best:

"No really authoritative account of this canal can ever be written, because the official records were once borrowed from the State Archives at Columbus and in some way were lost. All that is known is practically hearsay largely second-hand, yes, possibly third hand."

The significant dates are:

> Charter granted to incorporate January 11, 1828
>
> Engineer E. H. Gill hired
>
> Gill's 1834 plan called for a second tunnel and shortened the route by 15 miles
>
> Ground was broken for canal start November 24, 1834
>
> Work stopped by bank panic of 1837
>
> Work restarted in 1845
>
> First boat passed through Big Tunnel Jan. 8, 1848
>
> Last boat through Spring 1852
>
> Cold Run Reservoir breached April 12, 1852
>
> Portions of canal used until 1854
>
> Bankruptcy sale in Columbiana County Court House March 6, 1854

James Kelly's suit resulted in the Court appointing John Clark as Master Commissioner to carry out the sale. The recently discovered announcement of the sale, summarized in Tables 2-4, is believed to be the best source for makeup of the Sandy and Beaver Canal. The other sources, reviewed below, are summarized in Table 1.[*]

## Major D. B. Douglass

This survey, started 1828 for the Sandy and Beaver Canal Company Commissioners, was based on observations by Douglass together with surveys and measurements furnished by the Resident Engineer.

---

[*] The tables, which contain 82 entries detailing the sale, have been omitted here to conserve space.

He designated three divisions for the canal. There would be one tunnel, 924 yards long, with a sandstone roof and sides and a reservoir.

The Western Division would be 33 1/2 miles in length. The number of locks was not proposed but a total lockage of 222.66 feet was needed with lifts up to 10 feet. Three dams of 4 1/2 feet in height and three aqueducts were needed for crossing including one at the Tuscarawas River.

## R. Max Gard and William H. Vodrey, Jr.

Present-day understanding is mostly based on Gard and Vodrey's book written nearly 100 years after the sale of the Canal Company holdings.

The Eastern Division contained 57 locks and 20 dams and was 27 miles long.

The Middle Division was 14 miles long, no locks, 2 tunnels and 2 reservoirs. The Little Tunnel was stone lined. The Big Tunnel had a natural rock roof and the west end floor was timber lined because of quicksand. And endless chain was used to pull the boats through the Big Tunnel. Could this have been assumed from Major Douglass' suggestion of omitting a towpath as a means of saving money in constructing a 900-yard tunnel? Other depictions show the boats were poled through both tunnels.

The Western Division contained 33 locks, nine dams, one reservoir and one aqueduct and was 32 miles long.

## W. F. Gilmore

The date of this reference, sometime after 1901, is uncertain. The only date mentioned in the Stark County Historical Society report involves a drawing done in 1901.

Gilmore compiled his material while hiking the winding route of the canal from Bolivar to the Ohio River, but some of his dates are in error, for example, he states a charter for the project was granted in 1835, and that the canal was abandoned in 1852. The canal distance was 45 miles as the crow flies but covered 60 miles. He lists 21 locks between Guilford Lake, one of the two large reservoirs, and the Middle Beaver Creek, a drop of 105 feet, and probably 80 locks from Lisbon to the Ohio River in a fall of 400 feet. The report credits two tunnels, the one west of Dungannon nearly a mile long. The aqueduct at Bolivar carried the boats nearly 50 feet above in crossing the Tuscarawas River. He shows probably 60 locks in the 300 foot drop in the Western Division.

## Frank Wilcox

His story starts with the Middle Division, 14 miles long, and lists one tunnel, 900 yards long, and a timbered Little Tunnel nearly 1,000 feet long. He also proposes a few locks in the Middle Division to lower the canal down from the Little Tunnel to the West Fork of Beaver Creek. The only reservoir listed is Guilford Lake.

The Eastern Division was 43 miles long and there were 140 locks from Hanoverton to Smith's Ferry on the Ohio River.

The Western Division was 33 1/2 miles long and contained 40 locks. He shows 3 aqueducts, including one crossing the Tuscarawas, in this division.

Many references to historic trail locations and historic events are inaccurate. He too refers to a possible endless chain pulling the boats through the Big Tunnel.

## W. H. van Fossan

The Middle Division was 12 miles long from a point 2 miles above New Lisbon to 2 miles beyond Hanoverton. Two reservoirs, West (now Guilford Lake) and Cold Run, supplied water for this section. There were also two tunnels. The Big Tunnel was 900 yards long and with deep cuts at both ends making its length 2 1/4 miles. The Little Tunnel was 1000 feet long and arched with stone. One or two locks lowered the canal from the tunnel to the level of the West Fork.

The Western Division was 33 1/2 miles long, had 40 locks and a reservoir 2 miles west of Kensington. The Eastern Division was 43 miles long and contained 140 locks.

Several dates given for the area known as McKinley Crossing relating to the house and furnace are incorrect.

## <u>Ohio Patriot</u> by James Kelly, Master Commissioner

The court ordered a bankruptcy sale of the Sandy and Beaver Canal Company property to recover some of the $400,000 in mortgage. For sale purposes the Company's holdings were described in 82 parcels.

The order of sale was to be, first, an entity, then by division and, if still not sold, by parcel. The entire canal was appraised at $25,956.00, the Eastern Division at $6,960.00, the Middle Division at $12,921.00 and the Western Division at $6,095.00. […] The sale did not include that portion of the canal in Pennsylvania. A second sale for unsold parcels was held July 31.

The parcels making up the Eastern Division show it contained 60 locks and 19 dams. The Middle Division contained 2 tunnels, 3 reservoirs and 1 culvert. The Western Division contained 40 locks and 11 dams and 1 aqueduct.

Adding the two locks and one dam that Gard's book lists for Pennsylvania, provides a total of 102 locks, 31 dams, three reservoirs, one culvert, two tunnels and numerous tow bridges.

Clearly, this careful reading of the sale announcement, which indicates 12 more locks and one more dam than proposed by Gard and Vodrey, will change the numbering and location of the locks proposed by them.

§§§§§§§§§§§§§§§§§§§§§§§§§§§§

*Labeled as a "Canal to Nowhere," Herbert W. O'Hanlon walked the 25-mile length of the Walhonding Canal in 1942 in search of the feeder dam at its head near the Coshocton-Knox County line. This location is in the general area of Cavallo.*

Volume X (1972), No. 2, pp. 14-17

### WALKING THE WALHONDING – IN 1942 by Herbert W. O'Hanlon

The resurgent interest in Ohio's canals has focused attention on the major waterways that once were the life-lines of commerce for the state. Just as interesting are the branch or lateral canals that, in their own particular ways, aided in the development of certain localized regions of Ohio. One such waterway was the Walhonding Canal. It furnished an outlet for the produce of western Coshocton County and a small part of Knox County.

The Walhonding Canal, opened for navigation in 1841, was the initial portion of a canal originally planned to reach Mount Vernon on the Kokosing River as well as other towns in the Mohican and Killbuck River Valleys. The financial difficulties following the Panic of 1837 doomed this canal to its original 24 mile length till the State officially abandoned all but six miles in 1896. This latter portion was used as a feeder to the Ohio & Erie Canal till the 1913 flood put an end to all canal traffic.

In 1942, when my attention was first drawn to this forgotten artery of commerce, Roscoe had not yet been incorporated into the city of Coshocton. Its main thoroughfare, Whitewoman Street, was lined with old, moldering buildings that had apparently outlived their economic usefulness. An extension eastward from Hill Street led to Roscoe Bridge which was the main traffic artery across the Muskingum River to Coshocton. In that year, State Highway 16 had not yet pre-empted the bed of the Ohio & Erie Canal.

The most spectacular feature on the Walhonding Canal in 1942 was the now-famous triple lock, about 3/4 of a mile above Roscoe Village. Then, this structure was topped by an unusual plate girder trestle that carried the tracks of the old Toledo, Walhonding Valley, and Ohio Railroad through Warsaw, Walhonding, and Brink Haven to a junction with the main line of the Pennsylvania Railroad at Loudonville. The railroad, in 1942, crossed the Muskingum River from Coshocton, cut across the Lower Basin of the Ohio & Erie Canal on a long wooden trestle, angled over the triple lock, and paralleled the Walhonding Canal for about a mile.

The charred remains of an old canal boat were resting in the bottom of the triple lock. Local residents stated that this boat was drawn into the lower lock chamber by its captain when the main canal was abandoned and, according to these tales, he lived out his life there. He left instructions to burn the boat after his death. Another, less romantic, version is that the abandoned boat was burned accidently by local "neer-do-wells" who used it as a "hang out".

Although the canal had been abandoned for twenty-nine years, it still contained water from Six Mile Dam to the triple lock. The prime function of this section was to provide water for a hydro-electric generating plant near the triple lock.

Moving up the canal to a point just east of a small settlement called Randle, I found a stone waste weir that served the purpose of maintaining a proper water level. In the summer of 1971 this waste weir was still performing its original function. The surplus water diverted by this weir then passed under U.S. Highway 36 through a cut-stone culvert apparently constructed when the canal was built.

At Six Mile Dam, the canal crossed from the south bank to the north bank of the Walhonding River. There were two locks at the crossing, a guard lock on the south bank and lock #5 on the north bank; since they were both on private property, I was unable to examine them.

Approximately one and one-half miles west of the dam, on the line between Bethlehem and Jefferson Townships, were the remains of a single lock. When viewed from Highway 36, the profile of the lock appeared perfect. From a distance, an imaginative observer could almost visualize a canal boat "locking through". However, closer examination with the owner's permission, showed a gateless lock that was being used as a private dump. The stone-work showed the ravages of time, growing trees had sprung the stone walls. Remains of the "bypass" and "tumble" were still evident.

The canal was visible from Highway 36 to the outskirts of Warsaw. It appeared as a well-defined cutting. At the eastern edge of the village, the highway pre-empted the right-of-way of the canal. Here, a graceful, single-arch, stone culvert across Beaver Run had been converted into a highway bridge. (it still performs that job — 1971)

Evidence of the canal through Warsaw was non-existent, but a mile to the west, an undisturbed segment crossed a small stream bed on a fair-sized fill that contained a well-preserved culvert. Between Darling Run and the junction of present highways U.S. 36 and Ohio 715, the canal made several sharp turns in order to follow its level contour through a well maintained farm yard. Beyond this point, evidence of the canal was obliterated by construction of Mohawk Dam and the resultant highway relocations.

Just east of the village of Walhonding, in a tangle of undergrowth, were the remains of a single lock. Apparently after abandonment of the canal, someone had removed all the cut stone from the lock walls. Just the rough-stone used to shore up the finish wall remained. In places, this rough-stone wall had crumbled and fallen into the lock chamber.

Two locks, two basins, and a water-powered mill were once located at Walhonding. Construction work (perhaps destruction would be a better word) resulted in the demolition of much man-made culture in the lower environs of the village. The reason for this was to provide an uncluttered flood basin for the waters backed up by Mohawk Dam. The canal remnants perished in this effort. In 1942 the canal bed could only be seen as a long, curved depression in a field of ripening corn.

From Walhonding, the canal made a sharp turn to the north and followed the east bank of the Mohican River to its upper terminus near Cavallo. The towpath of this stretch had been turned into a scenic country road for approximately two miles. For another mile, the road was on the berm side of the canal, but not in close proximity to the canal prism.

Near Cavallo, the road climbed around the shoulder of a steep hill that had caused the river to make a sweeping curve to the west and then reverse its direction by flowing east for about a mile. The canal followed an east-west course through a flood plain on the south side of the hill.

In 1942, another segment of the abandoned Toledo, Walhonding Valley, and Ohio Railroad followed the river from Brink Haven to the quarries of the Briar Hill Stone Company located about two miles downstream from Cavallo. The quarries were situated above the west bank of the Mohican River which the Railroad crossed on a steel bridge known locally as Bridge 18.

A short hike on the railroad grade from Cavallo towards Bridge 18 was required to locate the spot where the railroad crossed the canal on a low fill. The canal at this point was on a tangent that led upstream to a junction with the river. This section was, then, in an advanced state of deterioration. Study indicated the possibility of a basin before the river was reached. Stone culverts were located in the outside of the towpath embankment, but how they functioned was a mystery.

I was informed by knowledgeable persons in the vicinity that a dam once existed across the river and it bore the appropriate name of Feeder Dam. It was at this structure that the canal entered the river via the slack-water pool created by the dam. That dam, I was told, was built of timber with very little stone work. Flood and neglect, however, had removed most vestiges of Feeder Dam. I was also informed that the remains were visible at periods of extremely low water. Unfortunately, I was never present at those times.

Then, the exact location of Feeder Dam was a mystery to me. Later, I was able to determine its tentative position thanks to information supplied by Knox County residents. The dam, actually in Knox County, was located on the bend of the river mentioned previously.

On the west bank of the Mohican River, where the lower bend swings back into Coshocton County, is a natural rock formation known as County Line Rock. About a mile upstream from this rock, Flat Run empties into the Mohican River from the Knox County side. Feeder Dam occupied a position midway between County Line Rock and Flat Run. To reach this spot on the river, the canal had to traverse about 0.29 of a mile within Knox County. This negates the story of some Coshocton County residents that the Walhonding Canal lay entirely within the borders of their county.

Despite its long years of abandonment and neglect, the Walhonding Canal has not suffered as much as some other canals from the ravages of time and the heavy hand of modern man. In the summer of 1971, the waterway was much in evidence for many of its original 24 miles. The railroad track south of Cavallo vanished just after World War II. The right-of-way is now a dirt road that still spans the canal just north of Bridge 18. The road continues south and crosses the Mohican River on the planked-over deck of the railroad bridge. For those so inclined, it is possible to drive to the spot where the steam trains once crossed the Walhonding Canal.

§§§§§§§§§§§§§§§§§§§§§§§§§§§

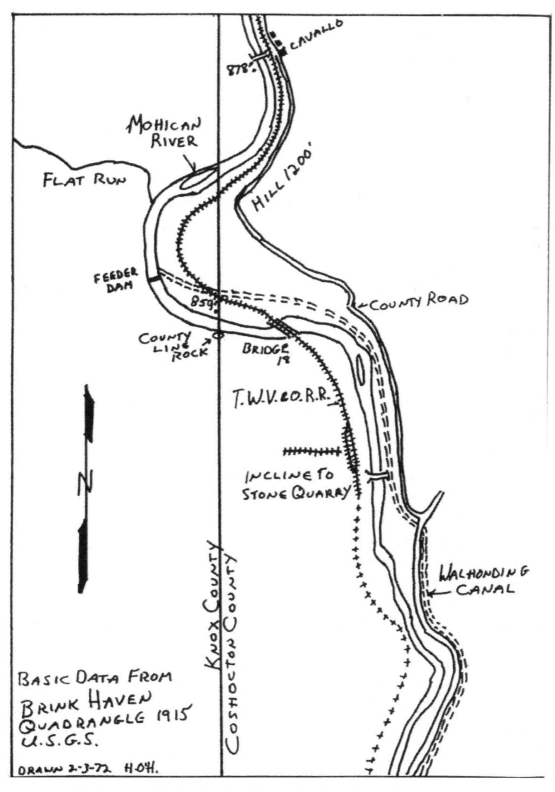

**Headwaters of the Walhonding Canal.** *Map drawn by Herbert W. O'Hanlon.*

*In preparation for the spring 1981 tour of the Muskingum River Improvement, Ted Kasper wrote a letter to modern-day lock tender Jim Thornton, keeper of Lock & Dam No. 9 at Philo. His reply on the responsibilities of a late 20th century lock keeper are printed here.*

Volume XIX (1981), No. 1, pp. 6-9

## WINTER ON THE MUSKINGUM PARKWAY by Jim Thornton

I have often wondered how the corps of full-time employees at the Muskingum River spend the winter months when navigation is suspended. Well, I did write a letter to my friend, Jim Thornton at Philo (southeast of Zanesville in Muskingum County). His answer takes much of the romanticism from the lore surrounding the profession of lock-master. The glory has vanished from the man who during the summer is the authority at the lock, and he is now like any other man winterizing his house and belongings. But here is his report. (Ted Kasper, Cuyahoga Falls.)

"Winter Events, November 1st through June 1st

"**November and December**. One of the first things that happens is that everyone is given a chance to take his vacation. I take the second and third weeks while a lot of the guys take the fourth week. Others wait until spring or around Christmas time.

"The first week of November we stay around the locks because a lot of people are taking their boats out for winter. Raking leaves and putting things away for winter. We take the buoys and dam markers out of the river, winterize the boat motors, lawn mowers and tractors. All the equipment is checked out and repaired, along with cutting brush along the canals. The lock valves and gates are checked and repaired when needed. Keep restrooms and park area clean.

"**January and February**. We scrape the buoys and dam markers, paint them anew and put new stickers on them. We flush the locks, shovel snow off lock walls and side walls. Clear snow around restroom areas and parking lots. We paint trash cans and parking signs. I also do carpentry work to lock houses and park office when needed.

"**March and April**. In March we do everything that we didn't get finished before. If we get a lot of snow, we get behind, so in March we catch up. But if we don't have a lot of snow during winter, then in March we put new signs up, get the picnic tables and benches out and fasten them and the trash barrels back out.

"We start working on the locks in April, repairing cracks in lock walls; and dredge out the lock and the approaches. We clean the area, cut grass and even lock some boats through.

"**May**. In May we open our boating season up again and are busy breaking in the newly hired help. We are putting the buoys and dam markers back in the river, locking boats through. With the warmer time comes painting time. All the caution lines around lock walls and the lock keeper's shelter are painted, including restrooms and parking lines. With cutting grass and brush and cleaning up, the circle of events is completed.

"In case of a flood or emergency, the river is divided into three groups, north, central and south. Each group has a boat in case we are needed. We also get water readings every day at the locks for flood control and ice jams. The past two winters we have had ice jams below Philo at the Narrows. The U.S. Army Corps of Engineers handles the ice, but it is our job to monitor the flow of water and assist them.

"There are ten full-time lockmasters and six full-time dredge operators on the Parkway. We work at times in groups of two or three. Clarence (Mr. Perry, Park Ranger and Lockmaster Rokeby Lock, No. 8), Bob (Mr. Grimes, Lockmaster at Zanesville, No.10), Don (Mr. Kleinhoffer, Lockmaster at Ellis, No. 11) and myself take care of the locks numbers 8, 9, 10 and 11. We each have different days off so that there is always someone working.

"That describes what it is like around the river in the winter time. Some days are real quiet, other days are real busy, according to the weather and height of the river.

Jim Thornton

Lockmaster"

Note: Ted Kasper will conduct the Canal Society's tour of the Muskingum River Parkway in June of 1981. He has done much research on the history of the Muskingum River, its locks and its present-day operation. Mr. Thornton's letter is part of that research.

Canal Society trustees arrange spring and fall tours of sections of Ohio's canals. These tours are open to the public in keeping with the purposes of the Society.

§§§§§§§§§§§§§§§§§§§§§§§§§§§§

*Originally titled "The Muskingum Improvement: Zanesville to McConnelsville," this piece was assembled by Brad Bond in preparation for the CSO 2007 Spring Tour. We focus here on the section in Zanesville.*

Volume XLV (2007), No. 1, pp. 1-6

### THE MUSKINGUM IMPROVEMENT AT ZANESVILLE by Brad Bond

**ZANESVILLE** is a schizoid city. If you visit the Muskingum County Historical Society's Stone House museum on the west side, you'd never know how Zanesville got its name. The historical story there is that Rufus Putnam bought the west-side property with nephews Levi Whipple and Dr. Increase Matthews for $4.25 an acre. They named it Springville, and it was renamed Putnam after Uncle Rufus died.

The east side of the river was claimed by Ebenezer Zane who with brother Jonathan, son-in-law John McIntire and nephew William McCulloch created a path – Zane's Trace – from Wheeling to the Ohio River opposite Maysville, Kentucky, under Congress's promise that he could thereby claim one square mile at the crossing of each of three rivers – Muskingum, Hocking and Scioto. The plan was to cross the rivers at a rapids or falls where there would be power for mills and a need for a ferry, both as sources of income. Ebenezer chose the Muskingum falls at the mouth of the Licking River rather than at what is now called Duncan Falls. He then hired Rufus Putnam from Marietta to survey the area and establish his claim. Lancaster, where Ebenezer Zane settled, and Chillicothe were the sites on the Hocking and Scioto. McIntyre built a log cabin in 1798 where today's Market Street meets the Muskingum and McCulloch set up a ferry nearby. Ebenezer willed the property to his brother and son-in-law on his death in 1800.

Thus the straight laced New Englanders settled on the west side of the river and the free-wheeling Virginians settled on the east side. Competition started early when a site for the new state's capitol was sought. Matthews (with Ebenezer Buckingham) and McIntire both built substantial brick buildings in hoping that would win the legislators' votes, but McIntire was the better politician and the county seat went to the east side. The state capitol was located there from October 1810 to May 1812, when it went back to Chillicothe while the final site in Columbus was being built. Zanesville also won the immigration battle and by 1840 had four times the population of Putnam. Putnam rejected annexation in 1868, and it was not until 1872 that it was approved for financial reasons.

McIntire proposed a dam and lock on the Muskingum in 1812, and the Zanesville Canal & Manufacturing Company was organized in 1814. By the time it was completed in 1816, McIntire had died. The National Road built in the 1820s and 1830s had a larger impact on Zanesville than the river traffic. Although it was not paved until 1913-1920, it was the only road across Ohio for some time. It departed from Zane's Trace in Zanesville.

Zanesville is famous for its Y bridge. The first two Y bridges bracketing the mouth of the Licking were wiped out in floods in the early 1800s. Ebenezer Buckingham, Putnam's son-in-law died in the collapse of the second bridge, trying to protect it from the flood. The third, a covered bridge built in 1832, lasted until the 1913 flood.

The first road parallel to the Muskingum between Zanesville and Marietta was completed in 1837. Even before the Dresden sidecut was opened goods produced in Zanesville arrived in Cleveland: for example, in 1830 three boatloads of linseed oil. With the opening of the Dresden sidecut to the Ohio & Erie Canal in 1832, traffic increased. F. Cogswell and Company announced July 27, 1839, that it would run a daily line of canal boats between Zanesville and Cleveland. River traffic increased again when the 11 locks and dams of the Muskingum Navigation were completed in 1841. John Alter. Jr., advertised in the Zanesville paper in 1847 "new canal boats" for use on the Muskingum Line, Ohio Canal, from the second warehouse above the dam. In 1833 he had partnered in building the *Zanesville* for conveying passengers and freight on the Muskingum River. The story of the traffic between the Ohio & Erie Canal at Dresden and Zanesville and thereby the Ohio River has been told in an earlier issue of **Towpaths**.

Railroads trimmed the traffic on Ohio's canals. The first railroad through Zanesville was the Central Ohio, chartered in 1847 and open to Newark in 1852, Cambridge 1854. A second railroad connecting to Cincinnati by way of the Little Miami Railroad was completed in 1856. The third to Muskingum County, originally named Steubenville & Indiana, bypassed Zanesville by going north of Dresden at Trinway. Competition for Muskingum valley traffic began with the Zanesville & Ohio Railway in 1888.

## The Zanesville Canal

Walking the canal island from the guard gate above the dam to the downstream lock passes five bridges – two for railroads, three for vehicles – and three Muskingum River falls no longer apparent. The river dropped four feet between the upper railroad bridge and Market Street. Just above the upper falls there was a ford passable at normal water levels. The 1816 and 1840 dams covered most of this drop. By crossing the National Road (US 40) and the railroad bridge, you'll find the guard gate at the upper end of the canal. It is one of the few remaining places where you can see the original winches used to open and shut canal gates. The 1816 dam was five feet high with a 30-foot upstream slope to allow log rafts to run over the top of it. The first canal was designed for keelboats and would have been narrower and shallower than the present canal with a smaller lock (probably at 3rd Street).

The present cellular dam was built in 1952 upstream of the 1840s crib dam. Wooden supports from the earlier era can be seen from the west side at low water. The upper end of the canal island supported two flourmills and a woolen mill in 1866 with glass works on the land side.

The middle falls dropped another 6-8 feet between the Y and 3rd Street bridges. Between these two is a railroad bridge. The City Water Works was located between the railroad and 3rd Street bridges in 1866. The riverbank at the Putnam end of the bridge housed woolen and flour mills with a dam just upstream providing water power. Later the Zanesville Pure Milk Company had a 3-story building on the island, and there was a toll house at the end of the covered bridge. The 1913 flood wiped out all but the piers. By 1920 […] there was a lift span for the canal and a trolley line crossing the 3rd Street Bridge with a stairway down to the island.

The 6th Street Bridge crosses the center of the lower rapids. The first of three bridges was built in 1885 and lasted until the 1913 flood. The rapids probably ran from 5th Street to where Slago Run entered the Muskingum. This run was carried under the 1840 canal in a culvert and its exit is framed in cut-stone in the river bank just upstream of the lower lock and locktender's house. Pre-1816 travelers complained about the effort it took to traverse these rapids often having to drag their canoes over them. If they were impassable, they portaged up a trail by present-day 7th Street and entered the river north of today's Zane's Landing Park.

The double lock at Zanesville is unique for the Muskingum Navigation. The lower gate, half the height of the upper gates, looks unfinished, but, of course, does the job of holding and passing boats just fine. The total lift is 18 feet.

**The *Valley Gem* at the public wharf headed upstream**. When she leaves, the 6th Street Bridge span behind her swivels open and she backs through to the double lock and into the river before turning around. The *Valley Gem* was built in Marietta's Knox Boatyard in 1897 and traveled daily between McConnelsville and Zanesville until 1917 when she was sold.

§§§§§§§§§§§§§§§§§§§§§§§§§§§

*Famous for his ever-present tape measure to determine the dimensions of canal structures, Barney Golding assembled this summary of the Hocking Canal with John Droege from official reports.*

Volume XXIII (1985), No. 4, pp. 47-52

### THE HOCKING CANAL REVISITED by John Droege and Barnett Golding

In 1969 Frank Trevorrow presented a description of the Hocking Canal with maps. In so doing he revived a story that had been largely forgotten. We trust Mr. Trevorrow will not take it amiss if we repeat the story and try to add a few details. (See *Towpaths* Vol. VI, No. 4, p. 53-60.)

**1826-1834:** The Ohio and Erie was completed to Carroll and Columbus in 1831 and to Portsmouth in 1832. The State had cooperated with the Lancaster Lateral Canal Company by locating its canal on the highest possible ground west of Baltimore, so that the Lancaster "side-cut" could pass over the divide between Walnut Creek and the Hocking River. The canal was formally opened in 1834.

**1835:** In response to a request from the Legislature, Samuel Carpenter, engineer on the Lancaster Lateral Canal and future engineer for construction of the Hocking Canal, surveyed the valley from Lancaster to Athens and laid out the approximate line of a canal. His report (2/2/36) described a canal 52 miles long (not including the 9 miles already built) with 22 lift locks and 8 guard locks. There would be 11 dams and associated with each dam would be a slackwater section of canal (no feeders). A total of 25 miles would be in slackwater sections of the Hocking River. He argued the advantages of so much use of the river bed. The cost of digging canal and constructing culverts and aqueducts would be reduced. Furthermore, each dam provided opportunity for a mill and consequent fees for the State from sale of water

**1836:** What a year!

President Jackson was in charge, and, finding a surplus in the national treasury, he instituted the first revenue sharing. Each state received a windfall based on its population. Ohio's share was about two million dollars, equal to about half the canal debt at the time.

Canal fever was about to reach its peak. The Legislature authorized the Muskingum Improvement, the Walhonding Canal, the Hocking Valley Canal and the Miami Extension from Piqua to Junction. The Warren County Canal was to be purchased and completed and loans were authorized to the Milan Canal Company and to the Mad River and Lake Erie Railroad.

The Legislature had received a report in February, prepared by Engineer Carpenter, outlining the vast extent of coal deposits in the Hocking Valley, so it was full steam ahead! The first 16 miles south of Lancaster were placed under contract. The Board of Public Works recommended that the State buy the Lancaster Lateral Canal, which lay between the new Hocking Valley Canal and the Ohio and Erie Canal and needed to be widened and deepened.

This year also marked the completion of the New Reservoir at the Licking Summit, with its two new locks, providing additional water which would be badly needed by the Hocking Canal.

**1837:** Was the canal fever running high in '36? In '37 it reached its crisis with the passage of the Loan Law, which opened the State coffers to almost any company wanting to be engaged in transportation - canal, slack water, railroad or turnpike. The State also gave away its discretion in the matter, making approval of the loans almost automatic. All this was just in time for the bank panic, followed in a few years by a general depression. In spite of the financial difficulties, the Fund Commission did an excellent job, for a while at least, in selling bonds for internal improvements.

Contracts were let on the Hocking Canal as far as Nelsonville. Progress was slow because of wet weather and scarcity of workers.

**1838:** The engineers and the Canal Commissioners had second thoughts about the original plan, which utilized long slackwater sections of the river. High water not only threatened dams and guard locks, it also caused changes in the river, eroding towpath banks and depositing sand bars in the channel. By converting to canal, the work could be better protected against damage, could be used with greater safety, and could be somewhat shortened. Three slackwater sections above Nelsonville were converted to canal. Several slackwater sections remained. Two below Nelsonville allowed for crossing the river without the expense of long aqueducts; these were still considered acceptable. Several long slackwater sections between Lancaster and Logan remained, because construction had already progressed to the extent that conversion to canal would be too expensive. In one section at Rockbridge the guard lock had already been built. When the slackwater was abandoned in favor of canal, this lock (Sheep Pen or Sheepskin) was converted to a lift lock. It remains today a curiosity among relics of the canal because of its guard lock construction. The two ends, which supported the gates, were built of well-laid cut stone. The part between was constructed with earthen banks, carefully riprapped. These changes eliminated the need for three dams with associated guard locks.

In March the Legislature authorized the purchase of the Lancaster Lateral Canal, and this purchase was completed in December.

**1839:** No part of the canal below Lancaster had been opened, but the work was nearly complete to Nelsonville. Progress had been slow because of unfavorable weather, a shortage of labor and lack of funds.

The generally depressed financial condition of the country now posed a severe problem for the public works under construction. No more contracts were to be let, and contractors were advised to postpone their work in progress wherever possible. In spite of the general slowdown, contracts were let for the final section of the canal from Nelsonville to Athens.

The Legislature required that the Board of Public Works explain why work was continuing on the Hocking Valley Canal and whether the Fund Board had authorized the expenditures. The Board referred the request to its Acting Commissioner for the Hocking, William Wall. Mr. Wall defended himself in a long reply. He reported that, although he had no assurance from the Commissioners of the Canal Fund that money would be available, he had learned, on what he believed to be good authority, that the money could be raised. Therefore he had signed the contract. He then proceeded to complain that $40,000 was due contractors but only $23,500 was paid, and that $8,000 was due under the new contract, but had not been paid by the State Treasurer.

**1840:** Early in the year the Board was reduced from 5 members to 4 and Mr. Wall was replaced as Acting Commissioner by Leander Ransom, long-time Canal Commissioner and member of the Board of Public Works.

As part of the general tightening of state finances, the Loan Law of 1837 was repealed. The Board found itself unable to pay contractors all they were due partly because the Fund Commissioners were not permitted to pay more than 6% or to sell bonds at less than par value. In the depressed economy they found it difficult to borrow money.

In September, the first coal boat moved northward, marking the beginning of large-scale commerce in coal.

**1841:** The canal was opened to Monday Creek.

For two months in late summer the summit section between Carroll and Lancaster was drained so that it could be widened and deepened. The two locks were removed so that the entire nine-mile section to Lancaster was at a single level. Hereafter the Hocking Canal would draw water through the Ohio and Erie from the Licking Summit Reservoirs.

**1842-1844:** The canal was opened to near Chauncey in '42 and to Athens in '43. A few years earlier Thomas Ewing and Samuel Vinton, with the backing of Nicholas Biddle and Elihu Chauncey, had opened salt works and laid out the nearby town of Chauncey. Salt was made by evaporating water from brine drawn from wells. Coal taken from the nearby hills was burned to boil off the water. Salt was to become the second staple of the Hocking Canal trade. In the years to come pig iron and sandstone also were to become important cargo.

Since it was now becoming clear that the canal would be used mainly for heavy freight, loads of sixty tons were being hauled and the Board of Public Works recognized the need for dredging and deepening the canal.

Every year the Board pleaded with the Legislature for money to pay its debts to contractors. By 1842 unpaid bills amounted to more than $90,000. By 1843, when the canal was finished, these difficulties had been overcome.

In their report dated January 9, 1844, the Board included a description of the completed canal, including especially detailed descriptions of the dams.

The canal was 56 miles long, included 26 lift locks with and aggregate descent of 202 feet, besides 5 guard locks, 34 culverts, 8 feeder and slackwater dams, and an aqueduct with a wooden trunk of 80 foot span, crossing Monday Creek, founded on abutments of cut stone. There were four slackwater pools, in addition to the slackwater crossing at Chauncey, for a total distance of 7 miles. By 1844 the canal had cost $975,000.

**1845-1849:** Every year the Board reported troubles on the Carroll-to-Lancaster section, still called the "summit" or "side cut." The nature of the soil was such that stable banks could not be maintained. Mud slides and silting made passage difficult. Every rain brought mud and sand with the streams that fed the canal. Frequent dredging and repeated suggestions for improvement brought only temporary relief.

The Monday Creek aqueduct gave trouble and required frequent repair. In 1849 it was rebuilt.

Freshets in 1848 caused considerable damage, especially below Nelsonville.

1849 brought a problem with vandals who damaged a number of lock gates, presumably with the intention of "keeping off the cholera."

**1850-1860:** In 1851 and again in 1856 drought cut down the water supply. Water in the Licking Reservoirs was low and the Hocking Canal could not be properly supplied. In 1852 and especially in 1858, flooding caused damage to structures of the canal, especially in the southern section. In 1858 the canal was devastated everywhere below Sugar Grove by a flood on June 11. Navigation was restored to Nelsonville by the end of July, to Athens only in September.

Every year mud slides and sand bars continued to obstruct navigation in the Lancaster-Carroll section. In 1856 this part of the canal was still only 28 feet wide at the surface and 14 feet wide at the bottom. For several years it had been necessary to keep two yoke of oxen available to pull boats through the mud.

In 1856, fortunately coinciding with a period of drought, there was a major effort to widen and deepen the sidecut. The most troublesome part was widened to 32 feet at the bottom. For two miles near Lancaster it was still only 20 feet wide. In spite of these efforts, 1858 found the canal filled from one to four feet for one half mile with sediment from the feeder streams. The Board now proposed that these streams he diverted, their water having become less than essential since the two-foot summit was removed.

In 1860 it was estimated that for under $4,000 Claypool Run could be diverted one-half mile downstream, then led by culvert under the canal and into the Hocking River. The Board further proposed that the entire level, including the six-mile level on the Ohio and Erie Canal, be raised one foot, which would require raising the banks in places, at a cost of under $6,000. Apparently no such measures were taken, and the side cut continued to be a source of trouble.

In 1860 the towpath bridge at Athens, which had washed out in 1858, was replaced one half mile south of its former location at Ballard's Salt Works. Athens County paid part of the cost so that a bridge suitable for general traffic was built.

By 1851 the Hocking Furnace was established in West Logan, followed by the Logan Furnace in 1854. The canal, if it could be kept open and deep enough, would be a convenient way to ship the pig iron produced in these and other blast furnaces.

The competition from railroads became more severe from year to year, beginning in 1856 for Athens. At the end of the decade, with the first service on the Hocking Valley Railroad, the canal and railroad ran side by side. The Board of Public Works responded with substantially lowered tolls.

**1861-1877:** If 1836 represented canal fever, the patient was now experiencing severe chills. Many wanted to abandon the public works as useless. But supporters still emphasized the positive, even asking for expansion. If New York could do it, why not Ohio? If we could only connect Lake Erie with the Ohio River by means of a modern ship canal! The Legislature took the former view. In April of 1859 it decided to lease the Public Works for 5 years. There were no takers. In 1861 they tried again, this time for 10 years. And this time a bidder came forward and agreed to rent the canal system for $20,075 per year. Sixteen years later the Lessees abandoned the canal system in a dispute with the State, thus returning control to the Department of Public Works.

After some initial uncertainty in 1861, the Board became an enthusiastic supporter of the Lessees. Every year brought praise, especially when the canals were faced with adverse weather. The annual reports show hardly a word of criticism. It should be noted that the members of the Board were partisans of the canal system. They feared that any public complaint about canal conditions (of which there were many) would discourage shippers and send business to the railroads. In fact, they accused critics of spreading false reports for just that purpose. It may be, therefore, that their reports were slanted a bit in favor of the Lessees.

The "Lancaster Side Cut" was the big problem. Boats only two thirds full could not haul coal economically. The Lessees moved swiftly on the problem of the Claypool Feeder, which was the chief source of sediment in the canal. In 1862 they excavated a large basin where the Claypool could deposit its sediment before passing water into the canal. They experimented with dredges and in 1863 began regular dredging of the sidecut. The results were dramatic, although the dredging had to be repeated year after year. In 1864 the soil was described as light and high in organic matter, like peat. When water was drawn off, the bottom rose and the sides flowed into the canal. Dredging had to be done while the canal was watered. This the new dredges did. Later a steam-powered dredge was introduced, with even better results. Twice the new Claypool basin was cleaned out.

A similar problem plagued the Deep Cut section of the Ohio and Erie Canal just south of the Licking Reservoir, which had been filling up with silt for years. When this was thoroughly dredged, the water supply in the Hocking was greatly improved. The Lessees, with the help of the State, also worked on the South Fork Feeder, thus improving the water supply in the reservoir. These improvements meant that coal boats could be loaded with 80 tons whereas formerly they had trouble with 40 as they passed through the sidecut.

Difficulties with the weather continued. Indeed, they probably increased, since clearing the land for agriculture resulted in rapid runoff followed by dried-up streams. From '62 to '64 rains were light and navigation was suspended in the fall when the reservoir dried up. In '65 and '68 floods caused extensive damage. 1870 to '72 brought drought again and heavy dredging of the Deep Cut. In 1873 a major flood took out all the dams below Lancaster and caused 30-40 breaks in the banks. The Lessees were required to excavate 20,000 yards of deposits from the canal and to move 70,000 yards to renew the banks. The canal was reopened in 75 days. A less-severe flood occurred in 1875.

The damage from the '73 flood was not repaired below Chauncey. This last 5 miles had done no business in the last few years, so there seemed to be no reason to maintain the canal below Chauncey.

During these years coal mining was increasing in the Hocking Valley, salt was being produced, and the iron furnaces were putting out pig iron. All these products were ideal freight for canal boats, and business increased steadily, even as shipments on other Ohio canals were falling off. In these latter days of the canal system the Hocking Canal was one of the bright spots in an otherwise dark picture.

**1877-1894:** Toward the end of 1877 just before the Lessees relinquished control, the Board of Public Works inspected the canal above Nelsonville. They found the locks to be in good shape. Some of the gates were in need of replacement, but others were new that year. The dams were all sound. The canal below Lancaster was well dredged. Above Lancaster they found the canal in fair condition, but as usual, in need of dredging. The Board said the side cut would probably require continuous dredging from the beginning to the end of every season.

One of the first actions of the Board was to sell the stone and other materials on the canal below Nelsonville. Salt was no longer being shipped on the canal

The iron industry had shifted to the Mahoning Valley. Coal was the lone remaining mainstay of the canal and this business now declined from year to year. In 1884 another disastrous flood hit the Hocking Valley. The canal recovered, hut the coal business did not. Very little traffic passed after 1890. When the Legislature pronounced the sentence of death in 1894, it only recognized what had already taken place.

The Hocking Canal was a carrier of heavy freight. After the early days, when it carried passengers and general merchandise, it settled into the slow-moving transport of coal, salt, iron and building stone. Had it not been for the unusual problem continuously faced and never really solved on the Lancaster-Carroll side cut, the canal might have had a much greater success. In the end, as usual, the railroads won. They could load at the mine, required less labor, used fossil energy, moved year-round. Compared to boats limited to 60-80 tons, there was no contest.

Today the prism can be traced through much of its length. Many culverts can be found. Traces of several dams can be detected. Locks 7, 8, 10, 11, 12, 17, 19 and 26 are substantially intact. Most of them are on private land, however, and are constantly in danger of being destroyed. Thus neglect of the Public Works, which marked the life of the canals, continues after their demise.

§§§§§§§§§§§§§§§§§§§§§§§§§§§

*As explained in the intro, the selection is an excerpt from Dave Meyer's book on the Hocking Canal. Here, we focus on some of the canal boats that used to operate at Logan.*

Volume XL (2002), No. 1, p. 1 & pp. 5-6

## LOGAN: HOCKING CANAL BOATER'S TOWN by David A. Meyer

The CSO tour last Spring covered the Hocking Canal from Carroll to the Falls of Logan. David Meyer, co-leader of that tour, is preparing a history of the Lancaster Lateral and Hocking Canal entitled Fifty-six Miles Into the Hills. The following is excerpted from a draft copy of his book with permission. Meyer wrote Life Along the Ohio Canal – Licking Reservoir to Lockbourne and the Columbus Feeder, published in 1998 by the Canal Winchester Area Historical Society. [...]

Logan was known as a boater's town. Some canal towns put up with the boat crew's antics since they brought in revenue, but boater towns welcomed the crews and many of the crews stayed there as much as they could. Some brief stories of the boatmen in Logan are as follows:

• The packet boat *Eagle* carried passengers up and down the Hocking Canal during Civil War. It was captained by Mark Pritchard of Logan.

• George Hatcher, who had lost his leg in a boating accident, operated the boat *Constitution* for many years on the Hocking Canal.

• The boat *Madam* was operated by Joe George and George Peters for many years.

• After the Civil War, the show boat *George Stewart* of Logan went to towns along the canals of central Ohio and the actors and actresses performed "tent shows" for the local citizens. Minstrel shows were especially popular in those days and youngsters were held in awe of the showmen and remembered their experiences for the remainder of their days.

• *The Statesman* was owned by John Ruff and operated for many years on the Hocking Canal. At the end of the canal era, it was towed to the boat graveyard at the end of Second Street in Logan and sunk there.

• High water on the canal was always a dangerous situation. Denny Noonan of Logan was on the boat *Friendship* when it went over State Dam Number 4 on the Hocking Canal near Enterprise during high water. Nick Rowe had a similar experience on the boat *Gale* when it went over a dam at Lockbourne on the Columbus Feeder Canal.

• Two old time boatmen named Charles Naile and Denny Noonan would congregate with others at public places after the canal was abandoned. Frequently they would fall asleep and this would be a signal for call "Low bridge!" They always ducked and many times would topple from their chairs amidst the gleeful shouts of their tormentors.

• Mayor J. P. Rochester of Logan recalled a trip he took to Lancaster as a boy aboard the canal boat *Amazon* captained by Mark Powers of Lancaster. The boat was described as being one of the finest on the canal at that time. The trip from Logan started at night and then returned the following night making the round trip in 24 hours.

• Killion Johnson of Lancaster first captained *The Twins* which was later sold to George Cook of Logan and then captained by Noah Cook.

• The boat *Chesapeake* was a peddler boat which plied the Hocking Canal in September 1838 with a Bill of Lading including 19 boxes of shoes, 3 boxes of sugar, 4 bags of coffee, 1 keg of liquor, 1 box of tea, 4 boxes of starch, 4 boxes of tobacco, 4 boxes of candles, 8 kegs of spice, 3 kegs of sugar, 1 keg of saltpeter, 8 half chests of tea, 12 bags of coffee, 1 box of hats and 2 boxes of soap. It would serve customers up and down the canal and was especially popular in rural areas. […]

§§§§§§§§§§§§§§§§§§§§§§§§§§§

*A picture is worth a thousand words. Lloyd Manley's terrific sketch of an unfortunate accident reinforces this old saying. The text is courtesy the Ross County Historical Society. From 1840-60, the Hocking Canal carried nearly as much coal (624,000 tons) as passed through Cleveland (720,000 tons).*

Volume XXXV (1997), No. 3, p. 44-45

### CANAL BOAT CUT IN TWO by Lloyd E. Manley

"One [canal-boat man] prided himself on being the only person whose boat was run over and cut in two by a railroad train. His boat was passing through a hoist bridge near Nelsonville, which bridge was at the foot of an inclined track, on which coal was carried from the mine above. The men in charge of the engine, at the top, failed to look and make sure that the track was clear, with the result that the loaded coal cars tore down the incline [beneath the hoisted bridge] and crashed into the boat. All hands jumped in time, but the boat was cut in two parts and two mules killed."

MINE CARS
SEVER A CANAL BOAT
The lift bridge was raised for the boat but the coal train operator did not know it.

**Mine cars sever a canal boat**. Hocking Canal coal boat cut in two by rail cars. *Drawing by Lloyd E. Manley.*

§§§§§§§§§§§§§§§§§§§§§§§§§§§§§

*Ohio's only surviving canal tunnel (the other two were on the Sandy & Beaver Canal) and one of only 12 in the entire United States, this detailed article on the Cincinnati & Whitewater Canal's Cleves Tunnel was written by Tom Fugate in 1996 and published in* Towpaths *five years later.*

Volume XXXIX (2001), No. 3, pp. 68-80

## CLEVES TUNNEL by Tom Fugate

### The Tunnel at North Bend

At the time of the construction of the tunnel at North Bend, canal tunneling was rare in the United States. In 1836 there were only four canal tunnels in the United States, all in Pennsylvania: one tunnel on the Schuylkill Canal, one tunnel on the Union Canal, and two tunnels on the Main Line Canal. The apparent model for the canal tunnels in the United States was the Harecastle Tunnel on the Trent-Mersey Canal built by the engineer James Brindley in England (Trevorrow 1973:39). However Darius Lapham was not the first American to consider a tunnel as the solution to an engineering problem in the trans-Allegheny region. When faced with the problem of negotiating Franklin's Ridge, located two miles above Brookville, engineers on the Whitewater Canal considered a tunnel as a possible solution. They eventually opted for a full open cut through the ridge because it was $8,000 cheaper than a tunnel (Potter 1963:8). Although tunneling was not unheard of as an engineering technique, it was still unusual and beyond the normal experience for most canal engineers. As a measure of how unusual canal tunnels were, rules promulgated by the State of Ohio for the construction of canals provided detailed specifications for every aspect of canal building - from grubbing to lock construction - but do not mention tunneling even in passing (State of Ohio 1974). The tunnel at North Bend represents the first canal tunnel in Ohio, and most probably the westernmost canal tunnel in the United States.

The North Bend tunnel was the creation of Darius Lapham. In almost all respects, Lapham was concerned with building a serviceable canal for the least cost. As a result, he frequently made adjustments in canal depth to minimize the amount of lockage required to cover the 25.04 miles of the canal. In his original 1837 survey, the bottom of the canal was located at six feet below the flood of 1832. This made the top of the canal bank in Cincinnati even with the high water mark, and the top of the canal bank at North Bend 4.5 feet above the high water mark (Lapham 1837a:3). In order to reduce the cost of constructing the canal, Lapham revised the plan by dropping the bottom of the canal an additional 4 feet (Lapham 1837a:3). Lapham reasoned that the 1832 flood was a century flood caused by a combination of frozen ground, deep snow, a warm south wind and eight inches of rain in one week, and that the chances of a similar flood occurring again were acceptably slight (Lapham 1837a:3).

The concern for cost control appears to have been the motive force behind the decision to build the North Bend tunnel. The ridge between the two rivers was a formidable but not impassable obstacle to the course of the canal. In the initial survey, Lapham recommended a tunnel rather than an open cut because it would reduce the amount of lockage required to equalize the water level from the Dry Fork crossing to the Ohio River (Trevorrow 1966:42). Apparently, it would have been too expensive to dig the open cut to the desired level, and therefore an additional lock would have been required. Moreover, the tunnel itself was cheaper to construct than the full open cut.

"The estimate of the expense of crossing the ridge by the plan of an entire open cut with an arch is as follows:

| | |
|---|---:|
| Excavation in open cut, 246,938 cubic yards @ .25 | 61,734.50 |
| Masonry in arch, 11,880 perches @ 2.50 | 39,700.00 |
| Total | 91,434.50 |

Upon the plan of a tunnel the estimate of the expense is as below:

| | |
|---|---:|
| Excavation in open cut; 55,392 cubic yards @ .25 | 13,848.00 |
| Excavation in tunnel;    12,450    "    "    @ 1.50 | 18,675.00 |

| | |
|---|---|
| Masonry of arch in tunnel; 6,600 perches @ 3.00 | 19,800.00 |
| Masonry of arch in open cut; 5,280 perches @ 2.50 | <u>13,200.00</u> |
| | 65,523.00 |

Making a difference of expense in favor of the plan of crossing by a tunnel of 25,911.50 dollars, and the saving effected in crossing the Miami river, by reducing the level, will be 11,000 dollars in addition to the above amount." (Lapham 1837a:2).

In either case, both the tunnel and open cut methods required a masonry arch, and excavation of a partial or full open cut. While excavation in the tunnel was more expensive per cubic yard, the sheer volume of excavation in the full open cut made that method more expensive than the tunnel method.

However, Lapham was instructed to re-survey the canal route, and in his report to Micajah T. Williams, president, submitted on December 28, 1837, Lapham reversed his recommendation in the earlier report. By Lapham's calculations, the summit of the hill rose 109 feet above the bottom of the canal and geological soundings of the ridge indicated that a tunnel was not practical. Lapham sunk two shafts to determine the hill's composition. The first was 37 feet deep and positioned along the canal course so that its lowest point came within a few feet of the proposed canal bottom. The second was 20 feet deep and ended 17 feet above the bottom of the canal. He discovered that the ridge was comprised of 2 strata. The lower stratum, extending 35 to 40 feet above the bottom of the canal was comprised of a tough blue clay, containing silex in minute particles, and becoming indurated on exposure to the sun; it is also occasionally interspersed with small rounded masses of stone (Lapham 1837c:3). The upper stratum was a bed of sandy soil and yellow clay. Lapham noted that in the surrounding ravines, springs appeared at the junction of these two strata, and concluded that the hill was ill-suited for a tunnel (Lapham 1837c:1-2).

Instead of a tunnel he recommended a full open cut in the ratio of 1.5 base to 1 rise, which he considered sufficient to prevent a collapse of the sides (Lapham 1837c:3). A brick arch, 14 feet high and 20 feet wide at water level, was to be built in the cut and then covered over with earth. Lapham designed the width of the canal so that it would accommodate not only a canal boat, but also provide excess water flow for hydraulic power in Cincinnati and allow for a tow path if one were deemed necessary. However, Lapham seemed to prefer a different method for propelling boats through the vault:

> "An endless rope passed along the crown of the arch, and kept in action by water power, drawn from the canal, will probably be found the best plan for passing boats through this tunnel." (Lapham 1837c:4)"

The revision in plan had financial consequences. In the re-survey report, Lapham estimated that the total cost of building the canal by tunneling through the hill would be $349,716. In estimating the cost for the alternative method of a full open cut, Lapham made the following adjustments:

| | | |
|---|---|---|
| "Amount of former Estimate (tunnel method) | | 349,716 |
| Deduct cost of tunneling | | <u>-65,523</u> |
| | Subtotal | 284,193 |

| | |
|---|---:|
| Add 142,540 c. yds Exc. in open cut @ 40 cts. | 57,016 |
| "    87,460    "      Exc. (in first 20 feet deep) @ .20 | 17,492 |
| "    6,930 perches masonry in arch @ 3.00 | 20,790 |
| "    29,700 Ft. Timber @ .12 ½ | 3,712 |
| Add        estimated cost of extending the canal to |  |
|                                 Western Row | 18,353 |
| "        12 per cent for contingencies, etc. | 48,186 |
| (Lapham 1837b:2)        Total | 449,742" |

The estimated cost of constructing the full open cut can be calculated by adding the additional expenses of open cut excavation, materials, etc (99,010) and adding 12% of the total (11,881) for contingencies (the cost of extending the Western Row is excluded because it is immaterial to constructing the full open cut). The cost of employing the full open cut was $110,891 or $45,368 more expensive than the tunneling method.

Despite Lapham's choice of a full open cut in the re-survey report, on July 4, 1838, four months after groundbreaking, contracts were amended to construct a tunnel instead of the full open cut (Bonsall 1839:2). None of the sources consulted during research indicated why Lapham's resurvey recommendation of a full open cut was abandoned in favor of a tunnel, except for Lapham's observation that:

"On the 4th of July, 1838, the character of the material of which the hill is composed, had been so far developed as to induce the belief that it was practicable to construct a tunnel; the contract was on that day, so modified, by mutual agreement, that the work should be constructed in the form of a tunnel, instead of an entire open cut (Bonsall 1839 2)."

The degree to which the cost savings associated with the tunnel influenced the final decision is impossible to say. At any rate, the tunnel was completed, but at a price: a cave-in cost 6 workmen their lives when the excavation struck one of the springs Lapham identified in his first survey.

Lapham's design called for 15 chains (990 feet) of masonry arch lining the tunnel through the hill, with the arch extended an additional 12 chains (792 feet) through an open cut, making a total of 1782 feet of masonry arch. The additional 12 chains of arch were needed to protect the canal from soil washing down from the high banks of the cut. Moreover, Lapham increased the interior width of the canal from 20 ft to 24 ft. with the arch increased commensurably. The tunnel bottom was also lowered 1 1/2 feet below the canal bottom, and the abutments changed from 4 feet to 5 1/2 feet. The original plan for a timber foundation for the arch was scrapped in favor of broad flagging stones, projecting 6 to 8 inches beyond the line of the walls (Bonsall 1839:3). Finally, the original stone arch was replaced by a construction of hard burned bricks (Bonsall 1839:2-3).

Much of the detail about the actual dimensions and construction of the North Bend tunnel come from the papers of Erasmus Gest (1820-1908). Gest, who went on to become a railroad magnate and street car entrepreneur, took his first job after leaving school as a rodman on the Cincinnati and

Whitewater Canal. He kept a diary and made the only known sketches of the canal tunnel (Ducket 1962:1). Gest's drawings and description indicate that the excavation was conducted in stages. The upper center and two side sections of earth were removed first, leaving the center and two upper side sections to support the roof. Brick masons built the arch immediately after removal of the upper side supports. The lower center portion of earth was removed last of all (Gest 1838-1841).

Gest's records describe the tunnel as 24 feet wide at the water line, with an arch that rose 15 1/2 feet above the water line and 20 1/2 feet above the bottom of the canal. According to this description, Gest's measurements make the canal, inside the tunnel, 5 feet deep, in contrast to Lapham's own report that the canal, inside the tunnel, had been lowered an additional 1 1/2 feet, presumably to a depth of 5 1/2 feet. Gest notes that the canal itself was 4 feet deep and the towpath was 4 feet wide. The width of the towpath is of interest because the towpath on the rest of the canal was 10 feet wide (Burress 1970:40). The narrowness of the towpath may be an indication that it extended into the tunnel. However, Neuhardt (1989) maintains that.

> "The animals walked over the hill, while the boat was pulled through by means of ropes hung in rings on the roof. Indeed, some longtime residents of the area remember seeing one such ring attached at one of the entrances."

By 1839 Gest had risen to the post of Assistant Engineer. However, suspension of work on the canal in 1839 cost Gest his job, and he set off to find his fortune in Pennsylvania canal building, armed with letters of recommendation from Darius Lapham and William Henry Harrison (Gest 1838-1841). As a result, he was not on hand to see the canal or tunnel completed.

By September 14, 1839, work was well under way on the tunnel. For administrative purposes, the tunnel comprised sections 20 and 21 of the canal, extending 63 chains (4158 feet). The contract for sections 20 and 21 was awarded to S. & H. Howard & Company (Bonsall 1839:4), and all evidence indicates that they remained the contractor from start to finish. Lapham reported that by September, 1839, the open cut at the south (North Bend) end of the tunnel was complete and that the open cut at the north (Cleves) end was far advanced. Moreover, workmen had excavated the tunnel 250 feet into the hill at the south end, bricked 175 feet of the arch, and masons were underway on 25 feet more (Bonsall 1839:4).

On the north side a shaft was sunk from the top of the hill down to canal level. The shaft revealed that the northern portion of the hill was made of the same tenacious blue clay as encountered elsewhere. From the shaft the excavation of a drift - probably a pilot tunnel along the axis of the canal - had progressed 50 feet (Bonsall 1839:4). The process of dropping shafts into the hill and excavating the tunnel from inside out is consistent with contemporary tunneling practices in Great Britain and at least one book (Strickland 1826:5-8) provided drawings and a discussion of the technique. One of the advantages of excavating the tunnel and building the arch in the middle of the hill was that construction could proceed throughout the winter, uninterrupted by inclement weather. Lapham predicted work could begin on the brick arch in the drift in a few days, and that about 1/2 of the brick necessary for the tunnel was already made (Bonsall 1839:4).

**Cincinnati & Whitewater Canal Co. $1 Promissory Note**. Engraved by William Woodruff. The bill shows the canal tunnel at Cleves, built on the farm of William H. Harrison.

The tunnel was built on the property of William Henry Harrison who was a subscriber in the company and a major landowner in the area. Harrison monitored the progress of the canal construction on his property and reported his observations to the president, Micajah T. Williams, from time to time. In one letter, dated August 10, 1838, Harrison related that the workmen were making preparations for making brick and were erecting a storage building. He suggested to Williams that the company pay $1,000 to S. & H. Howard in order to purchase the brick making machine, acquire wood from Kentucky, and lay a railroad and build cars (Harrison 1838a). Other letters from Harrison to Williams were far more acrimonious. In a letter dated November 15, 1838, Harrison demanded payment for earth removed from his farm to make brick (Harrison 1838b), and in a letter dated March 18, 1839, he demanded remuneration for 1200 cords of wood cut from his stands (Harrison 1839). The company issued its own scrip to pay its debt, some of which, ironically, bore an image of the canal passing through the North Bend Tunnel in front of Harrison's home.

The company paid landowners between $15.00 and $25.00 per acre for right of way through their property (Burress 1970:40), and where possible materials were obtained locally. However, acceptable stone for culverts and aqueducts was not so easily found:

> "The price of masonry is invariably higher in the contracts made, than I had estimated: 4 sections, embracing large stone structures have been given up and relet at greater prices, in consequence of the masonry being too low. The quarries in the vicinity of Mill Creek were abandoned, and the stones for the arch are procured from the quarries at Rockville in Scioto County (Bonsall 1839:3)."

Presumably, the arch mentioned above was the free stone arch aqueduct which crossed Mill Creek. In the course of research, no mention was found as to the source of the stone masonry which faced either end of the North Bend tunnel.

In August of 1839, the Cincinnati & Whitewater Canal Company encountered financial difficulties and construction of the canal was suspended. In his December 31, 1839, report to the Board of Directors, Darius Lapham described the state of construction on the tunnel and recommended that while construction on other parts of the canal could be suspended without ill effect, if possible, construction on the tunnel should continue. The open cut on the north end was nearly complete, and the tunnel had been excavated 353 feet into the hill at the south end and 311 feet of the arch was built. About 30 feet of arch had been bricked in the drift at the north end when work was suspended in August. By December the shaft had filled with dirt. The drift itself had been extended an additional 50 feet into the same tenacious blue clay, and Lapham had not detected any signs of springs. The clay was ideal for tunneling because it was easily worked, yet the roof would not collapse even when unsupported. About 2 million bricks had been fired using J. Reeder's patent brick machine (Lapham 1839:4).

Lapham was concerned not only with losing the momentum of progress that had developed in recent months, but also with the financial loss that would have been incurred by the contractors and the damages they would have been entitled to if the company breached its contract with them. Moreover, Lapham was concerned for the 50 men and their families, living in shanties, who would have been "thrown out of employment at an inclement season of the year, and unless assisted by the citizens in the vicinity, until the spring opens to enable them to find employment on other public works, they and their families must endure a great deal of suffering" (Lapham 1839:4). Finally, Lapham worried about the public distrust that would have been engendered by a work stoppage.

Whether Lapham was successful in his pleading is not clear, but there was work done on the tunnel in 1840. In his December 31, 1840, report to the Board, Lapham noted that at the north end the open cut was nearly completed and 150 feet of brick arch built. The arch was ready to be built in an additional 50 to 60 feet of prepared open cut. On the south end, 730 feet of tunnel had been excavated under the hill, but construction was stopped after a cave-in collapsed 70 feet of the roof. The cave-in was caused by a vein of sandy soil containing a great deal of water. The cave-in occurred before the brick arch could be built beneath it to support the roof. As a result, all work was stopped at the south end and the entire work force employed in excavating from the north end. However, before much progress could be made, a snowstorm forced a work stoppage for the season. Lapham estimated that a passage for water could be completed within six to nine months. All that remained was to tunnel and brick 225 feet under the hill, and excavate the rest of the open cut and construct the brick arch, which was to be covered by earth (Lapham 1840:2).

Given the concern he expressed for the hardships that faced laid-off workers, it is somewhat surprising that Lapham made no mention of the men who were apparently killed in the cave-in. On July 12, 1928, workmen unearthed a human skull at Cleves. Residents believed that the skull belonged to one of the workmen who died in the cave-in:

> "According to old residents, a force of men were engaged in digging a tunnel for the canal between Cleves and West Bend in 1840. A cave-in caused the death of six of the men, whose bodies were recovered later and buried on the plot of ground now being used for the erection of the school (*Cincinnati Gazette* 1928)."

In general, working conditions for canal workmen were very bad, and work on the Cincinnati and Whitewater Canal was probably no exception. Workmen were subjected to death and dismemberment on the job with little or no compensation, "canal fever" and assorted other ailments, as well as low pay and layoff. Marjorie Burress (1970:40) relates that workmen on the canal were paid $0.60 per day and $18.00

per month. By 1846 they were paid only $0.30 3/4 per day and worked 26 days a month.

It is unclear when the tunnel was actually completed, but the entire canal was opened for business in November 1843. When in operation, the canal was fairly profitable, however, a series of floods proved disastrous. In December 1846, a flood on the Whitewater River destroyed the feeder dam at Harrison, and the summer and fall of 1847 were spent making repairs. A flood in the fall of 1847 destroyed the canal at Harrison, and the canal had to be relocated to higher ground in 1848 (Wessler 1935:11). There were other floods in 1849. At the same time, the Whitewater Canal in Indiana experienced similar hardships, which, in turn, greatly reduced the amount of business on the Cincinnati and Whitewater Canal. The cost of repairs compounded by the loss of business and increasing competition from railroads proved too much for the Cincinnati and Whitewater Canal Company. On April 18, 1861, the Cincinnati and Indiana Railroad Company was incorporated, and, after the Cincinnati and Whitewater Canal Company went into receivership on May 31, 1861, the canal property was sold to the railroad on January 24, 1863 (Wessler 1935:11-12).

The railroad ran its tracks along the old towpath and through the tunnel. The comparable take-over of the Whitewater Canal by the Whitewater Railroad in 1863 preserved the water rights for power generation. It is unclear if a similar situation existed on the old Cincinnati and Whitewater Canal right of way. An 1868 plat map of North Bend shows railroad tracks going through the old canal tunnel. The railroad right of way changed hands a number of times, and it was an Indiana, Cincinnati and Louisville train that got stuck in the tunnel during a flood on July 7, 1876. The boilers were doused, the train immobilized and in danger of a head-on collision with another train due down the tracks at any moment. The accident was avoided by a quick thinking passenger who waded through the torrent and flagged down the oncoming train (Burress 1970:46).

In 1888 railroad tracks were laid in a new cut through the ridge to the west, and the last train ran through the tunnel in July of that year (Burress 1984). Around 1900 the railroad (Big Four) walled-up the south entrance to the tunnel as a safety precaution The wall was subsequently breached by hunters in pursuit of muskrat, and in 1937 the wall was washed away by a flood. By 1953 the opening at the south entrance was only 10 feet, and less at the north entrance (Feeger: 1953).

## Epilogue

Further exploration of the tunnel has taken place since Fugate's account, written in 1996. An architectural historian with Gray & Pape has confirmed the 1840s age of the materials in the tunnel face, the tunnel interior has been mapped by members of the Cincinnati grotto of the National Speleological Society, and the Engineering Department of the University of Cincinnati has analyzed cost and engineering of the restoration of the tunnel and surrounding property.

The tunnel property is now part of the park system of the Village of Cleves, and will be developed further for recreation, educational and historic activities. Cleves has enthusiastically adopted the tunnel as part of their village life and has installed signage on the nearby State Highway 50 that incorporates a painting of the tunnel as the logo.

**The North Bend (South) end of the Tunnel Before Route 50 Construction**. The south end shown here collapsed on February 16, 1960. The small circle of light near the top of the arch is the Cleves end of the tunnel.

§§§§§§§§§§§§§§§§§§§§§§§§§§

*Now the tale comes full circle. The idea for the Ohio canal system is generally credited to George Washington. One of his veterans fell dead at the dedication ceremonies for the Milan Canal. The story is from the* Norwalk Reflector *on July 24, 1839.*

Volume VI (1968), No. 2, p. 24

### ANOTHER REVOLUTIONARY WAR PATRIOT GONE

"Died, suddenly, in Milan, Ohio, on the 4th instant, Mr. Timothy Conklin, a soldier of the revolution – at the age of 96. Mr. Conklin served as a lieutenant in the army under Washington. The regiment is not known. His former residence was in Dutchess County, N.Y. He came to reside in Milan township in 1834, and although at that time far advanced in life, he manifested the Sprit of '76. On the morning of the 4th, he came from his residence, a distance of three miles, to the village of Milan, where he assembled with his fellow citizens for the double purpose of celebrating the national anniversary and the completion of the Milan Canal."

# EPILOGUE

*So, you've made it to the end. Such interest! Why not consider joining our merry little band? Contact us through our website at www.canalsocietyohio.org. And if you have an idea for a* Towpaths *article, send it along to towpaths@gmail.com.*

Volume II (1964), No. 3, p. 8

## IF YOU ARE INTERESTED IN AMERICANA, WHY NOT "CANAWL"?

While others have been speeding along highways in a hurry to visit a crowded historic site in some far away place, the "canawler" has leisurely followed an old back country road seeing Ohio as it was a century ago. He stops to examine an interesting remnant of pioneer days, an old canal lock, perfect in its neatly jointed masonry, with just a vestige left of the original wood and iron of its balanced beam gates – a small pool of water in the ancient channel – overgrown with vines and trees, trees as thick as a man's body – the great blocks of stone testifying to the painstaking skill of those long ago workmen. He shakes his head in wonder that it could be done with the crude tools of the pioneers and comes away with a renewed interest in our history and a better understanding of how our people lived.

# INDEX

*Following is a brief subject index. A comprehensive index to the entire* Towpaths *collection may be found online under the "Publications" tab at the CSO website.*

8735811R0

Made in the USA
Charleston, SC
09 July 2011